OECD Territorial

CAPE TOWN, SOUTH AFRICA

ORGANISATION FOR ECONOMIC CO-OPERATION AND DEVELOPMENT

The OECD is a unique forum where the governments of 30 democracies work together to address the economic, social and environmental challenges of globalisation. The OECD is also at the forefront of efforts to understand and to help governments respond to new developments and concerns, such as corporate governance, the information economy and the challenges of an ageing population. The Organisation provides a setting where governments can compare policy experiences, seek answers to common problems, identify good practice and work to co-ordinate domestic and international policies.

The OECD member countries are: Australia, Austria, Belgium, Canada, the Czech Republic, Denmark, Finland, France, Germany, Greece, Hungary, Iceland, Ireland, Italy, Japan, Korea, Luxembourg, Mexico, the Netherlands, New Zealand, Norway, Poland, Portugal, the Slovak Republic, Spain, Sweden, Switzerland, Turkey, the United Kingdom and the United States. The Commission of the European Communities takes part in the work of the OECD.

OECD Publishing disseminates widely the results of the Organisation's statistics gathering and research on economic, social and environmental issues, as well as the conventions, guidelines and standards agreed by its members.

Corrigenda to OECD publications may be found on line at: *www.oecd.org/publishing/corrigenda.*

Foreword

Across the OECD, globalisation increasingly tests the ability of regional economies to adapt and exploit their competitive edge, as it also offers new opportunities for regional development. This is leading public authorities to rethink their strategies. Moreover, as a result of decentralisation, central governments are no longer the sole provider of development policies. Effective and efficient relations between different levels of government are required in order to improve public service delivery.

The objective of pursuing regional competitiveness and governance is particularly relevant in metropolitan regions. Despite producing the bulk of national wealth, metropolitan areas are often characterised by unexploited opportunities for growth, as well as unemployment and distressed areas. Effective policies to enhance their competitiveness need to address their functional region as a whole and thus call for metropolitan governance.

Responding to a need to study and spread innovative territorial development strategies and governance in a more systematic way, in 1999 the OECD created the Territorial Development Policy Committee (TDPC) and its Working Party on Urban Areas (WPUA) as a unique forum for international exchange and debate. The TDPC has developed a number of activities, among which are a series of specific case studies on metropolitan regions. These studies follow a standard methodology and a common conceptual framework, allowing countries to share their experiences. This series is intended to produce a synthesis that will formulate and diffuse horizontal policy recommendations.

Acknowledgements

This Review was produced by the OECD Regional Competitiveness and Governance Division in co-operation with the Province of the Western Cape.

Special thanks are given to Ebrahim Rasool, who provided support to this project while he served as Premier of the Western Cape, as well as Edgar Pieterse (Director of the Centre for Cities in Africa, University of Cape Town), and Laurine Platzky (Deputy Director-General, Governance & Integration, Provincial Government of the Western Cape).

A team of peer reviewers participated in the research collection and offered counsel in the production of this review:

- *Canada*: Adam Ostry, Head of Unit, Policy and Strategic Initiatives, Cities and Communities Branch, Infrastructure Canada, Chairman of the OECD Working Party on Territorial Policy in Urban Areas;
- *Italy*: Flavia Terribile, Public Investment Evaluation Unit, Department for Development Policies, Ministry of Economic Development, Italian Delegate to the OECD Territorial Development Policy Committee;
- *United States*: Dennis Alvord, Deputy Director for Legislative and Intergovernmental Affairs in the U.S. Department of Commerce's Economic Development Administration (EDA).

The review similarly benefited from the insight of a team of international experts: Ash Amin (Professor of Geography, and Executive Director in the Institute of Advanced Study at the University of Durham); Jo Beall (Professor of Development Studies at the London School of Economics); Yonn Dierwechter (Professor of Geography and Planning, University of Washington, Tacoma); and Jeroen Klink (Director of Community Relations of the Federal University of the Greater ABC Region – Metropolitan São Paulo).

Susan Parnell, Shirley Robinson, Solange Rosa, and Anton Groenewald jointly co-ordinated the background report to the OECD Review. The OECD acknowledges the participation of several representatives from government, academia, nongovernmental organisations, and business associations who met with our delegations to Pretoria and Cape Town from 2007 to 2008.

The OECD Territorial Review of Cape Town belongs to a series of OECD Territorial Reviews on metropolitan regions produced by the OECD Division of Regional Competitiveness and Governance, headed by Roberto Villarreal.

This Review was co-ordinated and drafted by Lamia Kamal-Chaoui, Head of Regional Competitiveness, Governance Division, Raffaele Trapasso and Michael G. Donovan, Administrators in the Urban Development Programme. Olaf Merk, Administrator in the Urban Development Programme contributed to the urban finance section and Jeanette Duboys prepared the Review for publication.

Table of contents

Tables

Figures

Boxes

Assessment and Recommendations

A global reference for socio-economic …

The socio-economic conditions in the Cape Town city-region are in many ways more favourable now than at any time since apartheid was abolished fourteen years ago. As one of the most economically powerful metropolitan areas on the continent, Cape Town, with its 4 million inhabitants, has benefited from South Africa's macroeconomic stabilisation and its re-entrance into international markets. After a sluggish period in the 1990s, its average annual growth rate reached 5.5% in 2005. The region has modernised its traditional strengths in port logistics and trans-shipment and has developed innovative sectors in tourism, agro-food processing, viticulture and finance. The regional GDP per capita is USD 15 250, or 40% more than the national average, roughly equal to that of OECD city-regions like Naples or Mexico City. Though the Johannesburg-Gauteng city-region still dominates the overall national economy (with 31% of the national population and 33% of national GDP), Cape Town has been the only major city-region to increase its share of national output. The tenfold growth of population over the past 50 years is testament to its draw as the second-richest economy in South Africa, with the lowest unemployment rate and the best standards of health, education and housing in the country.

…and democratic transition

This dramatic transformation has occurred in the context of a national democratic transition. Since the end of apartheid in 1994, South Africa has undergone a rapid process of political democratisation, by developing more inclusive governance and conferring fiscal powers on local government. This period has been marked by a sweeping reorganisation of local authorities, which in 2000 were reduced from more than 1 300 to 283. Massive social transfer programmes to address long-standing disparities in education, health and housing have been initiated, complemented by cautious fiscal and monetary policies. This accompanied an enormous expansion of the social grant system, an acceleration of housing delivery and the institution of the Black Employment Empowerment programme. The effects of this radical overhaul were legion: in short order, local governments began to administer larger jurisdictions, collect revenue for the first time, deracialise the provision of public services, desegregate housing and public transportation and institute democratic, non-racial elections. In Cape Town, this political transformation completely reconfigured the institutional setting, and a single metropolitan authority took the place of a highly fragmented archipelago of no less than 61 public authorities. In a few years, dozens of different administrative entities, land use legislation, computer systems, accounting standards and contracts were standardised and collapsed into the Metropolitan Municipality. The creation of the Province of the Western Cape in 1994 endowed the region a vehicle for regional delivery of health services, education and inter-municipal co-ordination. Cumulatively, these reforms prepared regional and local governments to play a more prominent role in social and economic development. Few international precedents exist for such rapid institutional change.

A service-based and open metropolitan economy based on a set of promising economic drivers…

This new national and international context has resulted in a gradual shift of Cape Town's economic base. Spurred by the development of finance, business services, logistics and tourism, Cape Town is becoming a service-based city-region economy, which today represents 69% of the total regional GDP and employment. The integration of the region into the global economy has strengthened its position on a number of dynamic global value chains (agro-food, tourism and hospitality) and emerging clusters (financial and business services, logistics and creative and knowledge-intensive industries), while new demands for urban consumption (housing, retail and construction) driven by a positive business cycle and supported by public investments and social grants, have spurred internal dynamics. Each of these economic drivers holds great potential. For instance:

- *Agro-food.* Cape Town has developed more capital-intensive agricultural activities in specific niches, resulting in a number of success stories, such as the rapid growth in wine, citrus and table grape exports. Mainly driven by large firms, food processing has become the second-largest employer and the largest exporter in the region, producing about 20% of the manufacturing value-added.

- *Tourism and hospitality.* With its wide range of cultural and natural amenities, Cape Town is a destination of choice for tourists from Europe and North America. The recent significant increase of job creation in the tourism and hospitality sectors has been driven by the development of new niches in cultural industries and in conferences and exhibitions. Catering and accommodation has been the fastest growing sub-sector in the region since 2000.

- *Urban consumption.* Boosted by the positive business cycle, Cape Town's large urban market has typically generated demand for consumption of goods, land and services, especially in wholesale/retail, the second-largest contributor to the regional economy. The construction and housing sector has dramatically expanded, thanks to the boom in residential and commercial property development, which experienced 11.5% growth over 2004-2005, and to the massive sponsored housing delivery programme (16 000 units over 2006-2007).

- *Financial and business services.* This cluster has benefited from favourable macroeconomic conditions in South Africa, including the relatively low-interest environment and a better business climate. Thanks to the presence of head offices of a number large of firms, the contribution of finance and insurance to the regional GDP doubled in the decade from 1995 to 2005, making up 16.6% of the regional economy. An interesting development has been the recent rise in call centres and business process outsourcing (BPO).

- *Logistics.* This cluster establishes Cape Town as a transportation hub and transhipment point in Africa for agro-food, refined oil and steel. The two commercial ports at Cape Town and Saldanha, along with the airport, Cape Town International, freight rail and pipelines, handled 23.3% of South Africa's total cargo in 2006. In 2005, about one-third of the exports of crude oil from West Africa and nearly one-quarter of crude exports from the Middle East passed the Western Cape. This cluster has supported a petrochemical industry, with export potential in products such as pharmaceuticals, cosmetics and biofuels.

- *Creative and knowledge-intensive industries.* Cape Town has developed strong specialisations in biology, engineering and the life sciences. Given its medical expertise and global medical reputation – Professor Christiaan Barnard successfully performed the world's first heart transplant in Cape Town – medical tourism has grown. An increasing number of visitors, especially from the United States and the EU, have taken advantage of the skills of local surgeons, clinics and hospitals, available at a lower cost than in their home countries. Creative industries have also developed in film and publishing.

...with high unemployment and social exclusion

Notwithstanding these promising developments, serious concerns have accompanied this new growth. Unemployment, principally among medium- and low-skilled workers, stands at 22%, if discouraged workers are taken into account. Job scarcity is compounded by immigration from provinces with lesser economic potential. Social cohesion is additionally compromised by widespread poverty: nearly one-third of the population lives in poverty, up from nearly 23% in 1999. In the Cape Town city-region, 16% of the population has HIV/AIDS, and a large number live in informal settlements and inadequate housing (between 25% to 30% of households). Although not as acute as in other African cities, income inequalities in the Cape Town city-region are extremely high by international standards, South Africa being one of the most unequal countries in the world. Cape Town also suffers from one of the highest crime rates in the country. Employers in many sectors are critically short of workers with the appropriate skills, and tend to make up for the deficit with capital or foreign labour, thereby increasing the vulnerability of the city-region's economy. Cumulatively, this has created an imbalance between the demand for highly skilled workers and the large supply of low-skilled labourers, which in turn, reduces the competitiveness of the main economic drivers.

The sprawling growth of the city-region has produced a highly fragmented urban economy with strong spatial polarisation...

The evolution of the spatial structure of Cape Town has also resulted in several obstacles to the competitiveness of the area. The functional area, which, in addition to the core metropolitan municipality (3.2 million inhabitants in 2006) includes six surrounding smaller municipalities, has evolved into a sprawling and low-density multi-nodal city-region characterised by strong spatial fragmentation. This trend is not conducive to inter-firm networks and urbanisation economies and generates a spatial mismatch between employment and housing locations in the context of the limited transport available and the lack of information about job vacancies. Such sprawl also tends to be associated with greater capital costs related to school construction, the extension of road, water and sewer lines, and storm water drainage systems. Within this spatial pattern, the previous township areas of Cape Town and its informal settlements concentrate poverty and remain severed from economic opportunities. For instance, Khayelitsha, the super-township created for Africans in the 1980s, contributes only 0.7% to the overall GDP of Cape Town, even though it houses around 12% of the total urban population. The isolation of the townships has created a cycle of economic and social decline that has affected the entire region. The lack of skills, socio-spatial segregation, inaccessibility of public transportation and elevated crime rates have complicated the integration of these areas into the leading metropolitan value chains. As a result, Cape Town cannot take advantage of this large potential supply of labour, or benefit from future growth in consumption and productive activity within these areas.

…and significant environmental costs

The city-region has become particularly vulnerable to air pollution, flooding and fires, which in turn impinge upon health, tourism and Cape Town's image. In 2007, air quality monitoring stations recorded 128 days of poor air quality on which levels exceeded the World Health Organisation's international air quality guidelines. Cape Town's level of particulate matter (PM_{10}) has nearly doubled from 2003 to 2007, and the city's so-called "brown haze" is a common sight. Cape Town's ecological footprint (4.28 hectares per capita) has become so large that today it takes a land mass equal to the size of Greece to provide its inputs (for example, water, coal, gas, wood, etc.) and process its waste. Ground water contamination in areas suffering overcrowding, inadequate sanitation and chemically intensive farming practices compound the problems of flooding. Beyond the obvious health risks for Capetonians, declining air, soil and water quality, seriously limits the potential of the agro-food and tourism industries. Despite the abundant supply of land in the region, only a small portion has the soil conditions suitable for agricultural production. Finally, due to rapid urban growth, specifically in informal settlements, poor families face an increasing risk of personal and infrastructure loss due to fires that break out as a result of high unit densities, combustible building materials and the use of inflammable kerosene (paraffin) stoves. More than 41 000 informal homes were damaged or destroyed in fires between 1990 and 2004.

How to foster more inclusive and sustainable economic development?

In this context, the main challenge in the city-region is how to foster more inclusive and sustainable economic development. Recent economic growth has not generated sufficient employment to curb the entrenched social exclusion inherited from the apartheid system. Conversely, contemporary market forces have made mainstream economic activities socially selective. The distributional effects of such growth need to be considered to unlock the potential of the most disadvantaged. In addition, the city-region's recent economic performance has demonstrated its capacity to participate in the knowledge economy, but there are some doubts about its potential to anticipate and sustain the needs of such an economy. In the medium and long term, the lack of appropriate skills along with poor innovation capacity and inefficiencies in the transport system, seriously threaten Cape Town's global competitiveness. Meanwhile, a severe downturn in the business cycle could seriously harm the economy. Cape Town's particular context requires a focus on both knowledge-intensive strategies and socially based economic empowerment programmes. For this purpose, policy makers could optimise public investment by addressing a series of enabling conditions or public goods that would engender inclusive regional development, minimise socio-spatial exclusion and maximise economic linkages within the region. Such an approach would not be confined to one sector alone, but could be applied across multiple chains. These enabling conditions could encompass four areas: *i)* the labour market and skills; *ii)* innovation capacity; *iii)* built environment; and *iv)* environmental sustainability.

Upgrading skills and labour markets

The need to foster better skills…

The dramatic constraints on the supply side of the labour market are a result of the poor performance of the education system. Although the residents of the Cape Town city-region tend to have higher educational levels than the South African average – they are over a thousand times more likely to have a tertiary education – there often exists a disconnect between the skills being acquired in educational or vocational institutes and the skills that employers need. The rapid expansion of the student population due to the influx of migrant families, the relaxation of admission policies and the limited availability of good schools in poor urban nodes has taken its toll. The persistence of high unemployment can be partly explained by the legacy of apartheid and exogenous factors (*e.g.* global competition in the textile industry), but improved public policies could address rigidities in labour legislation, the regulatory environment for small and medium-sized enterprises, skill upgrading and job matching.

...and employment intermediation

Sub-national governments in the Cape Town city-region can play a more active role in fostering skills and jobs. For instance, skills training schemes delivered by provincial agencies could offer more skills training. Vocational schools could play a more important role if they were linked to new forms of public assistance for job searching and labour pooling. On-the-job regional learning could also be enhanced through policies that directly target small and medium-sized enterprises, which represent almost 93% of Cape Town-based firms. One relevant area of intervention would be textiles and clothing, which is moving into higher-end, fashion-conscious merchandise. The adoption of active labour market policies at the sub-national level would be particularly appropriate for the inclusion of unemployed, underemployed and informal workers. A specific approach towards the informal economy needs to be considered, given its capacity to provide income-earning opportunities. This will require a shift from the current national approach of simply "eradicating the second economy" into one that recognises that informal enterprises can become incubators for entrepreneurship.

Improving innovation capacity

Innovation capacity is low and disconnected from the regional key value chains...

Innovation capacity could be enhanced in Cape Town through the fine-tuning of existing policies. The competitiveness of the Cape Town city-region's economic fabric is limited by its shortcomings on the innovation front, which has tended to concentrate in the Johannesburg Gauteng city-region. In 2004, for instance, Cape Town generated only 13% of the total patents in South Africa, where Johannesburg generated 56%. This discrepancy shows every sign of growing more acute in the future. Public expenditure on research and development is relatively low and unevenly distributed in South Africa. Moreover, the manufacturing base in Cape Town lacks specialisation in high-value-added activities, which are generally associated with more active innovation. Despite its robust R&D infrastructure, including four universities and several research centres specialised in health care, biotechnology and environmental science, university-industry linkages in Cape Town are weak. Research initiatives are relatively disconnected from regional key value chains such as agro-food, logistics and tourism. Better collaboration between firms and universities would promote commercial applications of basic and semi-applied research projects in key regional value chains and industries such as medical and environmental equipment, agro-food and biotechnology.

and a regional innovation system could be encouraged

A concerted attempt to foster co-ordination between the main stakeholders would help to promote innovation in the region. National innovation policy has recently improved after the creation of public funding mechanisms, but the regional dimension, focusing on building effective networks among firms, universities and other public and private stakeholders, has been largely ignored. At the sub-national level, the Provincial Government of the Western Cape has made innovation a pivotal issue in its main strategic plan, the so-called Growth and Development Strategy. Policies are implemented by provincial bodies (agencies and Special Purpose Vehicles) through a model of sector promotion and private actor involvement that has delivered real benefits. This model could be considerably improved by increasing grants to the operating agencies, conditioned upon well-defined targets, and the adoption of a spatial approach that would support clusters of functionally related firms.

Large firms have a key role to play

Regional innovation policy would improve if large firms were more involved, given their importance to product development and employment in the Cape Town city-region. For instance, they could take a more active role in the governance of provincial agencies and special purpose vehicles. Such firms could also disseminate technology and skills to small and medium-sized businesses, especially in disadvantaged areas. Through the Black Economic Empowerment (BEE) legislative framework, they could foster collaboration with small and micro firms. BEE was launched in 1994 by the South African government to redress the inequalities of apartheid and give previously disadvantaged groups economic opportunities, through such means as employment equity or preferential procurement. Overall, it has proven difficult to implement, due to the lack of skills among the historically disadvantaged African population. However, its specific provisions for interaction between large firms and SMEs could be further exploited.

Expanding and maintaining the built environment

Despite tremendous improvements, Cape Town is still faced with a segregated and inadequate built environment

The task of mending a city divided by apartheid has presented public officials in Cape Town with a challenge as daunting as any in the most racially segregated and spatially fragmented cities of the OECD. In many ways, however, the built environment has been transformed by government intervention: residents in former townships benefited from one of the largest electrification programmes in the country, and educational access has dramatically improved. Entirely new neighbourhoods and office parks were developed, creating a polycentric structure that differs from the nuclear form of the past. Notwithstanding these improvements, the overall built-environment policy has been grossly insufficient in creating affordable, economically vibrant and accessible neighbourhoods. Apartheid's land use framework continues to shape urban planning in Cape Town, through the frequent use for social housing of cheap parcels on the urban periphery, often on land already acquired by the apartheid state for township development. In this sense, the need for speed (massive quantity) has trumped the logic of space (social and economic integration), as well as the logic of sustainable resource consumption and fiscal sustainability. Though the number of multiracial neighbourhoods has increased, the city-region remains highly segregated, ageing infrastructure, along with intractable replacement and maintenance backlogs in water and sewerage, the road and rail network and housing stock hinder the Cape Town regional economy.

Providing affordable housing is urgent …

Despite massive efforts post-apartheid to provide electrification and housing, current policies have not been able to satisfy the demand for affordable housing. In the Western Cape, the current scale of housing production and upgrading is insufficient to absorb a growing deficit, estimated to be as high as 410 000 units. This shortage is expected to grow by 30 000 per year as a result of natural population growth and in-migration. Following a sectoral approach, current housing policy reinforces the spatial mismatch by providing housing units in locations where employment is minimal. Paradoxically, the impressive delivery of individual units through the capital subsidy mechanism has left the urban form created during the apartheid era relatively undisturbed. Current housing funding mechanisms often reinforce segregation and curtail efforts to create mixed, dense neighbourhoods in central locations. Cape Town accesses conditional capital funds for infrastructure through national funding arrangements that allocate housing subsidies through bulk service extensions and new household connections. Few incentives are given for brownfield redevelopment that utilises existing infrastructure in central neighbourhoods. The supply of affordable housing is further reduced by a lack of mortgage loans for the purchase of low-income properties and an inadequate number of housing micro-finance programmes.

...and densification and mixed use need to be considered

The supply of affordable housing would increase if municipalities in the Cape Town city-region were allowed to require developers to set aside a percentage of moderately priced units in new developments. Inclusionary housing requirements are commonly utilised in many municipalities in OECD countries, typically requiring between 10% and 20% of large developments – usually between 50 and 100 units – to provide affordable housing. Local governments could also consider promoting heightened density levels, given the region's infrastructure constraints and environmental preservation goals (94.8% of residential land is of low density). Densification and mixed use, though widely acknowledged in the *National Spatial Development Perspective* and *Provincial Spatial Development Framework*, have been relatively ignored and overridden by the construction of basic housing through a conventional "one house, one plot" model.

Land use regulation is a major issue...

The difficulties in addressing the housing issue are in turn linked with the regulations surrounding land use. The City of Cape Town owns relatively little land in comparison to provincial landholdings and those of state-owned companies, such as the Transnet and South African National Defence Force. The latter own a large supply of land on well-located sites but are reluctant to release these properties at below-market values, since such areas often generate revenue. This, in turn, compounds land scarcity, raises the price for low-income housing development and forces housing authorities to concentrate developments on remote land plots. Moreover, land use suffers from unclear and contradictory plans, a plethora of building standards, environmental conservation decrees and provincial planning ordinances, each with different procedural requirements that increase red tape and transaction costs.

...requiring standardisation and readjustment

Several actions could help to address the current confusion surrounding land management. For instance, efforts such as Cape Town's Integrated Zoning Scheme (IZS), which is intended to standardise the multiple and overlapping zoning arrangements, could be supported and replicated throughout the Cape Town city-region. The provincial government could foster informed debate on the best strategic use of land and also conduct regular land institutions audits to ensure the synergy of programmes that aim to improve land access. At the national government level, the adoption of the Ministry for Agriculture and Land Affairs' Land Use Management Bill would help to introduce a coherent national regulatory framework. Clarification of concurrent mandates in land management, which are shared between provincial and municipal governments, would also contribute to a more efficient system. The central government might well follow the example of South Korea and Japan, which have implemented a land readjustment programme to regularise informal settlements and facilitate their service provision by transferring a proportion of the cost of equivalent land to local and central housing authorities to build low-income housing for the urban poor.

Underinvestment in transport has led to increased automobile use

By and large, public officials have not been able to accommodate the transportation needs of residents in the multi-nodal sprawl of Cape Town. On the one hand, the region faces congestion not only from commuting trips, but from long-haul freight. Road-based traffic volumes to or from Cape Town's central business district have increased by a rate of approximately 2.5% per year. On the other hand, limited connectivity between the different urban nodes throughout the city-region reinforces socio-spatial segregation. Internal mobility has suffered from underinvestment in the nationally renowned urban passenger rail network and its rapidly ageing fleet. Commuters have generally abandoned rail transport for private cars, buses and taxis, and the use of automobiles for work trips is higher than in many cities in Africa and the OECD. Paradoxically, the numbers of passengers on public transportation in the

Cape Town city-region have declined, due to competition from private minivans and taxis. This, combined with significant fare evasion, has reduced operating revenue.

New funding schemes are needed to increase mobility and ensure sustainable transport throughout the region

The fractured transportation network harms competitiveness. Much of the population cannot access the regional labour market, and those who do must contend with lengthy commutes and inadequate road safety. The Provincial Government has underinvested in provincial road maintenance, whose backlog for total capital maintenance and rehabilitation was estimated at ZAR 2 573 billion in 2006. Safety and connectivity in the region have been jeopardised, and given current limited funding and the deferred maintenance, the Provincial Government needs to seriously assess a range of options for financing that would encompass transportation districts, specialised taxes, public-private partnerships and municipal bond financing. In the region as a whole, multi-modal connections, especially rail/bus links, and links with non-motorised transportation, could also be improved. Prioritising existing plans for pedestrian and cycling networks could make the transportation network more carbon-neutral and help create a more environmentally sustainable and connected urban structure

Ensuring sustainability and liveability

Climate change will impact Cape Town, and sub-national governments have taken this seriously

Increasing pressure on the natural environment of Cape Town threatens the region's economic competitiveness and suggests an urgent need to implement a pro-active environmental strategy. South Africa's Western Cape has been predicted to be the area most affected by climate change, with a reduction in rainfall, a rise in sea level, increased fires and erosion. The transformation of Cape Town into a greener city would both respond to its increasing vulnerability and augment its appeal as a scenic destination, benefiting tourism, filmmaking and its ability to attract and retain skilled labour. Environmental sustainability has been increasingly prioritised on the agenda of city and provincial policy makers. The provincial government and the City of Cape Town have released strategic plans with ambitious renewable energy targets, and innovative projects are being launched in such areas as biodiversity, disaster management, coastal management, air quality, integrated water supply development and increasing energy efficiency. Monitoring has followed policy making and implementation, although additional indicators and improved reporting are called for.

The use of economic instruments and specific incentives could help…

Governments in the Cape Town city-region may well consider the use of economic incentives to implement their environmental policy. Removing distortions within the existing pricing and tariff structures in the energy sector and introducing additional financial incentives towards the reduction of pollution would entail a series of advantages. First, this would remove subsidies and price distortions for the major electricity users that produce the bulk of carbon dioxide emissions. Second, the revenue collected from environmental taxation could help finance the ambitious programmes at provincial and city levels. Such economic instruments promoting environmental technology and ecotourism could be reinforced by subsidising capital grants to the developers of renewable energy projects and accounting for environmental considerations in budgeting and tendering. Governments in the Cape Town city-region could also use financing measures and monitoring to encourage developers to adopt green building designs optimising natural light, improving insulation, using natural landscaping and containing fewer toxic building materials.

…but there is a need to find new funding

The Provincial and City governments' ambitious renewable energy plans can only be achieved with additional funding mechanisms. A finance plan was proposed in light of the Provincial Government's goal to purchase 15% of its electricity from renewable sources by 2010, but it has not been fully developed. Electricity accounts for 24% of revenues collected by the City of Cape Town, and it is not apparent how increased energy efficiency would affect the City's budget and how revenue lost from electricity fees could be recouped. Given the fiscal strain surrounding urban financial management, municipalities face a dilemma: they are mandated to maximise revenues and increase the services provided, while simultaneously promoting the conservation of water and electricity.

Environment is a cross-cutting spatial issue

Aligning transportation and land use initiatives with environmental management may help to create a more sustainable city-region. The increasing dependence on automobiles and the lack of intra-urban transport calls for increased intervention to protect the environment. Investment in public transportation programmes would increase mobility and decrease congestion, a critically important goal given forecasts that suggest that the number of cars in Cape Town will increase 41% by 2020. The transport sector accounts for 22% of carbon emissions in the Western Cape, which could increase if it continues to rely on petrol. Environmental policies aligned with mixed-use and densification initiatives that allowed jobs and homes to be located closer together would decrease both commuting and pollution. Though signs of alignment have surfaced, for example in the City of Cape Town's *Cape Town 2030* document, only a minimal level of environmental sensitivity and "cross-cutting spatial logic" informs investment decisions in infrastructure, housing, transportation and land use.

A specific approach to townships is necessary for community economic development

Reversing income inequality in the Cape Town city-region requires an explicit approach to community economic development. This is particularly highlighted by the absence within key policy documents (at both the provincial and the city level) of a discussion on strategies to create vibrant, resilient and sustainable local economies. The City's administration has advanced infrastructure-led development, improving water supply, housing, electricity and access roads, but it has not been sufficient to channel capital or employment to distressed neighbourhoods. The efforts to provide low-income housing have not solved the problems of a lack of employment, crime, health challenges and a generally degraded environment. Local economic development policies in the existing township areas should foster entrepreneurship, micro-finance and the social economy. Such an effort must involve the private sector as well as empowering civil society groups. The adoption of the still unapproved Community Reinvestment Housing Bill would help to create a regulatory framework capable of directing funds to disadvantaged areas whose capital and financial resources were drained during apartheid. Premiums could be provided for financial institutions that promoted innovations in poorer communities, for example micro-finance and rotating savings schemes, decentralised cashing systems and electronic banking in townships.

Priorities in economic development policies need to be widely shared

Fostering inclusive and sustainable economic development requires a shared vision among the main stakeholders. While most policy makers in the Cape Town city-region agree on the main challenges to be faced, the best approach for generating inclusive economic development is much debated. The city administration of Cape Town has primarily funded basic services and infrastructure. Although a wide number of complementary projects, ranging from the promotion of tourism to regulatory reform, transcend an infrastructure-led economic development approach. In contrast, the Provincial Government of the Western Cape finances sectoral agencies that support industries the Government views as favourable to job creation. At the central level, severe deficiencies hamper co-ordination between different national departments, including the national Department of Trade and Industry (DTI), which is responsible for regional industrial development. For instance, the programmes for cluster support, innovation and sector development developed in the Western Cape over the last decade have attracted only small amounts of funding from DTI. In general, new initiatives developed nationally are frequently not articulated with provinces and municipalities, and consequently, fail to take account of the progress being made with economic development policies at that level. More specifically, there are mismatches in relation to the number of priority sectors selected, the criteria used in picking specific sectors, and, finally, the institutional design of industrial policies. A web of frequently underfinanced regional development policies prevails.

The need for a second generation of governance reform

Overall, despite improvements in the effectiveness of public policy in Cape Town, a second generation of governance reforms is needed. The extensive government reforms after apartheid left many serious problems unresolved, including congestion, a lack of housing and a shortage of skilled labour. Grappling with the problems of immigration, poverty and the need to improve global competitiveness and foster inclusive economic development is not made any easier by South Africa's adoption of strict public spending restrictions, the entrenched legacy of racial inequality, ecological fragility and the volatile political environment. Reforms are needed to respond to these challenges, primarily to *i)* stimulate intergovernmental collaboration between the municipalities and the Province, *ii)* mainstream frameworks for regional planning, *iii)* improve public finance tools for economic development, *iv)* build and retain capacity in the sub-national civil service, and *v)* strengthen civil engagement to improve governance and foster a more inclusive economy.

Streamline intergovernmental relations

Functions among spheres need to be clarified…

Co-ordination initiatives between the Provincial Government of the Western Cape and municipalities in the Cape Town city-region could be improved to reduce the contradictions in public policies that may compromise its global competitiveness. Despite the imperatives for reforming governance between the Western Cape Province and municipalities in the Cape Town city-region, relatively few adequate agreements seem to have been designed to address multi-level governance problems in traffic, the environment, infrastructure and housing. Vaguely defined concurrent mandates often hamper the delivery of services and obscure which government sphere is responsible for government functions, particularly regional economic development. The legal ambiguity feeds into the budget process, reducing not only effectiveness, but also the amount of resources allocated to enhance spatial economic growth and competitiveness. A wide range of intergovernmental platforms have been launched, but monitoring of their effectiveness is spotty. Longitudinal evaluations are needed to analyse the level of participation and conflict management tools over time, especially given political volatility in the region.

Mainstream frameworks for regional planning

…with enhanced and more enforceable regional planning tools

Adherence to and co-ordination among spatial development frameworks could be strengthened by additional reforms. These frameworks provide conceptual guidance for regional planning, although the absence of a budget and any sanctions *vis-à-vis* municipalities makes it difficult to implement them. Aligned with the *National Spatial Development Perspective*, the

Western Cape *Provincial Spatial Development Framework* supports areas of economic growth and favours densification, urban growth boundaries and mixed land use. These principles, though widely accepted by municipalities throughout the Cape Town city-region, often remain rhetorical, given that the provincial government is confined to an oversight role and that municipalities approve their own spatial development frameworks (SDFs) and are therefore not legally required to be aligned with provincial policy. Co-ordination among spatial development frameworks could be enhanced by additional reforms. Legislation will be introduced by the end of 2008 – the Provincial Development Bill to replace the current Land Use Planning Act – that, if approved, would require SDFs to approve of more binding "land use planning acts". This would encourage municipalities to align land use with the thinking at the provincial and national level. Future land development may be better guided through such reforms, which aim to provide enforceable norms for both municipal and provincial government.

A regional authority could guide strategic planning for the Cape Town city- region…

To consolidate strategic planning, the creation of a new regional planning authority could help create horizontally co-ordinated regional development planning at the level of the Cape Town city-region. Given that different sectors – land use, housing and economic development – are intrinsically connected to the spatial economy, a cross-sectoral body would offer much more coherence. This institution would give its delegates the decision-making power to co-ordinate investments. Representatives from the national, provincial and municipal government would sit at its table and be given enforcement powers through a formal, legally binding tripartite agreement with a mandate and an accountability framework for measuring progress towards commonly defined outcomes. Municipalities would stand to benefit from the ongoing opportunity to influence policy, planning and investment decisions, on matters that affected them but over which they currently do not have jurisdiction. The Vancouver Agreement may provide useful reference for a ''territorial'' approach, where various scales of the state work together to maximise economic competitiveness.

...that could co-ordinate several operating sectoral regional agencies or platforms

This umbrella organisation could have the capacity to provide co-ordination in regional transportation, environmental or economic development bodies, if its members agreed. These agencies, in turn, would be represented on the regional co-ordinating body. In terms of transportation, consensus has been reached on the importance of a more efficient system in Cape Town, although no regional transportation body has been established. Significant institutional designs have been crafted in several OECD metropolitan areas, such as Frankfurt or Chicago that may prove helpful in forging sub-regional consensus on transportation challenges. Regional environmental governance institutions could also be adapted for improved enforcement. The state's inability to stem contamination of the regional water system, for example, suggests insufficient regional environmental enforcement. A number of different models may find resonance in Cape Town, particularly Helsinki's Metropolitan Area Council (YTV), which is charged with regional environmental enforcement and monitoring. Municipalities in the Cape Town city-region could also consider creating a regional development agency, a multi-stakeholder platform with the central government acting as a facilitator, and including trade unions and firms. Though Cape Town could look to Milan's "Metropoli" agency for reference, others options would include the strengthening of existing structures and the reinforcement of promising experimentation.

Improve public finance tools for economic development

A block grant for economic development could respond to the current fragmentation

The effective implementation of public policies requires strengthening funding mechanisms. Sub-national finance has undergone substantial reform: shares of sub-national expenditures and sub-national revenues in South Africa are now comparable to the average in OECD countries. Despite progress within the field of sub-national finance, several challenges remain, particularly the financing of economic development and an expansion of local tax resources. The City of Cape Town and other metropolitan municipalities could play a role in collecting revenues for municipalities that face difficulties collecting revenue. Grants for economic development are fragmented, and there is generally a lack of incentives to invest. Creating one block grant for economic development, in which several of the current conditional grants would be merged, could stimulate the financing of economic development. Similarly, the equitable share criteria could be adjusted to take better account of goods and services needed for the "near poor" in cities such as Cape Town, and also of recent population changes in growing provinces, such as Western Cape.

Build and retain capacity in the sub-national civil service

An efficient bureaucracy decoupled from politics needs to be put in place ...

Despite well-developed policies and strategies, government as a whole is often unable to deliver services effectively and efficiently in all areas. Relatively high turnover, staff shortages and a dependence on consultancies for work normally performed internally are some of the limitations on the public sector. Political volatility among levels of governments in the region further corrodes administrative continuity. Frequent political shuffles have made governance in the region unpredictable; policy priorities are often changed before programmes can be implemented, much less thoroughly evaluated. Political stability, coupled with improved capacity building, would help to build a professional bureaucracy sensitive to the inevitable political shifts, yet independent of them. In the long run, this would increase institutional memory and enhance the quality of implementation.

Strengthen civil engagement

...and a civil society more engaged in public governance

Meaningful participation may reduce the deep legacy of distrust between disadvantaged communities and local governments. An inclusive economy clearly requires a language of inclusive and plural governance, both to improve the efficiency of governance and to reduce state dependency on it. Signs of emerging participatory governance are visible in South Africa, though initial outcomes have lagged behind expectations. Municipalities could better draw upon civil society networks and strengthen the capacity of local politicians, who in turn could improve participation in the drafting of Integrated Development Plans (IDPs), which constitute the main conduit for citizen engagement in urban planning. In terms of accountability, participatory monitoring systems could be expanded to evaluate the effectiveness of governance and policy choices that emerge from the IDP drafting process. To reduce the region's large housing deficit, municipalities could facilitate community-driven housing delivery. The appropriation of some community organisations by opportunistic and corrupt individuals, along with increasing political apathy, presents a challenge to the consolidation of participatory governance.

National growth depends on the capacity of regions...

Finally, the national government might consider implementing a regional development policy in Cape Town and elsewhere as a component of its national growth strategy. Because South Africa's recent economic growth has been achieved in a context of persistent high unemployment and poverty, the central government launched the so-called *Accelerated and Shared Growth Initiative for South Africa* (AsgiSA) in 2006, setting targets for economic growth, unemployment and poverty reduction and identifying six binding constraints for policy action. A proper implementation of the AsgiSA strategy will certainly benefit from a regional development approach, which could at least directly address two of the six binding constraints – infrastructure investment and governance interventions. Indeed, in a context of strict public spending restrictions, the adoption of a regional development approach would enable the central government to allocate public resources to regions according to a tailored prioritisation, in co-ordination with sub-national governments. Currently, public infrastructure investment is frequently "siloed" amongst departments at the national level whose work is not informed by or performed in harmony with regional strategies. The 2003 Presidential *National Spatial Development Perspective*, the only strategic document that explicitly aims to include the spatial dimension in the national agenda, is disembedded from national policy and budgeting processes.

...and a regional development policy can help to reconcile urban with rural, equity and growth

A regional development strategy is needed to transcend the traditional cleavage between urban and rural and to target multiple regions. In South Africa, this paradoxical tension is presently at work around regional development. On the one hand, city-regions like Cape Town are increasingly viewed by national authorities as the main drivers of economic growth and as promising locations for the investment necessary to sustain national economic growth close to the 8% stipulated by the 2006 AsgiSA. On the other hand, urbanisation has brought poverty and unemployment to the largest urban regions, which now house the bulk of the nation's economically vulnerable population. Today, upwards of 60% of the South African population resides in urban areas, more than double the rate in 1930, and about 12% of the rural population migrates to urban regions every five years. This demographic shift has created diffuse territories where rural activities are often carried out in urban areas (*e.g.* peri-urban agriculture), and traditionally "urban" activities, like service industries, take place in rural or exurban areas. This new configuration is characterised by unprecedented flows of people, production, capital and information along a new urban-rural interface. A national regional development strategy needs to bolster interactivity along the urban-rural continuum, redress regional structural imbalances and strengthen competitiveness. Ultimately, such a focus will help reconcile the two policy objectives – equity and growth – that underpin AsgiSA's national strategy.

Chapter 1

Cape Town: An Emerging Growth Pole in South Africa

Introduction

Since the end of apartheid in 1994, South Africa has experienced a dramatic process of political democratisation and macroeconomic stabilisation. The democratic elected government has confronted the challenge of establishing macroeconomic discipline, opening the economy to the international market while at the same time developing inclusive and participative citizenship and upgrading and modernising a traditionally insular domestic economy, severely hurt by years of anti-apartheid sanctions. Central government has simultaneously implemented innovative social transfer programmes to address long-standing disparities and promoted cautious fiscal and monetary policies to control inflation and public debt and ensure a robust macroeconomic platform. These outcomes were achieved gradually, without nationalisation or large-scale asset redistributions. In addition, there is ample evidence that policy makers are acutely aware of the strategic role of strong institutional frameworks in building up a new nation, while successive firm policy commitments are also being made towards the acceleration of socio-economic and spatial inclusion of the communities that were marginalised under apartheid.

Despite considerable advances, the overall results of policies for South African society provide a mixed picture and continue to place disproportionate pressure on rapidly expanding urban areas. To some extent, the traditional social and spatial exclusion of racial groups – the black and coloured communities[1] – have been compounded by exclusion based on educational level and income. Although the South African economy continues to grow given its structural characteristics, including a large concentration of natural resources, this has not translated into substantial growth in employment. The national government has taken an active role in generating employment through the ambitious 2006 *Accelerated Shared Growth Initiative* (AsgiSA), which seeks to halve South Africa's poverty and unemployment by 2014 and raise the growth rate to 4.5% by 2009 and to 6% after 2010. South Africa's major cities and metropolitan areas, which provide the bulk of national output and a home and workplace for 56% of the South African population, will have to shoulder a substantial part of the burden. An ongoing demographic transition has enlarged the role of cities: whereas in 1930 only 30% of its inhabitants lived in South Africa's cities, the forecast for century later, in 2030, is that only 30% of South Africans will live in rural areas (UN-HABITAT, 2006). Social integration and an alleviation of poverty, however, remain elusive. Large cities concentrate extreme inequality and poverty, high inactivity and unemployment rates, and poor educational infrastructure, as well as security problems and the challenges of HIV/AIDS.

The Cape Town city-region, the second-largest metropolitan area in South Africa, reflects the national challenge of creating new economic opportunities while eradicating past inequities. For its geostrategic role during the eighteenth and nineteenth centuries, Cape Town earned the epithet the "Mother City", an accolade that is still apt, given its position as one of the most economically powerful city-regions in Africa. With a population of around 4 million, the Cape Town city-region has managed to modernise its traditional strengths in port logistics and trans-shipment functions, while at the same time developing innovative sectors in tourism, agro-food processing, viticulture and finance. Serious concerns, however, remain despite this new growth, including high unemployment and poverty, informal settlements, housing backlogs, mass transit inadequacies, crime and health disparities. Many of these daunting challenges constrain the objectives of the nationally led AsgiSA strategy.

This chapter provides a profile of the Cape Town city-region's leading economic, social and environmental trends and offers an analytical framework for future policy measures. Section 1 reviews the macroeconomic situation at the national level and analyses the trends in internal migration and urbanisation. Section 2 focuses on the socio-economic and demographic makeup of the Cape Town city-region as a functional area and illustrates the South African paradox in the Cape Town city-region, where 22% of the labour force is unemployed and 32% of the population live in poverty.[2] Section 3 addresses the Cape Town city-region's economic specialisations in the global context, outlining its main economic drivers, including key value chains (agro-food, tourism and hospitality, and urban consumption) and regional clusters (financial and business services, logistics, and creative and knowledge industries). While these sectors are the dynamic segment of the urban economy, generally linked to the global value chain, they coexist with the townships, a set of disconnected blind spots that have failed so far to generate sufficient employment and well-being across the social base. These aspects are emphasised in Section 4, which proposes a review of the specific conditions necessary to foster a more inclusive approach to development, as provided by AsgiSA, while maximising economic linkages within the region. These conditions include the need to improve urban infrastructure (particularly in transport and housing, given strong spatial segregation), to address labour market issues to deal with the shortage of skilled labour, to enhance innovation capacity, and last but not least, to maintain a sustainable and liveable environment. This leads to a discussion of policy analysis and co-ordination in latter chapters.

1.1. The macroeconomic context of South Africa

South Africa is a middle-income country and the largest economy in Africa. With a population of 48 million inhabitants, its total GDP was PPP USD 430.7 billion in 2006, and its national income per capita (PPP USD 9 087 in 2006), compared with a range of OECD countries and emerging economies, ranks just above Turkey, China and India, at the end of the list (Figure 1.1). Within the continent of Africa, South Africa is one of the most developed countries and accounts for 40% of the Gross National Income (GNI) in sub-Saharan Africa. For instance, it produces 40% of the electricity in Africa, it is home to the most advanced financial market of the continent[3] and it was the largest recipient of foreign direct investment (FDI) in the sub-Saharan region in 2005, experiencing a sharp jump in inflows, to USD 6.4 billion from only USD 0.8 billion in 2004 (OECD, 2007*a*). The national economy, although still dependent on natural resources such as gold and iron ore, is among the most diversified in Africa. Tertiary activities (excluding government services), at more than 51%, dominate the national economy. The "financial and business services", "transport and communication", "wholesale and retail trade catering and accommodation" sectors are all well developed, and South Africa plays the role of the gateway to sub-Saharan Africa as well as to West Africa for the oil and gas market. Manufacturing represents another important source of national wealth (Figure 1.2). The automotive industry is one of South Africa's most important sectors, with many of the major multinationals using South Africa to source components and assemble vehicles for both the local and international markets. The metals industry is also very important. Ranked the world's 19th largest steel-producing country in 2001, South Africa is the largest steel producer in Africa (almost 60% of Africa's total production). Finally, between 1905 and 2007, South Africa was the world's leading gold-producing country (China's gold production overtook South Africa's in 2008).[4]

Figure 1.1. **South Africa is a middle-income country**

GDP per capita – thousands USD PPP (2005)

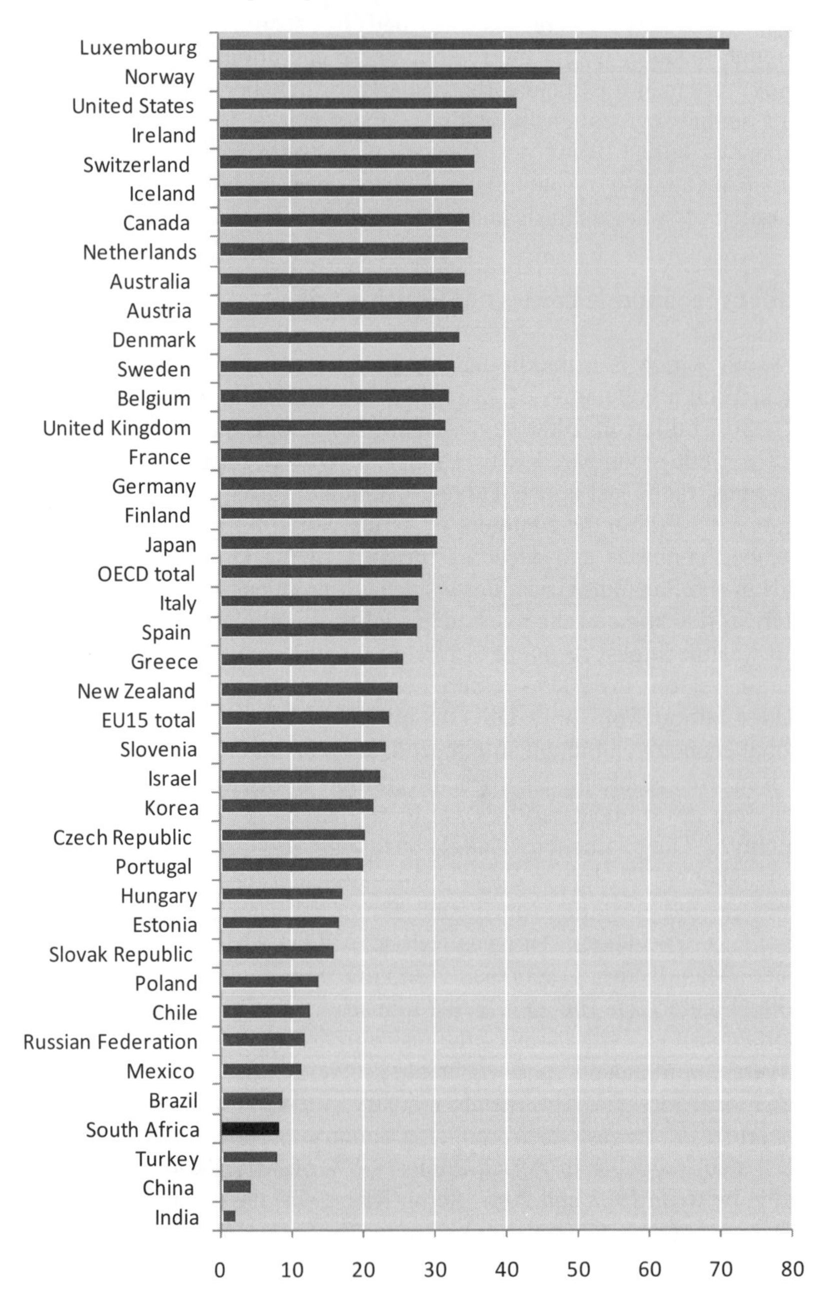

Source: OECD Factbook, 2008.

Figure 1.2. **Industrial mix in South Africa, 2005**

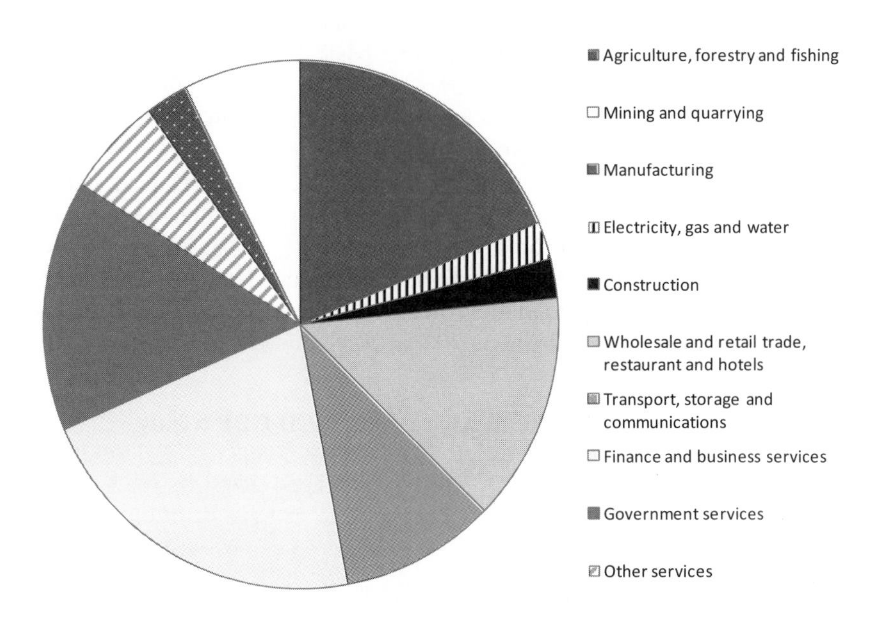

Source: OECD, African Outlook 2006/2007.

After sluggish economic growth right after the end of apartheid, democratic South Africa has experienced a positive trend, despite a slowdown in the beginning of 2008. South Africa experienced important boom and bust cycles over the 1980s, and to a lesser extent in the 1990s, but since 2000, it has progressively followed a more stable path of growth, surpassing that of the average for OECD countries (Figure 1.3). Between 1995 and 2005, GDP grew at an annual average of 3.4%, accelerating in 2004 and 2005 to 4.8 and 5.1%, respectively (OECD, 2007*a*). Between 2004 and 2007, average GDP annual growth reached 5%. Continued momentum in consumer demand, relatively low interest rates (until late 2006) and a wealth effect from rising asset prices, particularly within the property market, have contributed to growth. The average rate of fixed capital formation was 5% a year between 1994 and 2005, and picked up to nearly 15% in 2007. Gross fixed capital formation as a percentage of GDP also increased from a low level of 14.7% in 1993 to 20.6% in 2007. However, one important exogenous factor that has influenced national performance have been the international price trends for South Africa's main commodities, such as gold, iron ore, coal and diamond, since the early 2000s (OECD, 2008*b*). The short-term outlook continues to be positive, though the growth rate is expected to be lower in 2008, due to a series of factors, both exogenous and endogenous. Fresh oil and basic food price increases have fed into rising inflation, which is now above 10%, far beyond the inflation targeting band of 3% to 6%. This has prompted the South African Reserve Bank (SARB) to lift the interest rate from a low of 7% in 2006 to 11.5% in April 2008.[5] High inflation and high interest rates have reduced internal demand, which had acted as an economic driver over the previous five years. Compounding this problem is the electricity crisis. Frequent power cuts have affected national productivity and reduced the expectation for South Africa's future economic growth. All these factors have reduced projected real GDP growth by about 1% in 2008.

Figure 1.3. **South Africa and OECD GDP trends**

1980-2005

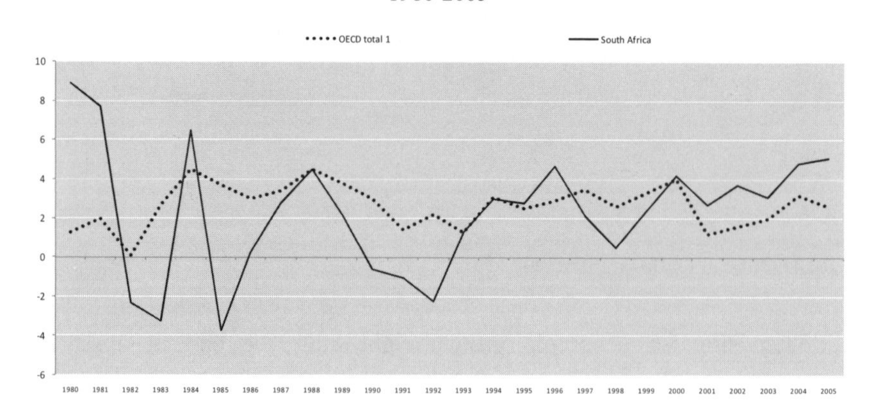

Source: OECD, Factbook 2007.

Recent years' positive growth performance has not translated into adequate job creation, and thus unemployment remains high. South Africa is still struggling to overcome the cumbersome social and economic legacy of apartheid. The democratic government inherited an economic framework based on natural resources (gold, coal and diamonds) and a poorly developed and highly protected manufacturing sector.[6] In spite of tertiarisation and the shift towards a relatively more knowledge-intensive economic structure that has occurred over the past 20 years, natural resources still play an important role in the national economy, and the labour market has been unable to generate enough employment to absorb the increasing national workforce. This has meant that a large part of the "broader black" working class continues to be excluded from the labour market, especially of unskilled workers.[7] Consequently, national unemployment stands at 25%; if discouraged workers are counted, the rate approaches 40%.[8] Overall inactivity rate is also very high, at 40% of the population. This is at least in part a function of a skills mismatch: the knowledge-intensive character of the formal economy and the capital-intensive activities have resulted in excess demand for skilled labour in a nation with a surplus of under-skilled labour, generating growing wage differentials across all skill levels. In turn, the lack of skills is linked to the failure of the educational system, with low enrolment rates, in particular for secondary education, which has considerable drop-out rates, as well as tertiary education. Huge educational disparities persist, with on the one hand, a substantial number of students performing even more poorly than in sub-Saharan African countries and a small proportion performing at OECD levels (OECD, 2008*b*).[9]

Poverty is still high in South Africa, and the devastating impact of HIV/AIDS and criminality have become major national concerns. Per capita income in South Africa advanced by less than 1% a year between 1994 and 2003, and the country continued to diverge from the OECD average (Figure 1.4).[10] Wealth is still abnormally concentrated, and South Africa still has one of the highest income disparities in the world. According to the United Nations, its Gini coefficient was 0.59 in 2005, worse than Brazil's, which stood at 0.58.[11] This compares unfavourably to Australia (0.35), for example, or to Spain (0.32), Denmark and Sweden (low 0.20s) and to other medium-income OECD countries such as Mexico and Turkey (both 0.33).[12] Although inequality in income is compounded by the social and spatial exclusion of the vulnerable "African" and "coloured" communities, race is no longer its sole cause. The persistent racial stratification is rather a legacy of the education system during apartheid, which served both blacks and coloureds poorly. Social stratification is also likely to result in higher crime rates. In the 2007-08 Global Competitiveness Index calculated by the World Economic Forum, for example, South Africa was ranked 126th out of 131 countries for the cost to business of crime and violence. The problem is not merely one of perceptions: South Africa has one of the highest homicide rates in the world, with particularly high numbers of gun fatalities. Finally, the high prevalence of HIV/AIDS infection (19% of adults aged 20 to 64) has struck much of the country and disproportionately affected the population of working age (Dorrington *et al.*, 2006). Indeed, while South African citizens represent less than 1% of the world's population, they represent more than 14% of the HIV+ population (Figure 1.5).[13]

Figure 1.4. **South Africa's GDP per capita diverges from the OECD average**

PPP 2000 – OECD = 100[1]

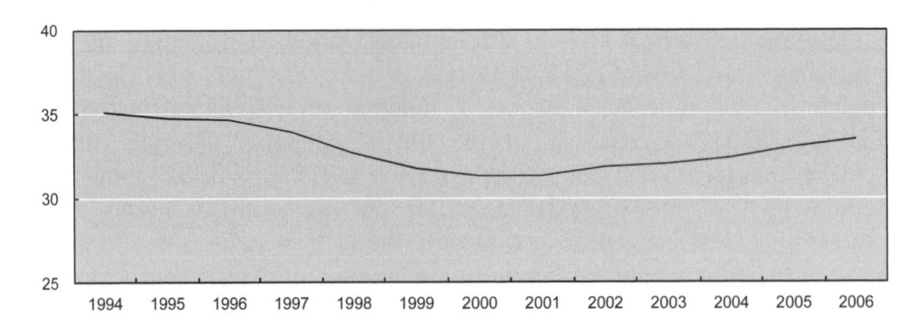

1. Excluding Hungary, Poland, Slovak Republic and Turkey.

Source: OECD Economic Outlook of South Africa (2008).

Figure 1.5. **Number of HIV+ individuals and percentage of AIDS deaths**

1986-2002

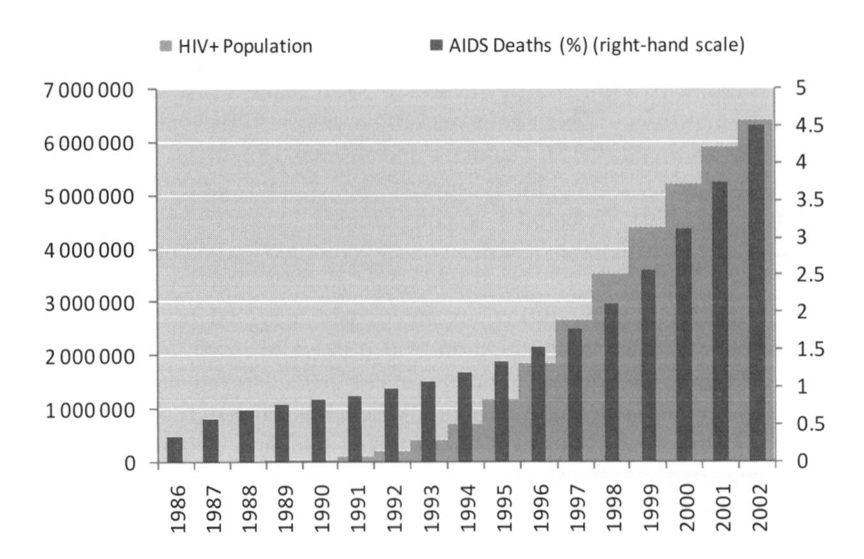

Source: UNDP, South Africa Human Development Report 2003.

Despite recent positive trends, South Africa's economic structure remains vulnerable to external shocks and is unlikely to generate the jobs necessary to adequately lower unemployment, at least in the short and medium term. As South Africa still depends on commodities, its economy is exposed to exogenous shocks, and currency volatility may constrain the national capacity to export. By most standards, and particularly in relation to OECD countries, the exchange rate of the South African has been highly volatile in the last 14 years.[14] The nominal effective exchange rate has seen several swings of 20% or more in a period of a few months, and its average variance over the post-apartheid era has been much greater than even most other middle-income countries, some of which have suffered severe balance of payments crises in that period (OECD, 2008*b*). This volatility is partly explained by the fact that South Africa's economy is unusually dependent on commodities, and the prices of its major export commodities have been highly variable. Mining still accounts for about 7% of GDP and more than a quarter of exports; non-ferrous metals and iron and steel alone represented 31.4% of national export in 2006. This is considerably more than even relatively resource-rich OECD economies such as Australia or Canada, as well as other quite commodity-dependent middle-income countries such as Brazil and Chile. The big swings in the exchange rate have largely followed fluctuations in key export commodities (OECD, 2008*b*).

South Africa's rapidly expanding urban areas face many challenges.[15] Since the end of apartheid, urbanisation has accelerated, reaching almost 60% of the total population in South Africa today. The national engines of growth are 26 major urban areas with high population densities (Table 1.1) and economies that include both labour-intensive and capital-intensive activities (Figure 1.6). The three major urban regions alone (Gauteng-Johannesburg, Cape Town and eThekwini/Durban) contribute more than 45% to national GDP.[16] Spatial disparities have increased between growing (mainly urban) regions and lagging (mainly rural) regions, but also within urban regions, where a large part of the population live in townships and informal settlements, with transfers and grants as a main source of income. The regions that lag behind lack conventional basic infrastructure because the apartheid system developed separate homelands – the despised Bantustan system – to concentrate Africans in peripheral regions and separate them from the white economy and society.[17] Today, these areas house high concentrations of people living in extreme poverty: about 1.5 million (or 6.5% of the total number living below the Minimum Living Level, or MLL)[18] live in rural regions with an extremely weak and underdeveloped economic base. In 2004, average per capita annual income in these regions stood at approximately ZAR 2 374 (PPP USD 367.50) which amounted to roughly 9% of the national average. Economic activity in such territories is largely survivalist; and state transfers and grants are generally the main source of income (Mohamed, 2007).

Poverty and unemployment have been displaced to the largest urban regions, which now face intense social problems, including criminality, HIV/AIDS and other social concerns, as migrants from less developed areas flood into the large cities.[19] Internal migration, mainly to urban regions, has been historically high in South Africa: every five years since 1975, 12% of the rural population has migrated to urban regions.[20] Of the 47 district municipalities that compose the country, 34 (or 72%) mainly rural districts have experienced net out-migration to major metropolitan centres and secondary towns and cities between 1996 and 2001 (*National Spatial Development Perspective*, 2006). However, this process has accelerated recently, as according to Census data (1996-2001), there has been a steady increase in the proportion of the urban population over time by race. The black African population is the least urbanised sub-population (Table 1.2), although the numbers are shifting steadily upwards (Figure 1.7). Latecomers are spatially concentrated in townships, which, with the "homelands", are the most evident legacy of apartheid.[21] This concentration in areas poorly connected with economic activities and cultural/social facilities has prevented the creation of a large integrated urban community that could generate an endogenous process of growth. As will be discussed below, townships house a large "reserve army" of workers without the skills to be integrated into the local economy.

Table 1.1. **Spatial concentrations of national population, Gross Value Added, and the poor in South Africa (2006)**

Concentration in the main 26 Economic Core Areas (urban regions)				
	National population	People living under MLL	National GVA	Land surface on national overall
%	62.62	53.21	77.04	27.15
Abs. val.	29.3 million	12.5 million	(ZAR) 940 billion	(ha) 12.7 million
Economic Core Areas (urban regions) extended into an accessibility radius of 60 kilometres from where 1 billion Rand of GVA is generated per annum				
%	84.46	77.31	95.59	31.24
Abs. val.	39.6 million	18.2 million	(ZAR) 1 167 billion	(ha) 38 million

Source: Republic of South Africa – The Presidency (2006), National Spatial Development Perspective.

Figure 1.6. **Spatial concentration of GVA in the 26 Economic Core Areas (2004)**

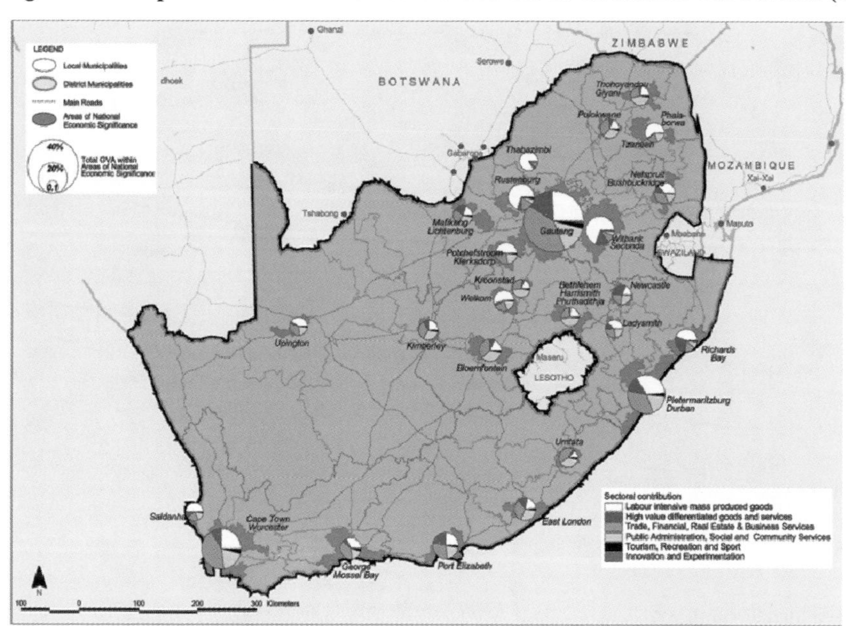

Source: Map prepared by CSIR Built Environment for NSDP, Presidency South Africa (2006).

Table 1.2. **Urbanisation level in South Africa in 2001**

Population group	Total population	Urban population	Rural population	Proportion urban (%)
Black African	35 433 492	16 820 234	18 613 258	47.47
Coloured	3 987 419	3 460 376	527 043	86.78
Indian/Asian	1 113 183	1 085 279	27 904	97.49
White	4 285 683	3 851 681	434 002	89.87
Total	44 819 777	25 217 571	19 602 206	56.26

Source: Statistics South Africa.

Figure 1.7. **South Africa's urbanisation trends**

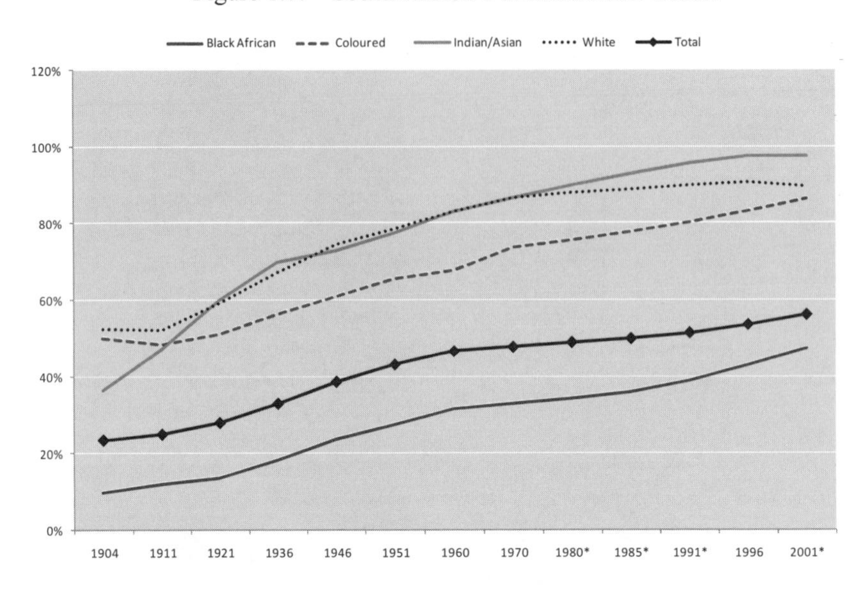

Source: Statistics South Africa, *Migration and Urbanisation in South Africa*, 2006.

1.2. Socio-economic and demographic trends in Cape Town

A large, low-density and sprawling city-region

With almost 3.9 million inhabitants, Cape Town is the second most populated city-region in South Africa, after the Johannesburg-Gauteng metropolitan area. With origins in seventeenth-century trade routes that first linked together the economies and cultures of Western Europe, South-East Asia and sub-Saharan Africa, Cape Town has evolved towards a poly-nodal city-region characterised by a series of essentially non-discrete "functional spaces" (Robinson *et al.*, 2007). This territory both spans overlapping geographies of function – commuting patterns and water supply, for example – and covers various scales of urban management and governance. Following a multi-criteria approach, a definition of the Cape Town Functional Region includes the Cape Town Metropolitan Municipality (3.2 million) and six smaller surrounding municipalities (Stellenbosch, Drakenstein, Swartland, Saldanha Bay, Theewaterskloof and Overstrand) (Figure 1.8 and Box 1.1). This city-region accounts for 8.3% of the population of South Africa and 92% of that of the Province of Western Cape (Table 1.3). As an international comparison, the Cape Town city-region has the approximate population of Ireland, New Zealand, Uruguay or Lebanon and OECD metro-regions such as Athens, Rome, Montreal, Melbourne or Seattle (Figure 1.9).

Box 1.1. **Definition of the Cape Town city-region**

The concept of a city-region is not in general use in South Africa, and only recently has the notion of the urban space economy been reintroduced into public policy debates. Though at times a functional city-region may be confined to existing administrative borders, it more often extends across multiple boundaries. In the Cape Town region, the relevant functional area for managing water (which encompasses the catchments of the Breede River and the Berg River) differs from the functional region for agricultural freight logistics, which stretches as far as Swellendam. These spaces, in turn, are not consistent with the commuting field, which tends to be narrower. The Province of the Western Cape responded to these concerns and created a definition that incorporates overlapping economic, political and ecological spaces (Provincial Government of the Western Cape, 2007*a*). This definition encompasses the spatial dimensions of economic relationships, infrastructure, ecology and political geography.

Economic definition: The range of economic functionality of a city region is sometimes calculated using commuter ranges as a proxy for defining the geographical extension of the territory. In the case of Cape Town, the commuter catchment for the region extends up to 100 kilometres and includes: (1) residents of outlying towns, such as Malmesbury, Paarl, Wellington, Stellenbosch, Grabouw, Rooi Els and Hermanus, who commute inwardly to the City of Cape Town, (2) residents of Cape Town who commute horizontally across the City, and (3) residents who commute outwardly to the towns identified above. Despite widely acknowledged connectivity, these patterns have not been quantified in a regional transport analysis of commuter origins and destinations. The mapping of connections between labour markets and employment nodes within the region would engender a greater understanding of the region's transport flows and functional economic area.

Infrastructure: The two commercial ports at Cape Town and Saldanha, along with road networks, airport, freight rail and pipelines, all play a crucial role in economic activity in the urban region. Because Cape Town is a coastal city, a tourist centre and an agri-business node, freight movement across the city-region is significant and forms a critical structure around which the functional economy operates. Though data are available on the number of passengers and freight tonnage, a more precise definition of flows within the city-region is limited by the lack of information about the origin of goods and passengers.

Ecology: The Table Mountain (1 080m) chain, together with extensive aquifers and the world's smallest floral kingdom (fynbos), has created an extraordinarily diverse yet fragile coastal ecosystem. A population triangle roughly circumscribes Cape Town, Saldanha and Hermanus, given the availability of arable land and water. Arguably the most important ecological features defining the region's economy are the shared resources of water and waste management. Regional collaboration is imperative, especially given projections that indicate that the region's climate will become hotter, more variable and prone to extreme events, including flooding, drought, fire, heat waves and water scarcity (Province of Western Cape, 2006). For these reasons, a regional definition takes into account local ecological assets.

Administrative units: A trade-off between measuring and defining metropolitan regions must be noted: the more the definition is detailed, the more it is likely to diverge from the political geography of the region. The disconnect between the definition and the existence of administrative units will affect the availability of data and statistics, making it is a challenge to measure the economic and social phenomena taking place within the region. For 20 years, Cape Town has experienced sweeping political change, morphing from a highly fragmented archipelago of no less than 69 public authorities into a single, consolidated metropolis. While fragmentation facilitated apartheid planning, consolidation has enabled the government to work towards integration by co-ordinating zoning, transportation and spatial policy. With a base of the "metropolitan municipality" of Cape Town (3.2 million), the Cape Town Region could also include the surrounding six smaller municipalities of Stellenbosch, Drakenstein, Swartland, Saldanha Bay, Theewaterskloof, and Overstrand, which collectively represent another 650 000 inhabitants. This definition of the city-region offers several advantages for both empirical analysis and policy making, reflecting practical administrative capacities, voting jurisdictions, and spatial planning districts – all of which are crucial in maintaining any kind of new urban development agenda.

Figure 1.8. **The Cape Town city-region**

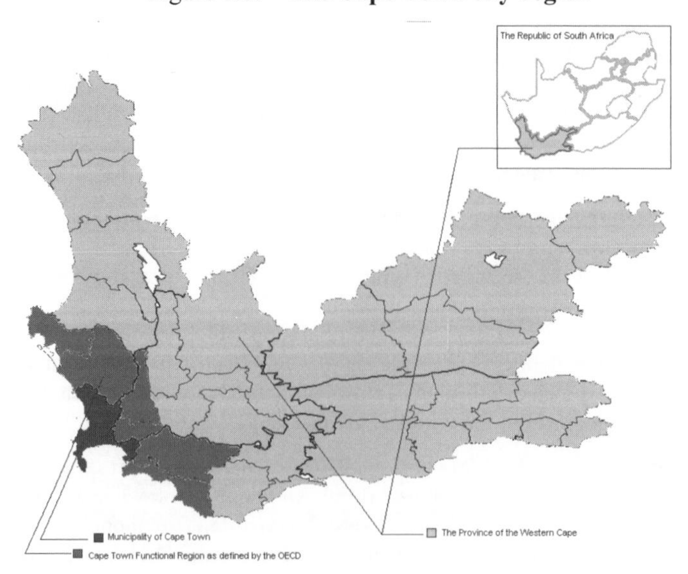

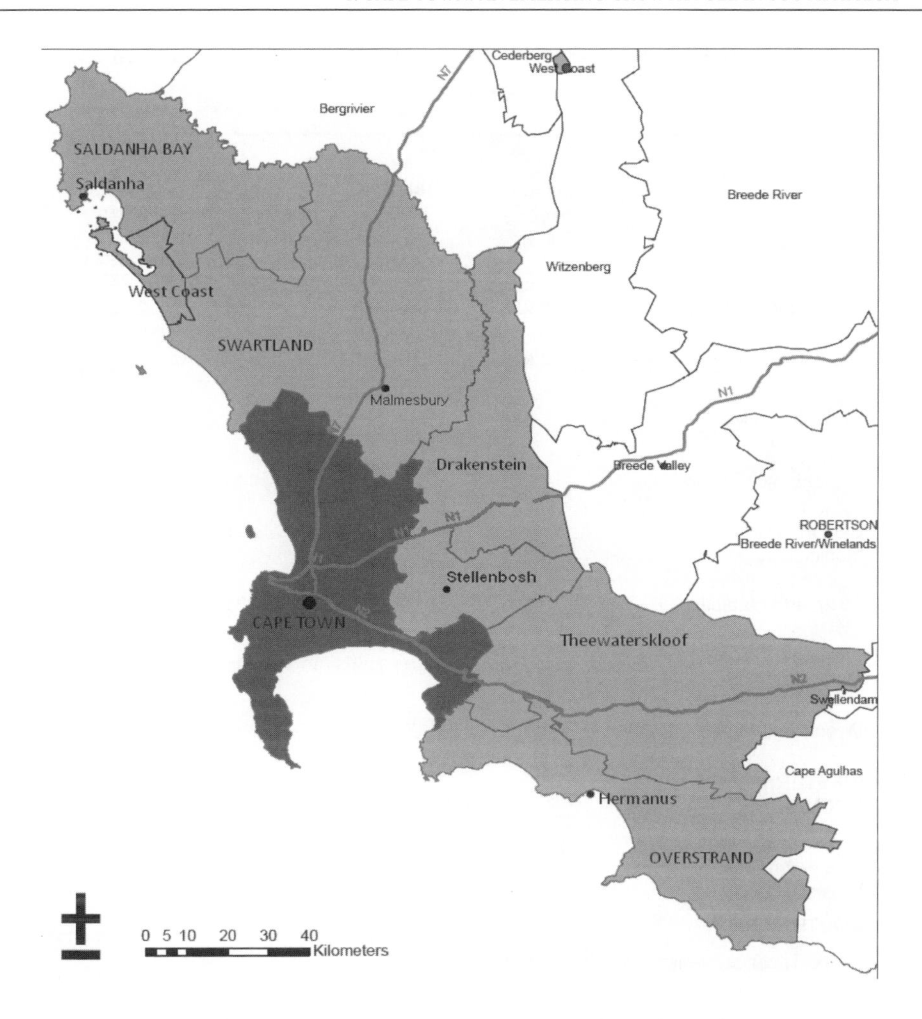

Source: OECD and City of Cape Town, Strategic Development Information and GIS (2008).

Table 1.3. **The Cape Town city-region (Functional Region) in the Western Cape and South Africa**

	Surface Area (km²)	**Population 2006**	**Density** (persons/ km²)	**GDP** (in million, PPP adjusted USD 2007) (share of Cape Town city-region GDP)
Cape Town city-region	**15 255**	**3 890 685**	**255**	20 630.32
Cape Town Municipality	2 461	3 239 768[a]	1 316	18 387.95 (89.1%)
Drakenstein Municipality	1 538	204 716	133	756.05 (3.7%)
Stellenbosch Municipality	831	116 605	144	475.36 (2.3%)
Saldanha Bay Municipality	1 778.56	81 121	46	317.49 (1.5%)
Swartland Municipality	3 692	76 225	21	284.46 (1.4%)
Theewaterskloof Municipality	3 248	101 798	31	230.68 (1.1%)
Overstrand Municipality	1 706	70 446	32	178.32 (0.9%)
WESTERN CAPE PROVINCE (Cape Town city-region as a percentage of Western Cape)	129 370 (11.79%)	4 994 244 (77.9%)	38.6	23 615.07 (87.4%)
SOUTH AFRICA (Cape Town city-region as a percentage of South Africa)	1 221 037 (1.25%)	48 502 063 (2007) (8%)	-	173 552 (2006) (11.8%)

a. Projected from Census data 2001.

Source: Quantec Research, 2007.

Figure 1.9. **Ranking of OECD city-regions and Cape Town by population size**

(2004 or last available year)

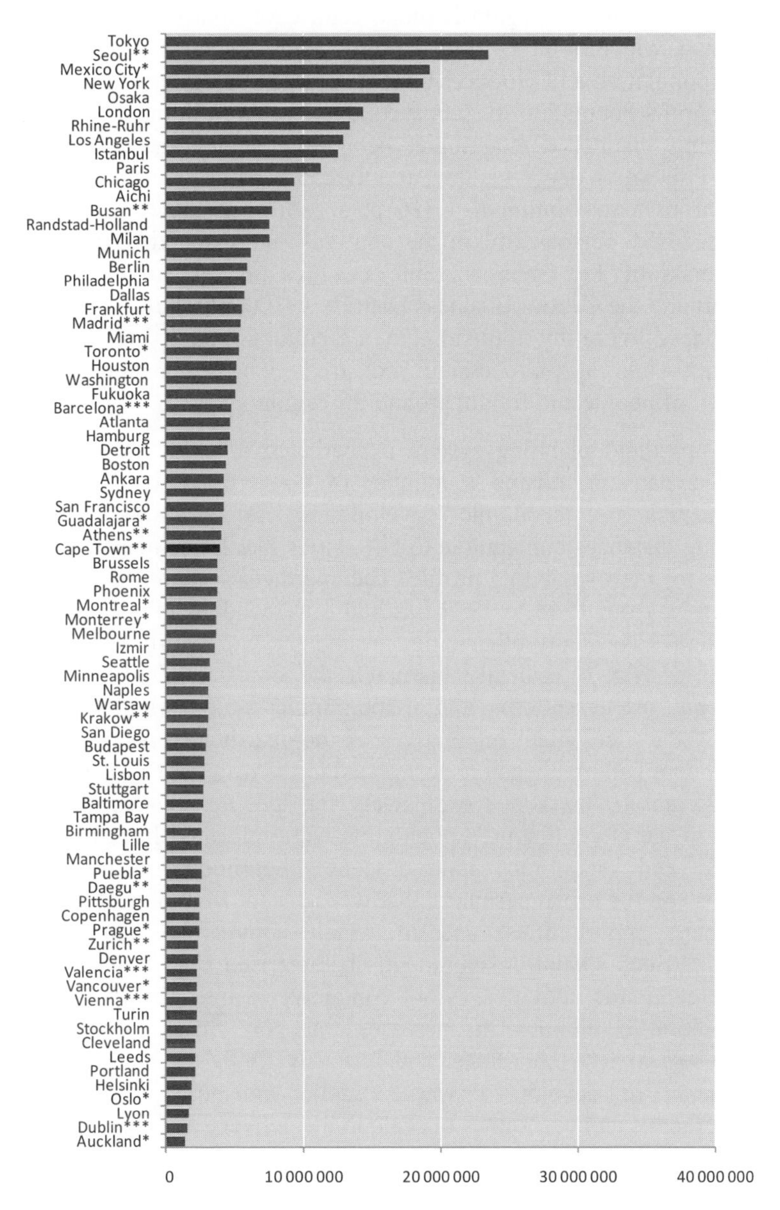

Note: (*) data as of 2005; (**) data as of 2006; (***) data as of 2002.

Source: OECD Metropolitan Database.

Cape Town is a low-density and sprawling city-region, covering 15 255 square kilometres, an area half the size of Belgium, and its population is dispersed throughout an area up to 160 kilometres from the city centre (Figure 1.10). The city-region is mono-centric yet multi-nodal; the City of Cape Town, which is the core of the city-region, contains 83% of the city-regional population and produces almost 90% of the regional GDP. The rest of the region's population lives in secondary, yet well-defined, urban nodes all showing distinct demographic, economic, social and environmental trends.[22] Population density is low, at only 255 persons per square kilometre, ranging from a maximum of 1 316 persons/km^2 in the central city to a minimum of 31 persons/km^2 in the relatively uninhabited municipality of Theewaterskloof. The main economic activities are concentrated around the city's port and the Central Business District (CBD), but the land use appears to be shaped more by tourism and agricultural activity, especially the agribusiness and agro-processing industries, which generate significant movement of people and freight around the region.

The apartheid planning system exacerbated a low-density, sprawling form of expansion, raising a number of concerns in terms of spatial, environmental and economic development. Today, Cape Town has commuting distances comparable to U.S. cities like Los Angeles, which are notorious for their sprawling profile. The apartheid system that prevailed in South Africa from 1948 to 1994 has had a tremendous effect on its urban morphology. Like many other cities around the world, urbanisation trends after World War II radically disrupted the city's original development pattern, but urban patterns and demographic trends were substantially shaped by the ideological imperatives of the apartheid state. In particular, car-dependent suburbs began to form outside the original city centre during the 1960s and 1970s, zoned exclusively for specific racial groups. Large numbers of the city's coloured population were relocated from functionally integrated and mixed-race inner-city neighbourhoods to new "super-townships" on the urban periphery that were distant from almost all existing employment opportunities, and in which commercial activities were outlawed.[23] Such spatial development, characterised by a fragmentation of nodes of economic activities, is not conducive to inter-firm networks and agglomeration economies. It increases transport flows, contributing to higher levels of CO_2 emissions, and seriously limits the capacity of local governments to develop a viable public transport system, liveable neighbourhoods and economies of scale in the delivery of public services.

Figure 1.10. **Population densities and distances from city centre in the Cape Town city-region**

2008

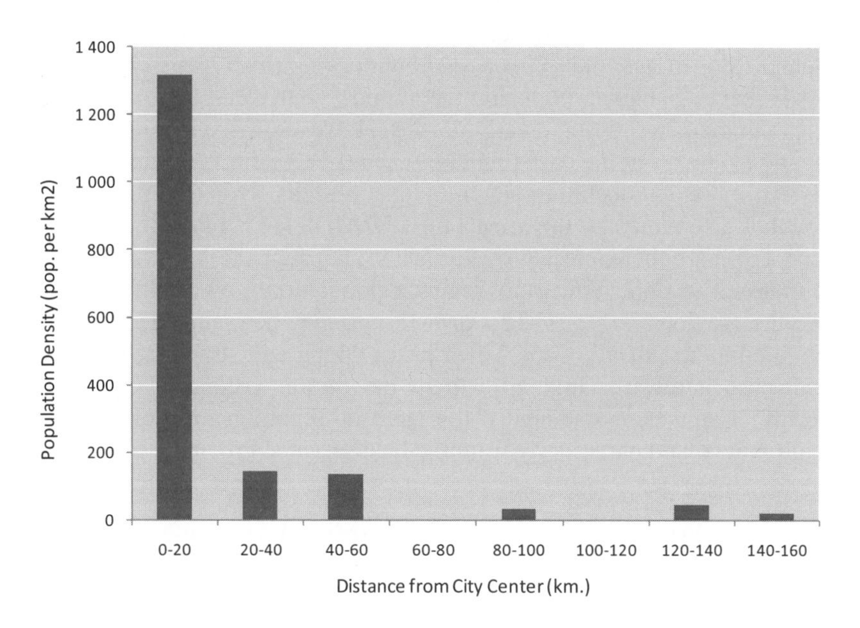

Source: Quantec Research, 2007 (based on SA Census data, 2001), OECD calculations.

...with a changing ethnic composition

Largely due to in-migration, Cape Town has experienced the highest population growth among city-regions in South Africa after Johannesburg (Figure 1.11). In the last 60 years, the regional population grew from 720 000 inhabitants in 1951 to about 3.9 million in 2006, *i.e.* at the rate of 3% a year (Figure 1.12). This positive demographic trend has been fuelled both by natural population growth, actually a national trend (Figure 1.13), as well as domestic in-migration, which represented the 35% of the overall demographic increase between 1996 and 2001 (Table 1.4). Most of these migrants arrive from areas within the Western Cape (66%), Eastern Cape (17%) and Gauteng (7%) (Boraine *et al.*, 2006).[24] Likewise, the city's population is young: residents between 15 to 34 years comprise 38% of the city's population. Cape Town is also increasingly attracting Africans from other countries, including young single male refugees and asylum seekers (between 60 000 and 80 000). In spite of a high dependency ratio, at 47%,[25] about half of new migrants coming from other regions of South Africa are young rural Africans between the ages of 15 and 34 years looking for better employment opportunities in Cape Town. These newcomers have enlarged that particular demographic segment in Cape Town, which now comprises 38% of the local population, many of whom are low-skilled and unemployed. In age and gender distribution, the urban areas of the region mostly have triangular population pyramids, with very large numbers of people in their twenties and early thirties. However, these pyramids are also starting to narrow at the base (children from 0-14 years), which suggests that the fertility rate is declining among younger adults. Projected natural urban growth is also muted by the impact of HIV/AIDS (16% of adult population). Cape Town's population is growing faster than Johannesburg or eThekwini (Durban). The Cape Town city-region's population grew at 3.3% per year over the previous 30 years. This growth rate may be maintained under two conditions. First of all, Cape Town has a young age structure, which may predispose it towards high growth in the future. Second, a high growth scenario would be maintained if the large in-migration from other parts of South Africa, and particularly from the Eastern Cape Province, continues.

Figure 1.11. **Average annual population growth rates in South Africa's provinces**

1996-2006

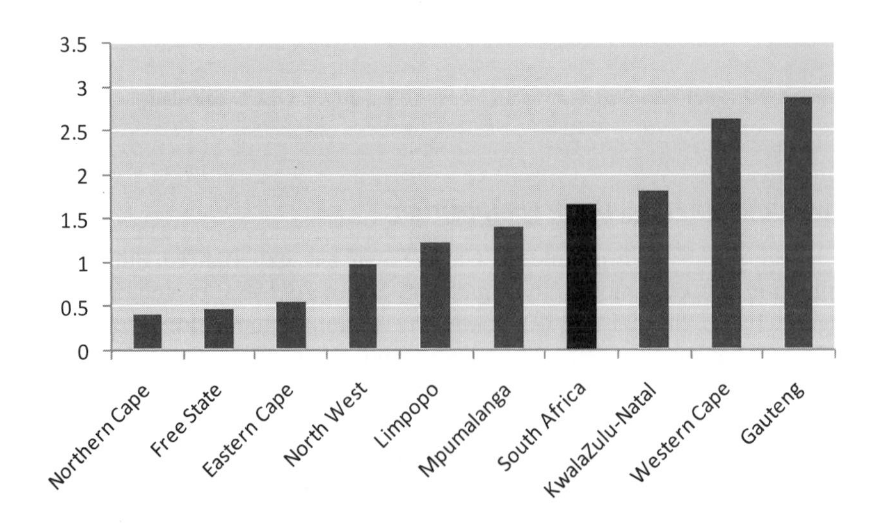

Source: Statistics South Africa.

Table 1.4. **Immigrant population between 1996 and 2001**

	Migrant population	% Migrant population
Eastern Cape	100 134	50.72
Free State	7 034	3.56
Gauteng	39 960	20.24
KwaZulu-Natal	18 098	9.17
Limpopo	2 912	1.48
Mpumalanga	2 785	1.41
Northern Cape	10 657	5.40
North West	3 653	1.85
Undetermined	12 175	6.17
TOTAL immigrants	**197 408**	**100**
Overall increase in population	**567 460**	
Percentage of immigrants		**34.79**

Source: Statistics South Africa.

The large influx of African population has changed the ethnic profile of the Cape Town region. Unusually for South Africa, the Cape Town region, and particularly the central city, was defined historically by the demographic dominance of the "Cape coloured" population, with far smaller populations of blacks and whites.[26] The Cape coloured community has consistently represented about half of the overall population of the region, constituting 48% of the population in 1911 and 51% in 2001. The steady increase of black Africans within the region in the past several decades is one of a handful of important macro-trends shaping territorial development (Table 1.5). African in-migration from the former apartheid "homelands", especially from the Eastern Cape, accelerated in the 1980s and continued at high rates into the 1990s. Often this resulted in large-scale informal settlements and infill on the spatial periphery, far from major employment centres. Meanwhile, the share of the white population is less than one-fifth, partly due to the exodus of many whites and coloured in the post-apartheid period to Canada, the United Kingdom, New Zealand and the United States. It continues to decline in relative terms.[27]

Table 1.5. **Demographic changes in the city of Cape Town since 1911**

	1911		1960		2001	
	Number of persons	%	Number of persons	%	Number of persons	%
African	4 115	1%	88 533	9%	1 007 823	30%
Coloured/ Indian	199 420	48%	510 409	53%	1 675 555	51%
White	215 124	51%	368 112	38%	627 359	19%
Other	35 493	8%		*		*
Total	418 659	108%	967 054	100%	3 310 737	100%

Source: Provincial Government of the Western Cape (2007*a*).

A growing but polarised economy

Since the beginning of the decade, the Cape Town metro-region has enjoyed positive economic growth, increasing its contribution to the national economy. After relatively slow economic growth in the 1980s and 1990s, a time of considerable political uncertainty in the country as a whole, the average growth of the region's real GDP reached 3.9% between 1995 and 2005, with acceleration over the period 2000-2005 at 4.7% (Figure 1.12). Within the national context, the Cape Town city-region's economic growth has been higher than for South Africa over these periods (3.3% in 1995-2005 and 3.9% in 2000-2005 for the country). The Johannesburg-Gauteng city-region still dominates the overall national economy (31% of national population and 33% of national GDP), but the Cape Town region has increased its local share of national GDP, unlike the other major metropolitan areas. With more than USD 20.4 billion PPP (ZAR 130 billion), the Cape Town city-region concentrated 13% of South African wealth in 2005,[28] *i.e.* more than its share of the country's population (8%), which suggests the agglomeration economies typical of many large cities (OECD 2006*a*) (Table 1.6).

Figure 1.12. **GDP trend in the Cape Town city-region as compared to the province and the country 1995-2005**

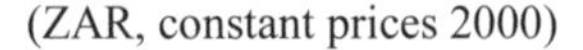
(ZAR, constant prices 2000)

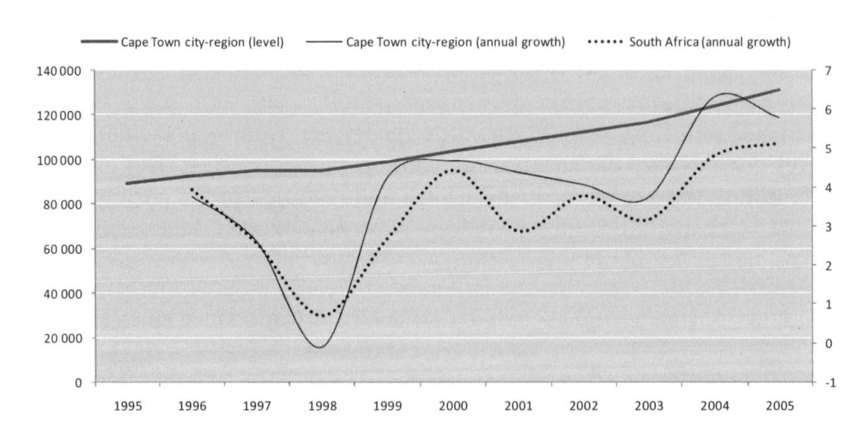

Source: Statistics South Africa and Provincial Government of the Western Cape (2007*a*).

Table 1.6. **Cape Town city-region's contribution to provincial and national GDP (1995, 2000 and 2005)**

Million of ZAR

	1995	2000	2005
Western Cape	103 112	119 098	150.176
South Africa	728 402	838 218	1 016 750
Cape Town city-region as % of Western Cape	86.48%	86.90%	87.36%
Cape Town city-region as % of South Africa	12.24%	12.35%	12.90%

Source: Provincial Government of the Western Cape (2007*a*).

Cape Town is the second-richest region in terms of GDP per capita in South Africa, after the Johannesburg-Gauteng city-region. In 2006, the regional GDP per capita amounted to USD 15 250, higher than OECD city-regions like Mexico City or Istanbul (Figure 1.13). In 2002, this indicator was more than 50% higher than the national average, which is comparable to OECD city-regions such as Izmir, Turkey, or Washington D.C. (Figure 1.13).[29] The income level in Cape Town has been above the national average (Figures 1.14-1.15). Although no clear data are available, the higher wages of Capetonians may depend on the higher productivity of labour (Figure 1.16).[30] At the regional level, tertiary activities pay wages that are comparable to those paid by manufacturing. The same is not true in South Africa, where tertiary activities, less developed and specialised than in Cape Town, pay lower wages than the secondary sector (Statistics South Africa, 2006*a*). The three major city-regions in South Africa (Johannesburg-Gauteng, Cape Town and eThekwini/Durban) display significant differences with their national average in terms of GDP per capita, while representing altogether around 22% of the total population of the country and 45% of the national output, an indication of significant regional disparities.[31]

Figure 1.13. **Ranking of OECD city-regions and Cape Town by income (2004 or last year available)**

USD PPP

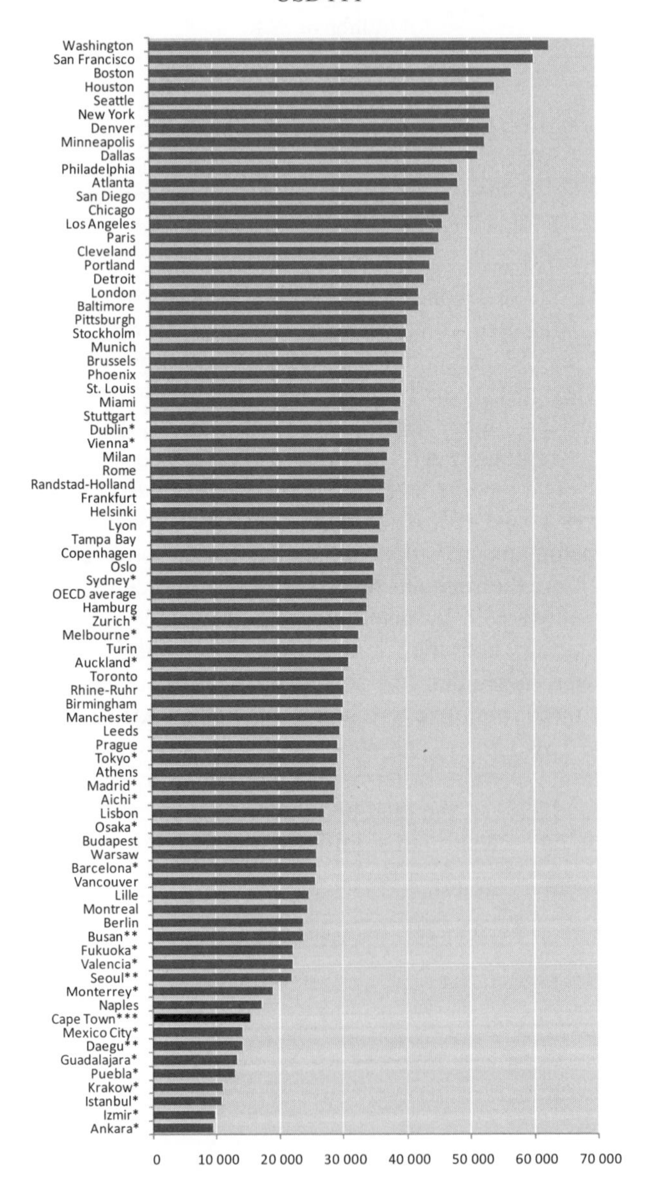

Note: * 2002 – ** 2005 – *** 2006.

Source: OECD Metropolitan Database and Provincial Government of the Western Cape (2007*a*).

Figure 1.14. **Difference in GDP per capita between city-regions and their national average (2002)**

(USD PPPs)

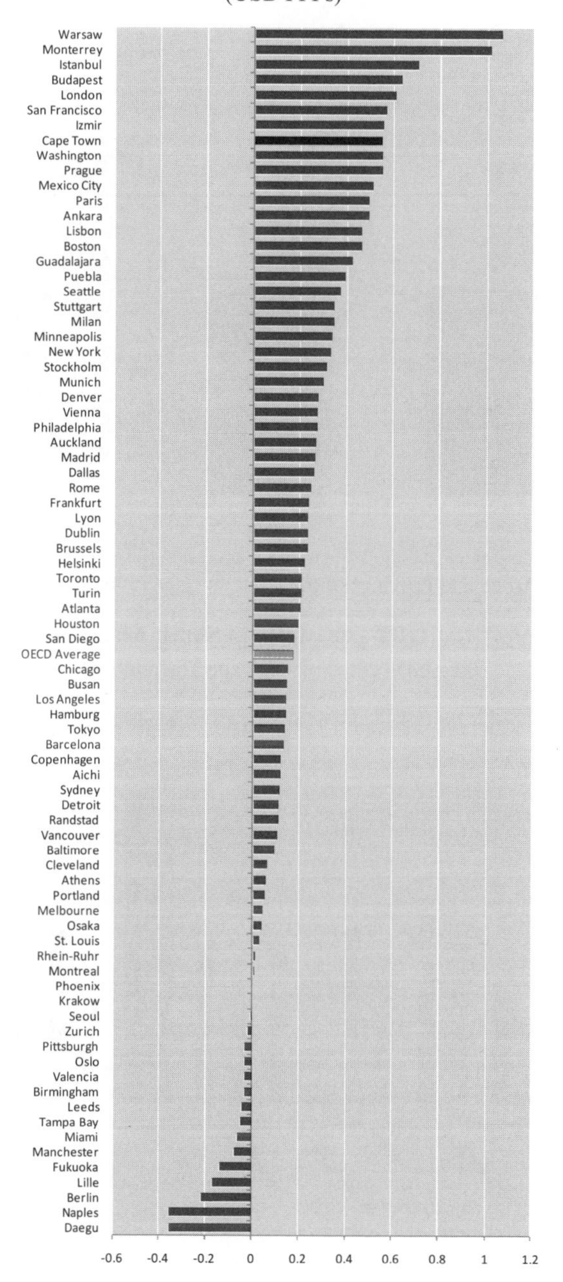

Source: OECD Metropolitan Database.

Figure 1.15. **GDP per capita trends in the Cape Town city-region and South Africa (1995, 2001 and 2006)**

USD PPPs

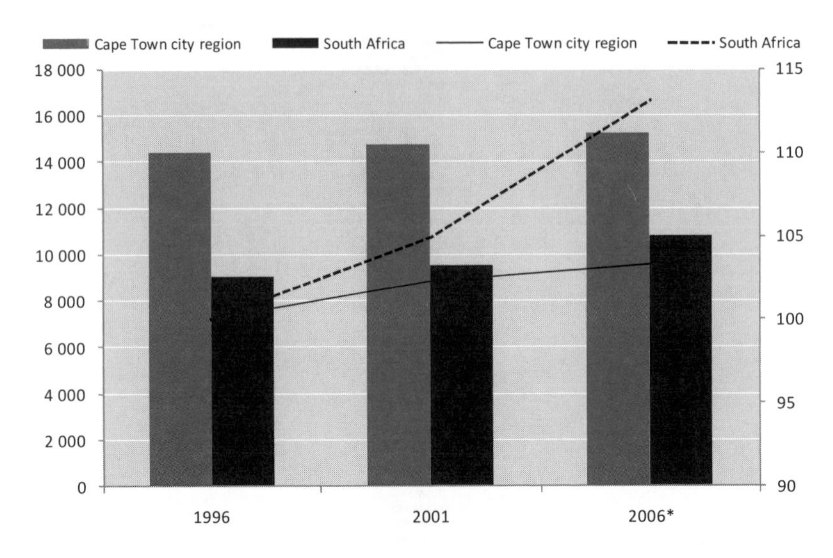

Source: Statistics South Africa and Province of the Western Cape (2007).

Figure 1.16. **GDP per capita in South Africa's provinces**

100 = GDP per capita in Cape Town in 1996

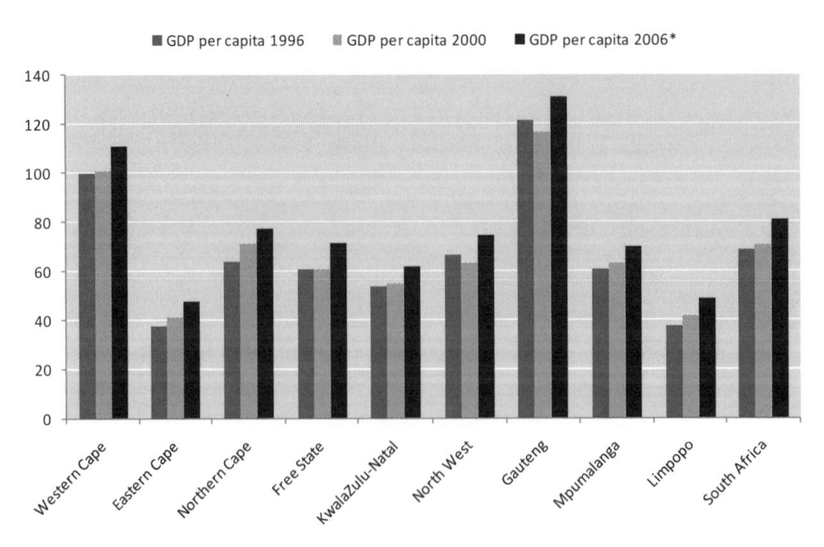

Note: GDP 2006 is calculated using mid-term Census data from 2007.

Source: Elaboration on Statistics South Africa (SSA).

Figure 1.17. **Distribution of monthly income of employees (in ZAR)**

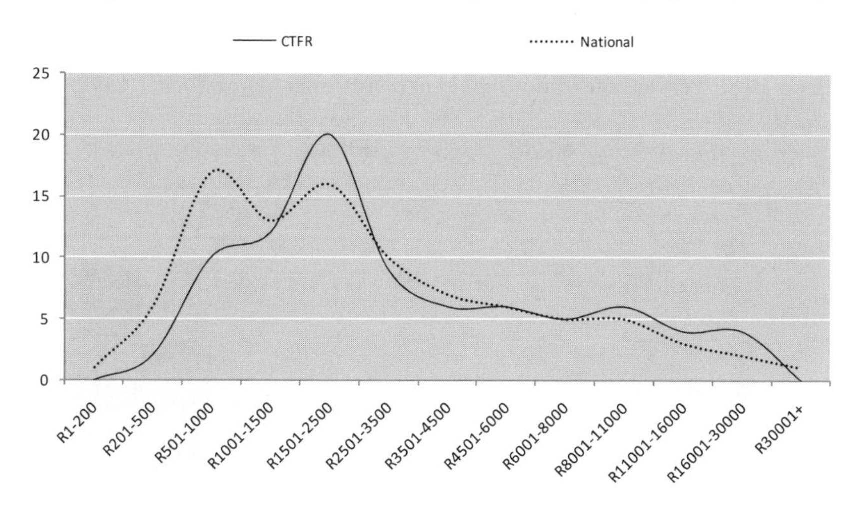

Note: Significant numbers of those surveyed refuse to disclose their income. The percentage of those who refused is not included in the graph. Refusal is far more common in the Western Cape than in the country as a whole: 12% and 4% respectively. Refusals are likely to be more common among higher earners.

Source: Labour Force Survey, Statistics South Africa 2006.

Poverty and inequality, although lower than the national average, remain extremely high in Cape Town. Despite recent economic growth, the incidence of poverty grew from 23% to 32% between 1999 and 2005 (Figure 1.18). The provisional "poverty line" used by Statistics South Africa includes households that earned less than ZAR 1 199 per month, some USD 150. By 2005, going below this poverty line, 19% of the City of Cape Town's households earned below ZAR 800 (around USD 100) per month, and an additional 13% earned less than ZAR 1 200 (USD 150). [32] In absolute terms, 761 000 people in the region earn less than ZAR 800 per month, and a further 583 000 live in households with earnings below ZAR 1 200.[33] Nevertheless, income inequalities are among the lowest compared with other cities in South Africa, as illustrated by the Gini index (Figure 1.19), but remain extremely high by international standards (Figure 1.20). While recent improvements in regional unemployment figures might limit these trends, the growth of poverty in the post-apartheid era remains a deep concern. Beyond purely income-based criteria, the disadvantaged have inherited a spatial structure from apartheid that constrains their mobility and access to areas of employment. Within this spatially polarised topography, disease, crime and underemployment have become especially entrenched in the former townships, where the concentration of poverty prevents upward mobility.

Figure 1.18. **Percentage of household expenditures below ZAR 1 199 per month**

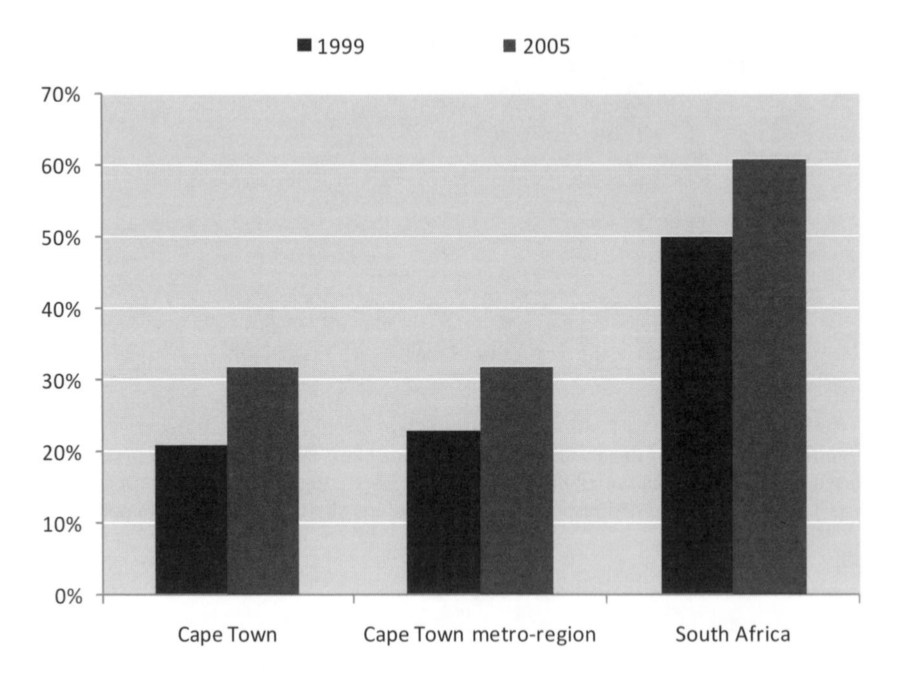

Source: October household survey 1999; General household survey 2005 (NB: The 1999 figure for the Cape Town city-region is designated as "urban Western Cape," which is used a spatial proxy for the 2005 figures).

Figure 1.19. **Gini index in the 10 largest South African cities (2001)**

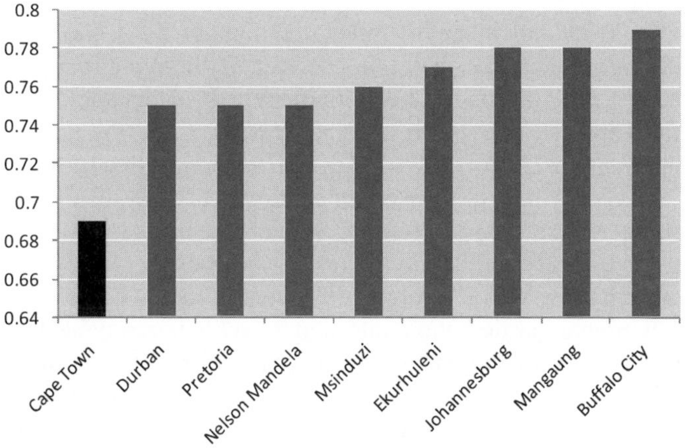

Source: Statistics South Africa.

Figure 1.20. **The 10 most unequal countries in the OECD versus the 10 most unequal in the world**

Gini index

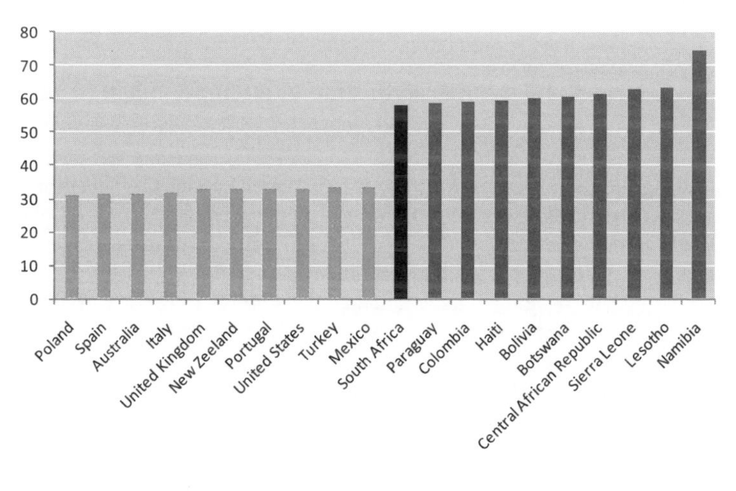

South Africa has the following percentage share of income or consumption:

Lowest 10%	Lowest 20%	Second 20%	Third 20%	Fourth 20%	Highest 20%	Highest 10%
1.4	3.5	6.3	10	18	62.2	44.7

Source: World Bank.

...with improved, although problematic, labour market performance

Unemployment and inactivity rates are high in the Cape Town city-region, although better than those in the rest of the country. Taking into account the broad definition of unemployment in 2006, unemployment rates for both the City of Cape Town and the Western Cape Province stood at 22%, compared to 37% for South Africa (Box 1.2). Already in 2001, the City of Cape Town had the lowest unemployment rate of all the largest cities in South Africa, next to Pretoria. Similarly, employment in 2006 was 14% higher in Cape Town than in the rest of the country (55% versus 41%) and the inactivity rate was 7% lower (29% versus 36%) (Table 1.7).[34] Cape Town has a higher participation rate and lower unemployment level for females than the rest of the country, a lower number of young unemployed workers of age 25 to 34 (and also unemployed seniors) than the national average. The Western Cape Province has among the highest education levels in South Africa, second only to Johannesburg-Gauteng. Cape Town, the Cape Town region and the Western Cape areas have a better profile than the country as a whole, with 2% as compared to 8% having no formal education (Budlender, 2007). Yet while regional GDP grew by 3.9% a year between 2001 and 2005 (19.5% in cumulative terms), the regional unemployment rate decreased only by about 1.5% over the same period (Labour Force Survey, 2006).

Box 1.2.**Broad and narrow definition of unemployment in South Africa**

Following the definition used by the International Labour Organisation (ILO), South Africa's official (narrow) definition of unemployment definition classifies individuals as being unemployed if they "(a) did not work during the seven days prior to the interview, (b) want to work and are available to start work within a week of the interview, and (c) have taken active steps to look for work or to start some form of self-employment in the four weeks prior to the interview" (Statistics South Africa, 2002). This places the "burden of proof" upon non-employed individuals, who must demonstrate that they have made some attempt at finding or creating a job for themselves.

The expanded (broad) definition of unemployment, on the other hand, does not include criterion (c). Although the narrow definition is the official definition in South Africa, the evidence suggests that the broad definition is better able to accurately identify the unemployed in countries like South Africa, where unemployment rates are very high and many individuals give up looking for work, becoming what is termed "discouraged workers". Taking into account the discouraged workers, the region's unemployment rate is 22%, rather than 14% (2006).

Thus, most of the analysis in this Territorial Review uses the expanded definition of unemployment. Simply stated, subjects who have not worked in the last week but want to work and would, if offered a job, be able to start working within a week, are classified as unemployed, according to the expanded definition.

Source: Western Cape Provincial Treasury, 2005; Statistics South Africa (2006*a*)

Table 1.7. **Employment, participation and unemployment rates by sex, September 2006**

Broad definition of unemployment

Area	Rate	Male %	Female %	Total %
CTR	Employment	62	49	55
	Participation	76	66	71
	Unemployment	19	26	22
Western Cape	Employment	62	48	55
	Participation	76	66	71
	Unemployment	18	27	22
South Africa	Employment	48	33	41
	Participation	69	60	64
	Unemployment	30	44	37

Source: Statistics South Africa, *Labour Force Survey September 2006.*

The service sector was responsible for the bulk of new jobs in the region between 2004 and 2006. Services alone absorbed 68% of total regional employment in 2006. Wholesale and retail, catering and accommodation grew the most between 2004 and 2006, creating more than 100 000 new jobs over the period. Today, this sub-sector accounts for 25% of total regional employment (Figure 1.21). This dramatic increase is partly due to the success of tourism-related activities, such as catering and accommodation. Transport and communication also increased their share of regional employment, which absorbed 5% of regional employment in 2006. Conversely, employment has increased in absolute terms but declined in relative terms in financial and business services and manufacturing (14% and 17% of total regional employment in 2006, respectively). Government is another important employer in the region. As the legislative capital of South Africa and the provincial capital, Cape Town is home to three spheres of government. The government sector guarantees stability in the labour market and helps disseminate knowledge and skills among many of the local workers.

Figure 1.21. **Sectoral trends of employment (2004-2006)**

Number of workers (in thousands) Percentage of total

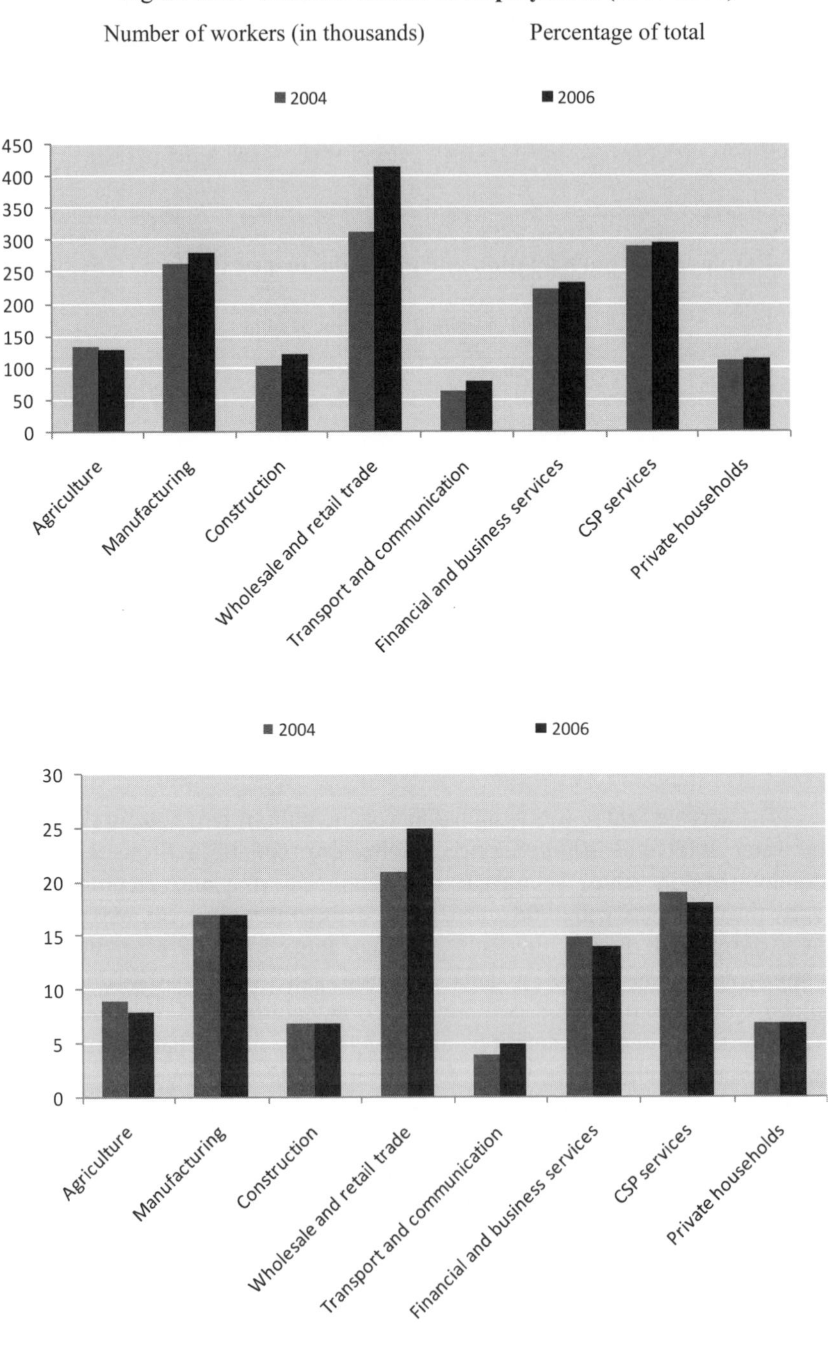

Source: Statistics South Africa Labour Force Survey 2004-2006.

The Cape Town city-region suffers from low integration of medium-skilled workers. The sectors driving regional GDP are increasingly knowledge and skill-intensive and have effectively absorbed the skilled workers. Typical of large metropolitan areas, this trend has also generated jobs in traditional low-productivity sectors, in domestic and community services and construction, as well as in the downstream hospitality and service industries. Meanwhile, medium-skilled workers (*i.e.* those who hold a secondary school certificate) are excluded from the regional labour market.[35] In 2006, almost 25% of these workers were not employed (according to the narrow definition of unemployment, as detailed in Figure 1.22).[36] Possible explanatory factors include a manufacturing sector that has suffered from international competition, particularly in the textile, clothing and leather industries.[37] As will be discussed later, the low capacity to generate employment is in part a function of a mismatch in skills – the knowledge-intensive nature of the formal economy produces an excess of demand for skilled labour, without a commensurate demand for less skilled labour.

Contrary to many other middle-income metro-regions, Cape Town's informal economy does not provide many employment opportunities. South Africa has the lowest rate of informal labour in Africa, but a relatively high rate compared to OECD countries. This trend may have been reinforced in recent years with increasing urbanisation, with more people unable to find formal employment. Though statistics on the informal economy are problematic, given informal moonlighting and multiple job-holding on evenings and/or on weekends, Statistics South Africa (2007) reported that 24.3% of South African workers laboured informally or in domestic work in 2006.[38] Interprovincial comparisons reveal that the Western Cape has a smaller informal labour force, averaging only 11% of total provincial employment. This compares to 39% in the Eastern Cape, 29% in Kwazulu-Natal (eThekwini/Durban) and 19% in Gauteng (Johannesburg). At the urban level, informal labour rates average 16% across the country's six larger metropolitan areas.[39] With the partial exception of textiles and clothing, the informal economy in the Cape Town city-region tends to focus more on non-base activities, and informal activities are not embedded in more extensive production chains. The region's informal sector is concentrated in the wholesale and retail trade; catering and accommodation sector (28%) and in private households (40%).[40] However, the low level of flexibility in the regional labour market could represent a clue that informality is used by SMEs to follow variation of demand (Table 1.8).

Figure 1.22. **Educational levels in the regional and national labour markets**

2006 – Official (narrow) definition of unemployment

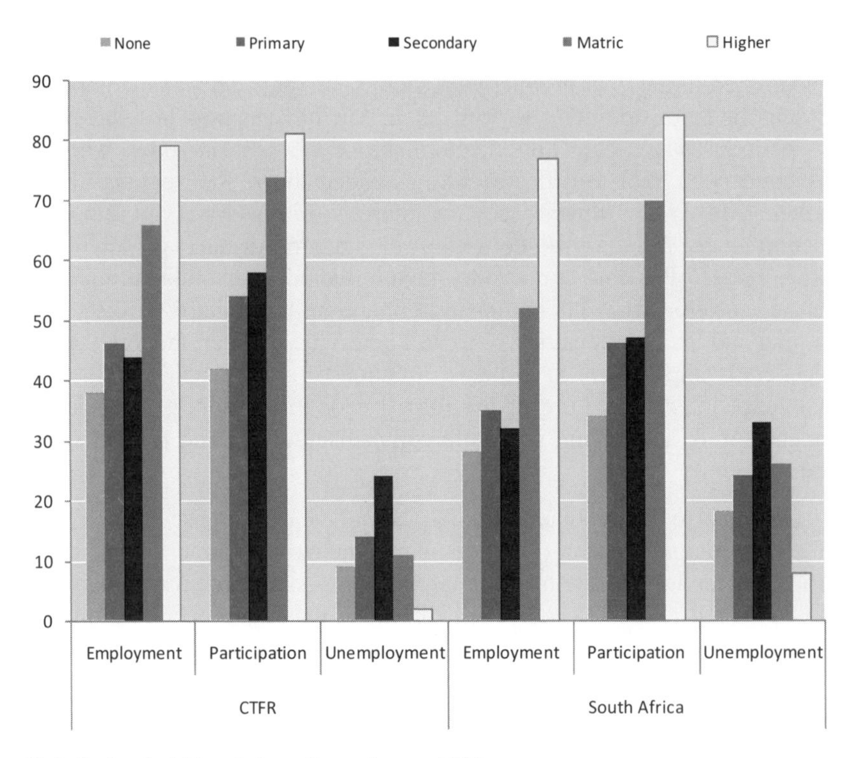

Source: Statistic South Africa, Labour Force Survey 2006.

Table 1.8. **Percentage of employees with fixed-period and permanent contracts by industry in the Cape Town city-region**

(2006)

	Fixed period	Permanent
Utilities	0%	99%
Financial intermediation	3%	88%
Community, social, personal services	9%	87%
Transport, storage, etc.	4%	80%
Manufacturing	3%	79%
Agriculture, etc.	4%	73%
Wholesale and retail trade	7%	67%
Construction	4%	60%
Private households	2%	55%

Source: Statistics South Africa, Labour Force Survey, September 2006.

1.3. A spatially fragmented and divided metropolitan economy

An increasingly diversified and open economy

Cape Town is becoming a service-based metropolitan economy, although manufacturing and agricultural activities are still important. Between 1995 and 2005, the regional economy has gone through a process of transformation that has resulted in a large development of tertiary activities (Figure 1.23). In 2005, the total service sector represented 69.5% of regional GDP, including financial and business services (more than 30%), wholesale and retail trade catering and accommodation (17.7%), transport and communication (11.6%) and government services (9.2%).[41] The primary sector, despite a reduction in its contribution to regional GDP (3% of the region's economy in 2005), is still the major exporter. This sector has a great influence on the regional landscape (in terms of land use, for instance) and underpins large sectors of the manufacturing economy (agro-processing) and the tourism industry (conference, ecological and winery tours).[42] Finally, manufacturing, despite an intensive process of restructuring in textiles, represents more than 17% of both regional GDP and total employment (Figure 1.24).

Figure 1.23. **Trends in sectoral specialisation in the Cape Town city-region**

(1995-2005)

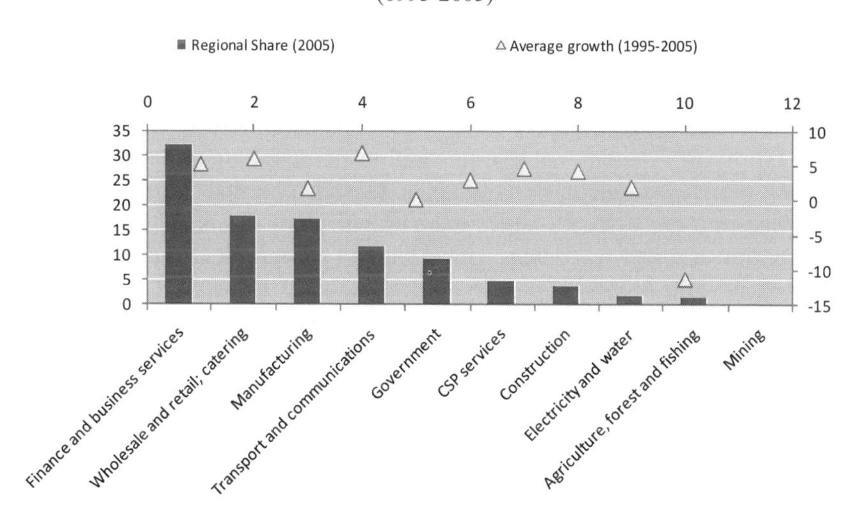

Source: Provincial Government of the Western Cape (2007*a*).

Figure 1.24. **Export growth in the Cape Town city-region by sector**

(1995-2006)

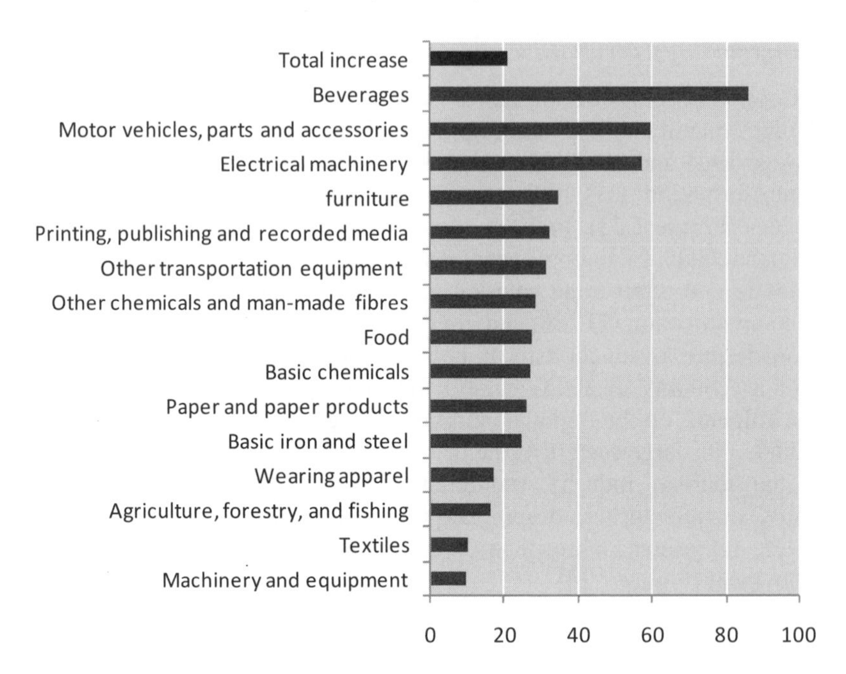

Source: WESGRO, 2007.

Cape Town has become an open economy, which presents an opportunity for economic growth but also a challenge, given its exposure to the volatility of international markets and to its emerging competitors. The specialisation in service (non-tradable) sectors and the restructuring of manufacturing are effects of the international competition with which the Cape region has had to contend since the end of apartheid, as Cape Town regained its role of "soft" gateway to Africa. For instance, transport and communication, along with wholesale and retail, developed most between 1995 and 2005. Although Cape Town has no mining activities, it features a regional trade-to-GDP ratio of 0.61, a figure in line with the national average and above the OECD average (Figure 1.25).[43] Due to exchange-rate fluctuations and specialisation in traditional manufacturing, regional competitiveness is now challenged by competitors such as China and India.

Imports have soared since the mid 1990s, only partially offset by the increase in exports. The region has seen a tremendous growth in imports: ZAR 69.9 billion (USD PPP 10.32 billion) worth of goods, or 37.7% of regional GDP, was imported into the Cape Town region in 2005, up from 20.5% in 1995. The regional increase of imports mirrors a national trend. Between 2000 and 2005, the national trade balance was negative both for goods and services, a peculiar dynamic for a middle-income country, which usually imports services and exports manufacturing goods (Figure 1.26). China has become the second most important supplier to the Cape Town city-region after the European Union, with an annual growth rate of more than 30% between 2000 and 2005 (Figure 1.27). A surge in clothing and textile imports followed the expiration of the WTO Multi-Fibre Agreement in January 2005, posing a challenge to local producers. Less important in terms of value than imports, regional exports have nevertheless recorded positive growth, averaging 15.5% annually between 2000 and 2004 (WESGRO 2005). Within this period, exports made their largest contribution to GDP in 2002 (24%), when the ZAR was relatively weak. In 2006, total exports from the Cape Town region amounted to ZAR 41.5 billion (USD 6.12 billion), and the leading export sectors were agriculture, forestry and fishing, printing, publishing and recorded media, and food and beverages. This trend reflects the expansion of the agro-food industry, while the share for other sectors, such as textiles, has almost disappeared from regional export. Within agro-food, deciduous fruit, iron and steel, and fish are the most important regional exports.[44] Growth in the beverage sector was the most pronounced; its share of regional export increased by 80% between 1995 and 2006 (Figure 1.24).[45]

Figure 1.25. **Trade-to-GDP ratio in the OECD and South Africa**

2004

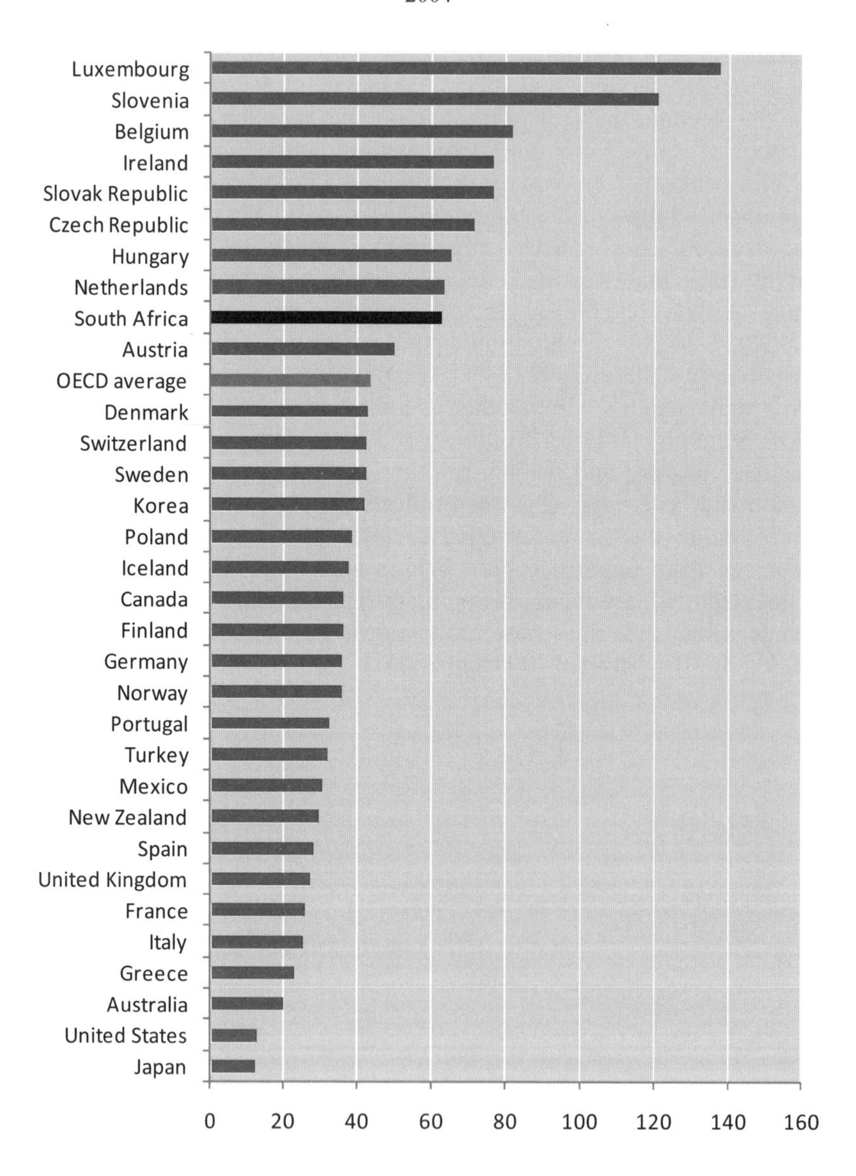

Source: OECD Factbook (2007) and Province of the Western Cape.

Figure 1.26. **Trade balance in South Africa and a selection of non-member countries**

Average 2000-2005

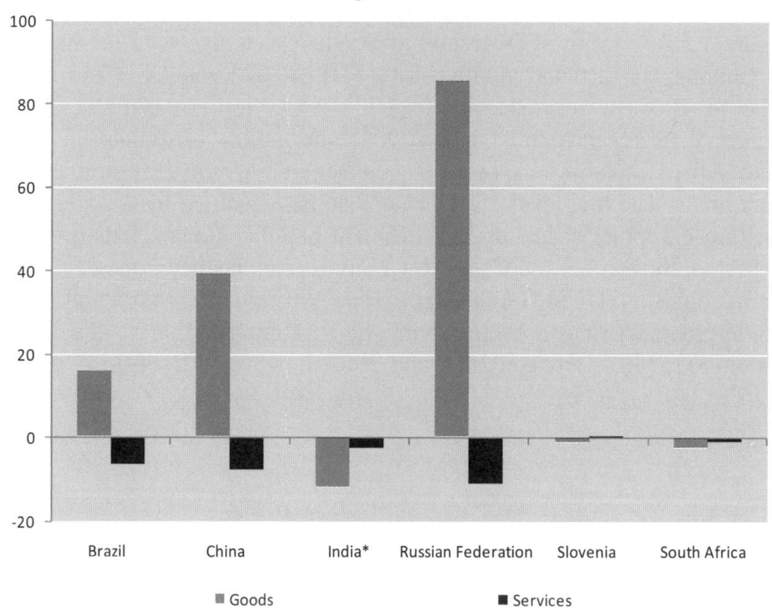

Source: Calculated from OECD Factbook 2007.

Figure 1.27. **Trade balance between the Western Cape and China, 1995-2004**

ZAR million

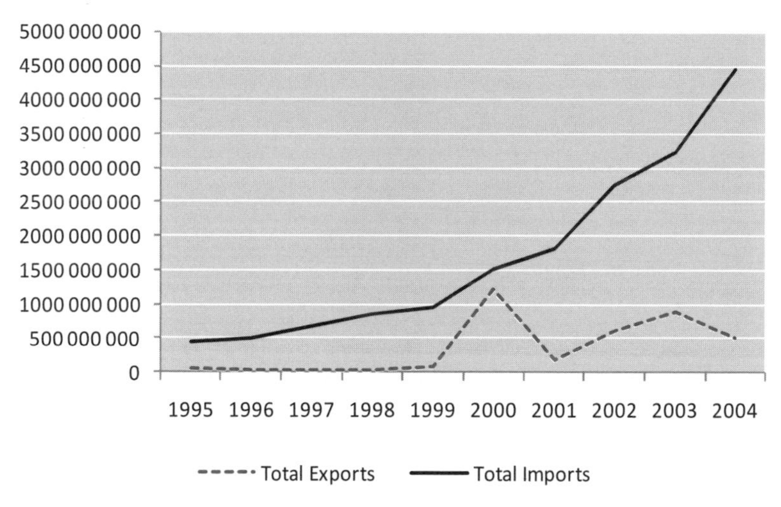

Source: WESGRO 2005 – Custom and Excise, South Africa.

Increased openness to international trade has also attracted Foreign Direct Investment (FDI) to the Cape Town city-region, although this trend has recently declined. FDI inflows in South Africa averaged 1% of GDP between 1999 and 2003, relatively low compared to OECD countries (Figure 1.28).[46] Inflow FDI trends to South Africa also tend to show deep fluctuations; for instance, South Africa FDI in 2004 was USD 701 million, while in 2005, it rose sharply to USD 6 133 million (OECD, 2008*b*). According to Thomas and Leape (2005), the major constraints for FDI in South Africa include lack of skills, exchange-rate volatility and the high crime rate.[47] The low level of FDI may also be explained by the presence of a mature corporate sector and an efficient national financial market. Over the period 2004-2006, the Cape Town city-region has been one of the main destinations for FDI in South Africa. The Western Cape attracted 33% of FDI in South Africa, a larger share than its contribution to the national economy (15%).[48] Between 2004 and 2007, however, FDI inflows declined by 75%.

Figure 1.28. **FDI in OECD and selected middle-income countries**

(2004-2006)

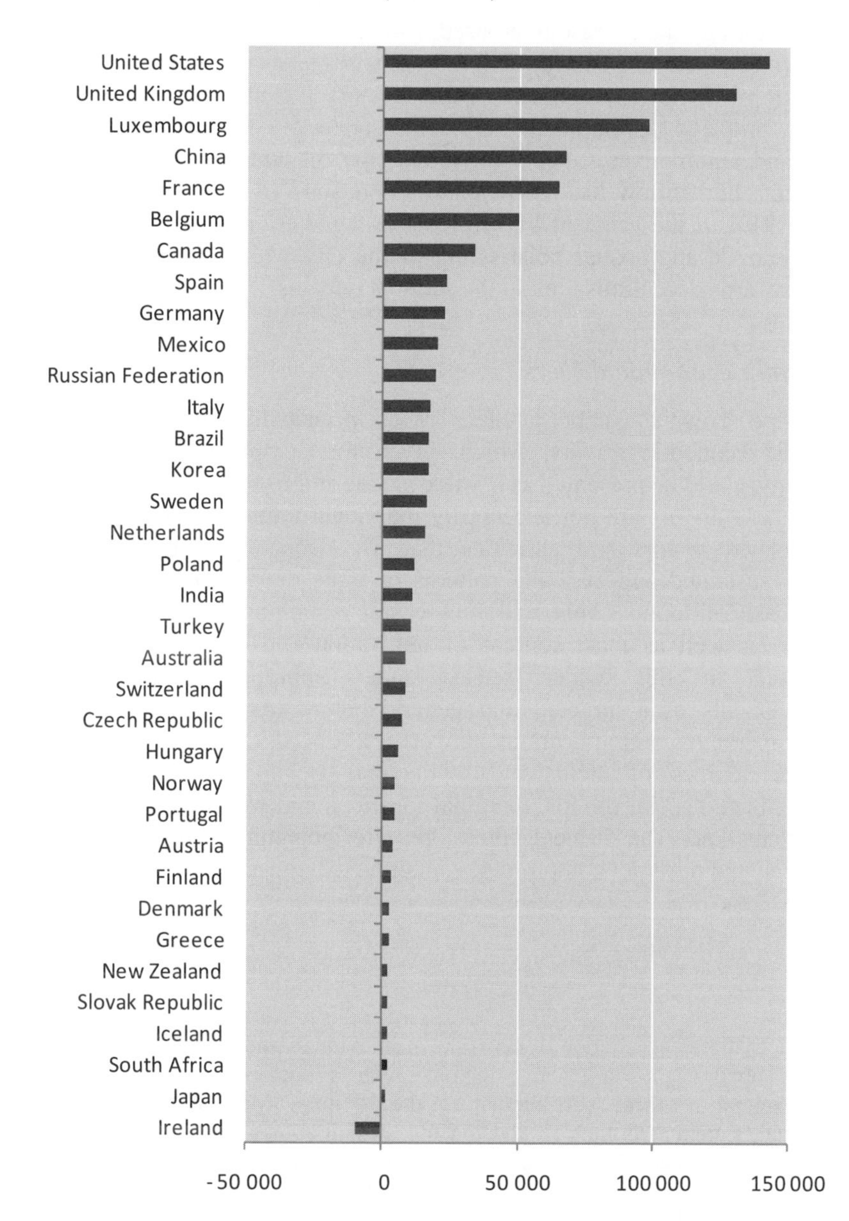

Source: OECD, Factbook, 2008.

Foreign direct investment primarily targets the Cape Town city-region's booming service sector, mainly located in the central city. The service sector attracts 83% of overall investment in the Cape Town city-region, while manufacturing and resource-based sectors attract 13% and 5% respectively.[49] Among service activities, tourism takes the lion's share, with 39% of provincial FDI inflows. Other sectors include: business services (14%), property development and construction (12%), BPO/call centres (5%) and automotives (5%).[50] Excluding the oil and gas sector in Eden District,[51] FDI inflow has so far mainly concentrated in the City of Cape Town (91% of the value of FDI inflows to the Western Cape), reinforcing the economic and spatial polarisation of the city within the region; yet a trend towards decentralisation to the suburbs remains.

The main economic drivers

Cape Town's competitiveness relies principally on a number of dynamic economic drivers, which, given the complexity of the urban economy, could be presented as *i)* value chains and *ii)* regional clusters (Box 1.3). These drivers are not necessarily individual industries, but clusters of inter-related sectors and activities that, if adequately supported, could deliver sustained and evolving patterns of trade drawing on a wide local asset base of inputs. This will secure self-sustaining growth with local returns, as well as local sources of innovation and creativity. "Drivers" discussed in this wider sense, under appropriate infrastructural improvements of a targeted and generic nature (*e.g.* business services, labour markets, communications networks, knowledge circuits, etc.), could become sources of inclusive growth, that is, involve smaller firms, disadvantaged social groups, marginal locations and weaker sections of the labour market. The drivers, therefore, are potential sources of social inclusion and need not compromise economic dynamism.

Box 1.3. **Which theoretical framework for a complex urban economy?**

The spatial concentration of networks of individuals and firms belonging to a single supply chain can generate agglomeration economies, *i.e.* advantages that are external to firms but internal to the territory (Marshall, 1920). Such advantages are due to the high division and specialisation of labour, the presence of a large number of qualified suppliers-producers and the fast circulation of information. Firms belonging to a supply chain transform local inputs into outputs through complex networks of backward and forward linkages (Hirschman, 1959). Agro-food industries work in this way, as do clusters of craft industries and knowledge-based industries that rely on strong urban learning and knowledge networks. Agglomeration economies positively affect firms' competitiveness by increasing their productivity, reducing production costs and enhancing learning and knowledge formation. This dynamic can be observed in a number of OECD regions, where the economic value generated by a given territory strongly depends on a single supply chain acting as a local economic driver.

When a large number of networks of individuals and firms belonging to different supply chains are spatially concentrated, positive externalities or "urbanisation economies" emerge (Jacobs, 1969). These range from local specialisation in the skill, knowledge, business service and financial needs of the value chains, to trade and learning proximities built between inter-connected firms and institutions. Backward and forward linkages among firms are usually more interconnected than the spatial concentration of a single supply chain. These economies generate collective goods and institutions that are by nature unspecialised, as they support the competitiveness of most regional supply chains. Urban collective goods can be highly sophisticated – world-class universities, large airports, etc. – and are usually involved in symbiotic relationships with the spatially concentrated urban markets that host them. The presence of a large market also attracts firms that (a) seek to benefit from the concentrated demand and (b) interface not with one supply chain, but with a number of them, *e.g.* financial activities or logistics. These firms are usually clustered in key nodes of the urban region. An urban region's competitiveness will depend on the economic value produced by a number of supply chains and clusters acting as local economic drivers.

Key value chains

The agro-food value chain

The agro-food value chain features the Cape Town city-region's image on the global market, evolving towards a more capital-intensive form of production. Agriculture has grown relatively rapidly over the past decades, and there have been a number of success stories, such as the rapid growth in wine, citrus and table grape exports, and the exploitation of foreign and domestic markets with smaller niche products. Agriculture production covers a large area within the city-region and is the main economic activity of key urban nodes within the functional region, such as Stellenbosch and Drakenstein. The Western Cape has more or less reached the limits of its potential spatial expansion for agricultural activities, and the chain is now evolving towards more capital-intensive productions and specialised niches (OECD, 2006*b*).

The food-processing industry is the most important segment of the chain. Western Cape demand for food is higher than in the rest of the country. This subsector is the second-largest employer (18.5% of the Province's manufacturing workforce),[52] the biggest exporter (17% of the

Western Cape's exports) and produces about 20% of the manufacturing value-added of the province (Western Cape Department of Economic Development and Tourism, 2006; WESGRO, 2006).[53] The bulk of the regional output comes from large and well-organised businesses such as Clover Danone, Parmalat, Delmonte and other large global players.[54] Similarly, four major global food retail chains dominate the consumer retail business – Shoprite, Pick n Pay, Woolworths and Spar.[55] Local small and medium businesses do not play a large part. However, the recent growth in demand for health products and niche foods has created new possibilities for small capital-intensive firms that may start taking advantage of these new markets (MEDS, 2006). The other important segment within the agro-food value chain is food and beverages, including the wine industry, one of the most successful regional products on the international market. This sub-sector is a large, complex industry with high degree of vertical integration. It added ZAR 2.3 billion in 2005 (PPP USD 361.6 million), or 2.3% of Cape Town's GDP.

The agro-food value chain is supported by the presence of a well-developed regional specialisation in research in food biotechnology, encouraged by the local concentration of agro-food activities.[56] Large corporations and leading research institutions have continued to play a role in encouraging the adoption of biotechnology, to improve the production and quality of agricultural produce and food within the Cape Town region. Moreover, local Cape Town-based food biotechnology has increased its specialisation in fields that are engaged to local competitive advantage in the agro-food chain. An example of such specialisation is the Stellenbosch Institute for Wine Biotechnology, which hosts a number of start-ups funded by the Cape Biotech Trust that are active in research in winemaking and nutraceutical (nutritional supplement) industries.[57]

The growth potential of the agro-food value chain is, however, compromised by a number of structural weaknesses. Business profitability is challenged by insufficient intra- and inter-industry linkages. In particular, functions such as distribution, marketing, tourism, logistics and transportation are not sufficiently integrated in the value-chain. Because of this lack of co-ordination/co-operation within agri-business, the chain is vulnerable to exogenous shocks such as currency volatility, and firms are not likely to anticipate major structural changes that could dramatically impact their profitability. Transport logistics also represent a major issue. In an international context of decreased relative prices, which require both a reduction in production costs and an increase in the quality of products,[58] firms in Cape Town have to bear the soaring logistical costs of getting perishable products to the market with limited transport infrastructure and port facilities. For instance, a 1997 study shows how the expansion of the local fynbos industry was hampered by a lack of affordable airline freight space into the European Union (Allerts *et al.*, 1998). Similarly, a study on the cold fruit supply chain between South Africa and the Netherlands identified various infrastructure capacity problems as barriers to industry development, for example insufficient cold storage facilities in certain regions, too few refrigerated trucks suitable for fruit transport, and bottlenecks in the fruit terminals (Broens *et al.*, 2000).

A major challenge for the agro-food value chain is climate change, which is affecting the Mediterranean-like micro-climate of the city-region and changing the spatial pattern of production. Only 17% of the Western Cape's land territory is available for agriculture, most of it for grazing. Accordingly, valuable land represents a scarce resource that should be highly protected. Nonetheless, decades of unsustainable agricultural practices and desertification are a threat to the agro-food value chain. Erosion, human activities (*i.e.* inappropriate road construction, informal settlements, etc.), alien plant infestation, limited water resources and uneconomic sub-division of land[59] are among the main concerns facing the development of agriculture in the Western Cape. Of course, climate change could result in geographical shifts in local agriculture, but the overall impact on productivity is likely to be negative in the medium term.[60]

Finally, the development of the agro-food sector is burdened by regulations that prevent SMEs participating in the market. Large businesses generate the bulk of the regional added-value, but the region also has a large number of small and medium-scale enterprises that are marginal within the local value-chain. The marginalisation of SMEs can be partly explained by regulations that were designed to respond to large firms' needs. Bureaucratic disincentives holding back the growth of SMEs include tax, environmental and labour laws (SMEs are bound by the same rules as large firms when hiring or firing). Because of such restrictions, SMEs have not been able to develop agro-tourism or other niche markets, which could become a rich new source of development for the entire value-chain.

Tourism and hospitality

Tourism and hospitality activities have generated significant job creation. With 8.4 million international arrivals in 2006, South Africa ranked 25th in the world's top tourist destinations, and the province of the Western Cape is the third destination in the country (the second in terms of international arrivals), after Gauteng (Johannesburg) and Kwa-Zulu Natal (eThekwini) (Figure 1.29). The Western Cape attracts a larger number of tourists from Europe, especially from the United Kingdom (32%), Germany (15%) and the United States, than the other provinces (Figure 1.30).

According to WESGRO, the region's trade promotion organisation, the Western Cape enjoys the highest average expenditure per domestic tourist for all provinces. WESGRO projects an increase of air passengers from 5 million in 2003 to 14 million by 2015. This positive trend is likely to be enhanced by the 2010 FIFA World Cup, which is leveraging public investment in the region. The rapid expansion of the tourism and hospitality value chain has directly supported the income of the local population, since more than half of regional SMEs operate in catering and hospitality.

Figure 1.29. **Provincial distribution of international arrivals**

(Q3 2005-Q3 2006)

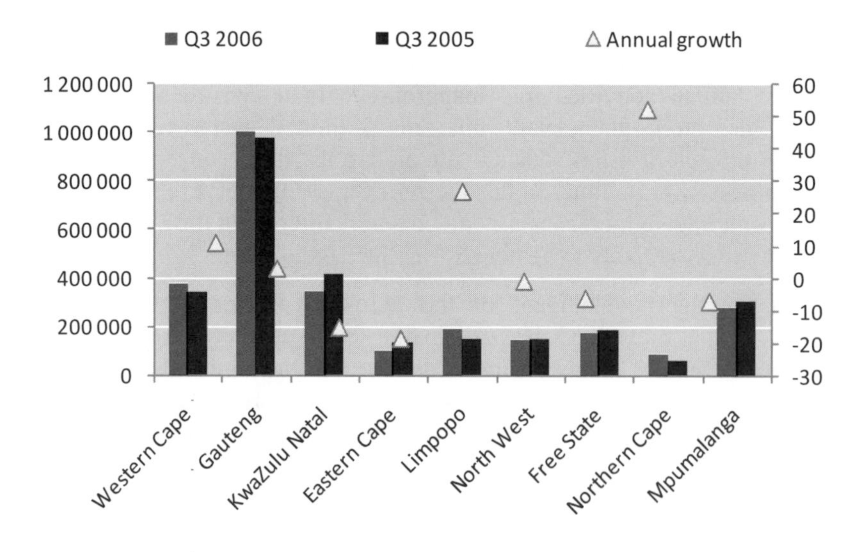

Source: Statistics South Africa.

Figure 1.30. **Provincial distribution of international arrivals by origin**

(Q3 2006)

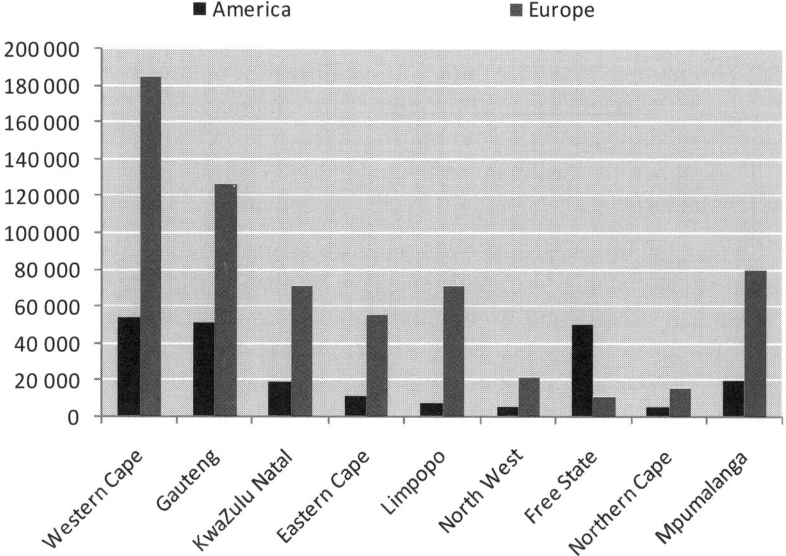

Source: Statistics South Africa.

Tourism and hospitality represents one of the most integrated and promising value-chains within Cape Town, being related to virtually every sector of the regional economy. The fact that wholesale and retail trade, catering and accommodation, construction, transport and communication have all increased by more than 6% a year in terms of GDP between 1995 and 2005 reflects in part the overall success of the tourist economy. More specifically, catering and hospitality activities have expanded their contribution to regional GDP by 77% in the years from 1995-2005.[61] Catering and hospitality grew faster (at 9.5% per annum) than every other sector in the regional economy, including finance and insurance, between 2000 and 2005.

Specific market niches in the tourism value chain include cultural industries, as well as the MICE (meetings, incentives, conferences and exhibitions). The Cape Town city-region benefits from a wide range of cultural and natural amenities, such as the Castle of Good Hope, the National Gallery, Robben Island (where Nelson Mandela was imprisoned for almost 20 years), the Victoria and Albert Waterfront, the Kirstenbosch

Botanical Garden, Table Mountain and the Winelands. In addition to its coastal location, it has a well-developed array of assets and competencies that draw on its "creolised" history and contemporary culture. Recreational amenities and cultural assets have boosted the MICE sector, as illustrated by the recent success of the Cape Town International Convention Centre (CTICC), which hosted 35 international and 40 national conferences in 2006, contributed ZAR 1.2 billion, and directly employed 2 350 people within the Western Cape Province. The International Congress and Convention Association (ICCA) put Cape Town in 29th position worldwide for the number of meetings per city in 2006 – ahead of Pretoria (209th position) and eThekwini (Durban), which ranked 168.

Challenged by other South African destinations, the Cape Town regional tourism value-chain is also constrained by weaknesses in international and regional accessibility and its negative image as a place with a high crime rate. Although recent trends are positive, the Western Cape's share of the domestic market has been declining by an average of 10% per year since 2002, showing that its appeal for tourists may be losing out to such cities as eThekwini (Durban), which has increased its international visitors by 19% since 2004 and hosted three times the number of domestic visitors to the Western Cape. There is room for Cape Town to increase domestic business trips, which currently represent only 9.5% of the national total. The upcoming events in 2010 will provide an opportunity to leverage potential in the sector, especially in sport and ecotourism. Growth in tourism is, however, inhibited by airlift capacity constraints and by the lack of an efficient public transport system that tourists may use when visiting the region. Another major issue is crime, which although concentrated in the townships, can spill over into areas frequented by the tourists, harming Cape Town's international image. Finally, climate change is likely to affect the competitiveness of the tourism value-chain in the medium term. The European Union is considering capping the greenhouse gas emissions in the aviation industry, which would raise the price of air travel for Europeans. Since about two-thirds of the Cape Town city-region's tourists arrive from Europe, generating ZAR 14.9 billion in spending in 2005, the province should plan a concerted effort to attract more international tourism. Estimates indicate that if a decrease in arrivals led to an equal decrease in expenditure, a 1% increase in the price of air travel could entail a loss of ZAR 68 million per annum for the provincial economy (Western Cape Department of Environmental Affairs and Planning, 2007).

Urban consumption

The Cape Town city-region, itself a large urban market generating demand for consumption of goods, lands and services, also acts as an economic driver, attracting economic activities that need a large and concentrated demand to flourish. The value chains that benefit most from a symbiotic relationship with the regional market are a) wholesale and retail, and b) construction and the housing sector.

a) Wholesale and retail value chain

Economic growth in Cape Town has been propelled by the demand for consumer goods, generating new retail areas. Wholesale and retail activities are numerous and complex and represent a proper value chain that has become the second-largest contributor to the local economy (17%). Besides the commercial activities linked to the agro-food industry, as discussed above, the region has become one of the most important urban markets in Africa. The central city, for instance, boasts some of the most developed shopping centres of the continent. The Victoria and Albert Waterfront, a mixed-use property development located around the original harbour, is now a regional retail attraction, attracting about 20 million visitors in 2006, a third of them international tourists.[62] Another important retail area is the newly established Century City, a 250-hectare enclosed "city" that combines office, residential, retail and leisure opportunities on a massive scale, which is driving intense commercial activity and retail growth along the northern axis of the city-region. Cape Town is the head office for the Foschini Group, PEP Stores, Ackermans, the Woolworths Group and Truworths – all major national players in the fashion industry. The Foschini Group, for example, is the largest specialty retailer in the country, with 13 trading divisions, more than 1 200 stores and 2007 retail turnover up 8.8% from the previous year.

In the retail industry, the increasing demand for variety and higher-quality products underpins the development of the fashion and design business. An increasing emphasis of the regional clothing and textile industry is improving the quality of output, through better design and production processes. These firms produced 2% of regional GDP (ZAR 2.2 billion) in 2005. Burgeoning imports from China and India, as well as from other South Africa provinces such as KwaZulu Natal,[63] have pushed local producers to compete on differentiation more than on price in fashion and apparel, and to cater to a more sophisticated and diverse clientele. In response to international trends, local clothing retailers have become more demanding with respect to price, quality, flexibility and variety, forcing producers to focus on design and to concentrate on the upper end of the fashion market. The consequent restructuring of the industry has polarised the regional textile and clothing industry, and resulted in downsizing by formal factories, many of which now outsource production to informal cut, make and trim (CMT) operators. While local leaders have increased the use of machinery in the production process and outsourced to small producers, small craft firms still compete on price by contracting informal workers. Because of informality they cannot export, and operating with very limited investment capacity, they are prevented from improving the quality of their output, thus creating a vicious cycle.

b) Construction and housing

The booming construction and housing industry has exploited a favourable investment climate, emerging as one of Cape Town's cardinal drivers. It has recently experienced massive growth as a result of increased urban consumption and low interest rates. While the construction sector contributed just over 3.6% of the city's value-added in 2005, its annual growth over 2004 and 2005 exceeded 11.5%, making commercial and residential property development one of the Cape Town city-region's most dynamic sectors. Indeed, in 2006, the Cape Town municipality passed more than USD 160 million of projects in building plans in 2006, the highest figure of any metropolitan area in the country. The development of a number of restoration projects, such as the Victoria and Albert Waterfront, have increased the activity in this sector. The construction sector benefits a web of connected industries in Cape Town, such as design, architecture, finance, road construction, taxis, and the hardware and home improvement retail sector. The massive state-sponsored housing delivery programme (16 000 units produced between 2006 and 2007)[64] has also boosted the construction sector within the region. Although the programme delivers low-income units, the quantity is so high that it represents a large portion of construction value.

Several recent commercial and residential projects illustrate the potential of this economic driver. In terms of commercial property, the gradual developments over the past 25 years has produced a sharp increase in the office space outside the Central Business District (CBD), in such areas as Bellville/Durbanville, Pinelands, Claremont and Century City. Challenging the dominance of the city centre, these projects provide more office space than the CBD. Construction in the CBD has not been stagnant during this period; central improvement districts (CID) and the creation of urban development zones that offer investors tax relief have led to a property boom in the downtown area. Simultaneously, construction in the residential sector has expanded the stock of primarily single-dwelling homes[65] and created a new generation of mixed retail/residential developments.[66] Entirely new residential developments have emerged in West Beach and Parklands on the city's north western axis and Capricorn in Muizenberg along the southern axis. This has been complemented by the construction of mixed-use projects, particularly the 250-hectare Century City development and the forthcoming Tembokwezi Life Style Estate.[67] However, as will be discussed later, because of strict land regulations and developers' preference for larger units, the construction sector, apart from the state-sponsored housing delivery programme, has not built an adequate supply of affordable housing for low- and middle-income residents. If this situation were to be addressed, the housing and construction sector could become an even more robust driver in the regional economy.

Emerging clusters

An emerging financial and business services cluster

The favourable macroeconomic conditions in South Africa, including a relatively low-interest environment and better business climate, has favoured the development of finance and business services in Cape Town. Although not as sophisticated as Johannesburg's – whose stock exchange is among the 20th largest in the world – the finance and insurance industry in Cape Town doubled its contribution to the regional GDP over 1995-2005,[68] accounting for 16.6% of the regional economy. Of significance is the location of a number of head offices of large financial and life insurance companies in South Africa, such as Old Mutual, Sanlam and Metropolitan Life, whose historical location within the city-region has enhanced local specialisation in these sectors.[69] An interesting development within this cluster has been the recent rise in call centres and business process outsourcing (BPO). These activities span a number of sectors, including telecommunications, financial services, and wholesale, retail and hospitality. Off-shoring is responsible for 36% of the industry's growth in the past five years. The United Kingdom accounts for 18 companies, the United States follows with nine, and Germany with three companies, although a number of companies serve multiple offshore markets (Deloitte and Touche, 2007). The number of local agents in BPO almost doubled in one year (2005-06), and kept growing in the following year (Deloitte and Touche, 2007). This sub-sector has stimulated the dynamic financial services sector but also reverberated across telecommunications, wholesale, retail and hospitality.

There are, however, several concerns over the current and future growth potential of this cluster, including:

- Lack of middle management. Poor interaction between the financial/business services and the local universities has caused a lack of specific training programmes, limiting the availability of middle management. While importing highly educated workers is still economically efficient, it is a costly proposition in the case of middle management, and could affect competitiveness of local firms in the medium term.

- Lack of skills. The main concerns are linked to the difficulties in implementing the Black Economic Empowerment (BEE) strategy, which is intended to increase the number of black citizens holding key positions in South African business community.[70]
- Lack of transportation facilities. Contact centre and BPO companies are located around major business centres or nodes, which in turn are situated with convenient access to main transport interchanges and highways. The major nodes are the CBD; the southern suburbs, particularly Claremont; the northern suburbs, particularly Bellville; and Century City. The industry's location is problematic for many of its staff, lengthening their daily average commute-time to between 30 to 60 minutes. While this compares favourably with other industry centres, such as Johannesburg, improving transport mobility still remains a challenge as far as staff retention is concerned.

Cape Town as an African logistics hub

The Cape Town region holds a strategic position as a coastal city and trading hub and has developed a successful logistic cluster specialised particularly in the transport of agro-food and oil. Cape Town has the geographical advantage of access to global markets and trade and acts as a gateway for a large part of sub-Saharan Africa. This has shaped the Cape's industrial mix, in which transport plays a disproportionately large role as compared to the South African average (Figure 1.31). The regional employment generated by transport and communications increased by 10% between 2004 and 2006. The bulk of transport activities are related to agricultural products (fresh and processed) and other key exports (such as refined oil and steel). These goods are transported from their nodes of production to regional ports and to the airport for national distribution and export purposes. The two commercial ports at Cape Town and Saldanha, along with the airport (Cape Town International), freight rail and pipelines, handled 23.3% of South Africa's total cargo in 2006 (National Ports Authority, 2007) (Figure 1.32). The Cape Town-based logistic cluster is specialised in food, especially deciduous fruit and fish. The former is consigned via Cape Town from as far afield as the northern provinces of Limpopo, Mpumalanga and Swaziland. Fish comes from the South African and Namibian fishing industries and is exported to Europe and the Far East. The logistic cluster also supports the oil industry in West Africa, as well as the development of other economic activities, such as repair and maintenance of ships and offshore drilling platforms.

Figure 1.31. **Trends of specialisation in South Africa and in the Cape Town city-region**

Shift and share analysis 2004-2006

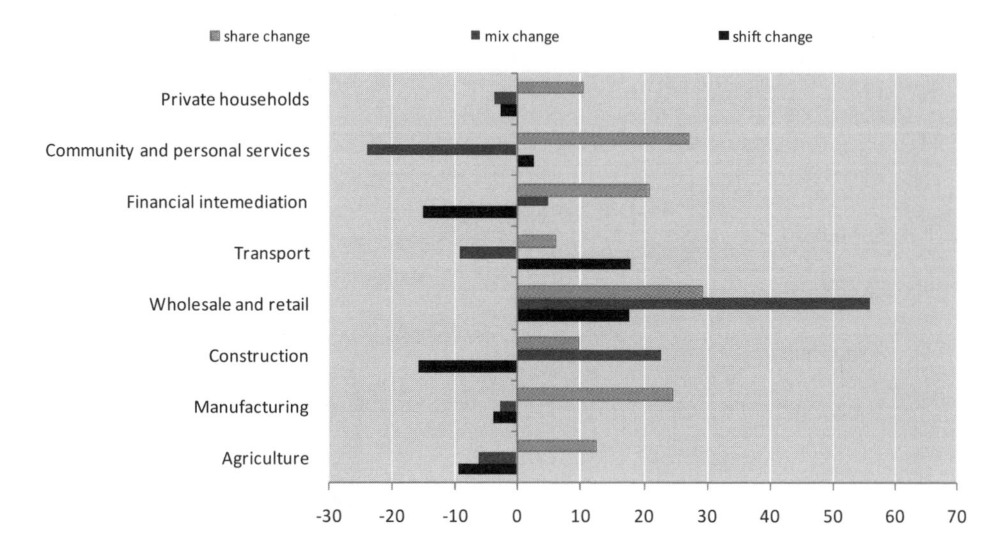

Note: eit+n – eit = share change + mix change + shift change = eit [Et+n/Et – 1] + eit [Eit+n/Eit – Et+n/Et] + eit [eit+n/eit – Eit+n/Eit]

Source: Elaboration on the Provincial Government of the Western Cape (2007*a*).

Figure 1.32. **Total cargo handled in South Africa's ports**

Metric tons

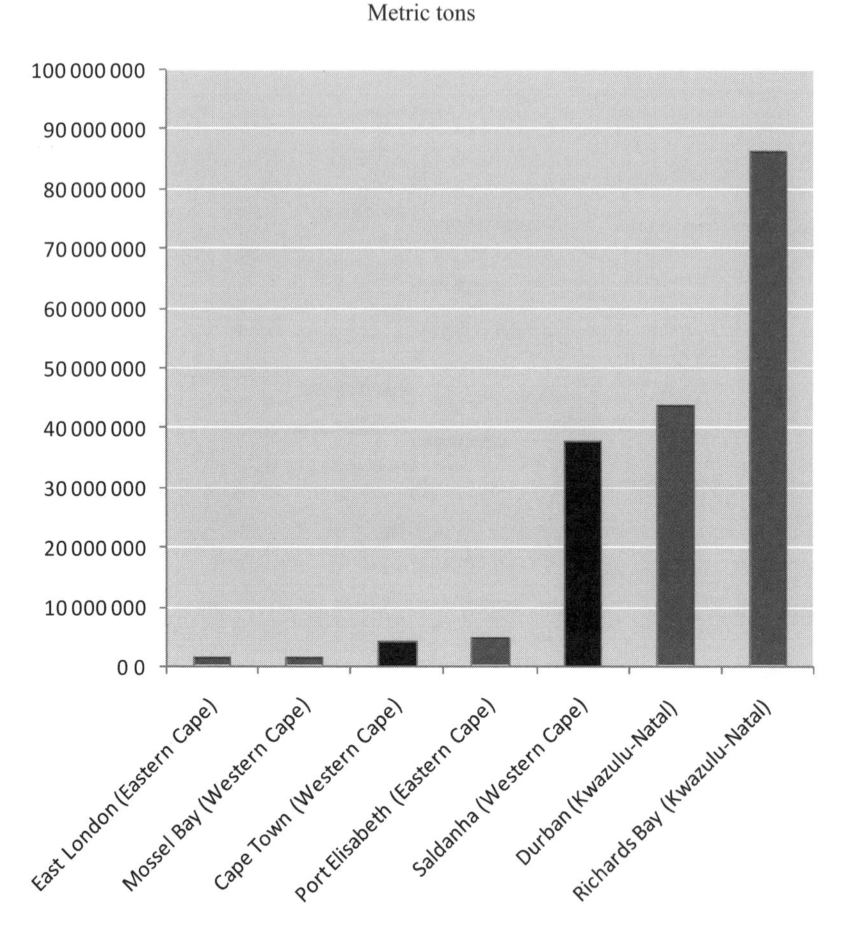

Source: South Africa Port Authority, Annual Report (2007).

The logistic cluster has also supported the development of a chemical industry, driven by oil company wholesale distributors, that relies on the city's logistical port capacities to service the oil and gas sector in South Africa as well as the West African offshore oil market. This is one of many reasons why the transport subsector contributed 7.1% to local regional GDP in 2005. The oil industry's refining functions in Cape Town, combined with the Port of Cape Town's ship-repair services and surrounding industrial fabrication capacity (the boat industry), make it possible for the city to promote a highly competitive oil and gas cluster, exploiting economic opportunities that arise as new supply potential opens up on the West African coast. In 2005, for example, about one-third of West Africa's and nearly one-quarter of the Middle East's exports of crude oil passed the Western Cape, providing "additional synergies from a shipping services perspective" (WESGRO, 2005). Some export potential exists also in chemicals associated with natural products, including pharmaceuticals, body care products, cosmetics and even biofuels.

Investment in port capacity and other transportation facilities has not kept up with the growth in service demand over the past few years, allowing inefficiencies to accumulate. Capacity constraints are conflated by the threat of a new competitor like the Maputo Port in Mozambique, which offers better prospects for exports of goods from Eastern Cape and Limpopo provinces, especially for citrus (Tralac, 2007). The competition of the Maputo Port underpins the City and Cape Town Port's recent collaboration under the aegis of the Port City Forum, developing appropriate responses in the field of planning, development, financing, the environment, security and basic service provision, in particular, water, rates, electricity and waste removal (Robinson, Crankshaw and Boulle, 2007). As for rail logistics, although South Africa has an extensive rail network (about 80% of the total in Africa), maintenance is poor and the average speed is low.

Creative and knowledge-intensive industries

Cape Town has a good mix between codified and tacit knowledge, thanks to the presence of a good public knowledge infrastructure.[71] The region's knowledge-intensive activities claimed a 14% share of national research and development investment in 2004. This cluster supports many other segments of the local economy, spanning primary, secondary and tertiary activities. For instance, the region's agriculture sector, an important low- and medium-skill employer, uses knowledge intensity to enhance its competitiveness in the international market. In the manufacturing sector, Cape Town has a promising cluster of automotive components. Although the national automotive pole is mainly located in the Eastern Cape, the Cape Town city-region has a competitive advantage as a location for component producers that manufacture assembly components with a high degree of precision engineering for the high-volume niche export market, both for assembly and for after-market. The Cape Town city-region also shows a strong specialisation in the natural, engineering and life science fields, all of which are important to emerging technological areas, such as food and plant biotechnology (as in the case of biotechnology as applied to the wine industry) and high-technology manufactures.[72]

The region's specialisation in medical science supports a robust medical and health tourism sector. Since Professor Christiaan Barnard successfully performed the world's first heart transplant in Cape Town, its medical reputation has been steadily growing in stature. In recent years, and especially in fields such as non-emergency dentistry and cosmetic surgery, increasing numbers of medical tourists, especially from the United States and the EU, have come to Cape Town to take advantage of the skills of the local surgeons, clinics and hospitals, at a fraction of the cost they would incur in their countries of origin. No data are available to quantify medical tourists, yet the increasing number of destinations that offer medical services is an indication of a growing global market.

Cape Town is also taking advantage of its diverse and creolised culture and draws on its historic legacy as well as contemporary developments to support tourism. Culture supports the tourism value-chain and acts as a bridge between different ethnicities and between the informal and formal economies. Culture is also a driver for restoration projects within the region, encouraging the development of film and publication industries:[73]

- The latest available estimates (2005/06) suggest that the film industry, including feature films, made-for-TV productions and commercials, contributed a total of ZAR 2 billion to Cape Town's economy (Province of the Western Cape). This development has been reinforced by new international film festivals. Unlike Johannesburg, which dominates the domestic film and multi-media market, the Cape Town region is the preferred choice for filming commercials and stills photography for catalogues, particularly for international commercials produced in South Africa.
- The printing and publishing sector (considering wood and paper activities) is worth ZAR 4.34 billion (PPP USD 676.1 million) or 3.9%, to Cape Town's GDP (2005). The value chain links the paper, the publishing and printing industries in the production process, whereas the distribution process draws down-stream linkages through the channels of delivery and circulation of print publications. In particular, the most important phenomenon is the growth in the black reader consumer market, which offers new opportunities for expansion of the industry in an emerging local market (Western Cape Department of Economic Development and Tourism, 2006c).74 Educational publishing is the largest market segment, accounting for 60% of all books published. A key event in Cape Town's calendar is its annual Book Fair.[75]

Knowledge-intensive activities and cultural industries need nevertheless to be integrated with the rest of the regional economy. In spite of the improvements of the last decade, a large part of the SMEs and individuals do not have access either to the knowledge facilities (universities and/or knowledge transfer centres) or to cultural hubs within the region. While the access to knowledge-intensive facilities would increase SMEs' productivity, facilitating the access of poor people to culture would be an extremely effective policy for enhancing integration and reducing cultural barriers among ethnic groups. For instance, in 2002, half of the respondents to a survey conducted in the region were unable to speak either Afrikaans or English, a figure that was relatively independent of whether or not they were recent immigrants; even among those who had had between and 11 and 12 years of schooling, 28% were unable to speak Afrikaans or English (du Toit and Neves, 2007). Clearly, the city lacks public spaces where people can exchange, communicate and generate common languages and values.

An isolated "economic" space: the townships

Cape Town's key economic drivers coexist alongside a set of disconnected blind spots, the townships, which have few and not well-known inter-linkages. Although spatial fragmentation is a common characteristic among many urban regions in developing countries, the socio-economic divide is even more visible in Cape Town because of the legacy of apartheid and the post-apartheid perpetuation of spatial segregation by class. Because of this legacy, as well as contemporary market forces, the bias of the growth industries and the scale of social deprivation and exclusion, Cape Town is a divided urban region in which mainstream economic activity – and the infrastructure that underpins it – is spatially and socially selective. The spatial structure of inequality inherited from apartheid remains almost unchanged, while the transition to a competitive economy has created new social inequalities associated with market integration and limits to regulatory compensation, including entrenched unemployment, job uncertainty, wage depression and welfare insecurity. The progress towards reduced social and spatial inequality – racialised and otherwise – has been limited. Precise data on population and economic activities in the townships are not available; these territories represent black holes in the socio-economic structure of the metropolitan region. Khayelitsha, the super township created for Africans in the 1980s, contributes some 0.70% to the overall GDP of the city of Cape Town, but concentrates around 12% of the total urban population (estimated at between 400 000 and 650 000 inhabitants). In the townships, the education system is poor and the economically excluded travel very little, due to transportation costs and poor spatial mobility.

At the moment, the value chains are not distributing gains across the social spectrum of the Cape Town city-region. There are some stunning examples of the economic inefficiency of the current spatial arrangement.

The two largest townships, Khayelitsha and Mitchell's Plain, are located in the geographic centre of the Cape Town city-region (Figure 1.33),[76] a sterile sandy plain that is not able to sustain any agricultural activities. The persistence of townships after apartheid is also the result of distortions on land regulation, financial and tax incentives, and specific policies aimed at suppressing community economic development.[77] Some of the conditions that gave rise to the townships during the old regime are still in place. Recent legislation, such as the Less Formal Establishment of Township Act (1991) essentially locked residents into existing land use patterns, precluding the development of mixed-use in township areas. The high cost of agricultural land and the extensive environmental protection of land parcels in the Cape Town region have perpetuated an unusual and persistent clustering of poverty along the city-region's urban spine and in the south-east of the City of Cape Town, where people living in the Khayelitsha/Mitchell's Plain area face acute poverty. The lack of an efficient system of public transportation is another factor isolating poor areas.

Figure 1.33. **Map of Cape Town's largest townships, Khayelitsha and Mitchell's Plain**

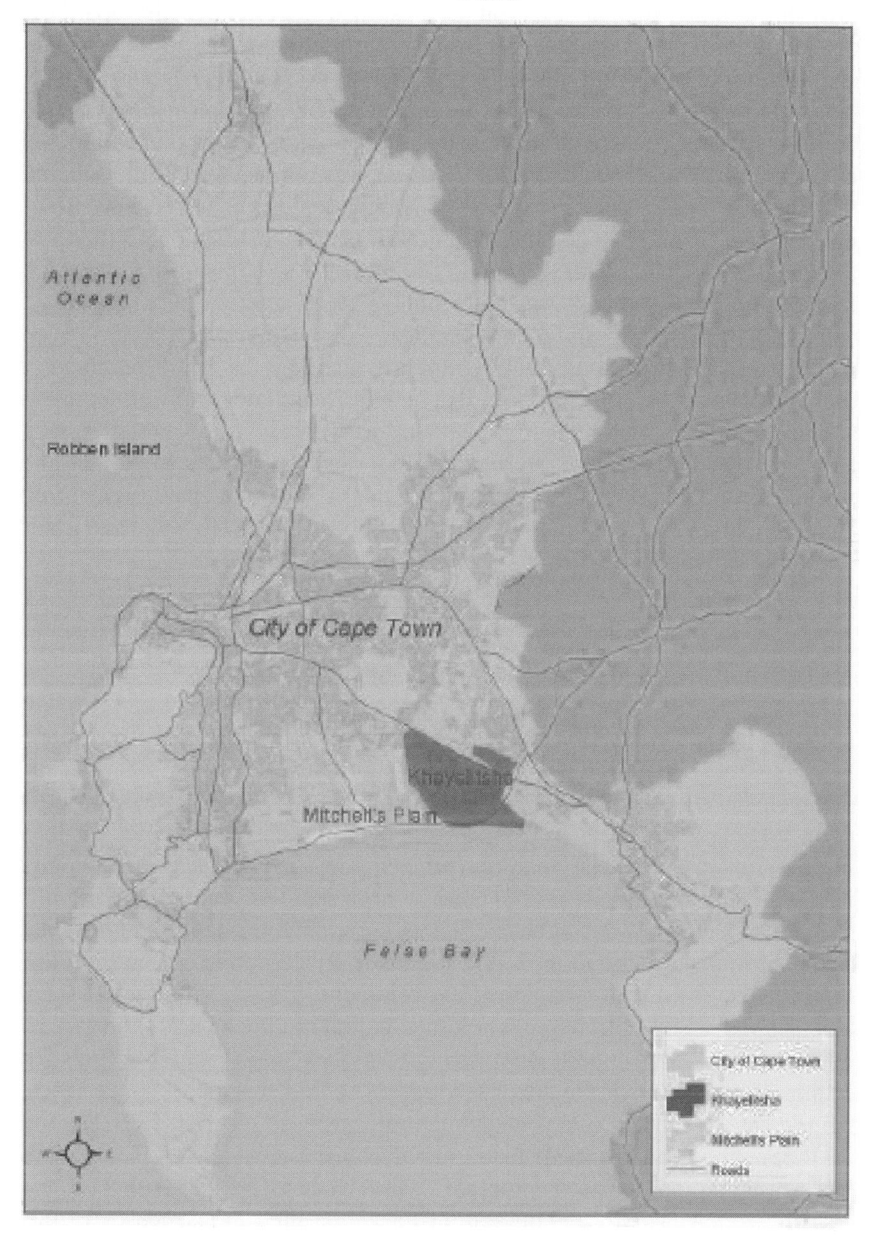

Source: Provincial Government of the Western Cape.

The isolation of township economies has created a vicious cycle of economic and social decline that affects the entire city-region. While townships represented a reservoir of unskilled workers for the apartheid economy, the re-integration of South Africa into the world economy challenges the access of these low-skilled workers to the labour market today. The lack of endogenous development potential in townships has also reinforced a persistent pattern of social, spatial and racial polarisation. As noted by Turok and Watson (2001), spatial decentralisation has not altered the traditional development trajectory, composed of an interrelated set of mechanisms of socio-economic, racial and spatial polarisation at the city-regional level. Under these conditions, people's abilities to draw on relationships with others, especially on the basis of trust (a critical asset commonly referred to as social capital), is severely prejudiced.[78] Such relationships of trust and reciprocity are also the basis of community organisations (*meso-institutions*) that might negotiate with government and/or the private sector for improved services. Networks and relationships between different strata of workers and between the owners of capital and workers or the unemployed is often the critical bridge that enables emerging entrepreneurs, the unemployed and the poorly paid to improve their economic situation.

Given their large populations, townships in the Cape Town city-region might represent more than a residual part of the regional economy, but current initiatives to create employment have failed to create job opportunities for them. Although Khayelitsha/Mitchell's Plain's GDP growth and GDP per capita figures are far below those of the Western Cape average, local GDP has increased gradually over the past decade (Khayelitsha's GDP grew by 2.4% between 2004 and 2005, while Mitchell's Plain GDP growth grew by 3.8% over the same period). According to a survey run by the national government on Khayelitsha's economy, wholesale and retail trade accounts for a large share of local GDP (and this sector also shows promising growth) and, surprisingly, finance and business also contribute strongly to the GDP (Figure 1.34) (Republic of South Africa, Department Provincial and Local Government, 2004). The formal local labour force is concentrated in wholesale and retail trade (18.9%), in private households (18.5%) and community services (14.4%). The relative economic expansion of the area has attracted some investment. For instance, the recently realised Khayelitsha central business district (KBD) is a ZAR 350 million investment made mainly by the Khayelitsha Community Trust, a city-support based initiative.[79] The KBD is a mixed-use business district located next to a train station through which thousands of people travel every day. It includes a large retail centre, a service station, public sector offices and facilities, offices for the private sector, sports facilities, residential units, a bus and a taxi terminal. However, in spite of its original aim of creating jobs within the township, the KBD tended to compete with informal street sellers, who cannot compete in terms of variety of goods and low prices. More generally, and as will be discussed in Chapter 2, further integration of this population in the regional economy would require better linkages between the different nodes of the functional area, specific skills, job enhancement programmes and a better and more affordable transport system.

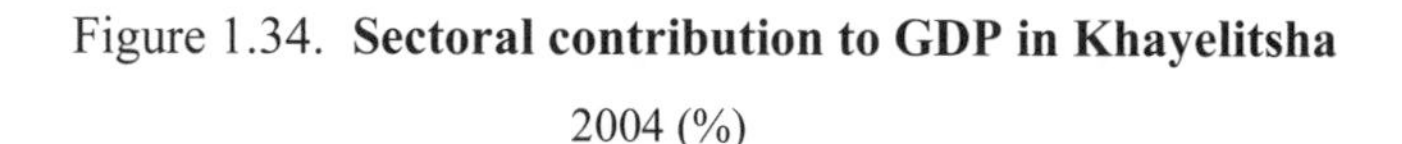

Figure 1.34. **Sectoral contribution to GDP in Khayelitsha**

2004 (%)

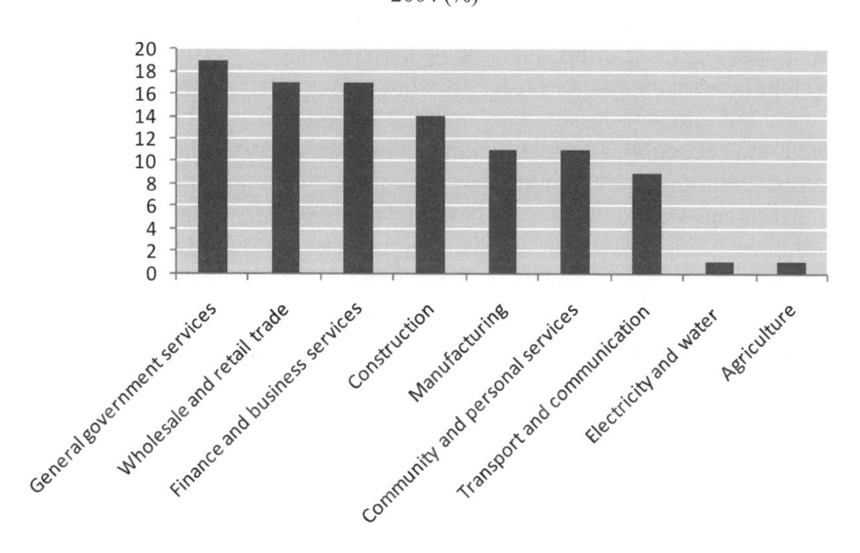

Source: Department of Local Governments, Republic of South Africa, *Khayelitsha Nodal Economic Development Profile* (2004).

1.4. Challenges ahead: Enabling conditions for competitiveness

Despite Cape Town's recent economic growth, entrenched structural and spatial divisions impede its potential to fully exploit its regional assets and to respond to national growth and poverty-reduction objectives. These divisions prevent a more inclusive growth model from materialising, thereby blocking an effective response to AsgiSA's goal to halve poverty and unemployment in South Africa by 2014. Despite a growth rate of around 4.5 to 5.5% since 2000 in Cape Town, a level that meets the poverty alleviation target set forth by AsgiSA, the scale of social deprivation in post-apartheid Cape Town remains massive: 32% live below the (unofficial but generally agreed) poverty line set at less than ZAR 1 199 per month, 16% have HIV/AIDS, 22% are unemployed, and most residents suffer from a regional housing deficit estimated at as much as 410 000 units, though this may be an overestimate.[80] The scale of economic exclusion in Cape Town hampers the spatial and social distribution of economic growth and reduces the potential of economic drivers. It is not only that the fruits of economic growth often do not benefit marginalised groups – those living in townships, informal settlements, the unemployed, underpaid and socially incapacitated sections of society – but that growth itself is constrained. Some nodes within the city-region perform far better than others, and this increases economic disparities within the city-region. A more economically inclusive system, which takes into account such multi-nodal pattern, has the potential to develop new economies, especially those in former townships, and to increase the interactivity between multiple sectors. This will have beneficial effects on economic competitiveness and on tapping latent economic potential through a combination of three factors: (a) international competitiveness depends on cost-based advantages, as well as quality-based advantages that draw on skills, motivation, know-how, and social participation; (b) social inclusion reduces the cost of welfare as well as the risks, uncertainties and hazards associated with crime, corruption and social breakdown; and (c) building social capabilities through improvements in townships, informal areas and among the socially marginalised, unlocks future economic potential through small-scale entrepreneurship, self-help and the social economy in general (which is reliant on local provision of welfare needs).

The Cape Town city-region lacks a series of integrated collective and public goods needed to enable inclusive regional development that could minimise social and spatial exclusion while maximising economic linkages within the region. For example, labour market upgrading or investment in learning and technological innovation can also benefit firms and other actors across a supply chain. Secondly, the enabling conditions can act as forms of supply-side upgrading to spark or support new economic ventures not necessarily linked to the leading value chains in the city-region, ranging from new forms of spin-off to entirely new growth industries. Thirdly, the enabling conditions, if tackled sensitively, can help to increase the breadth of social involvement in the economy, by ensuring, for example, that labour market reforms work for the poorest and the most spatially excluded, or that interventions in the knowledge economy also tap into local craft knowledge (see Chapter 2). Essentially, these conditions could lay the foundation to create "localisation economies" across specific fields and "agglomeration economies" between dissimilar companies that locate conterminously.[81] In addition, such conditions decrease mobility constraints. The benefits of these "links" would not be confined to one sector alone but diffuse across multiple value chains. Besides institutional stability and a functioning bureaucracy, which will be thoroughly discussed in Chapter 3, essentially, these enabling conditions include *i)* labour market and skills, *ii)* innovation capacity, *iii)* the built environment and *iv)* sustainability and liveability.

Labour market and skills

Persistent high unemployment and inactivity rates in the Cape Town city-region have been linked to a polarisation the labour market that tends in particular to penalise medium-skilled workers. As noted above, the shift towards a more service-based metropolitan economy has resulted in a change of occupational structure, with the formal labour force more engaged in higher skilled jobs. In 2006, 72% of the labour force worked in either skilled or highly skilled professions such as managers and technicians. Low-skilled elementary workers and domestic workers, mostly service-sector jobs, made up the remaining 28% of employment. In other words, the tertiarisation of the economy and the increased demand for personal and basic services penalises the medium-skilled (most of them former manufacturing workers), who are the worst hit by unemployment (25%), since they are under-skilled for the new vacancies and at the same time over-skilled for manual labour jobs.

The regional economy's weak showing in generating employment is due to dramatic constraints on the supply side of the labour market. Although the residents of the Cape Town city-region tend to have higher educational levels than the South African average (5.22% of workers in Cape Town have a tertiary education, versus 0.004% in South Africa in 2006), there is often a disjuncture between the skills being acquired in educational or vocational institutes and the skills needed by employers. According to the 2007 WESGRO Survey of Constraints to Investment, 45% of respondents cited skills and education of the workforce in Cape Town as a negative factor for investment and economic growth, and a lack of skilled workers was identified as the primary weakness of the business environment (cited in Robinson *et al.*, 2007). Twenty large firms surveyed by the University of Cape Town's Development Policy Research Unit indicated that they needed more graduates in science and engineering skills and that graduates, especially from "historically black" universities, lacked the crucial skills typically acquired in internships or apprenticeships. Beyond the need for "hard skills" in mathematics or financial management, firms noted that graduates often lacked "soft skills," that is, communication skills, presentation skills, workplace readiness and creative thinking (Pauw *et al.*, 2006; cited in DPRU, 2008). Accordingly, businesses have difficulty obtaining specialised labour in the Cape Town market and bring in workers from such countries as England and Australia. Similar bottlenecks were even claimed to apply to low- and medium-tech sectors, such as the construction and boat-building industry. A recent 2005 study by the Department of Labour also identified skill deficits in qualified and specialised labour (engineering etc.) along with medium- skill occupations such as artisans, trade and technicians.

Regional education bodies, although numerous, fail to produce profiles that meet regional firms' requirements, and their students underperform in basic literacy and numeracy. [82] The Cape Town City-Region lags in basic literacy, with a population that is 16.5% illiterate, only 24.6% of which have completed high school (Robinson *et al.*, 2007). After the end of the apartheid regime, education services have been dramatically expanded, but the quality of education has suffered, compromising workers' capacity to satisfy the requirements of the regional labour market. Tests conducted in Grade 3 in the Province of the Western Cape in 2002 show that 63% of students performed two to three years below the level appropriate for their age.[83] A similar test applied in Grade 6 in 2003 found that 15% and 35% of the students respectively had acquired a Grade 6 numeracy and reading level (Western Cape Education Department, 2006). On the secondary level, too few students in Western Cape enrol in mathematics: from an analysis of 2006 matriculation results, 4 137 students (10.4%) and 9 826 (24.7%) passed mathematics on higher grade and standard grade, respectively. Despite the additional focus and funding in mathematics, the pass rate for standard grade mathematics has decreased in every income quintile. In physical science, 4 053 students (10.2%) passed the higher-grade exams and 4 973 (12.5%) passed the standard grade exams. Moreover, there is minimal progress in the lower quintiles, despite the substantial amount of resources that go into poorer schools, limiting progress towards the nation's agenda of advancing skills. These skill gaps translate into poor secondary school graduation rates. Using a probit regression, which models the probability of advancing from one grade to another, Lam *et al.* (2006) found that grade advancement was associated with numeracy and literacy.[84] Poor attainment in these categories may explain, in part, why only 29% of Africans in Cape Town who begin the ninth grade are able to reach Grade 12.[85]

This poor performance can be partly explained by the rapid expansion of student population thanks to the influx of migrant families, the relaxation of admission policies and the unavailability of good schools in poor urban nodes. From 1995 through to 2004, the number of students enrolling increased by 104 000 students, because of the good reputation of local schools. This increase is due not only to the substantial inter-provincial in-migration of families into the province, but also to the relaxation of student intake/admission policies for Grade 1 students, which resulted in large numbers of students enrolling in Grade 1 in 2001 to 2004 (Province of the Western Cape). Due to the influx of immigrants, the number of illiterate and the functionally illiterate (people with less than seven years of schooling) in Cape Town is still relatively high, and the number of teachers has not kept pace with the number of students, resulting in a low student-to-teacher ratio. Also noteworthy are the differences within the city-region (Table 1.9). Finally, top-performing schools (with an average pass rate of over 90%, an exemption rate of over 70% and over 25% of students attaining a distinction) are located in the most affluent nodes of the region and, because of the lack of public transportation, remain inaccessible to low-income communities most in need of the skills.

Table 1.9. **Indicators of the education status of residents of the Cape Town city-region**

	Percentage of illiterate over 14	Educator to students ratio
Total	16.5%	1:39
Cape Town	15%	1:39
Stellenbosch	20%	1:38
Drakenstein	23%	1:38
Theewater-skloof	32%	1:37
Overstrand	19%	1:39
Swartland	31%	01:37
Saldanha	21%	01:38

Source: Data sourced from Treasury, District socio-economic profiles, 2006 (cited in Robinson *et al.*, 2007).

In addition to the skills mismatch, a spatial mismatch between the location of employment and housing is a drag on labour market pooling, given limited transport mobility and a lack of information about job vacancies. A large number of individuals live virtually isolated in poor nodes within the Cape Town city-region. As discussed above, the urban geography of Cape Town was conceived to exploit black and coloured workers, while keeping them separated from white areas, and the workplaces where black and coloured people were employed were usually far from their homes. Some progress has been made, and subsidised public buses and private mini-buses (a sort of cheap taxi service) now serve poor areas of the city-region. However, unskilled workers sometimes pay up to 30% of their disposable income on such transport and face long commute times (more than one hour from Khayelitsha and Mitchell's Plain to the city centre). Segregation also aggravates information asymmetries within the local labour market. Many workers remain unemployed simply because they are not informed about the existence of job vacancies that match their skills or expectations.

Finally, the informal sector may represent an untapped opportunity for generating higher employment. Official estimates place the region's informal labour at about 11% in 2006 (Crankshaw, 2007; Western Cape Provincial Treasury, 2007). In this respect, Cape Town is an exception vis-à-vis other middle-income metro-regions such as Mexico City, Istanbul, or Naples, where the informal economy represents more than 30% of the regional employment and plays a key role within the local economy.[86] Such a low level of informality could be a legacy of the old regime, which outlawed and restricted informal workers. However, official estimates are likely to be misleading, since people in Cape Town are even more reticent than usual to declare themselves informal workers. This may also reflect the attitude of public authorities and trade unions, which tend to perceive the informal economy as a marginal and underdeveloped part of the economy that needs simply to be eradicated.[87] The AsgiSA strategy is to eliminate the second economy by integrating informal activities into the formal market, but the reality is that Cape Town's informal economy has two levels. The region's marginal informal workers are involved in non-tradable low-value-added activities (street sellers, domestic workers, etc.), and about 77% of them have not completed secondary school (compared to 47% of the region's formal workers). The rate of functional illiteracy (below Grade 8 education) is very high (29% at the regional level) (Crankshaw, 2007; Western Cape Provincial Treasury, 2007). Public authorities tend to overlook the fact that the city-region has complex networks of firms and self-employed that use informality to reduce the cost of labour and of compliance with regulations.

In South Africa, the regulatory environment for businesses constrains SMEs' capacity to generate formal entrepreneurship and employment. Total regulatory and tax compliance costs for formal firms in South Africa are particularly high, representing respectively around 6.5% and 2% of GDP in 2004 (Chamberlain and Smith, 2006). Because small firms receive no special regulatory treatment, their competitiveness vis-à-vis large firms is drastically reduced (Small Business Policy Brand, Industry Canada, 2003). Lack of differentiation with large firms also affects small and micro firms as regards the wage-setting mechanism, since firms employing more than six workers (including the owner) fall under the jurisdiction of the bargaining councils and are required to pay as much in wages as large firms. Some of the region's small and micro informal firms are not marginal actors within the regional economy and interact with formal firms. This issue has already been noted as regards the agro-food sector as a main obstacle to the development of niche markets. In the textile and clothing industry, formal firms outsource to informal cut, make and trim (CMT) operators to reduce production costs. Enhancing these kinds of linkages could be an effective way to produce more formal employment in labour-intensive sectors as well as to enhance regional entrepreneurship in black communities (Box 1.4).

Box 1.4. **Main regulatory obstacles to the labour market**

Bargaining councils are registered bodies composed by employer and employee bodies (unions) whose aim is to set the wage level in a given industry or in a given territory. The condition to be registered by the Department of Labour is that the parties are sufficiently "representative", *i.e.* trade unions proposed as party to the council have more than 50% of employees in the specified sector as members. The bargain councils set wages, conditions of work and benefits. These agreements are subsequently formally registered with the Department of Labour and, in the same cases, can be extended to non-parties so that all employers and employees in the industry are covered all over the country. Currently, bargaining council agreements cover about 25% of national workers (Godfrey *et al.*, 2006).

The number of bargaining councils has fallen from 104 in 1983, to 87 in 1995, to just over 50 today. Mergers of regional and sub-sectoral councils into single, larger, national councils explain part of this decrease. Thus, despite the decrease in the number of councils, the number of employees covered has increased over the last ten years. Despite some mergers, councils still vary greatly in terms of their geographical and sectoral scope. Some are national, while others are restricted to a particular province, or even a particular city. Some cater to a very specific industry, such as Canvas Bag Manufacturing, while the Metal and Engineering Council covers a wide range of different products and is of national scope.

Source: Provincial Government of the Western Cape (2007*a*).

Technology, innovation capacity and the regional innovation system

The competitiveness of the Cape Town's economic fabric is limited by its poor showing in innovation by comparison with Johannesburg. Considering patents applications as a proxy for innovation, Cape Town generated 112 applications in 2004, *i.e.* 13% of national total, as compared to the 496 generated in Johannesburg-Gauteng, 56% of national total (Lorentzen, 2007). This is relatively low when considering that R&D investment per capita is almost the same in the two regions, meaning that Johannesburg has a higher capacity to transform input (R&D expenditure) in outputs (patent applications) (Table 1.10).[88] The innovation gap between Cape Town and Johannesburg is likely to grow, since Johannesburg keeps on attracting more R&D investment. Between 2005 and 2006 the spatial variation of business R&D in Johannesburg almost tripled that of Cape Town (Figure 1.35). There are several reasons for this trend.

- Post-apartheid South Africa inherited a weak innovation framework, almost entirely focused on defence and mining, favouring Johannesburg and its surrounding region to the detriment of Cape Town.[89]

- The share of private R&D in Cape Town is much lower than that of Johannesburg, whose business community is the largest in the country (Table 1.11). This is particularly relevant in a country where public R&D is relatively low and partially balanced by high private expenditure (Table 1.12).

- Finally, the manufacturing base in Cape Town lacks specialisation in high value-added activities, which generally tend to be more active in innovation. The concentration of firms in the Johannesburg-Gauteng region has not only quantitative implications: the Western Cape share in knowledge-intensive and creative industries, expressed as a percentage of that activity in the total national value-added (base 2004), is much smaller than the participation in that same sector from the Gauteng province. For example, for what is labelled as "innovation and experimentation," this amounts to 63.5% in Gauteng versus 15.7% in the Western Cape. The same figures for the high value-added sector amount to 52.6% and 11.3%, respectively. The Cape Town city-region's profile as a place for innovative firms compares to blue-collar provinces like the KwaZulu-Natal (eThekwini/Durban) region.

Table 1.10. **National (public + private) R&D Expenditure and Patent Applications (2006)**

Province	% R&D Expenditure	% of Patent Applications
Eastern Cape	4.7	2
Free State	5.1	3
Gauteng	50.7	57
KwaZulu-Natal	10.8	12
Limpopo	1.4	1
Mpumalanga	2.4	1
North-West	2.3	4
Northern Cape	1	1
Western Cape	21.6	13
Total	100	100

Note: Data for R&D expenditure are for 2006.

Sources: National R&D Survey 2005/6; Lorentzen 2007.

Figure 1.35. **Spatial variation of business R&D between 2005-2006**

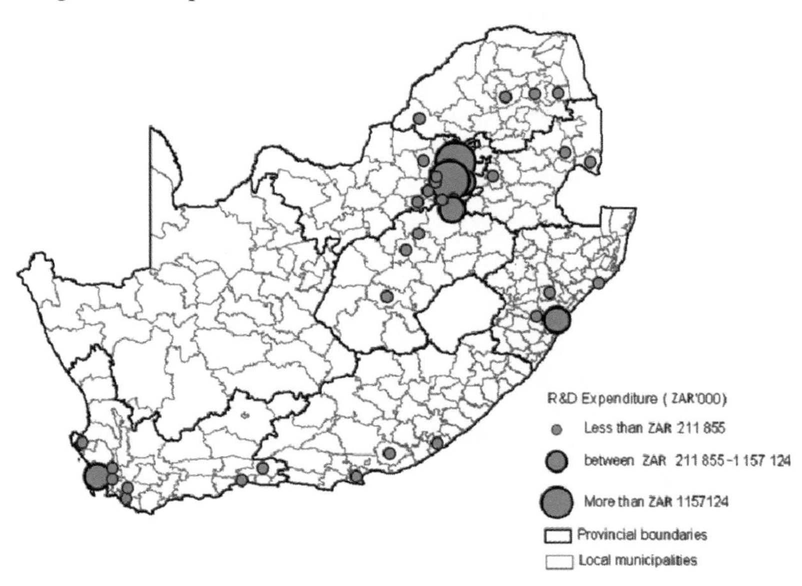

Source: National R&D Survey, Human Sciences Research Council (HSRC) of South Africa, 2006.

Table 1.11. **Provincial split of R&D: Private/public (2005-2006)**

Province	Private Amount		Public Amount		Total Amount	
	ZAR 000s	%	ZAR 000s	%	ZAR 000s	%
Eastern Cape	249 281	2.9	422 728	7.4	672 009	4.7
Free State	480 033	5.7	238 876	4.2	718 909	5.1
Gauteng	4 747 866	56.1	2 425 724	42.7	7 173 590	50.7
KwaZulu-Natal	878 535	10.4	653 623	11.5	1 532 158	10.8
Limpopo	89 516	1.1	107 539	1.9	197 055	1.4
Mpumalanga	198 172	2.3	142 601	2.5	340 773	2.4
North-West	183 774	2.2	140 065	2.5	323 839	2.3
Northern Cape	16 341	0.2	122 086	2.1	138 427	1.0
Western Cape	1 626 772	19.2	1 425 710	25.1	3 052 482	21.6
Total	8 470 290	100.0	5 678 949	100.0	14 149 239	100.0

Source: National R&D Survey (HSRC).

Table 1.12. **R&D performed by business enterprises in selected countries ranked by the GERD/GDP ratio**

	GDP per capita (2004 PPP USD)	GERD as a percentage of GDP (2004)*	% of GERD performed by business enterprises (2004)*
Sweden	29 540	3.95	74.1
Japan	29 291	3.13	75.2
Korea	20 471	2.85	76.7
United States	39 678	2.68	70.1
Denmark	31 914	2.48	68
Singapore	28 860	2.25	60.8
Canada	31 263	1.99	54
United Kingdom	30 821	1.88	65.7
Netherlands	31 790	1.78	57.8
Norway	38 453	1.61	54.8
Ireland	38 827	1.2	64.5
New Zealand	23 932	1.14	42.5
Spain	24 992	1.07	54.4
South Africa	**11 393**	**0.87**	**56.3**
Portugal	19 629	0.79	33.2
Turkey	7 752	0.66	28.7
Greece	22 205	0.62	30.1
Poland	13 316	0.58	28.7
Argentina	13 302	0.44	29
Mexico	9 776	0.43	34.6

* or latest year available – GERD = Gross Expenditure on R&D.

Source: OECD Reviews of Innovation Policy South Africa, OECD, Paris, 2007.

Innovation in Cape Town does not occur in the key value-chains of the economy, and technology transfer is mostly import driven.[90] Following the national trend, the sectors from which the most patents originated were "machinery and equipment" and "furniture", indicating that the bulk of regional innovation does not come from those value-chains and clusters in which the region has a comparative advantage, such as agro-food, logistics and biotechnology-life science. Therefore, it is possible that regional innovation is more linked to "process innovation" rather than "product innovation", as for instance in the case of the boat-building industry in Cape Town. Product innovation has been quite slow, and firms have mainly innovated their process of production by adopting (imported) machinery.[91] The result is that they still depend on international suppliers for key products, and their margins have been shrinking over the years. In the 1970s, some 50 firms were active in the boat industry in Cape Town, but in 2007 there are less than ten firms.

The Cape Town city-region does however have a good public R&D infrastructure composed of four universities and several research centres specialised in high technology fields such as care, food biotech and environmental science.[92] Reflecting regional specialisation, Cape Town-based universities focus on fields such as health. The University of Cape Town, in particular, has the highest number of A-grade scientists in the country and ranks among the top institutions in the world in areas such as biology, environment and ecology, according to a citation-based index on the performance of universities (OECD, 2007*c*). Universities represent a key asset for the regional innovation system. The four universities invested ZAR 770 million on R&D in 2006, and employed more than 2 200 researchers (FTE). Considering the average performance of the Cape Town-based innovation framework, the number of researchers (FTEs) in regional universities is not that far from OECD value. For example, Madrid – which has one of the most educated workforces within OECD city-regions – had 8 402 FTE university researchers in 2005 (OECD, 2007*c*). Universities also generate a total of 36 000 postgraduate students who were involved in research activities in 2006. The regional public R&D infrastructure is complemented by the regional offices of all of South Africa's nine statutory science councils, and a number of government research institutes, such as the Centre for High Performance Computing (CHPC)[93] and Cape Town's International Centre for Genetic Engineering and Biotechnology (ICGEB). Regional hospitals also play an important role within the regional innovation system. For instance, besides being the site of the world's first heart transplant in 1967, Groote Schuur Hospital is internationally renowned in the fields of anaesthesiology and internal medicine.[94] Together, these universities and institutes employed a total of some 4 000 researchers (FTE) in the Province (2006) (Table 1.13).

Table 1.13. **R&D expenditure and researchers in the Western Cape**

Value expressed in "full time equivalents" (FTEs)

	2005-06			2004-5		
Sector	R&D expenditure WC	Researchers (FTE) WC	Researchers (FTE) National	R&D Expenditure WC	Researchers (FTE) WC	Researcher s (FTE) National
Business	1 570 333		6 354.37	947 623		5 300.66
Government	239 630		723.28	131 912		491.05
Higher Education*	769 378	2 216.31	9 235	694 867	2 086.99	10 406
Science Councils	416 702		1 546	280 591		1 549
Not-for-Profit	56 436		228	46 169		234
TOTAL	**3 052 479**		**18086.65**	**2 101 162**	**3991.97**	**17980.71**

Note: *includes PhD and postdoctoral students.

Source: The National R&D survey 2004/5, 2005/6.

There are weak interactions between science-based institutions and firms, with only a few advanced firms engaged in innovation activities in isolation. As discussed above, the role of the business community in supporting regional innovation capacity is not as developed as in Johannesburg-Gauteng. Yet, the bulk of private R&D expenditure in Cape Town comes from large-high tech firms, which represent a very small percentage of Cape Town-based firms, at 7% (Table 1.14).[95] Small and medium firms' contribution to formal R&D activities is low, as is their interactions with large firms, universities and research centres. Given the importance of local academia and its comparative advantage in advanced fields of specialisation, the regional innovation system in Cape Town could perform better if university-industry linkages were further developed. Presently, not only are such linkages very low, but they do not focus on regional key value chains, such as agro-food, logistics or tourism (Table 1.15). The data shows that regional innovation has still "great scope and need for expansion […] and those weak institutional relationships between the provincial and metropolitan administrations and the High Education Institutions will need to be strengthened to mobilise potential" (Kruss, 2005).

Table 1.14. **Technology class of Western Cape manufacturing firms (2005)**

	High Tech	Medium High	Medium Low	Low Tech	All Manufacture
Cape Town	131	527	1188	2 333	4 179
Winelands	17	41	152	452	662
Overberg	na*	na*	na*	na*	na*
Westcoast	na*	na*	na*	na*	218
Total+	148+	568+	1 340+	2 785+	5 059+
%	2.9%	11.2%	26.5%	55.1%	100.0%

Notes: Data has been obtained for the RSC (Regional Services Council) Levy data base (2005), which does not include the entire universe of firms located in the Western Cape. High Tech is intended in terms of a reported Standard Industrial Classification (SIC) code that has been matched to OECD Manufacturing Technology Class descriptions (OECD, 2003).

"na" denotes "not available"; "+" denotes "actual number is greater than this figure, but not known" – Data are collected at the district level.

Source: RSC Levy 2005, arranged following OECD 2003.

Table 1.15. **Western Cape-based firms collaborating with higher education institutions**

Sector	No of firms
Electronic equipment	4
Chemicals	3
Agriculture, horticulture and fishing	3
Medical equipment	2
IT	2
Health	2
Food and beverage products	2
Business services	2
Clothing and textiles	1
Pharmaceuticals	1
Paper and packaging	1
Mining	1
Machinery	1
Defence	1
Automotive manufacturing	1

Note: Data are drawn from a limited random (non-exhaustive) sample of R&D companies and provides an indication of the regional collaborative R&D activities of firms with universities.

Source: HSRC/CeSTII.

The region also suffers from the lack of untraded interdependencies supporting innovation. Cape Town has not developed a "soft" infrastructure that the community of regional firms can use to exchange information and technology. In general, high transportation costs and the legacy of apartheid in the Cape Town city-region have constrained the location of both individuals and firms and thus stalled the formation of backward and forward linkages among SMEs. These weaknesses are further exacerbated by the paucity of dialogue between the business community and provincial/local government. As a result, in spite of the large number of SMEs within the region, the local economy is built on large firms and small and micro firms, which represent 93% of the total, play a marginal role and are mostly low-tech firms operating in traditional/mature industries.

Built environment

Cape Town public officials grapple with spatial integration, desegregation, service provision and infrastructure maintenance for a booming city across an urban structure that has become polycentric. Sprawling along the shores of the southernmost point of Africa, Cape Town is a complex landscape for which to plan: given the built environment shaped both by apartheid and more recent trends of suburbanisation; environmental protection; and the construction of informal settlements. The task of setting to rights a city stamped by apartheid presents challenges that daunt those even in the most racially divided cities of the OECD. In a relatively short time, public officials have deracialised service provision, desegregated public transportation and begun to consolidate building and zoning codes throughout the region. In many ways, this built environment has been transformed since their successful interventions: residents in former townships benefited from one of the largest electrification programmes in the country, and the region has witnessed a sharp increase in commercial buildings as its economy blossomed. Entirely new neighbourhoods and office parks were developed after these initiatives, creating a polycentric structure that differs from the nuclear form of the past. The underlying dynamics of the transformation in the built environment in Cape Town's metro area, however, are driven not by the desire to segregate or integrate but by internal population growth and the arrival of thousands of migrants in search of economic opportunities. This has increased the demand for housing beyond the point that the market can currently provide. Cape Town's population has grown tenfold in the past 50 years. Against this backdrop, ageing infrastructure, the road and rail network, old housing stock, and massive replacement and maintenance backlogs in water and sewerage are a drag on the regional economy.

As one of the driest areas in South Africa, the Cape Town Metro Region has been stressed to provide water and sanitation equally throughout the region, despite substantial infrastructure upgrades. The region relies on a wide number of sources, drawing from reservoirs of five dams within the region.[96] Access to water and sanitation, especially in informal settlements has increased, and recently significant upgrading projects in Bellville, Parow and Kraaifontein wastewater treatment works have been completed in the hope of raising the percentage of wastewater reused above its current low level of 7%. Whereas 90% of households had access to drinking water in 1996, by 2005, 93% enjoyed access. With respect to sanitation, 90% of households in 1996 had a flush toilet, increasing slightly to 92% by 2005 (Census of South Africa, 1996; General Household Survey, 2005). However, basic services are still not adequately distributed throughout the 105 utility wards that divide the City of Cape Town. For example in Ward

80, where 78.2% of the inhabitants lived in slums, 81.9% were without flush toilets and 84.5% had no potable water on site in 2001 (Figure 1.36-37).[97] Given the region's water scarcity and the continued absence of provision in particular neighbourhoods, the City of Cape Town estimates that ZAR 7.24 billion is required for new provision and replacement costs for water and wastewater provision over the next ten years (City of Cape Town, 2008*a*). These demands will likely become more acute given that the region's climate is predicted to become warmer and its water sources more polluted by the discharge of treated sewage and contaminated storm water.

Figure 1.36. **Percentage of Cape Town households without flush or chemical toilet, by ward (2001)**

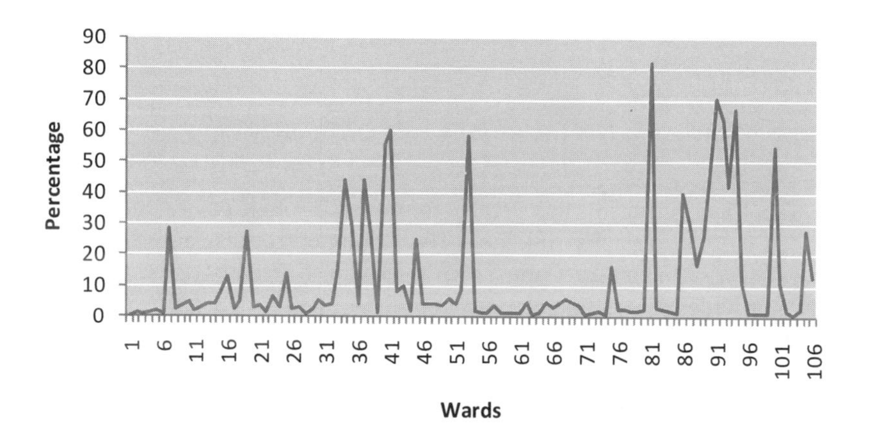

Source: Statistics South Africa (2001), cited in City of Cape Town (2008*b*).

Figure 1.37. **Percentage of Cape Town households without potable water on-site or in-dwelling, by ward (2001)**

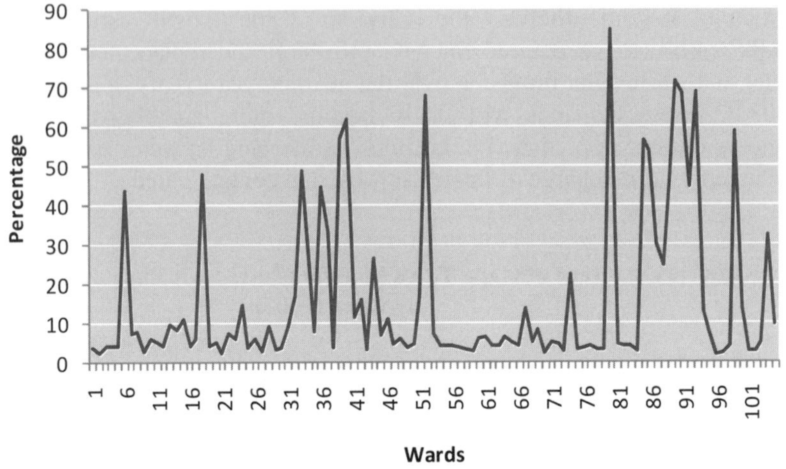

Source: Statistics South Africa (2001), cited in City of Cape Town (2008*b*).

Electrical provision has greatly improved, though power shortages and limited electric capacity militate against competitiveness and disadvantage the poorest segments of Cape Town's society. Currently, the City of Cape Town provides access to electricity for 75% of its residents; the other 25% is provided through South Africa's state-owned power utility, Eskom. Together these institutions improved household access to electricity in Cape Town from 87% of households in 1996 to 95% in 2005. This mirrors national electrification trends; whereas in 1990, Eskom supplied power to only 1.2 million customers, this number had expanded to 4 million customers in 2007 (Macnamara, 2008). In Cape Town, coal remains the main source of electricity power (88%), although its percentage is declining, given the contribution of the Koeberg nuclear power station (70 kilometres outside of Cape Town) and two new gas-fired power stations in the Western Cape and the Darling Wind Farm. Unfortunately, the maximum generation capacity has not substantially grown; underinvestment has led to dependence on an overstressed electricity grid that produces frequent blackouts. In 2007 alone, there were 17 forced power disruptions in Cape Town. On the national scale, these disruptions have caused a loss of output that has caused economic forecasters to scale back their projections for real GDP growth in 2008 by between 0.5 and 1 percentage points, and caused downward revisions to the AsgiSA strategy for economic growth (OECD,

2008*b*). These blackouts, along with the resulting increase in electricity fees,[98] especially hurt small and medium- sized businesses, which specialise in small orders and fast turnaround time. Beyond equipment failures and system malfunctions, Eskom has struggled to find electrical engineers to fill a growing number of vacancies in the Western Cape (Powell, 2008). In addition to maintaining existing connections, Eskom has yet to electrify several remaining neighbourhoods without power. In 2001, for instance, in 19% of Cape Town's wards, at least one out of four households lacked access to electricity (Statistics South Africa, 2001; cited in City of Cape Town, 2008) (Figure 1.38).

Figure 1.38. **Percentage of Cape Town households without access to electricity for lighting, by ward (2001)**

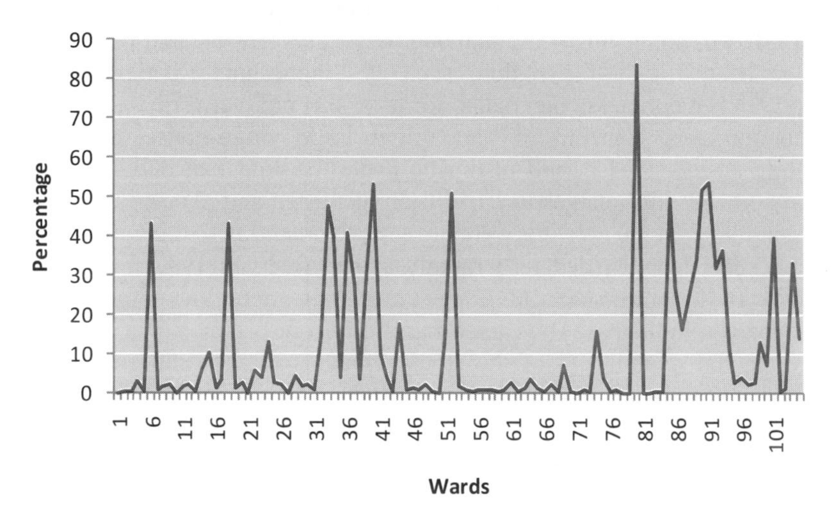

Source: Statistics South Africa (2001), cited in City of Cape Town (2008*b*).

Cape Town has an extensive road network with acute congestion. The region's road network, covering approximately 10 000 kilometres, was developed radially around the central business district. It features two main freeways, the N1 and N2, which run from the CBD in a north-east and south-east direction respectively, and four other freeways, the M3, M5, N7/Vanguard Drive and the R300, which act as link roads and primarily run in a north-south direction.[99] The Cape Town regional road network benefits from an unusual degree of connectivity to the rest of South Africa via the N1, which connects Cape Town to Bloemfontein, Johannesburg, Pretoria and Zimbabwe; the N2, which joins the city to Port Elizabeth, East London and eThekwini (Durban); and the N7, which links Cape Town with Malmesbury and the West Coast and onwards into the Northern Cape and Namibia. However, the roads, particularly in the city centre, face traffic congestion caused by population growth, rising car ownership and a dramatic increase in middle-class urban sprawl. Consistent overloading of roads for the haulage of freight has also placed a significant burden on the maintenance of the city's road network. Cumulatively, these factors have elevated congestion: road-based traffic volumes to or from Cape Town's CBD increased by a rate of approximately 2.5% per year (City of Cape Town, 2006*d*).

Underinvestment has impinged upon the service of Cape Town's nationally renowned urban passenger rail network. The most extensive in South Africa, the metropolitan rail network covers approximately 290 kilometres and plays a dominant role in the public transport system in Cape Town, conveying some 620 000 passengers per day and penetrating a range of towns in the region, such as Malmesbury, Stellenbosch and Paarl.[100] Nevertheless, the radial form of the rail network has difficulty accommodating demand in the current large, multi-nodal urban form. During an extended period of drastic underinvestment in public transport, many crucial rail linkages that had been identified and planned to close the missing links in the network were never developed. Lack of investment over many years has also led to a rapidly ageing fleet. In 1997, for example, 45.2% of the rail stock in Cape Town was more than 33 years old. Fortunately, in the past 10 years, a significant refurbishment programme has lowered the overall age of the stock, though averages still remain high. Other issues include unreliable service (88% of trains on time), antiquated stations, poor passenger information and a loss of patronage, especially during night hours, when trains are perceived as being unsafe.[101] These issues have resulted in a decline in market share and a general shift away from rail transport to private cars, buses and taxis for commuting. Though Cape Town has a robust rail network,[102] the dominance of the use of the automobile for work trips is higher than in many cities in Africa and the OECD. Conversely, commuters in the City of Cape Town depend on bus transit far less than other African countries during work commutes (Table 1.16).

Table 1.16. **Urban transport for work trips, select African and OECD cities, 2002**

			Transport Modal Split for Work Commutes (2002)			
City	Nation	Population (2005)	Private car	Train, tram or ferry	Bus or minibus	Other (motorcycle, bicycle, non-motorised)
City of Cape Town	South Africa	3 239 000[a]	67.0	17.0	16.0	
African Cities						
Accra	Ghana	1 938 00	34.7	4.0	50.0	11.3
Dakar	Senegal	2 313 000	8.1	1.3	77.2	13.4
Ibadan	Nigeria	2 375 000	45.0	0.5	45.0	9.5
Harare	Zimbabwe	1 527 000	18.0		32.0	50.0
Kinshasa	Democratic Republic of the Congo	5 717 000	13.0	42.0	30.0	15.0
Kumasi	Ghana	1 465 000	22.2	0.6	50.0	27.2
Lagos	Nigeria	11 100 000	51.0	2.5	45.5	9.5
Maputo	Mozambique	1 316 000	6.5		80.0	13.5
Nairobi	Kenya	2 383 000	6.0	1.0	70.0	23.0
Port Elizabeth	South Africa	998 000	52.4	1.8	45.8	
Rabat	Morocco	1 859 000	40.0		40.0	20.0
Select OECD Cities						
Birmingham	United Kingdom	2 215 000	73.9	1.4	9.1	15.6
Ciudad Juarez	Mexico	1 469 000	51.3		23.7	25.0
Katowice	Poland	2 914 000	46.2	9.4	19.9	24.6
Madrid	Spain	5 145 000	60.0		16.0	24.0
Manchester	United Kingdom	2 193 000	71.8	1.9	8.1	18.0
Prague	Czech Republic	1 164 000	33.0		54.5	12.5
Seoul	South Korea	9 592 000	20.1	32.3	38.8	8.8
Stockholm	Sweden	1 729 000	35.1	34.5	13.8	16.6

a. Projected Census data 2001.

Sources: Population: Figures were cited in UN-HABITAT (2007) State of the World's Cities Report 2006/7. Transport: For the City of Cape Town 2004-2005 figures were used from the *Summary of 2004/5 Current Public Transport Record* and refer to inbound passenger trips between 6 a.m. and 7 p.m. Other transport figures derive from UN-HABITAT (2002) Global Urban Indicators Database 2 and World Bank (2005) World Development Indicators 2005.

Cape Town's sprawling spatial form strains the capacity of its existing infrastructure and reinforces the isolation of the poorest and most isolated communities. The current situation is one where 94.8% of residential land is low-density (City of Cape Town, General Valuation 2000). This ribbon development pattern is dominated by single dwelling units which not only increase the cost of infrastructure and grid extensions, but contribute to a rapid land conversion. The City of Cape Town Building Plans Tracker (2006) reported that 88.1% of the building plans submitted from November 2005 to April 2006 were for single-dwelling houses. Indeed, over the last 25 years, 900 hectares (3 600 football fields) a year were converted to urban land uses. Combined with underinvestment in public transit, this spatial growth has reduced the mobility of Cape Town's citizens. Increasing numbers of developments, mostly to the north, are beyond easy reach of the rail network. New Greenfield middle-income urban developments within the metropolitan area in such northern areas as Durbanville and Blaauwberg are underserved by public transport, resulting in dramatic increases in congestion on the routes linking these areas to employment centres. Some areas remote from the rail network are connected to the rest of the urban region via bus and mini-bus taxi services. In some cases, these services are limited to commuter peaks, effectively isolating many of the smaller, poor communities, such as Red Hill, Fisantekraal and Sir Lowry's Pass, where passenger numbers cannot support frequent service from the broader urban region.[103]

The construction sector, though vibrant, has not accommodated the enormous demands of low- and middle-income residents. As the Western Cape's Department of Local Government and Housing argues in its *Road Map to Dignified Communities: Western Cape Sustainable Human Settlement Strategy* (2007), "The sophisticated institutional capacity of the formal housing system (including construction, materials, banking, bonding, loans, professional services, insurance, etc.) is not configured to work for pro-poor housing delivery". At this point, there are virtually no affordable formal housing options for the low-income (ZAR 3 500-7 000) bracket: only 3% of the population can afford to pay the average cost for affordable housing (ZAR 193 000). Builders are constructing fewer smaller units: the construction of units smaller than 80 square metres declined by 19.9%, while those over $80m^2$ increased by 29% over 2004 and 2005 (PGWC, 2007). As a consequence, the Cape Town Metropolitan Region finds itself in a severe housing affordability crisis, as the Provincial housing deficit has mushroomed to an estimated 410 000-unit shortage (Provincial Government of the Western Cape, 2006*b*). Contractors have generally neglected construction in former townships, despite their robust demand, and have often failed to decrease the cost of housing through alternative building materials and such initiatives as transit-oriented developments (TOD) along rail lines. Though the public sector delivered almost as many homes at the private sector in 2007, production of affordable housing needs to be accelerated. The Integrated Human Settlement Program, which built only 4 740 low-cost units per year from 2002 to 2006 in Cape Town, merits expansion. Significant changes in planning approval mechanisms and land development are required to correct the distortions of the property market and transform housing and construction into a stronger driver of the regional economy.

A growing informal housing market located on the periphery reinforces the polycentric urban form and provides housing in areas underserved by public transit. Responding to increasing levels of migration, low-cost developers have sold a range of inexpensive homes in areas unauthorised for housing (Figure 1.39). According to a count based on satellite photos from the City's Geographic Information Systems and Strategic Information Branch, the number of shacks nearly quadrupled from 1993 to 2007. Using a different methodology based on a sample of 30 000 housing units, Statistics South Africa counted 140 605 informal housing units in 2007, which represent approximately 16% of Cape Town's total housing (Statistics South Africa, 2007*a*).[104] Many informal settlements are located remotely from the city centre without public transportation facilities (Figure 1.40). Faced with few employment opportunities, the residents of informal settlements are often forced to travel long distances for employment.

Figure 1.39. **Location of informal settlements in Cape Town**

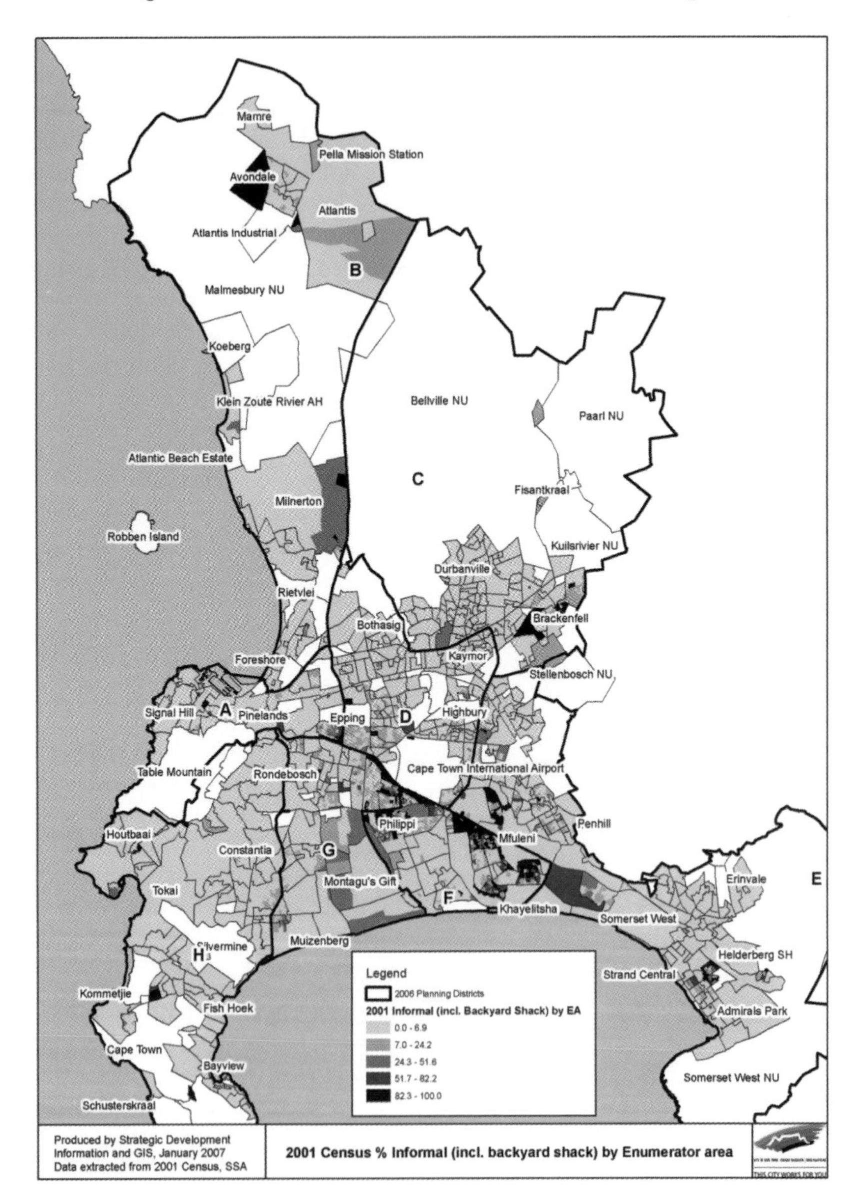

Source: City of Cape Town Strategic Development Information and G.I.S. (2007), data extracted from Statistics South Africa (2001).

Figure 1.40. **Mobility constraints in Cape Town**

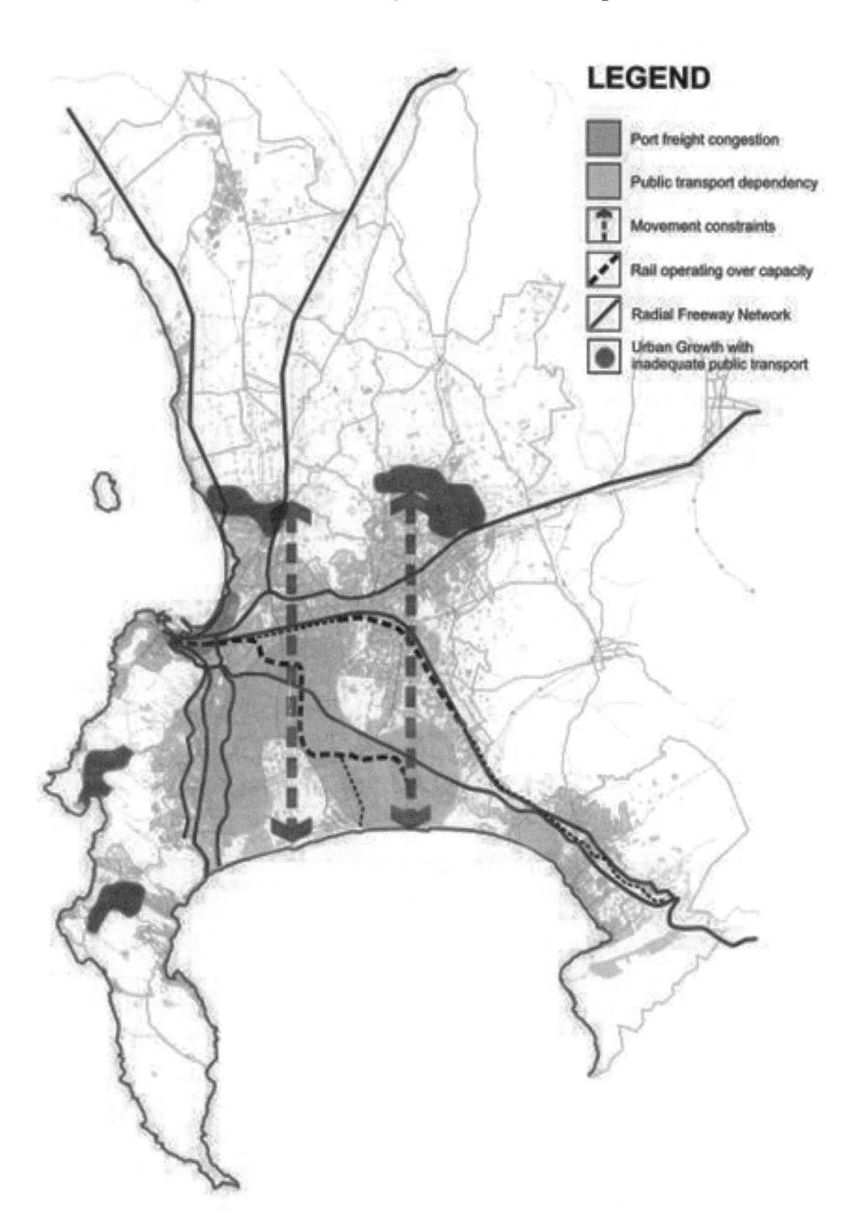

Source: City of Cape Town (2008*a*).

The inability of the region's transit system to provide services to residents in peripheral and suburban communities has constrained mobility, hindered productivity and increased commuting costs, especially for the poorest. The existing stock of roads was built on an East-West axis, which fails to serve the new settlements in the North and South. In the absence of public transit routes, thousands of private taxis and buses have entered the market, largely responding to commuter peak periods. The number of passengers who take taxis in Cape Town has risen to around 332 000 passengers per day, almost double the 197 000 passengers who take public buses (Cape Town, 2006). Taxis transport fewer people per vehicle, exacerbating congestion, poor inter-modal integration and burdens on road infrastructure. The cost of private transport – often as much as 30% of commuters' disposable income – disproportionately affects residents in informal settlements and former townships, who have the least to spend on transportation costs. Losses in productivity, which have not been measured in Cape Town, have probably increased due to the increased commuting time. A recent report from Cape Town's Department of Transportation (2006) noted "commuters have become accustomed to long travel times and for many public transport users, travel times of more than 2 hours to travel 30 kilometres are not uncommon. On the other hand many private vehicle users from the northern and eastern suburbs are accustomed to travel times exceeding one hour to travel the ± 30 kilometres to the City Centre." Ultimately, the asymmetry between existing road infrastructure and the sites of new communities in Cape Town impedes the movement of goods and people across the Cape Town Metro Region, with a prejudicial effect on the region's economy.

Environmental sustainability, liveability and attractiveness

Cape Town's attractiveness and main comparative advantage in tourism are largely based on its unique natural amenities. The deliberate emphasis on the coastal quality of city-regional development in Cape Town takes advantage of its geography as a port city and the ecological assets associated with its coastal setting and climate. While the city's many cultural features, such as the Castle of Good Hope, the National Gallery and Robben Island, provide local comparative advantages, the success of its tourist economy depends principally on the region's unique geographical and ecological features. Domestic and foreign tourists are drawn to Table Mountain and Cape Town's 308 kilometres of coastline (one of the longest of any city in the world), as well as its hiking trails and 327 square kilometres of nature reserves. The region has more green space per capita than almost any other major city in the world (City of Cape Town, 2007*c*). Other assets include a Mediterranean climate and the Cape Floral Kingdom, the smallest of the plant kingdoms. The recent impact of alien species and climate change in this isolated ecosystem has given Cape Town the unfortunate distinction of being the city with the highest number of threatened species in the world.

From an ecological perspective, Cape Town is one of the world's most valuable and ecologically fragile coastal city-regions. Increasingly, the city-region is starting to breach key ecological thresholds that will have economic costs and undermine both regional competitiveness and long-term growth. The region is beginning to face environmental and challenges, especially in energy conservation and water management. As mentioned before, a large part (94.8%) of Cape Town's residences are characterised as low-density, which places a heavy burden on the transport structure and tends to be associated with higher CO_2 emissions, as residents take longer commutes from peripheral suburbs. Though Cape Town contains a level of nitrogen dioxide (NO_2) that has decreased during the last four years, its level of particulate matter (PM_{10}) has nearly doubled, from 22 $\mu g/m^2$ to 39 $\mu g/m^2$ from 2003 to 2007 (City of Cape Town, 2007*a*). Despite Cape Town's relatively low concentration of air pollution, compared to other cities for which data are available, air pollution in particular neighbourhoods such as Khayelitsha often exceed the UK daily guideline of 50$\mu g/m^3$. For example, nearly 125 days in this district in 2006 reached a level of particulate matter that exceeded the guideline. Such levels represent a major health risk to citizens in Cape Town and portray an image that compromises Cape Town's competitiveness in relation to other cities, especially in the tourist industry (Figure 1.41).[105]

Figure 1.41. **Air quality in urban areas, 1995-2002, 2004, 2006**

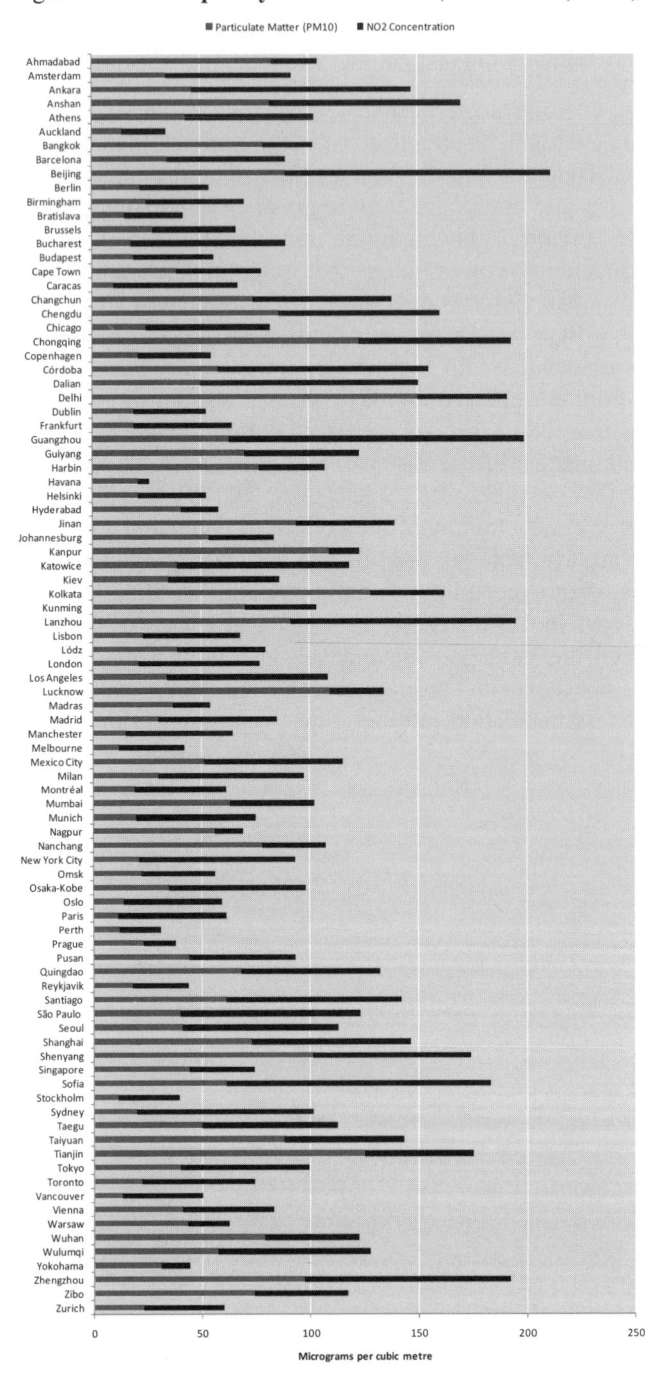

Sources: NO_2 measurements for cities in the OECD derive from OECD Environmental Data Compendium 2002, EEA (AirBase), and national statistical Web sites (cited in OECD, 2005) and refer to 2002. For non-OECD cities, NO_2 measurements are from WHO's Healthy Cities Air Management Information System and the World Resources Institute (cited in World Bank, 2007). They refer to years between 1995 and 2001; the most current year was used. Data on particulate matter concentrations are from Pandey *et al.* (2006) (cited in World Bank, 2007). These data refer to 2004. Data from Cape Town was sourced from the City of Cape Town Air Quality Monitoring Laboratory and were collected from the City Hall's air monitoring station in 2007; data from Johannesburg were found in City of Johannesburg (2007) and refer to the 2006 yearly average.

Cape Town is facing the consequences of climate change, and constraints on the natural resource base, particularly energy and water, are likely to have a significant impact on its economic position (Western Cape Provincial Treasury, 2007). In particular, as mentioned above in the case of agro-food and tourism, the climate is expected to become hotter and more variable, and subject to more extreme events, including flooding, drought, fire, heat waves and water scarcity (Province of Western Cape, 2006). There is a range of possible impacts of climate change on the Western Cape's key value-chains, clusters, resources and infrastructure (Table 1.17).

Table 1.17. **Possible impacts of climate change on economic sectors**

Value chain and cluster	Linkages and Impacts
Agro-food	Change in production Reduction of valuable agricultural land
Urban consumption	New markets (*e.g.* climate control, sea defence, water conservation and supply) Government policies (carbon, fuel taxes) Changing customer preferences Sea level rise and properties at risk Rehabilitation of degraded bathing beaches
Tourism	Change in tourist numbers due to temperatures, precipitation, price of air travel Sea-level rise and beach degradation Reduced freshwater stream flow and water-based recreation
Financial (insurance) cluster	Insurance for weather events Banks and asset managers affected through impacts on underlying secured assets, changing investment criteria
Logistics	Temperature, precipitation and physical infrastructure Temperature, precipitation and travel demand Traffic accidents Volumes and quality of production affecting trade Restrictions on international trade of carbon-intensive products or products produced in carbon-intensive production processes

Source: Adapted from Provincial Government of the Western Cape, 2005.

Because of urban sprawl and traffic congestion, the Cape Town city-region has become particularly vulnerable to air pollution, flooding and fires.

- Air pollution. As a city surrounded by mountains, which gives rise to temperature inversions, air pollution is an increasingly visible problem, despite the fact that there is relatively little industrial production in the region. Children, women and the elderly are exposed to dangerous levels of air pollution. In winter, regular episodes of the so-called "brown haze" are a common sight across the Cape Flats to the mountains that border the city. In 2007, the air quality monitoring stations recorded 128 days of poor air quality when levels exceeded international World Health Organisation air quality guidelines. These episodes and levels of air pollution are a major health risk to the citizens and cast Cape Town in a negative light to visitors, tourists and residents alike. Key hot spots are household fuel-burning areas, particularly informal settlements such as Khayelitsha – due to high particulate concentrations associated with fuel burning; the Central Business District and residential areas transected by highways, on-ramps and main feeder roads, residential areas close to industrial areas such as Bellville South, Milnerton and Vissershoek, as well as residential areas close to the airport.[106] Vehicles accounted for 65% of pollution, followed by industry (22%), wood (11%) and other causes (2%) (City of Cape Town, 2006c). The source of CO2 emissions mainly derived from electricity (69%), petrol (17%), diesel (9%), coal, kerosene, HFO (5%) (City of Cape Town, 2006c).
- Flooding. Groundwater contamination of the high water table as well as wetlands on the Cape Flats in areas suffering overcrowding and inadequate sanitation, as well as highly chemically based farming practices, compound the problems of flooding in many areas. This occurs in the burgeoning township of Masiphumele on the Cape Peninsula, along with several low-lying settlements in Khayelitsha, Philippi and Guguletu. In March 2003 and April 2005, Cape Town experienced damaging floods due to cut-off lows, which cause bursts of heavy rainfall and gale-force winds. The damage sustained by the Western Cape Province during this period exceeded ZAR 260 million (Holloway, 2005). Exposure and vulnerability to climate extremes of 136 port cities around the world was recently ranked. Cape Town ranks relatively low, but the study determined that USD 570 million of assets in the city-region are vulnerable to extreme changes in water levels and ranked it as the 107th most vulnerable port city (Nicholls et. al., 2008).
- Fires. Fires in the Western Cape normally occur on average every 15 years, with intervals between fires ranging between four and 40 years. With global warming, the prevailing warm, dry summers are conducive

to fires, which are common between November and March each year, especially when hot, dry and windy conditions prevail for several days (Midgley *et al.*, 2005). These fires destroy not only the natural vegetation, but also urban infrastructure. Due to rapid urban growth, specifically in informal settlements, the exposure of poor families to personal and infrastructure loss due to fires has increased in Cape Town. Most informal settlement areas are at risk from the rapid spread of fire as a result of high unit densities, combustible building materials and the use of inflammable kerosene (paraffin) stoves.107 In spite of recent electrification campaigns, in 2001 only 68.6% of households in the province were electrified,108 leaving the remaining 31.4% reliant on unhealthy and unsafe sources of fuel for cooking and heating. For these reasons and others, more than 41 000 informal homes were damaged or destroyed in fires between 1990-2004 (Holloway 2005).109 The number of incidents has been increasing: in 2006 alone, more than 6 000 shacks were destroyed by fires (City of Cape Town, 2007c).

In addition to the increasing pressure on natural amenities, rampant crime hinders the region's liveability and attractiveness. Although Capetonians live longer than in any other province in South Africa and 12.3 years longer than the average South African, life expectancy has suffered due to the HIV/AIDS pandemic and the rise of homicide over the last decade.[110] The city has one of the highest crime rates in the nation: Cape Town has 7% of the nation's population, but is responsible for 10% of the country's reported homicides and 21% of its drug-related crime. The current homicide rate of 62 per 100 000 inhabitants is among the highest in South Africa, despite its decrease from a peak of 84.4 from 2003-2004. Blighted areas throughout Cape Town are susceptible to homicide rates upwards of seven times the city average, equivalent to areas undergoing high-intensity warfare.[111] Comparatively, Cape Town's citywide homicide rate is approximately 15 times the average of the 33 EU cities monitored by Eurostat. Current levels compare to the rate in Rio de Janeiro (56 per 100 000 inhabitants) and Recife (72) in Brazil and with Compton (67) in the United States.[112] The city also has one of the highest reported rates of rape in the world, approximately three and a half times as high as the rate in the average city in the United States. With 5 700 cases of reported rape and indecent assault in 2006, Cape Town has 28.5% more rapes than the national average. In terms of drug-related crime, Cape Town's rates have tripled since 2001, at 748 crimes per 100 000 inhabitants (City of Cape Town, 2007*c*). Methamphetamine, colloquially known as "tik", has emerged as a serious health issue; from January to June 2003 only 2% of patients cited "tik" as their primary substance of abuse, but from January to June of 2007 this had ballooned to 41% (South African Community Epidemiology Network on Drug Use, 2007).

Table 1.18. **Summary of indicators of sustainable development, City of Cape Town, 2006**

Concept	Indicator	Level
Air pollution	Tonnes carbon dioxide & CO_2 produced	20 126 952
	NO_2 concentration (µg/m²)	39
	Particulate matter (PM_{10}) (µg/m²)	39
Coastal water quality	% compliance with SA water quality guidelines[113]	80%
Crime	Homicides per 100 000 inhabitants	62
Effluent reuse	Percentage of treated wastewater reused	7.0%
Energy use	% use of renewable energy	0.26%
Freshwater system quality	Percentage rivers with alien infestation, pollution	32.60%
Green space	Area (m²) per capita	160.79
Sprawl	Low-density residential land use	94.8%
Waste disposal	Waste disposal per capita (kilograms)	751.3

Table note: NO_2 and PM_{10} concentration are for 2007.

Source: Compiled from City of Cape Town (2007*b*).

Annex

Model Statute for a Land Market Monitoring System

(1) Any [regional *or* county planning agency] that includes an urban growth area in its regional comprehensive plan and/or any municipality [and each local government *such as boroughs, towns, or townships*] that is required to employ an urban growth area in a local comprehensive plan…shall establish a land market monitoring system. A [regional *or* county planning agency] [shall *or* may] establish, by [implementation] agreement, a land marketing monitoring system for municipalities [and other local governments] within its planning jurisdiction and may assume the responsibilities of a local planning agency for the purposes of this Section.

(2) Any [regional *or* county planning agency] or local government that is not required to employ an urban growth area may elect to establish a land market monitoring system pursuant to this Section and may inventory the supply of buildable lands pursuant to paragraph (4)(a) below. For the purposes of this Section, a local government may also enter into an [implementation] agreement with the [state planning agency], a [regional *or* county planning agency], another local government, a special district, or a private vendor to establish a land market monitoring system.

(3) The purposes of the land market monitoring system are to:

(a) periodically inventory the supply of buildable lands for the [region *or* county] and the municipality [or other local governments] to determine its adequacy;

(b) evaluate the impact of the goals and policies of the [regional *or* county planning agency and the municipality [or other local governments] on the prices and supply of and demand for buildable land;

(c) propose changes, if necessary, that will ensure the supply of buildable land within the planning jurisdiction of the [regional *or* county planning agency] and municipality [or other local government] meets projected needs for residential, commercial, and industrial development, and supporting public and community facilities in the land use element of the local comprehensive plan; and

(d) provide information to the public on the operation of the land market within the [regional *or* county planning agency's] and the municipality's [or other local government's] jurisdiction.

(4) Using a geographic information system as part of the periodic review required by Section [7-406], the local planning agency and/or the [regional *or* county planning agency] on at least a [5]-year basis:

(a) shall inventory the supply of buildable lands within the urban growth area. The agency or agencies may also inventory any other buildable lands within the local government's jurisdiction. The agency or agencies shall use the following criteria in determining whether land is buildable:

1. whether the land is vacant [or, in the opinion of the local planning agency and/or [regional *or* county planning agency]] or underutilised (*i.e.*, developed at less than the density or intensity allowed by the applicable zoning classification) and likely to be redeveloped];
2. whether the land is zoned for residential, commercial, or industrial use;
3. whether the land has physical constraints (such as excessive slopes, floodplains, wetlands, or environmental contamination, or is in a critical and sensitive area or in an area of critical state concern) that would prevent its development, either in whole or in part; and
4. whether the land is provided with central water and sewer and has access to a publicly dedicated street.

(b) may conduct surveys of landowners and developers regarding their intentions to develop over the next [5] years and may monitor, on a per acre or other basis, patterns of changes in the prices of buildable lands over the previous [5] years;

(c) may evaluate the effectiveness of any previous amendments to the local comprehensive plan and/or land development regulations made pursuant to subparagraph (5)(b) below;

(d) shall determine the actual density and actual average mix of housing types and the actual intensities and actual average mix of types or categories of commercial and industrial land use that have occurred since the last periodic review or previous [5] years;

(e) shall analyze housing need by type and density ranges and commercial and industrial land use needs by category or types and intensities [in accordance with any minimum standards of land use intensity and net density contained in a state land development plan pursuant to Section [4-204(5)(c)]] and/or in the regional comprehensive plan pursuant to Section [6-201(5)(c) and (g)]; determine the land needed for each housing type and commercial and industrial land use by category or type for the next [20] years; and compare that amount against the supply of buildable land. Such an analysis may take into account any information from surveys of landowners' or developers' intentions to develop over the next [5] years and patterns of changes in the prices of buildable lands over the previous [5] years; and

(f) shall prepare a summary report to be included in the review of the local comprehensive plan pursuant to Section [7-406].

(5) If, after reviewing the inventories, determinations, and analyses pursuant to paragraph (4) above, the legislative body of the municipality [or other local government] determines that the urban growth area does not contain sufficient buildable lands to accommodate residential, commercial, and industrial needs for the next [20] years, then the legislative body shall take one of the following actions:

(a) propose to the [regional *or* county planning agency] that it amend the urban growth area in the regional comprehensive plan…to include sufficient buildable lands to accommodate residential, commercial, and industrial needs for the next [20] years at the actual developed density or intensity during the period since the last periodic review or within the last [5] years, whichever is greater. As part of this review, the amendment shall include additional lands that are sufficient and reasonably necessary for public and community facilities or services, including transportation, to support residential, commercial, and industrial needs. After the [regional *or* county planning agency] has amended the urban growth area in the regional comprehensive plan, the municipality [or other local government] shall also incorporate and adopt the urban growth area into its own local comprehensive plan and shall delineate an urban growth boundary on the generalised composite comprehensive plan map…and on the future land use plan map…;

(b) amend its local comprehensive plan and/or land development regulations to include measures that will demonstrably increase the likelihood that residential development will occur at densities and types sufficient to accommodate housing needs, and that commercial and industrial development will occur at intensities and mix of types or categories sufficient to accommodate commercial and industrial needs, for the next [20] years without expansion of the urban growth area; or

(c) adopt a combination of actions described in subparagraphs (a) and (b) above.

(6) Using the analysis conducted under subparagraph (4)(e) above, the local planning agency and/or [regional *or* county planning agency] shall determine the overall average density and the overall mix of housing types at which residential development must occur in order to meet housing needs, and the intensities and mixes of types or categories at which commercial and industrial development must occur in order to meet commercial and industrial needs, over the next [20] years. If that overall density or intensity is greater than the actual density or intensity as determined under subparagraph (4)(d), or if those mixes are different than the actual mixes as determined under subparagraph (4)(d) above, then the legislative body of the [municipality][or other local government] shall adopt measures that will demonstrably increase the likelihood that residential development will occur at densities and at the mix of types sufficient to accommodate housing needs, and that commercial and industrial development will occur at intensities and at the mix of types and categories sufficient to accommodate commercial and industrial needs, for the next [20] years.

(7) Measures or actions under paragraphs (5) and (6) may include, but are not limited to:

(a) increases in the permitted density of existing residential land and in intensity of existing commercial and industrial lands in a zoning ordinance;

(b) financial incentives for higher density housing;

(c) reduction of on-site parking requirements in a zoning ordinance;

(d) reduction of yard requirements in a zoning ordinance;

(e) provisions permitting additional density or intensity beyond that generally allowed in the particular zoning district(s) in exchange for amenities and features provided by the developer;

(f) minimum density or intensity requirements in a zoning ordinance;

(g) redevelopment, infill, or brownfields strategies;

(h) authorisation of housing types or site planning techniques in a zoning ordinance that were not previously allowed by the local comprehensive plan or zoning ordinance

(i) authorisation of changes in the zoning use classification, including the employment of mixed use zones; and

(j) changes in standards for public and community facilities or services, including transportation, that require the use of less land.

Source: American Planning Association (2002), "Commentary: Monitoring Land Markets" in American Planning Association, Growing Smart Legislative Guidebook, (Chicago: American Planning Association), pp. 7-92 – 7-100.

Note: Some portions of this model statute are based on the working paper "Land Supply Monitoring Systems," by Professor Scott Bollens of the University of California at Irvine. This appeared in *Modernizing State Planning Statutes: The Growing Smart Working Papers*, Vol. 2, Planning Advisory Service Report No. 480/481(Chicago: American Planning Association, September 1998).

Notes

1. During apartheid, South Africa's population was divided into four main racial groups: Blacks, Whites, Coloureds and Indians (all four terms were capitalised under apartheid-era law). The term Coloured, in particular, referred to a group of people who possess some degree of sub-Saharan ancestry, but not enough to be considered Black under the law of South Africa. They were technically mixed race and often of ancestry from Europe, Indonesia, India, Madagascar, Malaya, Mozambique, Mauritius, St. Helena and Southern Africa.

2. South Africa has not set an official poverty line. The percentage refers to the number of households living below a monthly income of ZAR 1 199 (some USD 156). Households whose income is under such level are eligible for social assistance.

3. With a capitalisation of USD 579.1 billion, the Johannesburg Stock-Exchange (JSE) was by far the most important stock exchange in Africa and the 16th largest stock exchange worldwide in 2006.

4. *www.mineweb.com/mineweb/view/mineweb/en/page33?oid=50465&sn=Detail.*

5. This is an increase of the benchmark repo interest rate by 50 basis points.

6. Historically, the country was a resource-based economy where black unskilled workers were used as a cheap workforce (or even slaves), mainly in the primary sector and in mining activities. The apartheid regime institutionalised this system of labour exploitation in 1948. This economic system flourished between the Bretton Woods agreements, concluded in 1944, and 1971, when the ending of the *de jure* gold standard and the oil crises led to wildly fluctuating gold prices, foreign receipts and exchange rate. Such exogenous shocks called for a shift to a different economic model, which was impeded by the lack of a skilled workforce, limited investment capacity, and soaring inflation. International pressure on the country in the 1980s finally contributed to bringing down the regime.

7. The "broader black" group includes African blacks and coloureds.

8 . The narrow or official definition of unemployment is used for international comparisons; However, South Africa has continued to track a broader definition of unemployment that includes discouraged workers.

9 . For instance, according to a 2005 international test comparing the reading skills of children across 40 countries, almost 80% of primary school pupils in South Africa failed to reach the lowest benchmark.

10 . Note that the GDP per capita does not include any transfer payment, such as social security or unemployment benefits.

11 . One recent study by the Human Sciences Research Council (HSRC), a South African research institution, places this figure close to 0.70, which would be the highest in the world.

12 . The assessment of South Africa's disparities through a "Theil index" (which takes into account assets rather than income) shows that continued high Gini coefficients are being driven by "within-group" rather than "between-group". For instance, in 1993, the contribution of "within-group" and "between-group" inequality to total asset inequality was respectively 63.4% and 36.6%. After 11 years, in 2004, such contribution was 81.9% and 18.1% respectively (Bhorat, Naidoo, and van der Westhuizen, 2006). Although inequality is still a major issue, a black/coloured middle class is growing significantly and could play an important role in the future socio-economic development of the country.

13 . In the South Africa Human Development Report 2003, the United Nations Development Programme noted many of the consequences of this scourge: "The disease is compromising households and depleting their coping mechanisms. ... The result of the epidemic is the higher cost of employing labour (because of increased absences from work due to illness, decreased productivity and increased medical and funeral costs). Increasingly women, children and older members of households and some public facilities are carrying the burden of caring for those affected by the disease" (148). Based on this problem, South Africa has the largest treatment programme in sub-Saharan Africa for those with AIDS, with 210 000 people receiving anti-retroviral therapy (Economist Intelligence Unit, 2007).

14 . High volatility is also due to the impact of 1998 Asian financial crisis and to the current US-led financial bust, which has led to considerable speculation in emerging markets, whose central banks have been forced to build up significant reserves to ward off further speculative attacks. Curbing volatility of the e-rate is a key macro-level objective of AsgiSA, and interventions are centred on the coherence of fiscal and monetary policies.

15 . It is important to note that this report does not take into account South Africa's definition of "urban" and "rural". Typically, both a density and size criteria are used to indicate the proportion of the population deemed to be urban. South Africa uses neither of these definitions, nor does it invoke the UN's size-based definition of urban (settlements of more than 2 000 people are designated as urban). Instead, both Census 1996 and Census 2001 use variations on the old apartheid definition of urban, which was premised on an area that fell under the political jurisdiction of a municipality elected and run by white people. The South African definition is not only clearly very ideologically problematic, since it fails to counter colonial notions that Africans were rural and "traditional" and not urban and "civilised", but it is also totally misleading. Huge non-agricultural settlements, sometimes referred to as "displaced urbanisation", that are characterised by extreme poverty, continue to be designated "rural" simply because they fell under the old homeland administrations and not under a "white local authority" (Parnell, 2004).

16 . Data are from City Network (*www.sacities.co.za/left/stats.stm*) and refer to 2000. It must be noted that City Network does not use a definition for metropolitan regions that matches the one used by the OECD in this report for the Cape Town metro-region. The contribution of the three largest metropolitan regions is therefore likely to be higher than 45%.

17 . The apartheid policy exacerbated the dispossession and subjugation of black people, balkanising the country into ethnically based homelands, or Bantustans, where black people were forced to live apart from economic activity of any significance. The economically dynamic parts of the country were designated as white South Africa. It is in this context that South Africa's uneven spatial development must be understood – the result of a brutal and oppressive system of land dispossession of black people by white settlers, propelled by a deliberate policy of apartheid and historical growth patterns. This left the post-apartheid democratic state a terrible legacy of disparities in income and welfare (Mohamed, 2007).

18 . The MLL, which is not the official poverty line in South Africa, measures the minimum monthly income needed to sustain a household and varies according to household size. The larger the household, the larger the income required to keep its members out of poverty. MLL includes food, clothing, payments to municipalities in respect of rent, utilities, washing and cleaning, education, transport, contribution to medical and dental expenses, replacement of household equipment and support of relatives.

19 . Drivers of urbanisation in South Africa are both economic and social. While temporary migration is mainly prompted by job-hunting and seasonal employment, permanent migration is a more complex

phenomenon involving both economic and social motivations. Permanent rural migrants go to urban areas because they expect to improve their life conditions, and tend to join relatives or friends who have migrated there (Kok and Aliber, 2005). According to Cross *et al.* (2005), young, educated, black Africans tend to migrate to cities in South Africa. They look for a supportive cultural and social environment that does not oblige them to respect the tribal traditions that, in many cases, still regulate rural society. However, not all rural people can afford to migrate; poverty prevents many from moving away permanently, and a significant proportion of people in very poor areas are trapped there.

20 . The MLL figure is based on Census data covering five-year periods, namely, 1975-1980, 1992-1996 and 1996-2001 (SSA, Migration and Urbanisation in South Africa, 2006).

21 . The national and regional effects of apartheid are similar. Homelands and townships were intended to keep African (and coloured) separated from the white economy/society, but while the workforce in the homelands could not move long distances to work, African low-skilled workers living in townships were used for labour-intensive activities in sectors such as mining or agriculture.

22 . For instance, the City of Cape Town has a range of City Improvement Districts that span the Central Business District, Tamboerskloof and Greenpoint – which present a very different character from that of Epping, an industrial/manufacturing heartland, and the Century City-Bellville northern development spine. These, in turn, are notably different from the population and social densities of Khayelitsha and Mitchell's Plain on the south-east peninsula.

23 . This occurred in such areas as Cape Town's District Six, which abuts the CBD.

24 . Data related to the share of region of origin refer to the period 1996-2001 (Boraine *et al.*, 2006). According to the South African Cities Network, 129 400 people relocated to Cape Town in 2006, more than the number of people who migrated to Johannesburg.

25 . The dependency ratio refers to the ratio of dependent children 15 years and under (plus adults 65 years and older), to the working–age, productive population.

26. WESGRO, "Demographic Statistics 2005," *www.wesgro.co.za/assetlibrary/assets/281814428.pdf.* According to the old apartheid classifications, the population was divided into four racial groups: whites, coloureds, Indians, and Africans. The apartheid government attempted to maintain this predominance of white and coloured residents by restricting

African migration to Cape Town and preventing Africans for competing for jobs held by coloured and whites. In the Western Cape, the National Party pursued a deliberately preferential policy in favour of coloureds as regards employment and residential rights, in order to mobilise coloured racial identity (Goldin, 1987). The diversity of this region is also reflected in its polyglot composition. The dominant languages spoken in the City of Cape Town include Afrikaans (41.4% of population), IsiXhosa (28.7%), English (27.94%) and Sesotho (0.7%).

27. White and coloured migrants leaving the country are a drain on key sectors of the economy, such as health care. The South African Medical Association estimated that at least 5 000 South African doctors moved abroad between 2002 and 2003. According to DENOSA, the largest nursing union in the country, 300 nurses leave South Africa each month. Southern African Migration Project (SAMP), *The Brain Drain of Health Professionals from sub-Saharan Africa to Canada.* (2006).

28. GDP contributions are calculated in current prices.

29. Due to the displacement of poverty and unemployment to Cape Town in recent years, the value calculated for 2002 could be higher than the current one.

30. It is worth recalling that, because of the coloured preference policy, the apartheid regime provided the coloured population with better schools than African blacks. The fact that Cape Town is home to a coloured majority may explain why the concentration of skilled workers is higher than elsewhere in South Africa. This may also influence labour productivity.

31. Data are for 2001. The definition of the metropolitan region used in this calculation is that used by City Network (*www.sacities.co.za/left/stats.stm*) and is not consistent with the definition of Cape Town the OECD used in this report.

32. In the Cape Town metro-region, the poverty rate is calculated through a proxy: the Household Subsistence Level (HSL) rate. The HSL, the most widely used measure of poverty in South Africa, is defined as the minimum theoretical amount required to maintain a minimum level of health and subsistence for a family of four (ZAR 2 250, or USD 353.8). It consists of the total costs incurred in food, transport, fuel, utilities, rent, and cleaning and washing equipment (City of Cape Town Sustainability Report, 2006).

33. A household whose monthly income is ZAR 800 is considered indigent and is eligible for rebates or other assistance with rates and user charges.

The second level, ZAR 1 100 per month, gives access to similar social grants.

34 . As with other issues, time series are not easy to construct in South Africa with the available labour statistics. The problem relates to changes in political boundaries both in 1994 and later for municipalities, changes in data-collection instruments, and problems of geographical disaggregation. The disaggregation challenge relates to the drawbacks of South Africa's Labour Force Survey (LFS), particularly its relatively small sample size and the weighting at the provincial rather than district level of analysis. Given these problems, estimates are provided for September 2000, which was the first full round of the labour force survey, and March 2007, the latest round for which data are currently available. For September 2006, the estimates are provided for the Cape Town metro-region, the Western Cape Province, and the country as a whole. Specifically, the estimates for the Cape Town metro-region were obtained by combining data from Cape Town metropole and the three district councils of Overberg, West Coast and Winelands. While the individual total population estimate for each of the three district councils appears to be unreliable, when the four areas are combined, they give an approximate indication.

35 . However, the demographic bulge at that level is leading to both increased employment and increased unemployment, because the labour market is not able to supply jobs at the rate school leavers enter the market.

36 . Workers with more than 12 years of schooling made up 52% of the overall employed workforce in 2006.

37 . SMEs absorb 40% of regional employment.

38 . These categories exclude agricultural work: in 2007, 8.5% of the labour force was working in agriculture (Labour Force Survey, March 2007).

39 . The Cape Town region (11%), Nelson Mandela (10%), eThekwini (15%), Ekurhuleni, (20%) Johannesburg (20%) and Tshwane (15%) (Western Cape Provincial Treasury, 2007).

40 . This compares to a national concentration of 14% in agriculture, fishing and forestry; 28% in wholesale and retail trade, catering and accommodation; and 28% in private households.

41 . The public sector plays an important role within the regional economy. Cape Town is the legislative capital of South Africa and site of the National Parliament. General government services accounted for 9.2% of regional GDP in 2005. Parliament's 2007 budget pumped ZAR 1 billion into the regional economy, while also attracting a range of economic activities around political networking and lobbying. The Western Cape

provincial government and the large, metropolitan local government (City of Cape Town) also stimulated the economy, through budgetary allocations of approximately ZAR 30 billion.

42. The agriculture sector, through agro-processing activities, typically contributes 20% to 25% of the value-added in the manufacturing sector in middle-income countries (Wilkinson and Rocha, 2006). In this sense, despite the small size of the primary sector as a whole, maintaining and diversifying the competitiveness of agriculture is an important policy issue for developing lucrative value chains.

43. Data presented in this paragraph refer to the Province of the Western Cape and are for 2004. It is worth recalling, however, that the Cape Town metro-region accounts for more than 90% of Western Cape's economy, and that the City of Cape Town is by far the most important commercial node within the Province.

44. Exports of services will increasingly play an important role in the regional economy, but an effective way of monitoring regional trade in services has not yet been developed.

45. Although it enjoys a trade surplus with the rest of the world, the "beverages" sector is not highly traded at the national level. Approximately 10% of domestic demand is supplied by imports and 10% of output produced is exported. However, on average, this trade surplus is narrowing. Further classification of this sector shows that Vermouth and other wine of fresh grapes flavoured with plants or aromatic substances, as well as undenatured ethyl alcohol have suffered a negative trade balance in the past few years.

46. 2001 is an outlier in the data series. A large spike in 2001, at almost 6% of GDP, was the result of the elimination of the cross-holding of ownership between the UK-based Anglo-American Plc and De Beers. The figure for 2001 should therefore be excluded from the analysis, because it provides a somewhat misleading indicator of a surge of investment (Thomas, Leape, 2005).

47. According to Gel and Black (2004), a large number of foreign investors enter South Africa through full or partial acquisition of domestic firms, as opposed to new greenfield investments or joint ventures.

48. Over the period January 2004 to October 2007, 17 investments came from other provinces in South Africa, and 81 foreign direct investment (FDIs) transactions were recorded for the Western Cape. In value terms, total investment (national plus FDIs) over this period amounted to ZAR 17.4 billion (UDS PPP 2.5 billion at 2000 prices) creating 8 368 jobs (one job for every USD PPP 116 000 of investment). The source

countries for FDI in the Western Cape are still dominated by its traditional trading partners, which consist of emerging markets and developed countries with little diversification. Excluding oil investments in the Eden district, the key source countries for overall investment since 2004 include the United Kingdom (21%), United States (14%), Bahamas (10%), Belgium (7%), while 12% was national investment.

49 . Note that the FDI data used for this analysis includes both WESTGRO's record of foreign investment transactions and those supplied by the international consultancy firm OCO Consulting.

50 . Employment intensity varies on a sub-sector level; property development, construction, tourism and business services produce the highest shares of employment from FDI inflows to the Western Cape. FDI has created jobs in the Cape Town Metro Region: on average, one job was created for every ZAR 785 538 of FDI from 2004 to 2007.

51 . The resource-based sector dominates the FDI inflow in the Western Cape, representing a 66% share of total FDI inflows to the Western Cape Province since 2004. The largest share of these FDIs is focused on the oil and gas sector in the Eden District. This includes major investments by two foreign companies in oil and gas extraction in Mossel Bay, totalling about ZA R10 billion. Eden District, however, lies beyond the Functional Urban Region of Cape Town.

52 . The Labour Force Survey sample size did not permit disaggregation at the city level until September 2005. Until then, it had been possible to disaggregate to the city level, although given the small sample size at that level, statistical significance requires analysis at the Cape Town regional level.

53 . In particular, the beverage sector has increased its export performance by 86% over 1995-2006 (WESGRO, 2007).

54 . This subsector evidences very high (33.2%) national four-firm concentration levels in comparison to Malaysia (26.9%), India (172%) and Egypt (9.4%). The full extent of concentration is more evident at the sub-sector or product cluster level. High levels of industry concentration are largely attributed to the continued legacy of restrictive licensing practices under the pre-1994 agricultural marketing boards, as well as to technological barriers (Western Cape Department of Economic Development and Tourism, 2006b).

55 . Of these, Shoprite and Woolworths are headquartered in the city, while Pick n Pay has one of its two joint head offices in Cape Town.

56 . Besides traditional techniques, such as selective breeding, hybridisation and tissue culture, regional biotech is dealing with such cutting-edge technologies as recombinant DNA technology, marker assisted selection (MAS), gene splicing, gene silencing, bacterial mediated gene transfer mechanisms and mini-chromosome technology.

57 . "Nutraceutical", a portmanteau word combining nutrition and pharmaceutical, refers to extracts of foods claimed to have beneficial medicinal properties.

58 . From 1995 to 2002, producer prices for fruit, vegetables and viticulture products increased by 41.6%, 44.2% and 54.2% respectively. Over the same period, the cost of farming implements and intermediate inputs increased by 61.2% and 84.8% respectively (MEDS, 2006).

59 . This consists of excessive fragmentation of agricultural land into unprofitable units.

60 . As the impact of climate change becomes apparent, some of the larger wine farms in the Stellenbosch area (the node in the Winelands) are buying up land in Theewaterskloof, which is slightly cooler and expected to offer better returns in the future. This has resulted in an emerging and growing viticulture sector in the Theewaterskloof local economy.

61 . I.e. from ZAR 987 to ZAR 1.75 billion.

62 . As suggested by a local study, this development alone has already created 31 000 new jobs since it was built, and will probably create another 40 000 jobs by 2014 (Victoria and Albert waterfront, *www.waterfront.co.za/profile/company/introduction.php2007*).

63 . In rural areas of Kwa-Zulu Natal, wages in the textile and clothing industry are appreciably lower than in the highly urbanised Cape Town metro-region.

64 . Provincial Government of the Western Cape, Department of Local Government and Housing, Report 2006-2007.

65 . For example, in 2006, 88% of the building plans submitted were for single-dwelling homes, followed by town houses (11%) and blocks of flats (1%) (City of Cape Town 2006, Building Plans Tracker).

66 . For example, over the six-month period from March to August, 2005, 12.5% more square metres of residential space was constructed than in the previous six-month period (Rode, 2005).

67 . These projects provide residential and retail opportunities on a massive scale. While Century City caters to middle- and to upper-income residents and clientele, the Tembokwezi Life Style Estate aims to provide

affordable housing and catalyse commercial activity in the distressed neighbourhood of Khayelitsha. The Cape Town Partnership (CTP) and various urban regeneration public-private initiatives have spearheaded similar projects, including the revitalisation of the Grand Parade and Mandela Rhodes Place, along with the establishment of 14 separate CIDs.

68 . ZAR 9 billion to well over ZAR 18 billion.

69 . Old Mutual recently relocated a large part of its activities to Johannesburg.

70 . The Black Economic Empowerment (BEE) strategy aims to overcome the legacy of apartheid and promote growth and social inclusion. It promotes competitiveness of black-owned and -controlled enterprises as well as black employment. Large enterprises are required to hire black workers (with the goal of reaching an ideal level of 50% of black workers) and to include black people in the ownership of an enterprise.

71 . Cape Town's universities include the University of Cape Town (UCT), the University of the Western Cape (UWC), the Cape Peninsula University of Technology (CAPUT), and the University of Stellenbosch. The University of South Africa (UNISA), a distance-learning university whose main campus is located in Pretoria, has over 23 000 students registered in the Western Cape.

72. South Africa became the first country in Africa and only the third in the world to host a laboratory of the International Centre for Genetic Engineering and Biotechnology (ICGEB). The laboratory will be housed at the University of Cape Town's Institute for Infectious Disease and Molecular Medicine, and complement the two other facilities in Trieste, Italy, and New Delhi, India. The ICGEB is an inter-governmental organisation that operates as a centre for excellence for research and training in biotechnology and genetic engineering, with special attention to the needs of the developing world. The main focus of the Cape Town laboratory will be on diseases that predominate in developing countries, and in particular with a view to study the reaction of the body's immune system to infections and chronic diseases such as HIV/AIDS, tuberculosis and various cancers. These research efforts are critical in developing tailor-made programmes focused on health and agricultural biotechnology, contributing to the potential identification of related diagnostic tools and specific drugs or vaccines. The university's research profile includes strengths in biological sciences, industrial biotechnology and food sciences, electrical and electronic engineering, medicine, dentistry, medical physiology, medical biochemistry and clinical chemistry, pharmacology and pharmaceutical sciences, positioning United

States as one of the country's eminent research and development institutions (Lorentzen, 2007)

73 . A budding partnership between the city and the University of Cape Town seeks to redevelop the university's Hiddingh campus into a creative and cultural precinct. Located within walking distance from the central city area and the Parliamentary precinct, the proposed Hiddingh creative precinct would span the Iziko museums, Hiddingh Campus, Cape Town High, Centre for the Book, St. George's Cathedral, the National Library, Parliament, Tuynhuis, the Holocaust Centre, the Jewish museum and the proposed Cathedral Square (Cape Town Partnership, 2007), revitalising the upper end of the old city and connecting it to the catalytic Mandela Rhodes Place development and the bustling activity of St. George's Mall.

74 . The segment is mainly concerned with publishing textbooks for use in primary and secondary schools. While it has been helped by the government's prioritisation of learning materials in schools, lengthy tender and procurement processes and funding constraints complicate operations. General or trade books account for only 30% of the publishing market, confirming that South Africa still has a limited readership in comparison to its middle-income competitors. Increased public funding of community libraries, coupled with efforts to promote national literacy, are key in boosting a learning culture (Western Cape Department of Economic Development and Tourism, 2006c).

75 . This year, the city hosted its second annual Book Fair (with 50 000 visitors), sponsored jointly by the Publishers Association of South Africa (PASA) and the Frankfurt Book Fair, in association with the Sunday Times.

76 . The township of Khayelitsha (meaning "new home") was established in 1983. With 406 000 residents at the end of 2005, Khayelitsha is Cape Town's biggest township and the second-largest in South Africa. Close to it is Mitchell's Plain, built during the 1970s to provide housing for coloured victims of forced removal due to the implementation of the Group Areas Act, and home to 350 000 people. The ethnic composition of the two townships is different. Khayelitsha houses Africans and acts as a buffer for African migrants coming from the Eastern Cape or from other rural areas of the country. Conversely, the residents of Mitchell's Plain are overwhelmingly coloured and more stratified in terms of income. Both townships are located in the City of Cape Town's Metro South East Region, commonly known as its "poverty trap," approximately 30 kilometers from Cape Town's central business district (CBD).

77 . In particular, due to the high price of land, housing development programmes, which depend on the low cost of land, are concentrated in

the areas where land is cheaper. Thish dynamic enhances the pattern of segregation.

78 . Social capital can be eroded by stresses in social relations such as violence, drug abuse and other destructive behaviour, political instability, a breakdown of trust between communities and a lack of time invested in social relations. (*Human Development Report*, UNDP 1997).

79 . The Khayelitsha Community Trust (KCT) was established by the City of Cape Town in April 2003, with the overall objective to uplift the community of Khayelitsha. In achieving its objective, the Trust would procure and establish commercial, residential and community facilities in Khayelitsha.

80 . Poverty and HIV/AIDS figures refer to the City of Cape Town and are cited in the City of Cape Town Sustainability Report (2006).

81 . Localisation economies indicate geographic concentrations of *interconnected* companies and institutions in a particular field (Hoover 1971; Lambooy 1981; Lambooy, Atzema, Wever and Rietbergen 2002). Conversely, urbanisation economies, which are also known as urban agglomerations (Hoover 1971; Krugman 1996; Lambooy, Atzema, Wever and Rietbergen 2002; Lambooy 1998), emerge when *dissimilar* companies, but also households, locate near each other. This generates a diverse complex of social institutions that do not support a specific sector but facilitate the development of the overall regional economy.

82 . The Western Cape Education Department (WCED) is responsible for 923 primary schools (Grades R-7), 310 secondary schools (Grades 8-12), 42 combined primary and secondary schools, and 159 intermediate schools (Grades R-9). Of the total 1 452 schools, 730 (50%) are located within the City of Cape Town's boundaries.

83 . In international comparisons of learning outcomes for maths and science, the Trends in International Mathematics and Science Study (TIMSS 2003) shows that nationally, South Africa is the poorest-performing of the 50 countries studied, with a scaled score of 264 for mathematics (international average of 467) and a scaled score of 244 for science (international average of 474). Of the four provinces that scored above the national average, the Western Cape is the highest, with a scaled score of 389 for mathematics and a scaled score of 386 for science. However, differences amongst former African schools and former white schools in both these subjects is significant, again highlighting the huge inequity in learning outcomes between the previously advantaged wealthier schools and the previously disadvantaged, poorer schools (HSRC, 2005).

84 . The term "probit" was coined in the 1930s by Chester Bliss and stands for probability unit. Probit analysis is a method for analysing binary response data through the use of cumulative normal probability distribution. In the case of student performances, for instance, the two possible events are "the probability that the student will advance to the next year of schooling" versus "the probability that the student will not advance to the next year of schooling". The probit studies the distribution of probability and assesses which event will be more frequent than the other.

85 . This contrasts with the rates of 86% for white youth and 42% for coloured youth (Lam *et al.*, 2007).

86 . In Mexico City, informal labour is estimated at around 50% of the regional labour market; and in Istanbul, some 30% of the local workforce is informal. In Naples, although official data are missing, some on-field research has found entire clusters of informal firms (Meldolesi and Aniello, 1996).

87 . In August 2003, President Thabo Mbeki introduced the idea that in South Africa, "first economy" and a "second economy" operate side by side. In November that year, in an address to the National Council of Provinces, he stated: "The second economy (or the marginalised economy) is characterised by underdevelopment, contributes little to GDP, contains a big percentage of our population, incorporates the poorest of our rural and urban poor, is structurally disconnected from both the first and the global economy and is incapable of self-generated growth and development." (Devey *et al.*, 2006).

88 . In the Western Cape, 10% of business R&D investment is "Social Scientific R&D", making the Western Cape the province that invests the most in this area: up to 50% of the national total in 2006. Though the impact of such investment is likely to be positive, it is difficult to measure it, since it does not generate patent applications, used here as a proxy for innovation capacity.

89 . In the early 1990s, the apartheid innovation framework was badly affected by 20 years of low or zero growth rates, falling gross fixed capital formation (GFCF was 30% of GDP in 1960s and only 15% in early 1990s), and sustained high inflation (OECD, 2007*c*).

90 . An exception is represented by sectors such as ICT, engineering and medical sciences, which concentrate a large business R&D expenditure.

91 . Cape Town-based firms perceive external markets (competitors, customers, suppliers) as a key source of new knowledge and innovation, while universities and science councils in general are not considered to be relevant (MEDS, 2007).

92 . The four regional universities are the University of Cape Town (with 21 700 students), the University of the Western Cape (15 200), the Cape Peninsula University of Technology (27 800), and the University of Stellenbosch (22 000). While its main campus is located in Pretoria, South Africa's distance-learning university, the University of South Africa, (UNISA) also has over 23 000 students registered in the Western Cape.

93 . The Centre for High Performance Computing was established as a joint initiative by the Department of Science and Technology, the Meraka Institute and the University of Cape Town to provide computing power for research and innovation activities. The installation of the first phase of the infrastructure was initiated in December 2006, with the centre commissioned in March 2007 (Department of Science and Technology, 2007).

94 . Other key hospitals include the Red Cross Children's Hospital (Rondebosch), Tygerberg Academic Hospital (Parow) and Groote Schuur Hospital (Observatory). The Red Cross Children's Hospital stands out as South Africa's leading medical centre for post-graduate paediatric specialist medical and surgical training. The hospital employs over 1 100 specialist medical personnel and clerical/non-professional staff. The hospital has academic links to the University of Cape Town's School of Child and Adolescent Health, the University of the Western Cape Dental School and the University of Stellenbosch (Red Cross Children's Hospital, 2007). Tygerberg Academic Hospital is the teaching hospital for the University of Stellenbosch. Operating with an annual budget of ZAR 770 million, the hospital has just over 1 200 active beds and employs over 4 000 staff, providing health care to over 2 million people directly or indirectly through its secondary hospitals; Karl Bremer, Paarl and Eben Donges (Worcester). The Western Cape's leading health facility for trauma and other acute-case care, Tygerberg caters for all health-specialised services appropriate to a large academic hospital (Cape Gateway, 2007).

95 . ZAR 518.9 million in high-tech services. R&D is also reported by using a definition provided by the National Science Foundation, United States.

96 . These are the Steenbras Upper, Steenbras Lower, Wemmershoek, Voëlvlei, and the Villiersdorp. Facing growing demand, the City of Cape Town, in collaboration with the national Department for Water and Forestry, constructed the Berg Dam in 2007 at the cost of ZAR 1.5 billion.

97. For a breakdown of 2006 service levels by ward, see *web.capetown.gov.za/eDocuments/Ward_2006_Service_Indicators_3112006132426_359.pdf.*

98. An initial price increase of 14.2% came into effect in April 2008. Eskom has proposed a 60.8% increase in 2008 (inclusive of the 14.2% already granted) along with a further increase in 2009 that would effectively double the cost of electricity in real terms over two years (OECD, 2008*b*).

99. The R27 (Marine Drive) along the Atlantic coast is becoming an important and heavily used road, because it links the CBD with the rapidly growing Tableview area.

100. The City of Cape Town owns the majority of these stations (97), and Spoornet, the South African state-owned railway company, controls 33 stations (CPTR, 2005). Cape Town station is the largest station and also serves the most passengers, with 621 trains entering and leaving the station on a typical weekday. The Khayelitsha and Mitchell's Plain lines account for 45% of total boarding train passengers, and together with the Strand line, account for 61% of total boarding passengers. The Simon's Town line has significant ridership, with 92 788 boarding passengers, or 15.4% of the total.

101. During the morning commute, 30% of passengers use rail, while over the entire day, 17% use rail as the predominant form of transit (City of Cape Town Department of Transport, 2006). Cape Metrorail (2005) reported that "Since 1997, the number of rail passenger trips made over the entire City of Cape Town area has been decreasing at an average of 2.2% per year, from 729 000 in 1997 to 601 940 in 2004."

102. The Transit Department of Cape Town hopes to reverse this trend by investment in a bus rapid transit (BRT) network, as in Curitiba, Brazil, or Bogotá, Colombia.

103. For example, the Golden Arrow Bus Company runs its final daily service to the southern areas of Red Hill and Scarborough at 3 p.m., effectively stranding domestic workers.

104. The number of shacks has grown rapidly, increasing from 28 300 in 1993 to approximately 108 899 in 2007. An informal dwelling or shack is defined as "a wood and iron structure, which does not meet basic standards of safety in building." This count, however, excludes "those shacks that have appeared in semi-formalised townships where engineering services like roads, sewerage, water and electricity have been provided before recipients took ownership of a site and erected a top structure." Another 10 000 to 15 000 shacks could be added to correct for this omission, though a total number should be tempered by the

acknowledgment of a 5% error in the annual shack counts (City of Cape Town, 2006; correspondence with Craig Haskins, 2008).

105 . It should be noted that the recorded NO_2 rate has decreased from 44 to 39 $\mu g/m^2$ from 2003 to 2007 (Cape Town, 2007).

106 . Air Quality Management Submission to the 2006 City of Cape Town IDP (internal document).

107 . In 2003 the Paraffin Safety Association of South Africa (PASASA) dubbed the wick-type paraffin stoves, "firebomb stoves", given that they burst into flames after being knocked over and may create dangerous pools of fuel in homes through leakage (City of Cape Town, 2007*c*).

108 . Department of Environmental Affairs and Development Planning: Towards the Development of and Integrated Energy Strategy for the Western Cape – Initial Status Quo and Gap Analysis – Workshop Draft May 2005, p. 23.

109 . Framework for Adaptation to Climate Change in the City of Cape Town (FACT) DRAFT, June 2006 Energy Research Centre and Climate Systems Analysis Group, University of Cape Town.

110 . In 2003, the average life expectancy for residents in the Province of the Western Cape was 61.5 years, compared to the national average of 49.2 years. There has been a general drop in South Africa's human development, mainly as a result of falling life expectancy. Due largely to the AIDS pandemic, life expectancy decreased from 61.6 years in 1990 to 49.2 years in 2003 (United Nations Development Programme, 2003).

111 . In at least one of Cape Town's police precincts, 430 homicides were reported for every 100 000 inhabitants in the period from 2006 to 2007 (*www.capetown.gov.za/Censusinfo/CityStatistics/City%20Statistics%20Detail/Murders%20Map.pdf*)

112 . Homicide levels in Compton refer to 2005 and those from Brazil refer to 2004 (IPEA).

113 . South African Water Quality Guidelines for Coastal Waters: 95% of samples must contain not more than 2000 faecal coliform bacteria per 100 ml.

Chapter 2

Towards a Competitive and Inclusive City-region

Introduction

After having achieved relative macroeconomic stability, South Africa's government is now spearheading efforts to drive economic growth and reduce poverty. Prudent fiscal, trade and monetary policy stabilisation programmes, such as the Growth, Employment and Redistribution (GEAR) strategy, have normalised the economic and investment environment. As a result, the national economy is doing well: the national budget is relatively healthy, and inflation rates and interest rates have been relatively low since 2000. After a decade of sluggish performance, growth has followed a more stable path, above the average OECD rate. However, despite democratisation and improved economic performance, South Africa faces significant unemployment, poverty and inequality. To reverse this situation, the central government launched the Accelerated and Shared Growth Initiative for South Africa (AsgiSA) in 2006. AsgiSA was a result of the recognition that despite substantial economic achievements since the end of apartheid, the fruits of those successes were not widely shared. It focuses on unlocking binding constraints to higher economic growth and ensuring a wider distribution of growth yields, particularly with respect to increased job creation.

The Cape Town city-region exemplifies many of the income disparities found throughout South Africa. As discussed in Chapter 1, the city-region concentrates 8% of South Africa's population and generates 12% of national wealth. With an annual GDP per capita of USD 15 250 in 2006, the region is also 40% richer than the national average. The last decade's regional performance in terms of economic growth slightly outperforms national trends (4% in Cape Town versus 3.4% at the national level between 1995 and 2005), despite the fact that it has no mining activity, a significant contributor to national wealth. Agro-food, tourism and urban consumption represent the driver value-chains in Cape Town and exhibit promising potential. The city-region also boasts clustered financial and business services, logistics firms and creative firms. As with the nation as a whole, Cape Town's growth model is fundamentally based on the increasing ratio between capital and labour. Increasing investment capacity has improved the general performance of the economy, as illustrated by the economic data presented in Chapter 1, and helped foster new segments of the economy that compete successfully on the international market. Nonetheless, this growth is often not linked with the city-region. While a part of the city-region has flourished, the other lags behind, trapped in the old regime's spatial and social structure. The result is that, in the medium-term, Cape Town may not be able to support the positive business cycle, because of its deficiencies in human capital and the political and social pressure on local resources. This may weaken not only its international competitiveness, but its national role, which competes with the increasing centripetal forces generated by Johannesburg-Gauteng, the national engine of growth.

In such a context, a policy to improve sustainable growth needs to balance economic development with social inclusion. To support the economic competitiveness of the region and allow a more equal distribution of economic development, policy makers need to enhance the city-region's collective goods. In particular, these collective goods (or framework conditions) comprise: *i)* active labour policies and better schooling, particularly in some locations; *ii)* a regional innovation system; *iii)* a restructured built environment freed from the legacy of apartheid; and *iv)* a more sustainable use of natural amenities. For policy makers at the sub-national level, the spatial dimension of such policies is of crucial importance, especially in Cape Town, with its inheritance from the apartheid era, a sprawling multi-nodal city-region, with limited connections that detract from its competitiveness. Rather than simply implement a sectoral, nationwide, strategy, the central government should better assist sub-national governments in providing public goods that support economic growth and enhance social inclusion. Expanding programmes to assist urban municipalities are especially appropriate given that urbanisation has accelerated in South Africa, with almost 60% of national population living in urban regions, particularly in Johannesburg-Gauteng, Cape Town and eThekwini (Durban). This has caused a large displacement of poverty and unemployment to city-regions across South Africa (OECD, 2007*a*).

The first part of this chapter assesses South Africa's development policies, which after a long period of centralisation are now slowly evolving towards a regional approach. Under such a framework, the central government has initiated the *National Spatial Development Framework* (NSDP) and the Province of the Western Cape and the Municipality of Cape Town have both started to play important roles in implementing the national growth and inclusion strategy. The second section focuses on the assessment of the four current policies that address the above-mentioned collective goods, in light of their capacity to improve regional competitiveness and reduce disparities. The last section discusses the importance of developing such framework conditions in the blind spots of the Cape Town city-regions, the townships. Finally, the chapter concludes on the need of co-ordination among local stakeholders and suggests creating a multi-stakeholder platform charged with building social and political consensus around a strategic vision for Cape Town's development based on existing institutions and initiatives.

2.1. Strategy for regional economic development in the Cape Town city-region

At the national level: a new, but timid, interest in the spatial dimension of the national economy

As a relatively new concept in South Africa, the role of regions in fostering national economic growth has been notably absent from the main national economic growth strategic documents. Since the end of the old regime, the governments have paid much attention to enhancing the country's unity and macroeconomic stability. In raising the issue of regional policy, it should be remembered that apartheid was essentially a regional spatial strategy. At the national level, the creation of homelands/*Bantustans* confirmed colonial possession of prime territory for whites, including the most productive agricultural land. Apartheid also secured the major cities and their industries for white domination. Within urban areas, race-based spatial strategies entrenched racial segregation in the interests of the ruling minority. The challenge of the post-apartheid period was to create new spatial opportunities, while eroding past inequities. But the way this challenge was taken up was not, at least initially, through overtly territorial or regional strategies, other than the removal of overtly discriminatory legislation. In fact, until recently, the space economy was not featured on the national development agenda, and national economic policy strategic documents, including the more recent AsgiSA, did not sufficiently take into account the spatial dimension in laying out how to proceed towards macroeconomic stability and rapid growth (Box 2.1).

Box 2.1. The Accelerated and Shared Growth Initiative for South Africa (AsgiSA) and the National Industrial Policy Framework (NIDP)

Accelerated Growth for South Africa is the main economic development strategy. Set up in 2005, after a year of consultation, AsgiSA aims to halve poverty and unemployment by 2014. The strategy focus on six binding constraints for national development.

- *Volatility and level of the currency.* South Africa is exposed to Rand volatility. Given the high dependency of the country on imports, currency volatility exposes South Africa to inflation and instability of the interest rate.
- *The cost, efficiency and capacity of the national logistics system.* Backlogs in infrastructure and investment, and in some cases market structures that do not encourage competition, make the price of moving goods and conveying services over distance higher than it should be. Deficiencies in logistics are keenly felt in a country of South Africa's size with a considerable concentration of production inland, at some distance from the major industrial markets.
- *Shortage of suitably skilled labour amplified by the impact of apartheid spatial patterns on the cost of labour.* The most intractable aspects of the legacy of apartheid arise from its deliberately inferior system of education and irrational patterns of population settlement. South Africa's growth capacity is constrained by the lack of skilled professionals, managers and artisans, and the uneven quality of education remains a contributory factor. In addition, the price of labour of the poor is forced up by the fact that many live a great distance from their places of work.
- *Barriers to entry, limits to competition and a lack of new investment opportunities.* The South African economy is concentrated in upstream production sectors such as iron and steel, paper and chemicals and inputs such as telecommunications and energy.
- *Regulatory environment and the burden on small and medium businesses.* A sub-optimal regulatory environment reduces the capacity of SMEs to contribute to GDP and create employment. In the administration of tax, the planning system (including Environmental Impact Assessment), municipal regulation, the administration of labour law and, in specific sectoral regulatory environments, regulation unnecessarily hampers business development.
- *Deficiencies in state organisation, capacity and leadership.* Certain weaknesses in the way government is organised, in the capacity of key institutions, including some of those providing economic services, and insufficiently decisive leadership in policy development and implementation all constrain the country's growth potential.

A six-point strategy has been set to reduce these binding constraints. In particular AsgiSA interventions fall into six categories:

- infrastructure programmes
- sector investment (or industrial) strategies
- skills and education initiatives
- Second Economy interventions
- macroeconomic issues
- public administration issues.

A particular focus is on infrastructure, sector investment and education. Concerning infrastructure, government has increased the public investment by around 8% of GDP between 2005 and 2008 – an overall investment of about ZAR 370 billion (some USD 48 billion). Regarding sector investment, AsgiSA has promoted intervention in some sectors of the economy, selected according to their functional linkages with the rest of the industrial base and their capacity to generate employment. These sectors are: chemicals; metals beneficiation, including the capital goods sector; creative industries (crafts, film and television, content and music); clothing and textiles; durable consumer goods; wood, pulp and paper. Finally, in the field of education, AsgiSA aims to improve the number of skilled workers within the economy able to support the development of the national industrial base.

Despite the robust performance of the national economy (which has outperformed AsgiSA's target), the reduction of unemployment and poverty, despite some progress, has lagged. The diagnoses of constraints to growth appear largely sensible, although the concern with Rand overvaluation and exchange-rate volatility may not warrant the same importance as other factors. At the same time, the list might have been longer; some major issues with serious economic consequences, such as HIV/AIDS and crime, were not touched in AsgiSA. The main weakness of AsgiSA, however, is in the mapping from constraints to interventions. While much of the diagnosis of constraints concerns obstacles facing firms in entering markets, policy responses are predominantly state-oriented, and some may frustrate the objective of strengthening competition. Moreover, the emphasis on government investment, initiatives and programmes is at odds with the finding that limited public capacity for policy planning, implementation and co-ordination is a major constraint. In addition, AsgiSA could do more to recognise the synergies between different policies that would open up opportunities for the historically disadvantaged black population. For example, there are important complementarities between the pro-competitive measures in product markets and policies to facilitate mobility in labour markets, which would have the effect of permitting the economy to generate substantially more jobs in the face of cyclical upturns such as the one under way since 2004 (OECD, 2008*b*).

Source: South Africa Government Information (*www.info.gov.za/asgisa/asgisa.htm*); OECD (2008b).

There has, however, been a gradual shift towards a spatial approach with the 2003 President Cabinet's approval of the *National Spatial Development Perspective* (NSDP). This document, first discussed in 1996 in the national Reconstruction and Development Programme, released in 2003 and updated in 2006, clearly singles out the regions as reservoirs of growth and the main target for the implementation of public policies to alleviate poverty. The objective of the NSDP is to "… fundamentally reconfigure apartheid spatial relations and to implement spatial priorities that [while promoting economic growth] meet the constitutional imperative of providing basic services to all and alleviating poverty and inequality" (The Presidency of the Republic, NSDP, 2006). Basically, the NSDP provides guidelines through a set of principles and mechanisms on locations for the major infrastructure and economic development investments, including a common framework for facilitating the interaction of different government spheres in the planning and implementation of infrastructures. In essence, it mainly advocates allocating scarce funding and human resources to regions that concentrate poverty but have development potential, while arguing that marginal areas should strive to demonstrate their local comparative advantages in order to attract creative and innovative private-sector solutions and support from all spheres of government. Recognising these agglomeration effects, economic activities should occur in activity corridors and nodes linked to the main growth centres, of which 26 have been identified across South Africa (Figure 2.1). Despite its formal high-level status, the impact of the NSDP has remained limited so far. Although it represents a step in the right direction, it is still unclear how funding/initiatives would percolate from the national level to those sub-national territories identified as NSDP priorities. Finally, the NSDP has not so far been incorporated into the national policy and prioritisation of budget processes.

The role of urban regions in national development policies remains controversial for historical reasons. Despite important and rapid institutional changes (Chapter 3), the idea that city-regions and metropolitan areas require a specific and differential spatial approach within the national perspective has yet to be embraced. More specifically, the notion of sufficiently flexible arrangements, which should both incorporate a more spatial view on city-regions and metropolitan areas, and a logic that goes beyond strictly administrative and jurisdictional boundaries, has not been, at least until recently, a part of the National Policy Agenda (Clark *et al.*, 2007). While the new post-apartheid government eschewed the segregationist spatial practices of the past, it was initially unsure what alternative spatial policy would be developed. As a matter of fact, the creation of the provinces in 1994 was a concession to calls for federal autonomy of sub-national regions. Subsequently, provinces were given minimal powers and little autonomy. The initial post-apartheid policy documents were characterised by a concern for social development and poverty reduction, and were predominantly focused on rural areas. Cities were generally ignored, except insofar as they noted the special needs of the townships. Politically speaking, "urban" and "rural" are loaded concepts that connote different things to different people, and they are frequently used to disguise or frame bigger discussions about, for example, tradition versus modernity, redistribution versus growth. As noted in the previous chapter, no formal definition of either urban or rural is commonly accepted, and the term rural is sometimes even used to describe poor African township areas. These have an impact on politics in general in South Africa and explain in particular the absence of well-defined regional territorial concerns in the wider strategic policy arena as well as the suspicion of a national urban policy agenda.[1]

There is, however, some movement towards the recognition of cities' role in fostering national growth and the need for a national policy for urban regions. In the NSDP initiative, driven by the Presidency, the role of urbanisation and city-regions in triggering increased economic growth rates is explicitly mentioned, and the Cape Town city-region is defined as a major growth node. The NSDP can therefore be considered a first shift in the immediate post-democracy approach, insofar as it aims at concentrating interventions and resources in the most populated areas that have economic potential. In the same vein, the Departments of Provincial and Local Governments, Housing and the Presidency have issued an internal draft of the *National Urban Development Framework* (NUDP), a policy document that stresses the role of cities in South Africa in contributing to national growth and the need to increase urban issues across government policy and actions. The Department of Provincial and Local Government also joined the South African Cities Network, a membership organisation of the nine largest municipalities and other key urban stakeholders, which produced the *2004 State of the Cities Report*, an influential publication that proposes an overtly urban agenda (SACN, 2004, SACN, 2006).

Although these initiatives all point in the direction of a more conscious approach to the role of city-regions and metropolitan areas within the national and global economy, considerable doubts remain as to how the specificities of city-regions and metropolitan areas will be recognised and dealt with at the national level. The NSDP, which basically provides guiding principles for public infrastructure investment at the territorial level, does not spell out how its objectives could or should occur, leaving sub-national governments the task of applying national priorities. In 2007, in line with the Presidency's NSDP initiative, the Department of Trade and Industry (DTI) released the *National Industrial Policy Framework* (NIPF), an interventionist industrial strategy targeting specific industries by public sector agencies for shared growth, and issued a related regional industrial strategy that proposed targeted interventions to overcome failure in territories. As it stands, the industrial strategy does not explicitly mention places where interventions could take place, but it was noted that if three main metropolitan areas (Gauteng, eThekwini/Durban and Cape Town) that account for 66% of GDP, continue to grow at a faster rate than small towns or the rest of the country (24% and 13% respectively), the spatial inequality of the country will increase to unacceptable levels. This position has raised concerns and tensions with other key national stakeholders about the lack of an understanding of the reality of spatial development in South Africa, including the fact, for instance, that many of the secondary towns mentioned by DTI are actually part of the functional metropolitan areas. Finally, the status of the draft *National Urban Development Framework*, which is intended to form the basis of a potential future national urban policy, remains so far unclear. As it stands, the draft NUDF's main recommendations focus on the need for better alignment of functions and programmes, capacity-building enhancement and regulation improvement in urban areas. There are no specific details about a competitiveness policy agenda embedded in the national urban strategy, something that is increasingly acknowledged to be essential by public policy makers in charge of urban policies in OECD countries.

Figure 2.1. **The National Space Economy as defined by the NSDP**

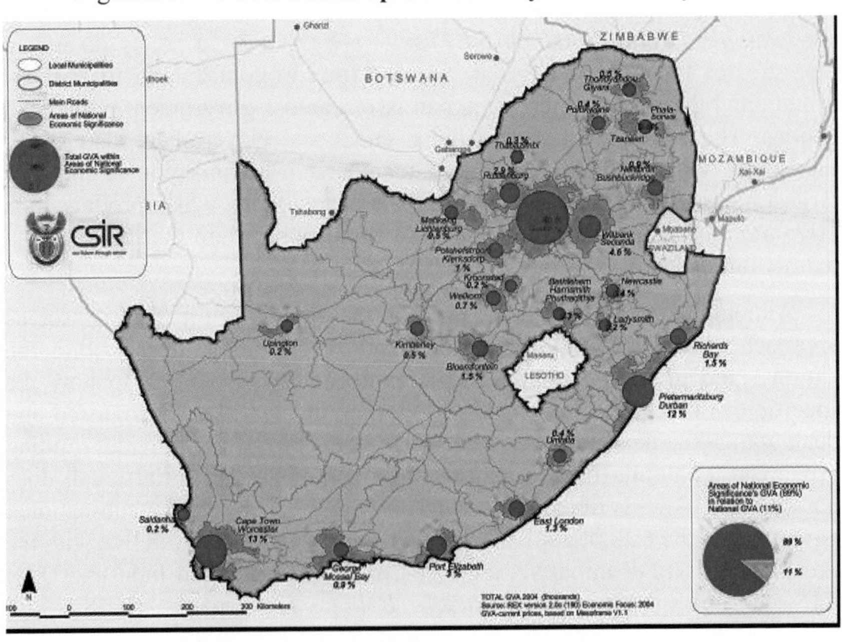

Source: Presidency of the Republic of South Africa, National Spatial Development Perspective, 2006.

At the sub-national level: Increasing attention to economic competitiveness but a limited spatial/regional perspective

The role of the Cape Town City administration in economic development strategy has largely been confined to a vision of infrastructure-led development, owing to an interpretation of Constitutional mandates, which call for municipalities to deliver basic services such as water and electricity. The Integrated Development Plans (IDPs), *i.e.* the development plan that must be produced every five years by all municipal councils in South Africa, reflects this approach. The IDP includes strategic objectives and informs the City's budget. Reflecting the City's main responsibilities to provide basic infrastructures and services, the IDP sees the improvement of local infrastructure endowment as the key element for creating an environment that welcomes business and generates employment. Although it is informed by local economic development plans, the Cape Town IDP primarily focuses on the improvement of the built environment through densification and better co-ordination of housing and transport. The concept of the city-region has often been given short shrift in the IDP and other local municipal plans. However, there are encouraging signs that the City administration is informing its economic development strategy through spatial considerations and regional development analysis. The City of Cape Town's *Cape Town 2030: An Argument for the Long-Term Spatial Development of Cape Town* (2006), *Sakha iKapa 2030: Long Term Metropolitan Spatial Framework* (2007), and most recently the City's 2008 Review of its 2007/8-2011/12 IDP, all stress the critical importance of a regional perspective. On the provincial level, this emphasis will also be echoed in the forthcoming *Human Capital Development Strategy for the Western Cape.*

A more explicit approach towards strategic economic development has been pursued by the Province through the Provincial Growth Development Strategy (GDS – called *iKapa elihlumayo* in isiXhosa), though in practice, insufficient intergovernmental co-ordination reduces its effectiveness. Since 2004, the new Government of the Province of the Western Cape has been consciously positioning itself on the rapidly changing South African policy scene, and has looked to international references to benchmark its conditions and its recent experiences, carefully articulating a more conscious and active role within the changing institutional, legal and political environment in South Africa. A major part of preparing this vision occurred within the context of the overall *Provincial Growth and Development Strategy*. The strategic document explicitly mentions the need for "broader economic participation" to reach "a higher than average rate of growth". It proposes a common strategic framework for long-term sustainable inclusive growth and identifies projects that support such a strategy on the regional level. Though it mentions the need to facilitate alignment across government and to promote common thinking on cross-jurisdictional issues, the current structure is impeded by the lack of joint planning and monitoring of progress (of which more in Chapter 3).

The provincial *Micro-Economic Development Strategy* (MEDS), one of the several sector strategies of the GDS, represents a remarkable in-depth and sustained effort to gather and discuss economic information about the provincial economy, with the involvement of regional stakeholders.[2] The MEDS is a cost-benefit analysis that prioritises public investment in key regional economic sectors to maximise growth and employment performance. It provides a detailed and elaborate analysis of the structural characteristics of the Western Cape economy and outlines the main dimensions of an economic strategy. The result is a series of studies on a range of sectors, varying from declining and restructuring low/medium manufacturing segments, such as textiles, to more knowledge- and skill-intensive sectors such as biotechnology, metals, engineering and electronics. According to the MEDS analysis, interventions in sectors such as tourism, information and communication technology and small and medium sized enterprises would have to be complemented with high impact/low cost interventions, such as those in call centres and business process outsourcing. Moreover, programmes aimed at financial services, biotech, fishing and electronics would feature low costs, but produce a comparatively low impact. Finally, a group of sectors were identified with medium impact and costs, such as the film and cultural industry, crafts, textiles, metals, engineering and agriculture.

Although the MEDS represents a remarkable advance in terms of data collection, key challenges need to be addressed to devise a more spatialised and regional economic development strategy. More specifically:

- *The MEDS is mainly concerned with the potentials of specific sectors, and rarely incorporates a spatial perspective on the forward and backward linkages (positive inter-firm linkages) that might be occurring within the economy.* In this sense, strategic policy information on the dynamic linkages between sectors is often missed, which calls for a more spatially oriented analysis.[3] Inter-firm and inter-sectoral linkages, along with learning effects within the regional economy, remain unexplored. For example, there is potential for synergy through expanding the linkages between engineering, electronics, ICT and call centres. Linking the implementation of call centres to an explicit spatial and relational perspective aimed at establishing local backward and forward linkages with clients, suppliers, local governments and universities (*e.g.* developing capacity for programming software for mobile phones, centres of technical assistance, incubators linked to university programmes, etc.), could be more promising from a endogenous development perspective. Likewise, it may be fruitful to analyse the possible linkages between the engineering, advertising and creative professions on the one hand, and specific segments such as boat-building and the petrochemical industry on the other hand. Finally, there is no clear perspective on the limits and potential of clustering initiatives aimed at establishing links and collaborative networks between agriculture, food processing and business services (advertising, marketing, creativity industry, etc.).

- *The absence of specific spatial/territorial analysis creates potential blind spots for the planning of microeconomic restructuring, and the spatial location of certain enterprise functions.* This analysis may provide a more precise picture of the limits and potential of specific sectors and may help shed light on such issues as whether textiles will be able to upgrade towards more design-intensive niches. Alternatively, a spatial perspective on productive restructuring may offer a better diagnosis on the perspective of smaller agro-producers to move aggressively into more global retail chains. Spatial analysis is useful in detecting to what degree specific business services – an important part of the Cape Town economy – are actually linked into more local or global value chains. Moreover, it helps in shedding light on the specific composition of this services segment; without a more detailed understanding of the spatial linkages, it will be difficult to advance with a more global strategy towards business process outsourcing.

- *SMEs and informal enterprises are mentioned as an explicit focus of possible interventions, but are not embedded in a more spatial view of the economic system in terms of subcontracting relations, restructuring, and linkages between the peripheral township economies and other sectors of the urban economy.* The mere size of the economies suggests that additional information is missing. Both relate to the lack of spatial knowledge in specific sectors (*e.g.* construction) and the need for a more profound analysis of the dynamics (or better, the lack of dynamics) of particular townships economies, specifically in terms of the survival strategies of families and individuals. There is a need to adopt aggressive policies that transcend standard recommendations of strengthening and deepening community networks, improving employment mediation, training and education. The approach towards the "second economy" also needs to move beyond general recommendations to strengthen and deepen community networks, improve employment mediation, and focus on early childhood development, training and education.

- *There is need for a more detailed analysis on the limits, potential, and costs of community economic development (CED) initiatives in township economies, specifically those embedded within comprehensive regional economic strategies.* The concrete threat of a vicious cycle of poverty in townships, fuelled by a continuous process of social and spatial polarisation at the city level, justifies increased attention on community economic development. This is not to say that several initiatives are not already under way. For example, large direct state investments have been undertaken in the establishment of a CBD in the Khayelitsha area and, as will be analysed in the next section, large amounts of housing and transportation subsidies are being channelled into the townships. At the same time, several experimental housing programmes for target groups somewhat above the direct poverty lines have been implemented. Nevertheless, and also considering the absence of any dynamic economies of agglomeration in the townships, fast-track and one-dimensional solutions will not be able to reverse the situation. Without a more detailed microeconomic understanding of territorial and socio-economic strategies of individuals and families living within the townships, massive area-based injections of funds will probably not be a panacea for the revitalisation of township economies. The complexities, rigidities and inertia associated with unequal land use patterns are the historical result of decades of apartheid policies, which will be difficult to erase rapidly by social engineering.

- *The MEDS still lack a more detailed database on specific learning and innovation networks.* As is acknowledged in the document itself, there is a broad intuitive awareness in the MEDS that this is indeed a missing link. More specifically, more field knowledge should be obtained on what we have labelled as non-codified or tacit sources of learning and innovation, specifically in sectors of relevance for the Cape Town region, such as engineering, medical equipment, boat-building and textiles.

- *A strategy based on regional competitiveness implies a fundamental restructuring and upgrading of information that will be required to underpin and guide the drafting and implementation of economic strategy.* The MEDS consists of a forceful first step, which will have to be complemented with explicit spatial and relational analysis on the profile of the regional economy. In that respect, the international experience with local economic observatories could be of interest to the policy makers of the Western Cape. These observatories involve public agencies, private stakeholders and academia to create and maintain dynamic information systems. The links with particularly important stakeholders, namely the business community, the Metropolitan

Government of Cape Town and STATS South Africa, would need to be forged to obtain better information on strategic directions and industry-specific trends.

Overall, the city-regional approach in the main economic development plans remains limited. At the regional scale, there has been only one recent experiment. During a Presidential *Izimbizo*,[4] in 2005, President Thabo Mbeki called on the City and Province to collaborate on developing a joint economic development vision and strategy. A joint team was established for this purpose, and an agenda for intergovernmental action plan developed in the months thereafter. Its top priority was job creation, as the main driver to link growth and inclusion, and it stressed the need to establish mechanisms at the regional level, but it did not offer concrete proposals to enhance specific capacity for its implementation. Moreover, while the plan was adopted by both the Province and City after a year-long process of multi-stakeholder consultation, its proposal for a regional spatial plan has yet to be formally endorsed.

2.2 Towards an inclusive economic development agenda

Linking value chains and framework conditions through a set of policies

To enhance regional competitiveness, local and regional authorities must abandon the sectoral approach and provide Cape Town's value chains and cluster with a series of framework conditions. Given the city-region's interconnected industrial base, regional competitive advantage does not depend on a single industry, but derives from interactions among networks of firms belonging to different sectors. Such interactions can be said to generate value-chains and clusters (Chapter 1), which are not easily grasped through traditional industrial policy interventions, which are largely sector-specific. Public policies need to address factors that are likely to strengthen supply chains and horizontal links between firms, focusing on such aspects as buyer-supplier exchange relations, or knowledge and learning capabilities of relevance to entire networks of interacting forms. To optimise public investment, the economic development strategy should not focus directly on firms, but should aim at generating *unspecialised collective goods* able to support the competitiveness of a number of different value chains while enhancing social inclusion. In particular, in the case of Cape Town, as will be discussed below, four critical framework conditions must be developed: *i)* an inclusive labour market and an educational system able to generate skilled workers; *ii)* a regional innovation system that matches the needs of regional firms; *iii)* a better built environment that reduces the spatial and social mismatches; and *iv)* a higher environmental quality that improves regional attractiveness.

Labour market and skills

As mentioned in Chapter 1, despite economic growth, unemployment in Cape Town (22%) is the most salient problem of the post-apartheid period.[5] The labour market is highly polarised, excluding coloured people with medium and low educations and most importantly, a large part of the African population group (mostly semi- to unskilled). The regional economy has increased the ratio between capital and labour, absorbing mainly highly skilled workers. Recent experience in Cape Town has demonstrated that firms, in the context of economic growth, have tended to substitute labour with capital, or to import the needed skills from abroad. In the construction sector, to cite one egregious example, some Cape Town-based companies have started importing foreign medium-skilled workers in order to deliver all the facilities for the 2010 FIFA World Cup on time. Such a solution, while it releases the constraints to economic growth in the short term, risks exacerbating social exclusion as well as competition among black Africans, who compete for jobs directly with foreign workers. Tensions between native Capetonians and immigrant labourers were exposed in a wave of xenophobic attacks in May, 2008.

While Cape Town needs a higher growth momentum to generate labour demand, there is room for public policies to address structural constraints on the regional labour market. The persistence of high unemployment in South Africa is partly explained by the legacies of apartheid (*e.g.* the failure to produce skills among the majority African population), some exogenous factors (*e.g.* restructuration in manufacturing and mining sectors) as well as factors linked with some structural problems in policies and institutions. At the national level, on the labour market policy side for instance, these include the difficulties of firing employees, due to cumbersome procedures that create a distortion favouring greater use of non-standard jobs, short-term contracts and low levels of training. On the education policy side, the mixed public-private state system, in which individual schools can charge fees and hire more or better teachers, has meant that the huge disparities in outcomes between different regions and ethnic groups have continued. In this respect, besides increasing the monetary support to pupils through fees, it may be worth considering moving to compulsory education to age 18 with free public education and no private co-funding of public schools. This would facilitate the evening out of teacher-pupil ratios, improve the quality of teaching within the public system and reduce the number of unskilled school-leavers (OECD, 2008*b*).[6] In addition to the need to address these problems, public authorities and in particular, local and regional governments, can be more active in providing active local labour market policies, addressing informal employment and complementing national education schemes with regional programmes. As will be developed later, changes in municipal laws and regulations and public transport development are crucial to ease mobility within the region, presently a major obstacle to an efficient functioning of the labour market, which contributes to the high unemployment, search costs and reservation wages in the region.

Public training schemes are part of the priorities of the South African government to address education and skills within the AsgiSA's objectives and are being applied by provincial governments, which have the responsibility for the implementation of education policies. These include training initiatives like the Joint Initiative for Priority Skills Acquisition (JIPSA) and the National Skills Development Programme – the NSDP, which funds the SETAs (Sectoral Training and Education Authorities). The SETAs are the national agencies in charge of training and apprenticeships in sectors such as agriculture, banking, business services, etc. These initiatives are however relatively small-scale or beset with implementation problems (OECD, 2008*b*). Moreover, these agencies are only moderately appreciated by the private sector, partly due to incomplete and unclear information on their precise role and rules. For example, several firms are not aware of the fact that there is no need to stop their ongoing apprenticeship programmes when working with the apprenticeship schedules adopted by the SETAs. The role of the Further Education and Training Sector (FET), *i.e.* vocational education institutions, could be improved as well. Given the low quality of basic education (literacy and numeracy), pupils' performances in vocational schools are poor. In that respect, there are interesting initiatives that would deserve to be strengthened and better connected to vocational schools (OECD, 2008*c*). For instance, to upgrade basic science and mathematics skills, the Western Cape Department of Education (WCED) has supported several initiatives, such as Dinaledi schools, public-private partnerships that aim both at improving the number and the quality of teachers and providing pupils with up-to-date learning equipment (Box 2.2). To date, there are 45 Dinaledi schools in the Western Cape.[7] The vocational schools could also play a more important role in delivering labour market programmes, by offering training to the unemployed, but conditioning the receipt of state benefits (including any new forms of assistance with search or mobility) on the acceptance of such training. This could help increase linkages between schools and the business sector, which are currently weak, and better tailor training programmes to the specific needs of small and medium enterprises.

Box 2.2. **Dinaledi maths and science schools**

The Dinaledi Maths and Science Initiative is a public-private partnership to improve the quality of maths and science in schools across South Africa. The project aims to increase the number of students in Grades 10 to 12 studying maths and science in the higher grades, particularly in the poorer communities. The initiative draws on a number of key private sector corporate social responsibility programmes. Telkom Foundation provides computer laboratories, which include up to 20 computers per school, and Internet connectivity. Microsoft SA supplies application software, and offers basic computing training. MultiChoice Africa Foundation provides multimedia maths and science programmes and training for school educators.

Dinaledi schools in the Western Cape receive further support from the WCED, including maths and science equipment; a well-resourced computer centre, provided and supported by the Province's Khanya Technology in Education Project; maths and science winter schools for Grade 12 students; career guidance for students, emphasising careers that require maths and science; and encouragement for the setting up of school science clubs.

The project has reported the following achievements and progress among the 45 schools included as part of the mathematics and science project, targeting:

- 675 students studying mathematics and physics at higher grade levels;
- Eight master trainers and 13 mentor teachers who have been trained, and current training for a further 98 mathematics teachers and 83 science teachers, focussing on content and pedagogy (to date 80 hours of training has been completed);
- A further two teachers from each of the Dinaledi schools have attended training sessions aimed at finding strategies for managing the high numbers of students entering high school without basic numeracy skills;
- Information and communication technology (ICT) training for educators has been offered to enable educators to use ICT in the teaching of mathematics; and
- On-site training sessions have also been held with science educators demonstrating the performance of science experiments.

Source : Lewis, 2007*b*; WCED, 2005; MultiChoice Africa Foundation, 2007.

Given the large regional disparities in education quality, a specific approach in the townships needs to be implemented. As mentioned in Chapter 1, good schools are generally located in affluent neighbourhoods within the city-region, and the few African pupils who attend them are forced to make long commutes every day because of the lack of public transportation. Moreover, the weak home support in families afflicted by poverty and HIV/AIDS increases students' drop-out rates and reduces their likelihood of achieving higher degrees. Finally, many schools have problems in recruiting valuable teachers in these sensitive areas, and the number of teachers has been reduced by the impact of HIV/AIDS. Given such a complex situation, the provincial government may aim at promoting a larger number of *flagship projects* targeting a small number of pupils, selected on merit. They and their families could be involved in tailored all-round education programmes supporting not only the gifted pupil, but each member of the family. Families in poor areas would begin to support the children's education by entering the aid programme and improving the socio-economic conditions of the family as a whole.[8]

On-the-job regional learning can also be enhanced through policies directly targeting small and micro firms, which represent almost 93% of Cape Town-based firms. These businesses account for 50% of output and 40% of formal employment in the city, and around half operate in the hospitality sector that services tourist industries (Boulle, 2007). Increasing the technology used by those SMEs would empower the local workforce. Enhancing the use of ICT in small firms, for instance, would spread basic know-how to a large number of workers. Such a policy might target SMEs in the poor areas of the city-region and in industries that generate a large part of regional employment. One relevant area for intervention is the textile and clothing industry, where concerted and collective action could enable a shift toward higher-end products and create niches in design. Technological and managerial upgrading would require the creation of high-level, internationally oriented courses in the areas of design, technology, marketing and management. In this respect, Cape Town may be assisted by the technology transfer and diffusion projects funded by the central government's Department of Science and Technology. Public sponsored programmes in the textile industry might also capitalise on some experiences of collaboration between the provincial and the central government, such as the Tshumisano programme, which increased productivity gains in SMEs using expertise from Germany to develop optimal sewing methods and modular production layout within firms (DST, 2005).[9] Cape Town might also be inspired by experiences implemented in Istanbul, which is also facing the challenge of productive restructuring in the textile and clothing sector. There, several co-operative mechanisms have been created to accelerate the delivery of strategic business development services (information, marketing, exploration and pre-viability studies of export markets, training, etc.), all of which were highly appreciated by the firms that were part of the cluster (Box 2.3).

Box 2.3. **Collaborative networking for collective efficiency: The case of the textile and clothing industry in Istanbul**

Within the context of restructuring due to the increased international competition from China and India, Istanbul, like Cape Town, has been challenged to engage into a productive restructuring of its textile and clothing sector. This sector accounts for more than 25% of Istanbul's value-added, nearly 40% of total exports and represents the largest share of employment. A main obstacle to this productive restructuring is the difficulty of implementing strategies of technological and managerial modernisation. In particular, the challenges of niches in design and fashion are that they operate according to informal work practices, generally with outdated managerial and technological production processes.

That said, there are promising signs that this segment is transforming into a business development system in which local stakeholders are taking a relatively active role in management and decision-making. The sector is represented by the Turkish Clothing Manufacturers' Association (TGSD), a private voluntary participation organisation with approximately 4 000 members, and the Istanbul Textile and Clothing Export Union (ITKIB), a semi-public organisation under the Under-Secretariat of the Prime Ministry for Foreign Trade, with some 28 000 members (working for approximately 5 000 clothing exporters). All textile and clothing exporters are required by law to be members. The number of firms in the industry quadrupled in the 1990s, a phenomenon fuelled by export incentives, a historical technical tradition of skills since the Ottoman Empire, strong international demand and relatively low labour costs. According to a recent survey of 159 textile sector firms done by Riddle and Gillespie (2003), 60% of those interviewed confirmed that their firm had been created in the 1990s. The newcomers to the sector, with relatively little know-how of and experience with new export markets, highly appreciated ITKIB services (in the 7-8 out of 10 range) specifically those related to export-oriented market research and other information-sharing mechanisms. IKTIB has successfully managed to improve mechanisms for information sharing, and co-operation among small and medium-sized enterprises and to facilitate penetration into export markets. New venture firms, and those exporting only to less developed markets (*i.e.* non European segments) rated the role of ITKIB as even more important.

A European Union's sponsored project is also about to be implemented, aimed at institutional strengthening and capacity-building of the sector. This will be done through the creation of a Cluster Co-ordination Agency, a Textile R&D centre and a Fashion Institute. This phase will strengthen and update the role of ITKIB in providing collective services for stimulating clusters, *e.g.* through joint business plans and investment proposals.

Source : OECD (2008*d*).

Besides the development of skills, much more attention needs to be spent on active labour market policies. In general, policies in the Western Cape have put priorities on improving and streamlining the policies for the development of skills. In the context of the enormous challenges that are faced in townships, this is a necessary but not a sufficient condition for social and economic inclusion of poorer communities. More ambitious programmes aimed at *active labour market policies* need to be implemented. An interesting example can be taken from Mexico, which, since the 1980s, has developed a relatively extensive track record of active labour market policies with a focus on poverty alleviation (Box 2.4). Most of these programmes were set up as complementary and compensating instruments in order to soften macroeconomic shocks, both associated with the restructuring of the Mexican economy after the end of import substitution and the promulgation of deregulation, privatisation and liberalisation. The early programmes were characterised by employment intermediation, training for the unemployed, improvement of the productivity in SME firms and modernisation of work practices (*e.g.* through the reduction of costs associated with the negotiation of labour conflicts.) Considering the persistent low performance of the so-called moderate poor, the recent post-2000 proposals aimed at strengthening the system focused on the implementation of a differential, more flexible regulatory framework for the social security regime in SMEs (as compared to the larger formal firms) on the one hand, and on the creation of an enabling environment that maximises, and formalises, the productive potential of the (informal) segments of the Mexican economy on the other hand.

Box 2.4. **Evolution of active labour market policies and poverty alleviation in the Mexican context**

Since the demise of the national import substitution system, the Mexican economy has built up substantial experience with active labour market policies. In 1978, the *National Employment System* (*Sistema Nacional de Empleo*, or SNE) was set up in order to facilitate the successful placement of job seekers through mediation services, training for the unemployed and the design of information-sharing services to map specific tendencies of regional labour markets. The SNE was implemented through regional decentralised offices that performed the role not only of a labour intermediation institution, but also of a front office for other active labour market services.

The Training Programme for the unemployed (initially called PROBECAT, after 2000 renamed as SICAT (*Sistema de Capacitación para el Trabajo*, or Capacity Building System for the Labour Market), was initially designed as an emergency employment programme after the 1982 debt and macroeconomic crisis, but was transformed into a permanent component of overall Mexican labour market policies. Its twofold design was to deliver temporary income relief and tailor-made training to help displaced workers to find a job. Training was both provided in the format of classroom vocational programs, and through job modules of three months. The programme was largely financed by government and included health and transportation subsidies, while businesses were committed to hire at least 70% of the participants.

In the 1990s, through instruments such as the *Modernisation and Integral Quality Programme* (CIMO), an increased emphasis was given to enhancing the productivity of business units through training and enterprise development (enterprise-based events, orientation to client development and export markets etc.). As documented by Sojo and Villarreal (2004), as a result of macroeconomic stabilisation, Mexican poverty indicators have shown broad overall improvements since 1996. However, several constraints still remain within the Mexican context, more specifically considering the weak labour market participation of the traditionally more vulnerable groups, such as women, youth and the long-term unemployed, over and above the relative low effectiveness of income and employment strategies of the so-called moderately poor segments of the Mexican economy. This set of constraints and bottlenecks is both reflected in a relatively high proportion of informality and underemployment, on the one hand, and relatively low productivity levels of small and medium sized business units, on the other hand.

In the last few years, a series of complementary measures have been discussed at the federal level to accelerate and strengthen the functioning of labour markets aimed at poverty alleviation and income and employment generation. The main thrust of this strategy is based on leveraging the entrepreneurial skills of the moderately poor and more vulnerable segments through training and capacity building, legal reforms and the enabling provision of a series of tailor-made real and financial services, in order to reduce risks and increase the expected returns of formalising self-employed business units. For example, in regard to the legal framework that surrounds small and medium sized enterprises (social insurance, unemployment benefits etc.), a differential and more flexible approach is suggested, as compared to the regulatory burden borne up by larger firms in the formal sector, taking into account the more vulnerable financial situation of many SME and the difficulty in monitoring the application of these laws (which, in many cases, has also effectively driven smaller units into informality). Moreover, more emphasis has been paid in recent years to increasing the effectiveness of many informal business units through micro-finance, income insurance schemes and simplified start-up procedures (all substantially reducing risk), in addition to the implementation of a range of real tailor-made services aimed at building entrepreneurial skills (support in formulating business plans, constituting a legal identity in order to separate personal and business assets, etc.).

Sources: Sojo and Villarreal (2004). WB 2005 Ex Post Evaluation Report of Active Labour Market Programs (No. ME 0186 ME 0118. (WB and IADB Labour Market Modernisation Project).

Sub-national authorities can play a role in delivering active labour market policies. Experiences in OECD countries have shown that economic growth and job creation can be improved if local agencies and authorities have more power and autonomy to adjust employment and training programmes to meet local needs (OECD, 2003). In emerging economies like Brazil, a series of interesting experiments have been implemented with such schemes as incubators for co-operatives, the creation of specific niche programmes for entrepreneurial development in vulnerable communities, with support from larger enterprises, and decentralised labour market intermediation, with active participation of the local stakeholders (enterprises, labour and local governments) (Box 2.5). Many of these programmes were then complemented with the provision of real and financial services – credit, capacity-building, etc. In some cases, this also led to creative experimentation, and learning by doing, in traditionally difficult sectors; for example, through the involvement of co-operatives in the collection, improvement, recycling and commercialisation of urban solid waste.[10]

Box 2.5. **Local labour market policies in Brazilian cities**

In a very large and disparate country such as Brazil, which is characterised by a relatively decentralised institutional setting, national and state agendas need to be complemented with a specific set of priorities at city level. This is all the more urgent in light of the ongoing Brazilian process of decentralisation of the active labour market and intermediation policies at the state and local level. As a consequence, since 2006, cities have had to take over the responsibility for the so-called labour intermediation centres that were previously managed at the national level with heavy intervention from the labour union. Thanks to the decentralisation process of the centres, cities now have a concrete perspective from which to broaden the policy agenda, from the previously rather narrow focus on formal sector wage-based employment within larger firms, on the one hand, towards new forms of self-employed and entrepreneurial forms of income generation, on the other hand. In the context of specific cities like Belo Horizonte, in the state of Minas Gerais, for example, programme activities are being concentrated on the transformation of several of the welfare-based service centres, which at present provide a series of unemployment benefits and services, into alternative vehicles for employment and income generation at the local level, often in direct partnerships with larger enterprises. In exchange, these larger firms receive official recognition and positive marketing in the media, which also leverages the business′ policy on corporate social responsibility. In other cities in the metropolitan region of São Paulo, the projects that are being developed are more directly focused on improving the role of the new local labour intermediation centres in linking several anti-poverty and income-generation strategies at the local level, such as upgrading, micro-credit, capacity building, collective marketing efforts, etc. Moreover, some cities directly explore strategies aimed at leveraging self-employment in the construction sector, specifically in light of the recently improved so-called National Accelerated Growth plan. This plan has set specific targets for the housing and urban development sector in general, and slum-upgrading investments in particular. As a result, some cities have started to set up dialogues with local stakeholder (community association, representatives of the business associations and the labour movement, NGOs) around the elaboration of specific decent work strategies in the construction sector. The work in progress is expected to be documented in a handbook (or manual), which could serve as reference material for other cities in Brazil and Latin America.

Source: ILO (2008) Manual on Local Decent Work – forthcoming.

A specific approach towards the informal economy needs to be considered, given its capacity to provide income-earning opportunities. As mentioned in Chapter 1, black entrepreneurialism was severely discouraged during the apartheid era, and the AsgiSA simply prescribes eliminating the second economy.[11] Although informal firms, in many cases, cannot guarantee safe and fair work conditions for workers, they may also represent incubators for entrepreneurship in the most impoverished areas of the city-region. Informal firms are also likely to interact with formal ones in mature/traditional sectors (such as textiles and clothing) where their flexibility and low operating cost represent a competitive advantage for the industry as a whole. Therefore, a regional policy aiming at improving the performance of the local labour market could detect the formal-informal networks and offer the informal firms the possibility of regularising their position, while retaining the advantage of being flexible and with low operation costs. Such a policy would also make it possible to analyse whether national and local regulations (*e.g.* labour market regulation or land use regulation) cause informality and marginalise some productive forces within the regional economy. An example that may inspire the Cape Town city-region is that of the CUORE (*Centri Urbani Operativi per la Riqualificazione Economica*) centres in Naples, where the municipality detects informal firms and networks and offers them tailored support towards a gradual emergence from the moonlighting economy (Box 2.6). Through the CUORE project, local authorities discovered economic potential that was stunted by strict regulations or the presence of organised crime. Even if the general context is different, Cape Town may suffer from the problems burdening the economy of Naples.

Marginal informal traders need to receive assistance to expand and improve their operations. Although the presence of informal street-sellers needs to be regulated and reduced, in some specific cases, a local policy could aim at their progressive empowerment and inclusion in the formal economy. Some steps in the right direction are the projects implemented by the Cape Town Partnership (CTP). As will be discussed in the next section, the CTP is one of the 19 provincial implementing agencies, and is in charge of managing and developing the central business district of the city of Cape Town. It limits informal trade to reduce congestion and to foster an image of Cape Town as a productive and orderly city.[12] In collaboration with the City of Cape Town, the CTP forbids hawkers except within designated markets and yellow-lined sidewalk sites. This strict regulation has led informal traders to mobilise in several organisations to demand more space for their activity. This represents a first, important step towards their inclusion in the formal economy, which they now perceive as the only way to regain the possibility of running their business within the CBD. Cities like Istanbul and Bogotá face similar issues and have designed a range of alternative programmes that may be of interest to policy makers in Cape Town; these include the construction of markets for relocated vendors, the use of zoning for informal commerce, and the support of skills training programmes for unskilled workers (OECD, 2008*d*; Donovan, 2008).[13]

Box 2.6. The Urban Operational Centres for Economic Renewal: The experience of Naples

Naples is one of the OECD city-regions whose economy includes the highest percentage of informal activity. In 2002, irregular or undeclared work amounted to 25% of total employment in the municipality. The city suffers from widespread crime, a lack of "social capital" (in other words, a civic network of trust and participation), and faltering municipal governance. At the same time, there is also evidence that the local economic infrastructure is not fully exploited, that entrepreneurs are marginalised and that workers violate labour rules.

In 1999, the Urban Operational Centres for Economic Renewal (*Centri Urbani Operativi per la Riqualificazione Economica*) or CUORE project – the Italian word "*cuore*" means heart, courage and passion – was set up, led by the University of Naples Federico II and the Municipality. It consists of a network of neighbourhood service centres for entrepreneurs and potential entrepreneurs. A total of four CUORE centres operate in four areas of the municipality of Naples – north, north-east, south and central.

The primary objective is to develop co-operation between the state and informal entrepreneurs; the government offers help, but requires something in return. A group of specially trained young professionals are charged with disseminating information through direct contact with entrepreneurs and craftspersons regarding: identifying the most appropriate incentives; establishing centres offering free consultancy; applying current regulations as a basis for formalising work arrangements; agreeing on conventions with national development agencies to guarantee a level of professionalism otherwise hard to achieve; organising the participation of companies at trade fairs; promoting co-operation among entrepreneurs for product marketing, exporting and technology transfer. The project had to contend with mistrust and reticence among entrepreneurs (who feared being exposed to organised crime). However, field research has resulted in some important findings, shedding new light on the motivations of both the local government and community residents, and making possible an evaluation entirely different from an assessment focusing strictly on crime. About 8 000 contacts were made by telephone, in person at the centres or during fieldwork; 3 580 people received support for setting up a business, 1 500 of whom were women; 1 280 companies engaged in undeclared work received advice on their situation, and 326 problems were resolved, showing that informality can be a trap for entrepreneurs rather than a rational choice.

The CUORE project has demonstrated that regulating businesses and workers takes time, due to economic and cultural factors. Furthermore, external factors play a role, such as competition from abroad, poor government support in crime prevention, and inadequate rules that adversely affect regularisation.

Source: European Foundation for the Improvement of Living and Working Conditions (*www.eurofound.europa.eu*)

Innovation capacities and the regional innovation system

Since 1994, there has been a conscious effort by policy makers to improve and streamline the governance of the national innovation system. As mentioned in Chapter 1, the level of research and development spending is relatively low in South Africa and mainly driven by a strong and growing nucleus of private sector firms, with limited participation from universities. In this context, the South African government has developed a number of positive initiatives. According to the *OECD Review of Innovation Policy of South Africa*, the country has built up a strategic competence that enables it to provide broad policy support to both increase the amount and improve the direction of R&D expenditure. A number of new mechanisms for public funding of R&D have been created. Among these, the *Technology and Human Resources for Industry Programme* (THRIP) has effectively integrated the training of researchers into industry-university co-operation in R&D. South Africa has also developed measures for providing strategic intelligence and analysis to support policy. The Human Sciences Research Council (HSRC) has played a leading role in this, in particular creating the Centre for Science, Technology and Innovation Indicators (CeSTII) to undertake basic R&D and innovation surveys and to build analytical work on the results (OECD, 2007*c*).

Despite the significant progress that has been made in consolidating a national innovation system through these new institutions, several challenges remain. First, supply and demand for design, engineering and management-intensive services are still very far from being aligned. This is likely to become a severe bottleneck when the national gross capital formation increases. Moreover, the present level of university-driven R&D

is unsustainable in light of the ageing of university professors and researchers and a dearth of successors to replace them. A brain drain is under way, given crime and racial exclusion, as well as the restructuring of the international knowledge economy. Second, fragmentation of funding and duplication of initiatives has spread financial resources too thinly over too many organisations and across too many activities in science, technology and innovation (OECD, 2007*c*). Within the overall process of establishing priorities, the private sector is weakly involved in the fine-tuning of programmes. Third, little attention is paid to the territorial and spatial aspects not directly related to Research and Development. Open and intangible sources of innovation that can arise from interactions within production chains (for example, engineering advances through learning by using, and technical assistance provided to users by suppliers, etc.) are relegated to a minor role in national policy. The National Council on Innovation would do well to take account of this dimension of the innovation system, for example by commissioning studies on the tangible and intangible sources of innovation in specific regional economies.

According to OECD's *Review of Regional Innovation – Competitive Regional Clusters* (OECD, 2007*d*), the major task of the central government is to stimulate, channel and empower the forms of creativity and entrepreneurship that can contribute directly to:

- Structural change, away from heavy dependence on the growth of resource-based industries and towards more knowledge-intensive production, including through the diversification of these industries into specialised supplier industries and services.
- Closing the gap between the first and second economy in order to disseminate the benefits of the national policy, enlarge the pool of human resources that can be engaged in innovative activities and increase domestic demand for innovations.
- Enhancing the linkages between academia and the national business community.

When pursuing strategies for growth through innovation, governments in the OECD countries are increasingly coming to realise that the regional dimension is critical in this regard (OECD, 2007*d*). In Cape Town, where dependence on natural resources is not a major concern, the limited dissemination of innovation throughout the regional fabric and the linkages between firms and academia help to explain why the city-region ranks so low internationally, and as compared to its national competitor, Johannesburg. Many of the solutions for enhancing innovation capacity in the region will depend on how public policy responds to these concerns. The central government might well consider developing strategies for enhancing regional innovation in Cape Town by building and leading effective networks among firms, workers, higher education institutions and other public and private stakeholders. This requires better co-ordination between other sub-national governmental actors that are involved in innovation policy and that remain close to the main stakeholders.

At the sub-national level, the Province of the Western Cape has turned its attention to innovation policies, although limited funds are available. Innovation is ranked as a high priority in its main strategic plan, the *Growth and Development Strategy* (GDS), one of whose objectives is to create a regional innovation framework involving the private sector and universities. Rather than implementing a comprehensive strategy for innovation, the GDS supports a series of initiatives within the Western Cape through provincial agencies and special purpose vehicles (SPVs). The agencies usually have a broader objective (as in the case of WESGRO, which has the responsibility for attracting FDI to the Western Cape), while SPVs, non-profit bodies, implement a sectoral approach for enhancing regional development and innovation capacity (Box 2.7). Through these institutions, over a ten-year period, the Western Cape has developed an increasingly robust model of sector promotion and private-sector involvement that is delivering real benefits. There are now 19 agencies and SPVs, which rely on public funds and operate within the Cape Town city-region (Table 2.2). The Municipality of Cape Town, although it is not responsible for innovation policies, contributes to SPV funding and participates in SPV governance. Nevertheless, the scale of resources applied by governments to fund agencies and SPVs in the Western Cape is limited: 1.25% of the combined budgets of the Municipality and the Western Cape Province. More specifically, an amount well below ZAR 500 million a year (some USD 65 million) is being allocated to these agencies, considering a context whereby the combined budgets from the City and Provincial governments alone exceed ZAR 40 billion, while the estimated value-added of the Cape Town city-region is ZAR 120 billion.

Box 2.7. **Provincial Agencies and Special Purpose Vehicles (SPVs)**

The Western Cape has 19 agencies and SPVs operating to improve the regional economy. They are principally funded by the Provincial Government, although the City of Cape Town also contributes to their funding and governance. Although the difference between agencies and SPVs is more legal than substantive, the agencies generally have a broader scope, while the latter, non-profit bodies, focus on a given industry and offer direct support to firms. The most important among them are the Western Cape Investment and Trade Promotion Agency, or WESGRO; Cape Town Routes Unlimited, or CTRU; Destination Marketing and Cape Town Partnership, or CTP.

- WESGRO is an agency with a budget of ZAR 18.5 million, funded mostly by the Municipality of Cape Town and the Western Cape Province that aims to provide investors and exporters with information and training. WESGRO's effectiveness in promoting the region is limited by its weak ties with the DTI (Department of Trade and Industry) and state-owned enterprises (SoEs), major players in the provincial economic environment. Furthermore, WESGRO cannot broker incentives or access outside the province, which means it can often only refer investors to other agencies or departments.
- CTP is a Special Purpose Vehicle in charge of managing the central business district of Cape Town. It acts as an urban development facilitation agency that includes property owners, chambers of commerce, the City of Cape Town and other stakeholders. The CTP is funded by property owners through an additional levy on rates and by government grants. Its aim is to develop, manage and promote Cape Town's CBD. Some critics see the CTP as presiding over a process that effectively excludes the poor from access to accessible and affordable housing in the inner city. Still, it is involved with projects to assist the poor and with organisations that champion social housing within the CBD.
- Cape Town Routes Unlimited (CTRU) is a SPV charged with marketing Cape Town on the global market that focuses on expanding existing markets, helping emerging markets to grow, linking markets to emerging entrepreneurs, and improving the ratio between business and leisure tourism. Tourism in the region is subject to market seasonality because of the cold, wet and stormy winter, and a key aim is to create a year-round destination through a sustained campaign. CTRU is the result of the merging of the City of Cape Town's tourist agency in 2004 with the Province of the Western Cape's. However, it is still struggling with a complex variety of external and internal issues, and the complex process of unifying the strategies of two different bodies.

Source: Province of the Western Cape.

Table 2.2. **Agencies and SPVs in the Cape Town city-region**

Name		Year founded	Number of staff	Budget (R-m)	PGWC contribution	CoCT contribution
Wesgro	Western Cape Investment and Trade Promotion Agency	1983	39	18 500	10 400	7 700
Casidra	Cape Agency for Sustainable Integrated Development in Rural Areas	1989	143	80 000	41 040	1 000
CLOTEX	Western Cape Clothing and Textile Services Centre	1996	4	2 300	0 550	0 200
CITI	Cape Information Technology Initiative	1998	5	2 900	1 500	0 600
TMNP	Table Mountain National Park	1998	120	76 000	-	3 270
CTP	Cape Town Partnership	1999	25	9 000	-	2 000
CTC	Calling the Cape	2001	20	15 000	3 870	1 000
CFC	Cape Film Commission	2001	7	4 537	3 700	0 837
CCDI	Cape Craft and Design Institute	2001	16	9 000	3 000	0 900
CBT	Cape Biotech Trust	2002	12	34 500	-	-
CN	CapeNature	2002	511	119 400	73 800	-
CTRU	Cape Town Routes Unlimited	2004	69	63 000	24 000	32 000

Name		Year founded	Number of staff	Budget (R-m)	PGWC contribution	CoCT contribution
CTBi	Cape Town Boat-Building and Technology Initiative	2004	2	0 610	0 350	0 260
CIMM	Cape Initiative in Materials in Manufacturing	2004	1	0 600	0 500	-
CCTC	Cape Clothing and Textile Cluster	2004	3	1 600	1 300	-
SAOGA	South African Oil and Gas Alliance	2004	5	5 500	1 500	0 675
CS	Cape Shiprepair	2006	3	1 600	1 400	0 200
WCTI	Western Cape Tooling Initiative	2006	2	1 000	1 000	-
CTFC	Cape Town Fashion Council	2007	-	0 900	0 900	-
		Totals	**987**	**445 947**	**168 810**	**50 642**

Source: Financial statements and interviews. Information is for the financial year 2006/7, except for TMNP, where 2005/6 budget figures are used. The majority of CapeNature and many Casidra staff work outside the Cape Town city-region. About ZAR 18 million of the Casidra budget relates to the staffing and management of the nine RED Door offices in the Province, six of which operate in the Cape Town city-region. The list above excludes SEDA, the national Small Business Development Agency, which has offices and programmes in the Cape Town city-region but not, at present, a regional governing board.

Given the importance of large firms as employers within the Cape Town city-region, they could be involved in the regional innovation system, acting as a main driver of a well-organised regional innovation system and enhancing their linkages with small firms. As demonstrated in Chapter 1, the Cape Town city-region, despite the presence of good universities and research centres, does not perform well in terms of innovation capacity, either in comparison to Johannesburg-Gauteng (the most innovative region in South Africa) or from an international perspective. The participation of the private sector in overall research and development expenditures is high, but mainly involves large firms, while SMEs, given their limited resources, on average, use external markets (competitors, customers, suppliers) as a source of know-how and technology (MEDS, 2006). This shows a disconnect within the Cape Town business community. Important interdependencies between big business and the local economy have not been explored yet by local and provincial policy makers. Linkages in business services and finance, for instance, would allow larger firms to be much more flexible and to experiment with new niche products through collaboration with SMEs. On the other hand, interaction with large companies would allow SMEs to increase their technological know-how, as well as their capacity to manage complex projects and to deliver on time. The objective is to enhance such interdependencies by associating public and private sectors, to compose networks of firms and disseminate technology and innovation throughout the regional fabric. The case of Munich, for example, illustrates how pro-active interaction between local leadership and large corporations like Siemens has helped transform a conservative city-region into a pro-active entrepreneurial innovation system (Box 2.8).

The Black Economic Empowerment (BEE) legislative framework could be used to enhance collaboration between large and small firms. To promote a dynamic similar to that in Munich in Cape Town and in South Africa overall, the central government might use the BEE to ask large firms to collaborate with small and micro firms, the majority of which are owned by black entrepreneurs. The BEE, launched in 2004, aims to empower groups negatively affected by apartheid. BEE set seven main criteria upon which empowerment credentials of businesses are assessed: (1) participation of "broader black" individuals in the ownership base; (2) management representation; (3) employment equity; (4) preferential procurement; (5) skills development; (6) enterprise development; and (7) corporate social investment. The last two points in particular could help large firms develop networks with small and micro firms to enhance their skills and technological endowment. Respecting the key conditions of the BEE (*i.e.* hiring black workers in key positions within a company and including black investors in the ownership base) has proven to be difficult for large firms because there are so few black professionals in the Cape. This alternative solution, to implement BEE through the interaction of small and micro firms, would allow large firms to participate in the creation of a black middle class.

Box 2.8. **Large companies and state governments as innovation brokers: The role of Siemens and Bavaria in transforming the Greater Munich Region**

The successful transformation of Bavaria from an impoverished agricultural state in the 1950s into one of Germany's high-tech centres was spearheaded by both the state government and large local firms. On the one hand, the state government was committed to stimulate the emergence of knowledge and information-intensive sectors within the provincial economy. Through its state-financed enterprise "Bayern Kapital", for example, it provided ample financial support to local technology-based start-ups, matching resources provided by local venture capital enterprises. This helped to reduce the initial risk of exposure for local venture capitalists with little experience in such matters. In addition, the province succeeded in attracting further technology-based foreign investors, such as Microsoft, and in establishing critical mass for technology-intensive restructuring. Fast-track approval procedures for high-tech businesses proved crucial in the transformation of the economic structure.

On the other hand, large firms such as Siemens started to play an active role in transforming an economy that was perceived to have excellent levels of technical skills but a comparative deficit in entrepreneurial innovation. To stimulate this restructuring, initially at the level of the firm itself, it began to invest in firms in the Silicon Valley, which it saw as possibly the most entrepreneurial regional innovation system in the world. As part of this investment strategy, cross-cultural teams between Munich and branches in the United States were set up to intensify cross-fertilisation within Siemens itself. Siemens subsequently started to disseminate these new approaches within the Greater Munich region through spin-offs, incubators and natural employment rotation, and labour pooling within the functional labour market. Backed by institutional and financial state policies supportive of high-tech, a series of smaller technology-based firms have since spread over the Munich metropolitan area.

Source: Based on Saperstein and Rouach (2002)

The innovation strategy could capitalise on the experience of agencies and SPVs active in promoting development within the Western Cape. The constellation of these examples constitutes a model for public-private co-operation and social capital formation that is well adapted to the regional needs. A recent evaluation conducted by the Provincial government found that SPVs, in particular, have met the demand for innovation from regional SMEs. The institutional and financial strengthening of some of the better working institutions (SPVs and public/private partnerships) could both help form dynamic learning networks between private and public stakeholders and strengthen the efficiency of the Western Cape economy. To further enhance SPVs' performance, sub-national government must leverage financial support to such bodies, identify well-defined targets and increase the participation of the private sector in governance. In particular, the private sector should have a key leadership role in defining and implementing SPVs. Greater involvement of private business would make SPVs less vulnerable to political cycles and instability. Finally, a focus on the implementation of specific strategic programmes would improve SPVs' credibility vis-à-vis other local actors, which could become involved in the development strategy.

Agencies and SPVs might also adopt a spatial approach to develop clusters of functionally related firms. As highlighted in Chapter 1, the apartheid regime, besides segregating people, also determined the location of firms. This is still evident in Cape Town, where clusters of functionally related SMEs are rare, even though SMEs represent more than 93% of regional firms.[14] For instance, the *Micro Economic Development Strategy* (MEDS), promoted by the Provincial government, is mainly concerned with the potential of specific sectors and rarely incorporates a spatial perspective. Strategic policy information on dynamic linkages between sectors and the capacity to exchange technology and information is often passed over, and inter-firm and inter-sectoral linkages that could provide collective efficiencies and opportunities for learning in the regional economy remain unexplored. For example, linkages between engineering, electronics, ICT and BPOs (call centres) could reduce costs and increase workers' productivity.[15] There are obvious links between the low value-added segments (call centres, etc.), information technology and knowledge-intensive engineering, which are relatively strong in the Cape Town context (and, in the case of "Calling the Cape", also have an active business representation). The missing link is organising the value chain. Given the large number of SMEs in the region and the presence of value-chains that generate regional wealth, Cape Town could follow the example of the Lombardy region (Italy) and implement a holistic approach to clusters that, rather than delivering specific services to firms belonging to the same industry, aims at enhancing cross-sector relationship within value-chains and including a larger number of small firms (Box 2.9).

Box 2.9. **The meta-district policy in Lombardy, Italy**

Recognising the evolution of Marshallian industrial districts towards a more complex and interconnected industrial fabric, the regional government of Lombardy issued a law in 2001 to support the development of "metadistricts" (*i.e.* cross-sectoral value-chains). A "metadistrict" is defined as a territory where the concentration of firms belonging to knowledge-intensive value chains is higher than the regional average. In contrast with the "industrial district" policy, territorial contiguity of firms is not the key indicator for identifying networks, and metadistricts focus instead on the density of networks between firms for exchanging input/output goods and information within the same value chain. In order to be eligible for public funding, firms, universities and research centres active in a given metadistrict must set up a network and present a joint research project. After evaluating the quality of networks and projects, the Region of Lombardy allocates support funds (total of EUR 25 million for five years, *i.e.*, EUR 5 million per industry). The policy targets five major industries: biotechnology, nanotechnologies, new materials, ICT, fashion, and design.

The metadistrict policy offers several advantages. First, it complements and improves upon the industrial district policy, which was strongly conditioned on the territorial contiguity of firms. Whilst the industrial district policy aimed to strengthen spatial agglomerations of firms, the metadistrict policy embraces entire value chains, unlike previous policies, which were confined to statistically defined territories and passed over potential synergies with firms that were part of a cluster but located outside the statistical boundaries. Second, the idea of financing networks linking firms, universities and/or research centres rather than individual firms is an efficient way to promote the competitiveness of local SMEs through knowledge spillovers and improved innovative capacity, and could in the long run promote the creation of meso-institutions co-ordinating innovation along the entire value chain.

Source : Bellini (2002), OECD (2005).

Universities should become crucial partners in the regional innovation system in Cape Town. As discussed in Chapter 1, regional firms (especially SMEs) consider external markets (competitors, customers and suppliers) a primary source of new knowledge for learning and innovation and rarely take into account the universities and other regional scientific institutions (MEDS, 2006). Collaboration between firms and universities could promote commercial applications of basic and semi-applied research projects in key regional value chains and industries, such as medical and environmental equipment, agro-food and biotechnologies. Universities play a critical role in many OECD regions, both for their research capacity and because they can interact with a variety of different entities at the local and national level

(Box 2.10). Conversely, improved linkages between universities and industry would also generate spin-offs and attract capital for research activities. In the United States, for instance, universities have become key actors in levying research grants. The University of Washington in Seattle, for instance, attracted USD 750 million in 2004, directly stimulating the regional economy as well as providing new intellectual platforms for regional cluster initiatives in the life sciences, IT, biotechnology and other high-tech growth sectors. Johns Hopkins University, located in Baltimore, Maryland, attracted USD 1.3 billion in 2004 (Centre for Measuring University Performance, 2007). In Cape Town, universities are an untapped resource for regional development. In South Africa, the interactions between universities and the private sector are more favourable (in terms of regulations, incentives, the possibility of extra earnings for university professors involved in project with businesses, etc.) than in countries such as Turkey, Spain or Brazil. However, the fact that university professors may act consultants to some firms does not necessarily mean that the universities are producing intellectual spillovers or spinoffs. A possible solution would be to link academia with agencies and SPVs, to take advantage of the social capital already available in the region and focus on collaboration in science, technology and innovation. University faculty could also participate on the boards of agencies and SPVs and assist in "soft" co-ordination and evaluation of their activities, in close collaboration with the private sector.

Box 2.10. **The role of higher education in Regional Innovation Systems (RIS)**

Knowledge infrastructure, notably research institutes and higher education institutions, are the main pillars of Regional Innovation Systems (RIS). Knowledge bases, communication channels and mechanisms for learning and sharing of knowledge are also crucial for articulating innovation systems. As several case studies show, universities at the heart of many regional strategies (for example in north-east England, Overijssel/Netherlands, Busan/Korea and Jyväskylä/Finland). In many countries, however, the number of universities that include liaison offices or centres of entrepreneurship is still limited (only one in four universities in France has a commercial service department). Such departments, often understaffed and with limited budgets (*e.g.*, Denmark, Norway, Spain or Italy), often put too much emphasis on obtaining patents and too little in exploiting them through licences. A number of good practices have nevertheless emerged in Europe and the United States. Most higher education institutions (HEI) with research facilities have created or reorganised industrial relationship offices. The Industrial Liaison Office at the Massachusetts Institute of Technology (MIT), for instance, is one of the best-known models for collaboration between universities and business.

Providing that they pay a membership fee, companies are given several privileges: i) unlimited access to specialised information services and seminar series; ii) a monthly newsletter that includes details of ongoing research and outlines new inventions; iii) the directory of MIT research activity, organised by area of expertise to make it easier to track down specific interests; and iv) faculty visits and expert meetings for companies that often result in consultancies or research sponsorships. The programme is particularly attractive to business because it is managed by a panel of Industrial Liaison Officers, each one being responsible for a focused portfolio of companies and with the responsibility for serving their unique interests and needs. While these offices usually do not differentiate between regional firms and others, some HEI are starting to clearly identify their activities with state or regional firms, and innovative models are emerging. For example, Purdue University (Indiana) has established an "innovation commons", Discovery Park, on its campus, to identify technologies with special promise for commercialisation in the state. The university has also completed its regional strategy by creating an Office of Engagement and the Centre for Regional Development to manage the resources assigned to regional involvement.

In line with a growing commercial awareness on campuses, universities, principally in the United States, but also in Europe, are increasingly hiring executives and entrepreneurs from the commercial world to lead their institutes. In Finland, Research Service units have been created to assisting researchers with planning IPR and providing other commercial services. Many universities also employ development managers (*e.g.* Jyväskylä) and hire professional personnel to identify client firms and deliver transfer of technology, licensing or consulting services.

Finally, with regard to incubation and the production of university spin-offs, while some universities have been highly successful (for example, Twente University, Cambridge/UK or Grenoble/France), in a majority of HEI the chairs of entrepreneurship are very dispersed, not exceeding 100 in Europe, as compared with 400 in the United States.

Source: OECD Report on Regional Innovation (2006).

Built environment

Overall policy governing suburban development has fallen far short of creating affordable, economically vibrant and accessible neighbourhoods. Despite the impressive number of houses built on the outskirts of the city in the post-apartheid years, the "bricks and mortar" approach to low-income housing delivery continues to trigger unexpected side-effects and frustration. There is an urgent need to improve the delivery system, both in terms of its capacity to provide land in better locations and to increase the leverage of governments over unfettered segregated land markets. Contrary to a mere infrastructure-driven approach, this will require changes in legal parametres and regulatory approaches. In addition, this agenda should aim to increase the environmental sustainability and available amenities of the city, which are critical to maintaining Cape Town's competitive edge. The reform of dysfunctional policies underlying the built environment would need to be embodied into a cross-sectoral strategy aligned with housing policies. In essence, such a strategy would *i)* put a definitive end to apartheid land regulation that still governs the location of individuals and firms; *ii)* improve land management, *iii)* expand affordable and well-located housing and *iv)* build an efficient network of public transportation.

Given the city-region's polycentric spatial framework, policies the built environment must be drawn up within a nodal spatial economic analysis. The collection of spatial data on commuting flows, regional infrastructure and labour markets would make possible the sophisticated cartographic and mathematical modelling that guides policy making in many OECD metro regions. Equally important, it would finally provide a dynamic view of interaction patterns in Cape Town. Essentially, such an analysis could throw light on (1) the *diffusion* of population throughout the Cape Town city-region in real time, and (2) *interaction* dynamics in which outcomes at one location are influenced by outcomes at other neighbourhoods or municipalities. Most important, developing measures of spatial interaction in Cape Town could benefit greatly from advances in geographical epidemiology, economic geography and environmental criminology that offer fertile avenues of inquiry (Haining, 2003). Studies that illuminate and define the strength, directionality and dominance of flows in polycentric networks would be most helpful (Limtanakool *et al.*, 2007). Such a high-level nodal analysis would highlight the interrelationships between the nodes and inform policies for integrating and enhancing connectivity. For instance, a cluster analysis might illustrate what might be gained by linking Khayelitsha, for example, to the proximate nodes of Somerset West and Stellenbosch, rather than simply to the CBD. A spatial analysis using block or tract level data could project how investment in physical infrastructure and public transportation could ultimately serve spatial integration.

Apartheid's enduring legacy on land regulation

Apartheid's regulatory framework that surrounds land and urban development continues to shape urban planning in Cape Town. The economic and social forces that emerged under apartheid did not expire with the advent of democracy and are deeply embedded in layers of social and institutional practices that frequently defeat progressive policy aspirations (Low, 2003; Turok, 2001). Apartheid urban planning left multiple physical legacies intact, above all, its low-density, discontinuous, mono-functional, racially segregated and auto-dependent landscapes. The *Less Formal Establishment of Townships Act* (113 of 1991), for example, entrenches apartheid-style land development and reinforces differential land development rules for poor areas of the city (Box 2.11). The frequent use of cheap parcels on the urban periphery for social housing or land that had been acquired by the apartheid state for township development, has led to a situation where, as Huchzermeyer (2003) puts it, many apartheid era urban plans have been implemented by post-apartheid governments. In this sense, the need for speed (massive quantity) has trumped the logic of space (social and economic integration), as well as the logic of sustainable resource consumption and fiscal sustainability. For this and related reasons, racial desegregation in Cape Town and elsewhere has been so slow that "the post-apartheid city continues to look remarkably like its predecessor, the apartheid city" (Christopher, 2005). Though momentum is building for neighbourhood desegregation, especially in low-cost housing areas and previously "white" middle-class suburbs, multiracial integrated neighbourhoods are a rarity in Cape Town (Lemanski, 2006).

Box 2.11. A brief history of apartheid planning and its aftermath in South Africa

Dense layers of legislation, norms, rules and institutions were instituted to organise, plan and finance the apartheid city. Historically, the process of segregation of the "African" and "Coloured" communities took place in several stages; formative policies included the 1901 emergency measures, the Native Urban Areas Act of 1923, the establishment of a model native village at Langa in 1927, and the incremental development of public housing estates on the Cape Flats, which were specifically designated for "Coloured" people. Historically, African townships had no commercial zoning, since the Native Urban Areas Act was intended to ensure that the black population funded its own urban development through municipal monopolies on retail and brewing. In addition, because black residents were forced to shop in the white town, the rates base of the white city was bolstered. During World War II, the rate of population growth, especially among the "African" group, rose sharply due to an increased demand for labour. Consequently, a rapid growth of informal squatting ensued, stoking white anxieties over the "native question". When the Herenigde Nasionale Party ("Purified National Party") took power in May 1948, it passed sweeping apartheid legislation, most notably the Group Areas Act (1950) and the Reservation of Separate Amenities Act (1953). From the 1960s to the 1970s, the Group Areas Act facilitated large-scale slum removal and displaced black communities from the inner-city areas to the townships, such as in the multiethnic District Six, where 60 000 individuals were forcibly evicted and an entire neighbourhood razed and left vacant. Overall, an estimated 150 000 people were removed to public housing estates in the Cape Flats. At the same time, strict control on the inflow of "African" and "Coloured" people was enforced, linked to a series of legal and financial instruments that, in practical terms, suppressed the economic development of townships by obliging black communities to shop in white CBD areas.

As apartheid was being dismantled in 1991, the Less Formal Township Establishment Act (LFTEA) was passed to fast-track land development for the poor, but allowed developers to ignore underlying zoning scheme requirements, building regulations and other construction standards. Under the LFTEA, the Cape Town Council, although it is not legally obliged to, has generally continued to provide land for public use (such as schools, clinics and sports fields) and has thus passed ownership and control for these portions of land to the relevant departments in the City and Province. Once the Member of Executive Council has signed off on an LFTEA development proposal, the zoning schemes no longer legally apply, and political pressure can be wielded to increase residential densities and decrease other land use allocations such as open space. Though "The 1991 reforms could be seen as a minor breakthrough by introducing simplified procedures to promote African housing, they were conceptualised within a very paternalistic and dictatorial paradigm … [the LGTEA] provided for much speedier procedures, but at the expense of transparency and decentralised decision-making" (Urban Sector Network, 2003). Community participation was kept to a minimum. Second, because the City's own zoning schemes no longer apply to the LFTEA development area, land is not required to be set aside for commercial use. This means that the poor are often forced to undertake commercial activities directly from their homes, which limits opportunities for expansion, given small plot sizes, proximity to neighbours and the improbability of securing loans from banks. More importantly, the higher bulk standards associated with commercial zoning are rarely enforced in areas developed under LFTEA, leaving these neighbourhoods without appropriately sized and serviced plots that are a minimum requirement for providing the bulk service connections that attract businesses. With almost no mixed-use developments, LFTEA areas are thus bound from conception to be residential areas, their residents compelled to travel to formal commercial amenities elsewhere in the city. This situation further perpetuates the spatial mismatch by providing housing in locations of minimal employment. Cumulatively, these regulations have inscribed an apartheid spatial structure on the Cape Town city-region, as illustrated in the diagram below.

Sources: Davies (1981), Jackson (2003), Mabin and Smit (1997), Platzky and Walker (1985), Urban Sector Network (2003).

Land management

A constellation of factors conspire to reduce land availability and escalate its price in Cape Town. The region's development is restricted by valuable agricultural land to the east, the mountains and Atlantic Ocean to the west and the False Bay Coastline to the south (Figure 2.2). Built on the fynbos floral kingdom and the habitat for many rare plant and animal species, the area features several environmentally protected areas where the development of large tracts of land is restricted. The City of Cape Town owns relatively little land in comparison to provincial landholdings and those of state-owned companies, such as the Transnet and South African National Defence Force. Key potential sites for low-income housing include Cullemborg, Ysterplat, Two River's Park, Stikland and Wingfield. Though state-owned enterprises own a large supply of land on well-located sites, they are reluctant to release these properties at below-market values, since these areas often generate revenue. This, in turn, compounds land scarcity, raises the price for low-income housing development and forces housing authorities to concentrate developments on remote land plots.

Figure 2.2. **Physical geography of the City of Cape Town**

Source: City of Cape Town Strategic Development Information and GIS (2008).

The issue of unclear and contradictory land use plans lies at the heart of the land question in Cape Town. A plethora of building standards, environmental conservation decrees and provincial planning ordinances, each with different procedural requirements, increase red tape and transaction costs.[16] Lengthy approval processes, associated with the application and interpretation of the National Environmental Management Act and environmental impact assessments, have resulted in frustration within the private development sector at perceived delays and excessive bureaucratic requirements. The new regulations, in addition to planning processes already complicated by complex and varied zoning/land use regulations, demand intensive professional capacity within local government and the private sector. The resulting contradictions are left for officials to mediate and residents to navigate. To correct this confusion, efforts such as Cape Town's *Integrated Zoning Scheme* (IZS) could be supported and replicated throughout the Cape Town city-region. This ambitious plan aims to standardise the overlapping zoning arrangements and would greatly clarify land use planning in the City.[17.]

Land use standards are unevenly enforced in rich and poor sections of the city. In old white residential areas, citizens generally expect that illegal land use can and should be stopped and that a simple letter or phone call to the Council will ensure that this occurs. A similar pattern exists in many old coloured areas, especially those characterised by home ownership. Here inspectors still visit building sites and can be expected to respond to complaints such as noise pollution or illegal commercial activity. In contrast, throughout the old public housing sections of the city, where the majority of the low-income population reside, land use enforcement is lax, and intervention by the state is perceived as either illegitimate or irrelevant. As a result, whole neighbourhoods are under-policed. While councils that governed the townships guaranteed a minimum level of compliance under apartheid, today little enforcement exists at all. Thus in poor quarters of the city that used to be regulated directly by housing departments, residents have no expectation that they can call on the state to enforce land or environmental regulations. The *ad hoc* use of residential land for commercial and industrial purposes is thus carried out with little regard for health and safety, and the already understaffed enforcement officials are often reluctant to apply the municipal laws designed to protect citizens in those areas. Because wealthy areas generate large amounts of waste, poorer communities in the Cape Flats often host illegal garbage dumps that compromise the health of local residents (Swilling, 2006).

To implement a land management strategy, the central government needs to accelerate land policy reform in South Africa, by clarifying concurrent mandates shared between provincial and municipal governments. At present, no one agency or level of government controls land management, and roles are often vaguely defined. While zoning and land use planning constitute a responsibility of municipalities, land management and housing reflect concurrent mandates with the provincial government. The provincial role, in turn, is constrained by the national government, which has delayed introducing a coherent regulatory framework. This could be corrected if the Department of Agriculture and Land Affairs' Land Use Management Bill (B27-2008) were approved. Currently undergoing comment, it is intended to promote co-operative governance in relation to land development and land use management, and facilitate the co-ordination and alignment of the land use scheme of different municipalities and the plans, strategies and programmes of national and provincial organs of state. The Bill would greatly clarify the roles and responsibilities of different spheres of government and endow municipalities with *enforceable instruments* that would allow them to charge the private sector for the real economic opportunity cost of investment decisions. Needless to say, the pending Bill faces some resistance from real estate developers, who argue that it may increase their development costs.

By employing regular land market assessments, the Provincial Government of the Western Cape could foster more informed debates on the best strategic use of land. The Provincial Government could institutionalise such a debate by including a wider number of actors involved in land management, such as representatives from different provincial government departments, parastatals, municipal government and housing associations. This forum would be charged with *i)* periodically inventorying the supply of buildable land, *ii)* evaluating the impact of policies of the actors on the supply and demand for buildable land and *iii)* proposing changes that would ensure a larger supply of buildable land within the city-region. With this framework, a serious and regular analysis of the land market is essential. A land market assessment could provide an inventory of land in the region that could be developed, including a review of land supply (buildable, vacant, occupied/serviced), housing stock (informal and formal), access to infrastructure, population levels and land prices. Though South African cities will undoubtedly develop land market monitoring systems differently than the United States, the Annex includes a model statute mandating land monitoring from the American Planning Association's *Growing Smart Legislative Guidebook* (2002). It provides basic statutory language that may be adapted to fit various political structures and legal systems, as illustrated by previous assessments in such different contexts as Bangkok, Jakarta and Recife.[18] In cities like Cape Town with high numbers of informal settlements, the land market assessment could integrate spatial data from mapping software such as Geographic Information Systems (GIS) and reference information from aerial photographs. Such data would allow the designers of land market assessments to map the private and public areas that could be released to increase the affordable housing stock and the areas suitable for infill development, to maximise the use of existing infrastructure and encourage smart growth.[19] The Provincial government could follow the example of policy makers in Washington, Oregon and California in the United States by legislatively mandating land market reviews at the state level.[20]

Given the multiple institutions and parastatals involved in land holding and release, the Provincial government could conduct regular land institutions audits to ensure the synergy of programmes that aim to improve land access. While municipalities in the Cape Town city-region keep records on programme beneficiaries and budget levels, they fail to comprehensively analyse the collective impact of a web of programmes on land access. A land institutions audit would facilitate "a systematic study of the legal institutions, legal instruments and adjudicative processes" that affects land access (Farvacque and McAuslan, 1992). Particular attention to time and the costs of current systems for residents would identify the most pressing inefficiencies that merit reform. This is especially needed given the high number of informal settlements in Cape Town and the cost and bureaucracy required to legalise irregular plots. Such critical assessments could tie into performance budgeting and be used to reward institutions that release land and ensure its legalisation most effectively.

Planners in the Cape Town city-region may find it beneficial to implement a land pooling or land readjustment (LP/R) programme to regularise informal settlements and facilitate their service provision. This approach will be particularly relevant given the high registration costs of the traditional land titling projects in informal settlements.[21] Some of the best-known examples of successful land readjustment are in cities throughout South Korea, Japan and Taiwan, where the technique has been used as an effective planning tool for more than 70 years (Box 2.12). Although used generally to plan cities, in the mid 1980s the South Korean government also began transferring a proportion of the cost of equivalent land to local and central housing authorities to build low-income housing for the urban poor. In South Korea between 1962 and 1981, 95% of urban land was delivered through land readjustment. Likewise, in Japan from 1977 to 2000, 40% of the total annual supply of urban building plots has been secured through land readjustment (Povey and Lloyd-Jones, 2000). Through this process, the region may strengthen existing efforts to regularise informal settlements and standardise land use throughout the Cape Town city-region.[22] Two caveats, however, should be addressed. First, land readjustment should be carefully designed in co-ordination with local communities and highly skilled community mediators. If done in a compulsory manner, LP/R may arouse resentment as a top-down compulsory acquisition exercise and exacerbate conflict between municipal authorities and residents (Farvacque and McAuslan, 1992). Second, though such a strategy has the potential to integrate informal areas into the city and contribute to infill development, it should not be seen as a means to increase housing supply per se. Land readjustment could complement a range of more appropriate planning tools designed to increase housing supply, of which many are discussed in the next section.

Box 2.12. **Land pooling/readjustment in East Asia**

A typical LP/R process begins with the preparation of a zoning plan by the municipality. On the zoning plan, within the site blocks formed by the streets, lots are allocated for private development. The areas for public use are then determined by measuring the square metres in the planned streets, parks, and so forth, and comparing this to the total area of project. In other words, all land parcels within a project area are grouped together and a percentage of each land parcel calculated to determine a contribution to public areas. This percentage depends on the size of the project area and the total size of required public-use areas. The remaining land is then reallocated within the blocks defined by the plan. Each site block is first subdivided into suitable new lots, then land redistribution is carried out. The basic principle in the distribution is to keep land in its original location, at least in the same block. After the physical and legal subdivision of land into streets, parkland and sites for buildings, the government may sell some of the building sites to recover costs and repay the loan. Finally, the serviced sites are distributed to the landowners, who are allocated final cash adjustments proportionate to each landowner's precise share of the project (Doebele, 1982). A graphic below from Archer's (1983) research in Kaohsiung City, Taiwan, visually presents the replotting of land due to LP/R.

Pattern of separate landholdings before pooling | Pattern after pooling, including the new street layout

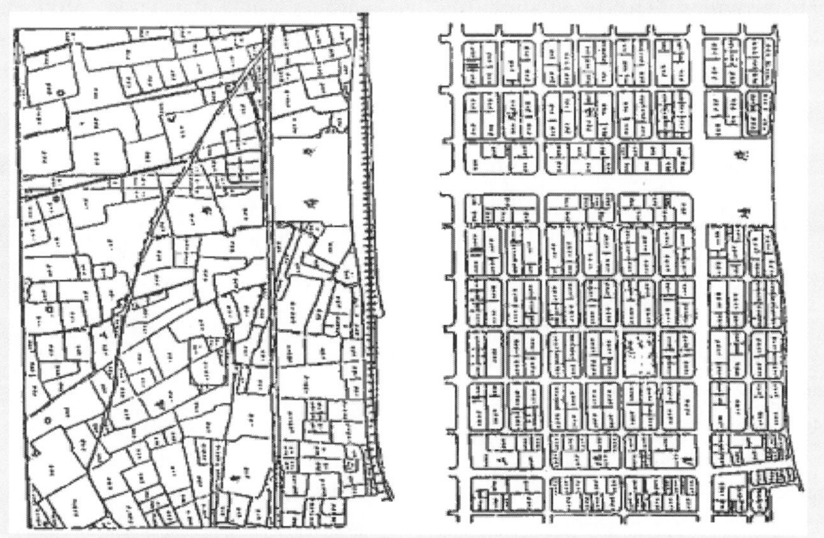

Sources: Archer (1983), Doebele (1982), Farvacque and McAuslan (1992).

Expanding the supply of affordable housing

Current policies have not thus far been able to satisfy demand for affordable housing. The post-apartheid state has delivered an astounding amount of new urban housing and related services to some of the poorest households in the country – putatively over one million units in the first seven years – but this has not kept pace with new demand. This policy is delivery through the capital subsidy mechanism, which provides a lump sum per unit, aimed at low-income target groups. In the Western Cape, the current scale of housing production and upgrading cannot absorb the growing deficit, estimated to be as high as 410 000 units. This deficit is expected to grow by 30 000 per year as a result of natural population growth and in-migration (Provincial Government of the Western Cape, 2006*b*). In the short run, it will be difficult to provide affordable formal housing: the number of informal dwellings stood at 140 000 in Cape Town in 2007, representing housing expectation, if not housing need.[23] Data from Statistics South Africa illustrate suggest that the region's informal housing constitutes a large portion of the housing stock in Cape Town (15.5% of units), Cape Winelands (10.6%), Overberg (10.1%) and West Coast (5.2%) (Table 2.3). The inclusion of the large number of "backyarders," residents who live in depressed physical conditions not acknowledged as "dwellings" in the Census, would produce a larger estimation of informal housing than current data provides. The population of "backyarders" in Cape Town alone is estimated to be in excess of 150 000 households.[24] The inclusion of this population into housing statistics would entail that between 25% and 30% of Cape Town's households currently live in inadequate housing.

Table 2.3. **Proportion of housing units per type: Cape Town and neighbouring district municipalities, 2007**

	Cape Town	Cape Winelands	Overberg	West Coast	South Africa
House on separate stand	65.9%	61.5%	83.1%	84.7%	59.3%
Traditional dwelling	0.4%	0.5%	0.9%	0.9%	11.7%
Flat in block	9.1%	6.9%	1.0%	2.0%	4.8%
Cluster/ townhouse	6.4%	12.7%	2.6%	5.5%	2.7%
House/room in backyard	1.2%	1.2%	0.9%	0.7%	2.9%
Informal dwelling in backyard	6.2%	5.5%	4.7%	3.5%	4.7%
Informal dwelling not in backyard	9.3%	5.1%	5.4%	1.7%	9.7%
Other	1.5%	6.6%	1.4%	1.0%	4.2%

Source: Statistics South Africa (2007*a*).

Following a sectoral approach, current housing policy reinforces the spatial mismatch by providing housing units in locations of minimal employment. Paradoxically, the impressive delivery of individual units through capital subsidies has not significantly changed the urban format established under apartheid. Land is an upfront cost, and the combination of high financial costs and limited budgets has obliged local governments to develop in the outskirts, which lack amenities and socio-economic infrastructure. This has trapped communities in suboptimal employment circuits, with low income and employment multipliers (mainly informal employment). Moreover, evidence collected by Turok and Watson (2001) suggests that the excessive cost of commuting has further reduced disposable income in low-income communities, *i.e.* in the range of 8% to 15% of disposable income, compared to the international standard of between 2% and 5%. This housing policy has been inconsistent with the emphasis on functional integration and urban compaction that characterised official local and national planning debates since at least the early 1990s, most notably in South Africa's *Urban Development Framework* (1997). The general principles that could have reversed the spatial mismatch – compaction as opposed to sprawl; integration as opposed to fragmentation; mixed use rather than separation – that informed metropolitan spatial policies, such as Cape Town's *Metropolitan Spatial Development Framework* (1996), but were never formally adopted.[25] This has been replaced by a fragmented "sectoral" agenda emphasising rapid delivery and urban design concerns that are often disconnected from economic and political limitations of the city-region.[26] The failure to use holistic life-cycle costing is symptomatic of the current approach; using this type of costing could show how the cost of transport subsidies for peripheral areas are significantly more expensive over the long term than the higher initial costs of building housing in well-located higher-density neighbourhoods (Urban Sector Network, 2003).

Dysfunctional co-ordination between housing and infrastructure funding stifles housing delivery. Cape Town accesses conditional capital funds for infrastructure through national funding arrangements that allocate housing subsidies through bulk service extensions and new household connections. The City of Cape Town benefits from a "one plot, one house model", since it can document larger bulk service extensions than those required for denser types of buildings. In other instances, the reverse situation occurs: sufficient funding may be available for housing but not for the requisite accompanying infrastructure. As will be developed in Chapter 3, the Municipal Infrastructure Grant (MIG) offers little funding once demands for new bulk infrastructure have been addressed, which curtails home construction, upgrading and densification. In the case of smaller municipalities such as Cedarberg, house building has had to stop altogether because infrastructure funds were exhausted. The central government could play a larger role in fast-tracking the processes underlying affordable housing development, as foreseen by the Ministry of Housing's pending Housing Development Agency Bill (B1B-2008). If approved, this would establish an institution that would "identify, acquire, hold, develop and release state and privately owned land for residential and community purposes … [and] ensure that there is centrally co-ordinated planning and budgeting of all infrastructure required for housing development".

Insufficient mortgage loans for the purchase of low-income properties reduce the poor's access to formal housing markets. Banks have made few housing loans available for subsidised households, as a result of very strict borrower eligibility criteria and alleged informal "redlining" of distressed areas perceived as being high risk. Many borrowers, especially those who receive housing subsidies, are often ineligible for the minimum mortgage loan (typically between ZAR 50 000 to ZAR 100 000) because they cannot provide evidence of stable employment or earn the minimum income level required for the mortgage (approximately ZAR 3 000 to ZAR 6 000 per month). Particular micro-lenders, in turn, have responded by offering micro-loans, which often contain high interest rates and are usually restricted to workers in formal employment or those whose employers use payroll deduction facilities. In order to increase mortgage loans to low-income households, financial institutions could consider adopting non-traditional methods such as those used by Cape Town's Kuyasa Fund, which acknowledges informal employment and judges creditworthiness from an individual's experience in saving funds. The high repayment rates from their micro-loans illustrate the financial solvency of many low-income individuals in Cape Town who seek affordable housing (Urban Sector Network, 2003).

Municipalities in the Cape Town city-region need to better stimulate the private sector to construct more affordable housing through proportional impact fees, waivers and housing enterprise zones. Currently, local governments maintain a pricing system under which developers are charged relatively equal amounts of fees for new or expanded infrastructure based on housing type, *e.g.* apartments or detached homes. Such a technique is problematic given that larger homes and more peripheral ones tend to have greater impact on infrastructure than smaller, more central homes. One solution is to adjust the impact fees to the size of the house and its stress on local infrastructure; such a "proportional" system would favour developers who hope to build on smaller lots in centrally located areas. Municipalities might also completely waive impact fees for those developers who build affordable housing. Designated housing enterprise zones could also help encourage new residential development in targeted areas. To counteract suburbanisation, Atlanta implemented such a programme, allocating a full property tax abatement for homes constructed in these areas for the first year. This was followed by a gradual reduction of 90% in the first year, 80% in the second year, and so on. Particularly attractive to developers, impact fees were waived for new housing in the zones and financed by a housing trust fund. For the municipalities in the Cape Town region, new housing enterprise zones could benefit from "a stronger future property and sales tax base, and an increased supply of all housing, including units affordable to working families and pensioners" (Nelson 2003). Though the City of Cape Town has catalysed commercial development in particular zones through 14 "city improvement districts" (CIDs), it has not instituted a new housing enterprise zone. A more ambitious affordable housing policy may feature both voluntary incentives such as proportional impact fees, waivers and housing enterprise zones or may include stronger mandatory approaches, as described in the next section.

The supply of affordable housing would increase if municipalities in the Cape Town city-region were permitted to require developers to set aside a percentage of moderately priced units in new developments. Inclusionary housing requirements are common planning powers utilised throughout many municipalities in OECD countries, which typically require between 10% and 20% of large (usually between 50- and 100-unit) developments to provide affordable housing. Developers are given the option of paying into an affordable housing fund managed by the municipality if they do not wish to include moderately priced units. In return, developers are typically given density bonuses. For example, according to the "Moderately Priced Dwelling Unit Ordinance" of Montgomery County, located on the fringe of Washington, D.C., developers of more than 50 detached residential units are required to set aside 12.5% to 15% of all units over 20 years in return for density bonuses of 20% to upwards of 22% (Nelson, 2003). Supported by the South African Property Owners Association (SAPOA), proposals were drafted but were challenged by particular developers. Given frequent opposition to affordable housing developments and existing racial tension in Cape Town, municipalities may adopt policies such as a "home equity assurance" programme to allay home owners' often unsubstantiated fears that their homes may lose value in such a transition.[27]

Box 2.13. Inclusionary housing approaches and their application in United States and Canada

Inclusionary housing approaches encompass the following tools:

- *Housing Fair Share Zoning Override*. This method was conceived in New Jersey as a result of the famous Mt. Laurel I and II court decisions. Under this scheme, the state determines the housing needs and assigns each municipality its "fair share" of the need.
- *Anti-Snob Zoning Override*. State laws in Massachusetts, where it originated, and practiced in New England, require all municipalities to maintain 10% of the housing in their communities as affordable.
- *Builder's Remedies*. Jurisdictions require that builders set aside a certain percentage of a development's units as affordable (between 10% and 20%) for those making less than 80% of area median income. Other variants of these programs allow the developer to pay a fee, donate land or place an affordable unit elsewhere, in lieu of meeting the required percentage of affordable units in a given project. The fees are usually placed in a fund to be used to build affordable housing elsewhere in the jurisdiction.
- *Linkage Programs*. These zoning programs link commercial uses to affordable housing. As an incentive, commercial developers have to build a certain amount of affordable housing relative to a certain amount of commercial square footage constructed.
- *Price-Based Programs*. These programs (primarily in California and Montgomery County, Maryland) aim to provide housing affordable to specific household income categories, such as 50% to 80% of area median income.

Inclusionary housing policy has been implemented throughout Canada. One example consists of the Province of Ontario's Land Use Planning for Housing Policy Statement. This policy, a response to rising housing costs in the late 1980s, required municipalities to include in their official plans and zoning regulations policies and regulations that would provide opportunities for the development of affordable housing. Thus, while developers did not necessarily have to provide the affordable housing themselves, they did have to provide the opportunity for such housing through appropriate zoning and secondary plan policies. The revised statement, in 2005, maintains this requirement by stipulating that the municipality must establish and implement "minimum targets for the provision of housing which is affordable to low- and moderate-income households".

Inclusionary housing policies were introduced in British Columbia initially in downtown Vancouver and shortly thereafter in the neighbouring city of Burnaby. In 1998, the Government of British Columbia passed enabling legislation so that local governments could introduce inclusionary policies. By 1997, 31 local governments were using Comprehensive Development Zoning (which allows for inclusionary zoning, density bonuses and municipal housing reserves) and 10 had some form of inclusionary requirements. In the larger cities, inclusionary policies had become a regular part of negotiations for large, high-density projects. In Vancouver, "Income Mix Zoning" requires major downtown redevelopments to dedicate a minimum of 20% of dwelling units as non-market housing. Collectively, these policies allowed Vancouver to secure sites capable of accommodating 2 670 affordable units. Burnaby's "Non-Market Housing Policy" which has been in effect since 1986, requires 20% of non-market housing on publicly owned development sites. Burnaby's policies, which have been pursued creatively with other mechanisms, such as density bonusing, land swapping and overall negotiations with developers, have been effective in creating 1 473 affordable units in 40 projects.

Sources: Tustian (2000), Koebel *et al.* (2004); Canada Mortgage and Housing Corporation (2008).

To expand housing opportunities, local government could more forcefully promote heightened density levels, given the region's infrastructure constraints and environmental preservation goals. As noted earlier in this Review, 94.8% of residential land in Cape Town is low density (City of Cape Town, General Valuation 2000). Without adequate infrastructure, congestion has dramatically increased, resulting in pollution that has stained the attractiveness of Cape Town. Densification and mixed use, though widely acknowledged in the *National Spatial Development Perspective* and *Provincial Spatial Development Framework* as a tool to use land more effectively, have been relatively ignored and overridden by the policy objective of supplying vast amounts of basic housing through a conventional "one house, one plot" model. The next generation of housing and infrastructure planning would be improved if it introduced densification overlay zones, accessory dwelling units, revised subdivision regulations and density bonuses. Such tools could be argued to reduce infrastructure costs and commuting times, while preserving farmland areas. To create the conditions necessary for densification, the city councils in the Cape Town city-region could adopt the *Provincial Spatial Development Framework of the Western Cape*'s (2005) recommendation of density levels of 25 dwelling units per hectare. Already the City of Cape Town's Department of Planning has proposed such measures, which would effectively call for a doubling of current base gross residential density, which stands at the low level of 11 dwelling units per hectare (City of Cape Town, 2006*a*).[28] Such a policy would respond to the Province's call for a multiplicity of housing and location types – upgrading, rental and social housing in mixed developments – that is articulated in its policy on integrated human settlements, *Isidima* (Dignity). Momentum is building around densification and containment: a document was recently approved by the Cape Town's City Council that "strongly advocated that new developments are located on vacant and underutilised residential, industrial and commercial land" (City of Cape Town, 2008*a*).

Densification and the provision of affordable housing could also be achieved through adopting zoning that promotes independent housing units created within single-family homes or on their lots. Technically known as accessory dwelling units (ADUs) and informally recognised as "granny flats", "carriage houses", "mother-in-law units" or "garage apartments," these structures have the potential to increase the housing supply, especially for students and the elderly. In terms of design, the units could be interior – modifying the outside of the dwelling to accommodate a separate unit – or detached from the main dwelling but still "accessory" and smaller than the main house.[29] Common rental arrangements throughout South Africa, where landowners lease detached backyard shacks or interior "flatlets" point to the demand for such tenure, especially from relatives of the property owner (Watson *et al.*, 1994). Cities throughout Canada and the United States, such as Portland, Oregon, have developed models for ADUs based on different designs and neighbourhoods. Similarly, the State of Washington has aggressively supported ADUs by requiring jurisdictions with over 20 000 residents to adopt ADU ordinances (Nelson, 2003).[30] The City of Cape Town's proposed *Integrated Zoning Scheme* (IZS) has adopted a revised approach, by including a second dwelling as a permitted use. In light of the current situation, where most of the 27 existing zoning schemes do not make provisions for a consent use of an additional dwelling, this IZS revision would streamline and simplify the requirements; land use applications would generally not be required.[31] Beyond the City of Cape Town, the Provincial Government of the Western Cape could better facilitate the production of ADUs by providing model zoning language and housing designs to municipalities.

Public transportation policies

The system of public transport provision in South Africa has been a product, as well as an instrument, of the apartheid planning mentioned earlier in this section. Together with the capital housing subsidies, it has locked urban development into increasingly unsustainable patterns. The consolidation of the apartheid system in the 1950s introduced two new acts, the Black Services Levy Act (1952) and the Black Transport Services Act (1957), which were intended to provide a general mechanism to subsidise transportation in peripherally located black townships, through a combination of levies on employers and central government subsidies.[32]

The urban transit system faces increasing financial constraints. From 1975 onwards, the central government gradually assumed a higher share of the total subsidy costs for the transportation sector, in reaction to the international oil crisis and employers' resistance to shouldering their full share of transportation costs. Although it is difficult to estimate the exact amount of the transportation subsidies, in light of the fact that some of the responsibilities for urban passenger transport were delegated to the provinces in 1997, total subsidy levels have risen, though only bus and rail commuter costs are directly subsidised by the state. Paradoxically, the number of passengers on public transportation in the Cape Town city-region has declined due to competition from private minivans and taxis, which have taken over half of the urban black commuter market. As a result, operators have closed down lines and/or cut back schedules, further reducing the demand for public urban transport and increasing leakages to the informal private mini-bus taxi industry. This has been compounded by situations where operators of public transport only receive six-month contracts. Rail services, which are operated by Metrorail, receive a large deficit subsidy from national government, and on average, only 30 to 40% of the total operating costs are covered by operational receipts (Behrens and Wilkinson, 2003). One reason for this is the widespread extent of fare evasion, as high as 70% in areas such as Khayelitsha. Meanwhile, bus operators receive a deficit subsidy from the provincial government and extra funds for bus lines that access the most remote areas in the Cape Town city-region. The subsidy mechanism is based on an incentive whereby the subsidy share, as a proportion of the full economic cost, increases in function of the distance from the CBD.[33] Some local governments also complement this amount with subsidies allocated from their own municipal budget.

The fractured public transportation network harms competitiveness. Despite Cape Town's good rail and road infrastructure, poor transport planning and co-ordination means that much of the population cannot access the regional labour market, and those who do face large commuting distances and inadequate road safety. Rail transportation and shipping are national government competencies, implemented via the parastatals, such as Transnet and SA Ports Authority. Public road transport in the form of buses is managed by provincial government but outsourced, while the taxi industry is both private and semi-formal but comes under the aegis of national transport policy. As mentioned in Chapter 1, commuting distances in a city like Cape Town are comparable to U.S. cities like Los Angeles, which are notorious for their sprawling profile. The distorted urban passenger-transit system has increased wage costs and overall costs of living, restrained economic dynamism of Cape Town and compromised environmental sustainability. Without structural changes, the people of Cape Town "will be working harder and harder in order to finance the moving of people, goods and waste into an increasingly fragmented metropolis" (Swilling, 2006). The additional traffic on the roads has increased traffic accidents to "almost crisis proportions" (Behrens, 2004). Cape Town has fewer road accidents per 100 000 inhabitants than Pretoria, Seoul or Johannesburg, but three times the rate in Jakarta, Toronto, Tokyo, Hong Kong, Beijing or Singapore (Vanderschuren and Ojungu-Omara, 2006). Moreover, the increase in fatalities from road accidents is particularly of concern in Cape Town where 59% of the dead are pedestrians (City of Cape Town, 2005*b*).[34] Such a dire situation is in sync with global forecasts which predict that by 2015, road accidents will overtake HIV/AIDS as the main cause of death and disability for people aged five to 19 in developing countries, according to the World Health Organisation (Toroyan and Peden, eds., 2007).

Provincial road maintenance merits immediate funding, given large backlogs and potentially unsafe road conditions. The Province of the Western Cape's Department of Transport and Public Works estimated that the total capital maintenance and rehabilitation backlog stood at ZAR 2 573 billion as of April 2006.[35] Current funding levels prevent the Province from attaining even the minimum standards on surfaced and gravel roads. The magnitude of the backlog is so large and the infrastructure provision costs so high that only a portion of this can feasibly be reduced. Additional funding is necessary to maintain minimal standards and meet safety requirements (Provincial Government of the Western Cape, 2007*b*). To the detriment of safety and connectivity in the region, the Provincial Government has drastically underinvested in this sector: only 1.1% of the Western Cape's GDP was programmed for public investment in road and rail transport infrastructure, as opposed to the generally accepted standard of 2.0 to 2.5% of GDP.[36] Given these alarming backlogs, the Provincial Government needs to seriously assess a range of options for financing that would encompass transportation districts, specialised taxes, public-private partnerships and municipal bond financing.

Transport policies need to better respond to safety issues. Though an exhaustive criminological study is beyond the scope of this review, police forces need to improve safety levels on buses and especially on trains, given the importance of public transportation for integration and mobility. As was mentioned in Chapter 1, the perception that public transport is unsafe at night has led many workers to use public transit during the day and cars in their nocturnal commute. This, in turn, has led to elevated traffic levels and declining disposable income for disadvantaged residents. Targeting safety in public transport corridors would no doubt improve ridership levels throughout the region. More generally, combating criminal networks, which so often harm citizens and prevent investment in areas perceived as dangerous, requires intergovernmental co-ordination. As the city with the highest homicide rate in South Africa (albeit concentrated in Khayelitsha and Mitchell's Plain) the City of Cape Town must strengthen crime prevention by aligning initiatives between non-governmental groups, community policing forums, law enforcement agencies and the criminal justice system. Already promising work is being done through Bambanani Neighbourhood Watches, community policing forums, inter-departmental programmes to reduce drug selling and gang initiation at schools, and the community-based Social Transformation Areas programme, which intervenes in the most distressed areas.[37/38] When Cape Town hosts the FIFA World Cup in 2010, significant safety and anti-terrorism countermeasures will be called for, and this period could be used as an opportunity to build adequate intergovernmental systems that will last when the fans go home. Through such measures, Cape Town could more systematically prevent crime and respond to emergencies, allowing the City to begin to repair its tarnished image as a dangerous city.

Multi-modal connections, especially rail/bus links and synergy with non-motorised transportation, could be improved. Part of the problem could be solved by utilising designs in stations and vehicles that foster interactivity between bus, rail and bicycle use. Rail stations, for example, could provide secure bicycle parking, and buses could accommodate bicycles more efficiently. These have become commonplace throughout OECD countries, particularly in Copenhagen and Amsterdam. Cape Town could also improve multi-modality by integrating bus schedules with train schedules. This would minimise the passengers' waiting time and contribute to higher ridership. Finally, Cape Town could better integrate pedestrian access to transport stations by fast-tracking its plans for pedestrian and cycling networks. Changes such as these would make the transportation network more carbon neutral and help foster a more environmentally sustainable urban structure, a concern that will be explored in the next section.

Realising sustainability, liveability and attractiveness

Increasing pressure on the natural physical environment of Cape Town threatens the region's economic competitiveness and suggests an urgent need to implement a more pro-active environmental strategy. As detailed in Chapter 1, the region's environmental vulnerability has increased due to poorer air quality, water pollution, frequent fires, urban sprawl and a low use of renewable energy. Continued power load shedding, given Eskom's underinvestment, spiralling food and petrol prices, looming water shortages and pricing rationing, all bring environmental sustainability to centre stage. Cape Town's ecological footprint (4.28 hectares per capita) has become so large that today it takes a land mass equal to the size of Greece to provide its inputs and process its waste. In other words, if everyone lived as people do in Cape Town, 2.3 planets would be required, a rate that is comparable to Canada's, but less than half that of the United States.[39] Beyond the obvious health impacts on Capetonians, rising contamination, namely declining air, soil and water quality, seriously jeopardise the growth the agro-food industry and tourism. Although a vast supply of land covers the region, only a small portion has the adequate soil conditions necessary for agricultural production. In response to its ecological fragility, Cape Town governments could place more stress on reducing the increasingly unsustainable ecological footprint. Together, these efforts would benefit residents' health and quality of life. The transformation of Cape Town into a "green city" would augment its appeal as a scenic destination, benefiting its image, as well as tourism, filmmaking and its ability to attract and retain skilled labour. Conversely, ignoring this urgent problem would be short-sighted: forecasts show the Western Cape to be the area in the nation most likely to be affected by climate change, with a reduction in rainfall, rise in sea level, increased fires and erosion.

The Cape Town city-region is well positioned to be a leader in environmental innovation, though additional monitoring is required. Environmental sustainability has been increasingly prioritised by municipal and provincial policy makers. Innovative projects have been launched in such areas as biodiversity, disaster management, carbon footprint reduction, coastal and marine management, air quality and health, integrated water supply development and increased energy efficiency.[40] Many of these programmes are ambitious, such as the Kuyasa Energy Efficiency Project, in which the city retrofits existing houses in low-income neighbourhoods with solar water heaters, insulates ceilings and supplies energy-efficient light bulbs. Monitoring has followed policy making and implementation: the City of Cape Town regularly monitors the state of the environment through a wide number of indicators covering air pollution, energy, biodiversity, water quality and waste (City of Cape Town, 2005*a*). However, a series of indicators covering areas of emerging importance have been overlooked. Both the City of Cape Town's *Sustainability Report* (2006) and the Provincial Government of the Western Cape's *State of the Environment* (2005), for example, exclude data on recycling, new cases of asthma and the percentage of alternatively fuelled cars. A macro analysis at the city and provincial levels, moreover, does not identify sustainable or polluting industries and firms. Improved reporting could identify, for example, those manufacturers that use recovered secondary materials as raw material and conversely, the industries and firms that produce high levels of groundwater contamination. This would allow for improved targeting and heightened transparency in the area of sustainability.

Although the City of Cape Town should be commended for its recent adoption of green technology, its dependence on fossil fuels requires an ambitious approach using economic pricing instruments intended to penalise polluters. To its credit, the City of Cape Town has acknowledged its energy use as the largest employer in Cape Town and has begun to foster pilot projects; in one project, the city government reduced the electricity bill of a municipal building by 22% through efficient lighting (CFLs), solar water heater installation and user behaviour information dissemination (mainly affecting air conditioner use). Similarly, the City is considering various options to extract energy from waste, including waste-to-methane gas, waste-to-energy, co-generation and sewerage gas energy generation. Though the City provides a strong example of energy reduction in the commercial private sector, low-income households still rely on kerosene (paraffin) gas for cooking, space heating, water heating and lighting. The City of Cape Town needs to strengthen its solar energy programmes to better provide electricity for low-income groups and provide an alternative to paraffin heaters, which are so often the source of the ubiquitous fires mentioned in Chapter 1. Likewise, environmental policies that make use of economic instruments aimed at pricing for pollution are only in the initial stage of design in Cape Town. The introduction of an environmental tax on fossil fuels, for example, would be within the responsibility of national policy makers, and has not advanced beyond the stage of exploratory studies. However controversial this subject might be, removing distortions within the existing pricing and tariff structures in the energy sector, and introducing additional financial incentives towards pollution reduction, would have a series of advantages. First, it would remove subsidies and price distortions that favour large electricity users that, in practice, produce the bulk of carbon dioxide emissions. Second, the revenue collected from environmental taxation could help finance the ambitious programmes being elaborated at the provincial and city level.

The use of economic instruments to stimulate environmental technology and ecotourism could be better leveraged in the Cape Town city-region. This could become a promising instrument in the South African context, where a substantial part of R&D is already being underwritten by larger firms. Economic instruments could also provide an additional incentive to avoid missing opportunities in strategic sectors of emissions reduction and alternative technology (solar and wind energy, for example). Sub-national governments may choose to replicate some of tools provided by the Department of Minerals and Energy's Renewable Energy Finance and Subsidy Office (REFSO), which subsidises capital grants to renewable energy project developers. The use of start-up funds for renewable energy providers, "soft" loans and grants or loans for detailed feasibility studies could be both a source of assistance and also provide models for local government replication. Governments in the Cape Town city-region would also benefit from implementing techniques such as environmental considerations in budgeting and applying environmental criteria in purchasing and tendering (OECD, 1996). There are signs that momentum is building in these areas; for example, a draft submitted to City of Cape Town authorities in February 2008 stipulates that all new buildings larger than 100 square metres should have a solar-water heater, potentially making Cape Town the first South African city to pass a law requiring that new buildings be equipped with solar water heaters (Smetherham, 2008).

Governments in the Cape Town city-region could provide financing measures and monitoring to encourage developers to adopt green building designs that optimise natural light, utilise geothermal heating, improve insulation, use natural landscaping and use less toxic building materials. Intervention is especially needed given that banks tend to bond only homes that receive a certificate from the National Home Builders Registration Council, which has refused to certify houses that use non-conventional materials and designs (Swilling, 2008). To its credit, the City of Cape Town has recently begun compiling guidelines for the construction of resource-efficient buildings in light of ongoing electricity shortages and impending drought. Further actions throughout the region are needed to update building codes and require new structures to meet energy and water efficiency targets, use non-toxic materials and recycle or reuse construction debris. To enable governments to establish quantified policy targets in sustainable building, authorities in the region need to agree on a framework to regularly monitor the environmental performance of the building sector. This would facilitate the establishment of specific strategies to minimise waste in the building sector across the design and demolition phases. With respect to existing buildings, governments may follow the example of such cities as San Francisco and implement residential energy conservation ordinances (RECOs), which require owners to implement specific low-cost energy conservation measures, such as weatherisation, when a building is sold or renovated (OECD, 2003). Cumulatively, however, these efforts should not be considered a substitute for the establishment of solid and transparent standards, which could be improved in Cape Town, as the next section attests.

In light of the fiscal strain that surrounds urban financial management, municipalities in the Cape Town City region face a conflicting interest: they are mandated both to maximise revenues and augment the volume of services distributed, while at the same time promote water and electrical conservation. The Provincial Government of the Western Cape and the City of Cape Town have pursued ambitious renewable energy targets that will only be achieved with additional funding mechanisms. In light of the

Provincial Government's goal to purchase 15% of its electricity from renewable sources by 2010, a finance plan was proposed, but has not been fully developed (Box 2.14). The delay of this plan and accompanying financial mechanisms suggests that it is highly unlikely that the Province will meet its targets. Likewise, though the City should be applauded for its innovative programmes for wind generation and solar heaters, some of its renewable energy goals appear to be more inspirational than achievable; for example, the objective to generate 20% of energy needs through renewable resources by 2020 exceeds the present use (0.26%) by a factor of nearly 80.[41] Given that electricity accounts for 24% of revenues collected by the City of Cape Town, it is not apparent how increased energy efficiency will impact the City's budget and how the City would recoup revenue lost from electricity fees.

Box 2.14. **Energy Targets: Provincial Government of the Western Cape and the City of Cape Town, 2007**

Provincial Government of the Western Cape	City of Cape Town
Energy supply	
• 15% increase in renewable energy generation (electricity only) by 2015 • 10% increase in overall energy efficiency by 2015 • 15% increase in overall energy efficiency by 2020 • Quantity of CO_2 emissions reduced by 10% from 2000 levels by 2015 • Quantity of CO2 emissions reduced by 15% from 2000 levels by 2020.	• 10% renewable energy supply by 2020 • 100% of formal households connected to electricity from 2005 • 90% of informal households connected to electricity by 2010 • Quantity of CO2 emissions reduced by 10% from 2005 levels by 2010
Transportation	
• 30% increase in transport energy efficiency by 2015 • 50% increase in government vehicles converted to cleaner fuels	• 10% increase of rail transport share of total transport modal split by 2010 • 10% decrease in the number of private vehicles commuting into city centre by 2010 • A fully operational "Non-motorised Transport Strategy" by 2015

Commercial and industrial sector

- 15% increase in commercial energy efficiency by 2015
- 10% increase in industry energy efficiency by 2015
- 10% increased energy efficiency in industrial and commercial facilities by 2010

Residential sector

- 15% increase in residential energy efficiency by 2015
- 10% of all households to have solar water heaters by 2010
- All City-owned housing to use efficient lighting by 2010
- 30% of all households to use efficient lighting by 2010, 90% by 2020
- All new subsidised houses to have ceilings from 2005
- All existing houses to be retrofitted with ceilings by 2020

Government

- 10% increase in renewable energy purchased by the Provincial Government
- 12% increase in energy efficiency in all municipal buildings by 2015

Source: Provincial Government of the Western Cape (2007a), "Integrated Energy Strategy" and City of Cape Town (2007), "Cape Town Energy and Climate Change Strategy".

High rates of automobile use in Cape Town entails environmental implications that rationalise increased intervention, especially in sustainable public transportation and land use. The transport sector currently accounts for 22% of carbon emissions in the Western Cape, a figure that will rise, given forecasts that the number of cars in Cape Town will expand by 41% by 2020 (City of Cape Town, 2006*b*; Provincial Government of the Western Cape, 2007*c*). A substantial increase in petrol consumption and the continued use of poorly maintained diesel vehicles will lead to a further deterioration of air quality. This future scenario would only increase the "brown haze" in Cape Town, with adverse implications for health and tourism. To address these concerns, the City of Cape Town has implemented a variety of initiatives. Existing or planned transport efficiency projects include: transport interchange upgrading, liquefied petroleum gas (LPG) conversion of City vehicles, dedicated BMT (bus, minibus, taxi) lane on major routes and the upgrading of 90 kilometres of cycle routes within the city (City of Cape Town, 2006*b*). The momentum behind some of these projects has stalled, however, and only ten of the City's 5 500 vehicles have been converted to LPG.[42] In turn, the Provincial Government of the Western Cape has conducted three initial simulations of how a modal shift towards greater use of public transportation, the conversion of taxis to diesel vehicles and a switch to biodiesel for 15% of automobiles would reduce CO_2 and SO_2 emissions (Provincial Government of the Western Cape, 2007*c*). Rising oil prices coupled with increasing air pollution would guarantee large gains for environmentally sustainable transportation initiatives that would be followed by monitoring and public reporting (OECD, 2002). Both the municipal and provincial governments could lobby for the further development of environmental programmes at the central government level, particularly the subsidisation of carbon neutral buses and the creation of income tax credits for hybrid cars.

Environmental policies in the Cape Town city-region that are aligned with mixed use and densification initiatives would ideally allow jobs and homes to be located closer together, thereby decreasing commuting and pollution. Sprawl tends to be associated with greater capital costs related to building more schools and extending roads, water and sewer lines and storm water drainage systems. Likewise, daily vehicle miles travelled per capita tend to be higher in sprawling cities, which leads to greater air pollution/ozone levels. The most complete empirical work on sprawl, "*The Costs of Sprawl – 2000*", applied scenarios based on estimates of uncontrolled (sprawl) and controlled (some sprawl allowed, but overall more compact, higher-density growth) for 15 economic areas in the United States. The result of five years of research, the study found that sprawl would result in USD 227 billion in additional costs in the United States over a 25-year period (Burchell *et al.*, 2002). Controlled growth, it was found, could be accomplished with only a 20% increase in density and a 10% increase in floor area ratio for non-residential uses. This produced considerable cost savings: Burchell *et al.*'s simulations estimated that a saving of 188 300 lane miles of local roads and USD 110 billion could be achieved by 2025 with more compact patterns, at a saving of 11.8% in state and local road costs. Water and sewer savings, though significant, were smaller; with compact growth patterns, the combined cost savings of lower tap-in fees and 4.6 million fewer lateral lines would offer infrastructure savings of USD 12.6 billion, or 6.6%, over 25 years (Burchell *et al.*, 2002). Although a provincial law on land use planning is being prepared for "urban restructuring" (reducing sprawl, exclusionary land uses and private car use while stimulating mixed land uses, pricing for pollution, etc.) there seems to be little clarity on the phasing and prioritisation of the diverse components that are part of this package. While a wide variety of forecasting indexes chart the benefits of sustainable environment policies in Cape Town, especially land use, local governments need to develop more comprehensive sequencing plans to implement these policies (Swilling, 2006; Mukheibir, 2007).

The Province and municipalities' environmental governance institutions need to be adapted for improved enforcement. The government's inability to stem the contamination of the regional water system, for example, indicates that regional environmental enforcement has fallen short. Within the Cape Town city-region, increased population and poor environmental enforcement has led to harmful, and in some cases, irreversible damage to river ecosystems. Indeed, six of the ten catchments receive effluent from sewage treatment works, and an alarming number have a water quality unacceptable for household use or even irrigation. Nevertheless, Western Cape's Environmental Agency is painfully aware of the gap: "Co-ordination of environmental governance is difficult because environmental management encompasses a broad range of concerns and is by nature cross-sectoral, whereas government administration, in contrast, is divided into narrow functional areas" (Provincial Government of the Western Cape, 2005). A number of different models may find resonance in Cape Town. Helsinki, for example, has a strong regional environment agency (Helsinki Metropolitan Area Council, or YTV) that co-ordinates transport system planning, regional public transport provision, waste management and air quality management across the four municipalities that comprise the Helsinki metro region. YTV also produces and compiles regional data on traffic, waste management and air quality that informs planners and decision makers across the 745 square kilometres of its area. It also features a governance structure run by a 22-member Regional Assembly that is proportional to the regional population: Helsinki elects 11 representatives, Espoo and Vantaa elect five, and Kauniainen one to each meeting (YTV, 2008). The Province of the Western Cape intends to create stronger intergovernmental fora, such as the Provincial Intergovernmental Water Management Team and the Provincial Energy Agency, that show potential for bolstering environmental governance. However, these initiatives run the risk of producing silos of experts around particular environmental sectors rather than coherent dialogue and cross-cutting programmes that reflect the holistic approach required for environmental policy.

Additional measures could be taken to develop an environmental jobs creation model. International evidence, particularly from Mumbai's Self Employed Women's Association (SEWA), suggests an ample possibility of establishing labour-intense projects that combine income and employment generation with increased recycling. Such an initiative would be welcome in the City of Cape Town, where only 6.5% of residential and community waste is recycled, compared to upwards of 40% in many European cities. The remaining waste either goes to regulated landfills that are projected to be completely full by 2011 or illegal sites that constitute 42% of Western Cape's landfills (Provincial Government of the Western Cape, 2005; Swilling, 2006). This contrasts with cities such as San Francisco that have taken dramatic steps to increase not only recycling, but the use of recyclable products (Portney, 2003). To this end, local governments could design job-creation strategies to integrate linkages between research institutes, environmental protection services and recycling-focused micro-enterprise programmes (OECD, 1996). In light of the expanding global market for environmentally friendly goods and services, Cape Town could benefit from policies that encourage the development of businesses in the fields of renewable energy and innovative new low-carbon technologies. Similarly, with an entire floral kingdom at its door and an emerging international food crisis, additional biological research programmes in the region could better identify native plants that require small amounts of water and are resilient to climatic change. Once areas of focus are selected, the region would also need to host meetings with likely investors – for example, renewable energy technology firms, green building companies, and manufacturers of environmentally preferable products – as a sign of Cape Town's interest in and commitment to this sector. Additional programmes could be developed to enlarge ecotourism and "green hotels" in the Cape Town city-region, especially for biosphere and nature watching in Overstrand.[43] This strategy would complement a set of innovative community economic development initiatives that will be discussed in detail in the next section.

Addressing community economic development in poor neighbourhoods

Improving the gross economic performance of the city-region will not be enough if a large part of the regional population is still ghettoised; policy actors private and public have not only to increase the linkages between distressed and productive nodes of the city-region, but also to look for ways in which local potential can be unlocked within the distressed nodes. The townships and poor neighbourhoods in general are locked in a cycle of poverty, with few opportunities for generating sustainable economic development. As discussed in Chapter 1, a large part of South Africa's population has relocated to urban areas during the last decade, and in Cape Town, many newcomers have been concentrating in townships and the surrounding informal settlements. The lack of skills, the socio-spatial segregation, the lack of public transportation, and elevated crime rates make it difficult to integrate these parts of the metropolitan region into the leading value chains. As a result, Cape Town cannot take advantage of this large potential supply of labour, nor can it benefit from future growth in consumption and productive activity within these areas.

There is presently a surprising lack of policy guidance on unlocking latent economic potential in the poor neighbourhoods. For instance, little mention of the issue of community economic development is made in the key policy documents, both at the provincial and at the city level. The city administration seems eager to push forward infrastructure-led development and the provision of basic services such as water supply, housing, electricity and access roads. An infrastructure-driven approach will not be enough to create sustainable and inclusive livelihoods, as shown by the fast-track delivery of housing policy in the townships in the post-apartheid era, which reinforced spatial exclusion without creating local endogenous development. Indeed, the various efforts to provide low-income housing have left settlements "beset by lack of employment, crime, health challenges and a generally degraded environment" (Huchzermeyer, 2003). Moreover, there is evidence that many who benefited from housing subsidies have sold their homes, often at below market rate, simply because they are too poor to run and maintain them.

Community economic development policies could complement infrastructure-led policy. They could focus on unlocking local potential in a variety of forms, from learning and skills to entrepreneurship, micro-finance and the social economy. Such an effort, crucially, must involve the private sector and empower the third sector, rather than leaving all responsibility to the state. Such a community development programme might focus on:

Direct engagement by large firms. Besides hiring black Africans, firms might explore ways of directly supporting entrepreneurship in townships and other poor neighbourhoods. Small firms could be integrated in value-chain, and large firms could be involved to disseminate technology (through machinery or management skills) and help SMEs to deal with labour regulation and tax collection. Such a policy could be integrated with a broad micro-credit policy. The example of the Kuyasa Fund demonstrates that there is a huge potential for such initiatives.[44] Integrating micro-credit with collaboration with large firms may help small firms define a better strategy for their investment. Large firms could also participate in this programme and finance, for instance, the purchase of machinery to be used in a given, specialised production task that would interface with value chains and increase the skills of entrepreneurs and employees alike.

Redirecting financial resources – "patient capital" – to the townships. For decades, capital and financial resources have been explicitly drained from the townships. With the financial sector red-lining poorer areas, there is a need to establish a regulatory framework that is able to invert this distorted and historical trend, and to redirect financial flows towards previously disadvantaged areas. The *Community Reinvestment Act* (CRA) in the United States provides an interesting example. Approved in 1977, the

CRA established for the lending performance of banks and mortgage institutions in poor and middle-income areas. Though the initial monitoring proved difficult, the CRA proved to be a powerful instrument for channelling financial resources to disadvantaged and previously redlined inner-city communities. Although it has been changed several times since its creation, the CRA has succeeded in channelling some USD 400 billion to poorer neighbourhoods. Interestingly enough, in 2002 a Community Reinvestment Act was also discussed in the South African context. This even led to the elaboration of the (still unapproved) Community Reinvestment Housing Bill, which focused on the allocation of housing finance to previously disadvantaged communities. It should be analysed, therefore, how the role of regulatory instruments in general, and the CRA in particular, could be used in order to leverage community economic development programmes in South Africa. For instance, the CRA could provide specific incentives and premiums for those financial institutions that promote financial innovations targeted at poorer communities, for example through micro-finance and rotating savings schemes, decentralised cashing systems and electronic banking in townships.

Implement community economic development programmes. In spite of the enormous complexities within the context of the townships in Cape Town, several decades of experimentation in the United States with community economic development programmes designed to revitalise inner cities may be of relevance to Cape Town.[45] Policies to reverse socio-economic and racial segregation between poorer inner cities and the more affluent outer suburbs, like the fair share housing and inclusionary zoning mechanisms, have corrected unfettered housing markets or exclusionary zoning policies.[46] Successful cases of economic revitalisation appear to have been driven by a combination of restructuring of federal programmes and regulatory frameworks that guided the organisation and finance of central cities and grassroots initiatives (Box 2.15). These included interesting elements of social learning with inner-city revitalisation over the last few decades, in terms of the creation of horizontal and vertical policy networks between local, state and federal governments, the tapping of credit from the broader financial sector for CED strategies, and, finally, the direct involvement of poorer local communities that effectively pushed for changes in the design and implementation of policies.

Developing the social economy. The social economy refers to creating markets for socially useful goods for poor people and poor neighbourhoods by creating opportunities for social enterprises – run by communities or the third sector – to supply these goods. In many parts of the world, the social economy is increasingly coming to the fore as a policy instrument in these contexts. States and markets usually avoid such contexts, while social needs remain high. This creates a space for social enterprises to grow, providing affordable services and goods such as child care facilities, recycled furniture, recycled waste services, housing improvement schemes, small-scale craft or industrial goods, and so on, for local families, communities, and neighbourhoods. The principle is to generate a local market around social needs, but by ensuring, through proper regulation and conditions tied to incentives, which provisions are of good quality, meeting needs and enhancing local skills and capabilities. In many cases, the ventures also insist on employing the poor and the disadvantaged in delivering the goods and services, helping to activate and renew labour markets. The Cape townships and poor neighbourhoods are places of massive under-met need, and with appropriate support for community organisations, co-operatives and emerging social entrepreneurs (micro-finance, facilities, training, etc.), this need could be met through local social entrepreneurship and the employment of local people. This is precisely the kind of effort required to correct inequities.

Overall, differentiated, multifaceted strategies to unlock the economic potential of township economies are needed to build on social improvement programmes, such as housing provision. This will make it more possible to see the Cape economy as a multi-nodal economy, allowing, in turn, a different infrastructural policy. At present, the policy focuses on getting commuters into the high-growth areas and ensuring the circulation of inputs and outputs into these areas. A community-development programme might seek to enhance growth within the poorer areas by looking for ways of enhancing linkage with areas that can support local growth. For instance, it may be better to link Khayelitsha to the geographically closer nodes of Somerset West and Stellenbosch than to the CBD. This requires investment in physical infrastructure (transport) as well as economic facilitation/sector interventions (*e.g.* tourism strategies linking the Winelands to township catering).

Box 2.15. **The revitalisation of inner-city areas in the United States: Towards real come-back cities?**

A growing number of cities in the United States have successfully designed and implemented inner-city revitalisation programs. At the same time, the federal government has introduced new approaches that enable the private sector, government and communities to work together in specific revitalisation programs. For example, the Community Reinvestment Act, which was introduced after heated debate, was an important turning-point in a long history of redlining and under lending to poor communities. This legislation, which required banks and formal financial institutions to demonstrate to the monetary authorities and Congress how well they had served low-income communities, as part of a process under which banks applied for approval of mergers or expansions, proved strategic. From the 1980s onwards, at the time of the restructuring of the American banking sector, substantial flows of funds were channelled to traditionally neglected communities. This cash flow channelled to poorer communities proved decisive in increasing the scale and professionalism of some of the incipient local initiatives.

Secondly, the grassroots movements, which in the 1960s had taken a confrontational stance over collaboration with the private sector, became interested in forming partnerships. A new generation of so-called Community Development Corporations, which in the 1960s and 1970s had restricted themselves to the operation of small-scale housing and physical upgrading projects, symbolised this new approach. They started to interface with the financial sector and helped channel cash flows to inner cities on a large scale. Finally, communities themselves had become increasingly aware of the dramatic impact of decades of failed state and federal programs intended to promote inner-city revitalisation, and began to scale up community-led initiatives. Grassroots initiatives thus assisted in the integration of communities into neighbourhoods through employment generation, maintenance of public spaces and crime reduction.

Concrete advances in revitalising U.S. inner cities were realised, in part, by a segment of society in the United States that had become aware that problems of inner cities had a negative impact on neighbourhoods and economies outside distressed areas, and that the severe reduction of federal contributions to cities' budgets necessitated the creation of regional programs. In 1980, federal contributions to city budgets were 18%, but by 1990, this had dropped to 6.4% (Wilson, 1996). Low-income residents were particularly affected, given that the HUD housing programme funding was slashed by 76% from 1980 to 1988 (Venkatesh, 2000).

Source: Paul S. Grogan and Tony Proscio, *Comeback Cities. A Blueprint for Urban Neighborhood Revival*, Westview Press, Boulder, Colorado, 2000.

Wide distributional benefits could flow to the local community through co-operatives and other kinds of "meso-institutions", a strategy left relatively unexplored in Cape Town. Co-operatives, as extensive research has shown, offer their members and the general public many benefits, including the following:

- political representation of ethnic minorities in an environment where they were previously neglected (Wells, 1981),
- better prices for consumers, and savings in transport for consumers who previously travelled long distances to stores,
- diffusion of training and technical/managerial advice from co-operatives to the public and those engaged in the establishment of co-operatives,
- spillover effects: the provision of public goods (roads and road maintenance, potable water, schools, etc.) to the community and the diffusion of practices and technology in collectives to the community, as is the case with many agricultural techniques and seeds that are transferable to observing neighbours (Tendler, 1988),
- village banks registered in South Africa as Financial Service Co-operatives (FSCs) can provide deposit, credit, banking and other financial services to those who cannot meet the minimum requirements set by most banks for opening a savings account or for obtaining loans (Nigrini, 2002).

2.3 Conclusion: towards a regional development strategic framework

The effectiveness of public policies in fostering inclusive economic development in the Cape Town city-region has been stymied by the lack of a shared vision among the main stakeholders. While in general there seems to be clarity among policy makers over the main challenges to be faced, there is a lack of consensus on the strategic approach for generating inclusive economic development. On the one hand, the City of Cape Town prioritises basic infrastructure and service provision, and an infrastructure-led economic development approach governs budgeting and expenditure priorities (of which more in Chapter 3). This is complemented by a raft of programmes, such as tourism business development, investment promotion and the streamlining of land use and building codes to accelerate property development. Though the City has traditionally been concerned with matters within its jurisdictional boundaries, political documents such as the 2008 Review of the Cape Town's 2007/8-2011/12 IDP illustrate an awareness of Cape Town's interconnectedness to other areas and an interest in formulating a regional development strategy. The Provincial Government takes a different approach, financing sectoral agencies that provide support to industries the Government views as conducive to job creation. These are favoured through various programmes on skills development, data collection, economic development (*e.g.* the MEDS), and technological innovation.[47]

The same lack of shared goals affects relationships with the central government. Although substantial progress has been made from the *National Spatial Development Perspective* onwards, severe deficiencies hamper co-ordination between provincial authorities and national departments, including the Department of Trade and Industry (DTI), over the scope and competencies in regional and city-regional economic development policies. New initiatives and planning approaches developed nationally are frequently not articulated with the provinces and metros, and fail to take account of the progress being made with economic development policies at that level. More specifically, there are mismatches in relation to the number of priority sectors selected, the criteria used in picking specific sectors, and, finally, the institutional design of industrial policies.

A growing disjuncture in formulating strategic direction and implementing programmes has inhibited economic development planning in the Cape Town city-region. While there is in general sufficient capacity to formulate strategic policy frameworks with the Provincial Government and neighbouring municipalities, the implementation of specific programmes has been cumbersome, given the politically contested environment and the institutional fatigue brought on by seemingly endless institutional reforms. In particular, the provincial government has improved its strategic capacity for policy formulation, but commands insufficient fiscal leverage for its implementation. The programmes for cluster support, innovation, and sector development developed in the Western Cape in the last decade have attracted small amounts of funding from the Department of Trade and Industry (DTI), the national department responsible for regional industrial development. Another example of systemic weakness in economic governance concerns the Specific Purpose Vehicles. While many of them still lack sufficient buy-in from the private sector (both financially and in political backing), the city of Cape Town has recently threatened to withdraw financial support for some of these agencies, which are at present jointly financed by the province and the city. As a result, the city-region must support a large number of poorly funded policies and tools. Agencies and SPVs, which have proved to be effective in dealing with SMEs and promoting development, are hampered by the lack of co-ordination.

Efforts to enhance the co-ordination of economic development policies across levels of government have produced limited consensus. For instance, the existing co-ordination forums, like the *National Economic Development and Labour Council* (Nedlac) and *Provincial Development Council* (PDC), are consultative bodies without the power to co-ordinate the various national and regional initiatives. Conceived to increase debate, Nedlac provides a platform for the central government to build social consensus on social and economic policy. It meets quarterly and is supported by four chambers, the Labour Market Chamber, the Trade and Industry Chamber, the Development Chamber and the Public Finance and Monetary Policy Chamber. At the provincial level, the Provincial Development Council (PDC) mirrors Nedlac, and provides for multi-party engagement between the state, businesses, labour and civil society in the Province. Moreover, attempts to catalyse consensus for achieving a shared development strategy beyond iKapa GDS, for example through the MEDS, have not been able to involve the other local actors, and particularly the Municipality of Cape Town, which seems locked into a strictly legal and jurisdictional perspective.

The Cape Town city-region could consider empowering regional institutions, either through strengthening existing organisations or creating a Regional Development Agency. Both of these options would consist of a multi-stakeholder platform that could involve the central government, acting as a facilitator, trade unions, and large firms, to create a new social consensus for a regional development strategy. Basically, two main options could be pursued:

- *First option*: *Strengthen existing structures*. Policies could be informed by and reinforce promising experimentation in the field, which is frequently being driven by the private sector in co-ordination with government. These innovations may provide the basis for dynamic processes of social learning for new metropolitan institutions. In this respect, examples such as Accelerate Cape Town (in which some of the larger companies maintain an important presence), the Cape Town Partnership (oriented towards the revitalisation of the CBD, as discussed above), and several of the SPVs could be taken up as benchmark examples and replicated on a larger scale, especially towards area-based revitalisation in informal settlements. This view is to a certain extent supported by a recent evaluation by the Provincial Government of the agencies and SPVs. While all the SPVs and entities have operating problems to various degrees, the review found that SPVs represent a strong operative linkage between the private and public sector.[48] The Province concludes that the current involvement of the business community would probably be ended if SPVs were brought into one agency controlled by the local government. Therefore, instead of centralising the control of SPVs and agencies, these bodies could be directly involved in the organisation and management of a regional forum of agencies that would define a common strategy and select which programmes to allocate a larger amount of resources.[49] Thanks to such an allocation mechanism, based on the actual performance of SPVs and agencies, local government financing could be gradually phased out in favour of increasing contributions from the private sector. Of course, other regional stakeholders could participate in the governance of the forum and in this process of resource allocation. In this way, the action of the best agencies could be enhanced and supported by a larger network of local stakeholders.

- *Second option*: *Create a Regional Development Agency*. Another possible option is to facilitate co-ordination among regional stakeholders through the creation of a Regional Development Agency (RDA). Creating a RDA in charge of co-ordinating and implementing policies is already under debate within the Cape Town city-region. In OECD city-regions, some precedent exists for development agencies playing a pivotal role in co-ordinating and implementing policies and strategies within functional urban areas. This is the case, for instance, with the "Milano Metropoli" agency (Box 2.16), which operates within the province of Milan in Italy. Although this option was rejected in the provincial evaluation of SPVs, a "soft" co-ordination and the merging of some agencies would allow a concentration of resources and the implementation of cross-sectoral policies.[50] To maintain, at least in part, the current structure, regional agencies and SPVs could be actively involved in the creation of the RDA, and the largest of them could drive the RDA. Of course, local governments (the Municipality and the Province) would participate on such a board in order to control efficiency of public investment. Moreover, the participation of the central government, as a facilitator, could bridge the Cape Town-based business community with the Province of the Western Cape and the Municipality. This would represent a departure from the current situation, in which large local firms directly interact with the central government. In any case, the design of the RDA should be adapted to the specific context of the Cape Town city-region and respect the following five conditions. First, it should act on a well-defined region and have the potential to co-ordinate all the policies implemented in this territory. Second, the creation of the RDA should be gradual and based on learning-by-doing process, rather than a "quick fix" institutional and top-down solution. Third, the participation of the private sector in the management and the funding of the RDA should guarantee the independence of the agency and its resilience in the highly volatile and conflict-driven political environment. Fourth, the RDA should have a strong relationship with trade unions, which should be involved in the design of some regional interventions that aim to reduce unemployment.

Finally, as will be broadly discussed in Chapter 3, the implementation of a co-ordination policy will require a fine-tuning of regional responsibilities, and a stronger interaction between policy designers and policy implementers.

Box 2.16. **The "Milano Metropoli" development agency**

The "Milano Metropoli" agency promotes sustainable development within the Metropolitan Area of Milan. "Milano Metropoli" is a joint-stock company, with mixed public (mainly) and private capital, promoted by the Province of Milan to enhance economic and social development. It was formed in early 2005 and grew out of a smaller development agency, ASNM (*Agenzia di Sviluppo Nord Milano* – Development Agency of North Milan). ASNM had been the local agency in charge of the re-industrialisation and socio-economic conversion of North Milan, following the closure of the area's largest factories in the 1990s.

"Milano Metropoli" works closely with public authorities operating in the metropolitan area of Milan and in partnership with local town councils, development agencies, universities and research centres, trade unions, the business community, banks, foundations and non-profit organisations. Shareholders in "Milano Metropoli" include the Province of Milan (majority shareholder), the Milan Chamber of Commerce, Finlombarda (the financial body of the Lombardy Region), some municipalities of the Greater Milan area, as well as private enterprises.

"Milano Metropoli's" mission focuses on the following strategic areas: territorial marketing; support strategic economic sectors; special re-industrialisation, urban regeneration and development projects. "Milano Metropoli" directs the following strategic activities.

- *Place-based marketing.* It plans and develops regional and communication marketing in order to heighten awareness – both at home and abroad – of local specialisations, skills and opportunities.
- *Support of strategic economic sectors.* It devises schemes to support and relaunch businesses in economic sectors that are particularly important for the Milanese area, from the net economy and biotechnologies to the creative industries.
- *Reindustrialisation and brownfield redevelopment.* It supports local agencies with plans to reconvert brownfield sites and improve the manufacturing system; it creates integrated urban redevelopment schemes to improve territorial, environmental, social and economic interventions.
- *Support for local agencies.* It devises and co-ordinates strategic planning and participation plans to help local agencies design a shared vision of development and to improve regional governance.

Finally, "Milano Metropoli" runs a network of services dedicated to promote new commercial and social entrepreneurship, support existing small and medium-sized enterprises and heighten awareness of energy saving and social responsibility.

Source: OECD Territorial Review of Milan, 2005; *www.milanomet.it/en.*

The national government needs to streamline its approach towards regional development in the Cape Town city-region. For instance, the weak performance of economic development initiatives in the Western Cape depends on the approach of national departments and state-owned enterprises. To counter such tendencies, the central government needs not only to act as a fulcrum and facilitate regional development both by accurate and narrowly focused funding (*e.g.* by becoming a shareholder of the RDA if this option is followed), but also support regional governments and the business community. Currently, there are emerging signs of such trends. As assessed above, the central government, through the NSDP, has recently adopted a spatial vision to improve the performance of those regions acting as engines of growth. This policy focuses on producing the necessary infrastructure at the local level to support growth dynamics and job creation. This approach could be extended by allowing regions to identify their own assets and promote investments to enhance comparative advantages.

More generally, South Africa might well consider regional policy as one of the chief ways to implement its AsgiSA's national growth strategy. Many countries recognise the importance of balancing macroeconomic policies with territorial approaches so that the special challenges and opportunities of diverse regions can be coherently addressed. So far, only the NSDP has abandoned the sectoral approach to economic development that is more conventional in other areas of South Africa's national policy, as evidenced in the Department of Trade and Industry's Regional Industrial Development Strategy (RIDS). Moreover, currently, around 40% of infrastructure investments are made through public enterprises, and the rest is being shared by the three spheres of government. These are capital investments made through a range of national department levels, with projects being distributed to provincial and local governments through the municipal and provincial infrastructure grant programmes, and the rest being funded by their own revenue sources for capital expenditure. This approach does not follow any regional strategy, with line ministries working in silos. A regional development policy in South Africa could better address the main binding constraints identified in the AsgiSA (*e.g.* infrastructure investment and governance and institutional interventions) through a more effective allocation of the scarce public resources for investment. Because of budget constraints, this calls for individually designed paths to regional development, which requires prioritisation of investments in public goods and services.

Regional development policy can also help to reconcile equity and growth, the two policy objectives that underpin AsgiSA's national strategy. Efficiency will help progress toward competitiveness in the exploitation of local opportunities for growth. Such opportunities concern both individuals and firms and are strictly linked to the regional economy. Equitable provision of essential public goods and services throughout the country requires integrated place-based policies. In South Africa, a paradoxical tension surrounds territorial development issues in the debates on poverty. On other one hand, city-regions like Cape Town are increasingly viewed by national authorities as the main drivers of economic growth and as worthy of more investment, in order to push sustained national economic growth closer to the 8% called for in the 2006 AsgiSA. On the other hand, as already noted, the historical experience of "regional" or "territorial" development in South Africa is too closely associated with oppressive and disastrous apartheid era concepts like "separate development". In the popular and policy imagination, this conjures up profound divisions between rural and urban regions, with concomitant overtones of race relations. An analysis of socio-economic trends in South Africa, as developed in Chapter 1, reveals increasing disparities between urban and rural areas but also a steady urbanisation of poverty within metropolitan areas. Here again, regional development policies in OECD countries have redressed regional structural imbalances while strengthening territorial competitiveness. Such initiatives hinge upon improvements in governance in the Cape Town city-region, as will be developed in Chapter 3.

Notes

1. Partly because closer settlements in rural areas concentrated poverty and limited access.

2. The two main other sector strategies include the *Strategic Infrastructure Programme* (SIPS) and the *Provincial Spatial Development Framework* (PSDF).

3. For example, within the MEDS, the HRD (Human Resource Development) sector is considered as a possible target for intervention. It is not clear, however, what could be the effective impact of such an intervention on labour pooling and the positive territorial spillovers on the more knowledge-intensive segments.

4. Imbizo is a forum for enhancing dialogue and interaction between government and the people. It provides an opportunity for government to communicate its Programme of Action and the progress being made and promotes participation of the public in the programmes to improve their lives. Imbizo also highlights citizens' concerns and grievances, as well as advice about the government's work

5. As mentioned in Chapter 1, this figure refers to the "broad" unemployment rate, *i.e.* it takes into account discouraged workers. The "narrow" unemployment rate was 18.94% on March 2007 (Statistics South Africa, 2007*c*).

6. It might also facilitate moving trained teachers to where they are most needed, which could potentially address the relegation of so much of the majority black population to unemployment, low-paid informal employment, or unskilled manual labour in the formal sector.

7. They include 34 in the City of Cape Town, seven in the West Coast and Cape Winelands districts (Paarl, Vredenberg, Vredendal, Saldanha and Stellenbosch), two in Worcester and Ashton, and two in the South Cape.

8. The implementation of such a policy may generate a "tunnel effect". Albert Hirschman's (1973) famous "tunnel effect" argues that if a person is stuck in a traffic jam in a two-lane tunnel, and the opposite lane begins to move while his lane remains still, his immediate reaction is not anger but hope, because he imagines that the traffic jam is broken and that he, too, will move soon. Similarly, in the case of the townships, supporting the education of gifted children, and supporting and empowering their families as well, could be a way to involve families in the support of the education of pupils in poor areas.

9. The Department of Science and Technology (DST) initiated the Technology Stations Programme (TSP) to create support for SMEs in targeted business sectors. The primary objective of the programme is to increase the innovative abilities of targeted SMEs through university of technology and technikon programmes. The Tshumisano Trust (which means "Co-operation" or "Partnership") is the implementation agency for the TSP. The Trust provides technical and financial support to Technology Stations, which are based at Universities of Technology/Technikons. TSP was developed by Department of Science and Technology (DST) to strengthen and accelerate interaction between Technikons/Universities of Technology (UoT) and SMEs.

10. Interviews with the municipal staff from Cape Town revealed that, at this point, there are no innovative solid waste projects in the pipeline. Despite the high probability of capacity problems in dealing with the volume of solid waste in the near future, there are no programs aimed at improving recycling or separating solid waste at the source. Apparently, there are also institutional and financial bottlenecks deterring the private sector from stepping into these areas (according to one of the municipal officers, risks are relatively high, so that a municipal or public guarantee would be necessary to leverage private investments in this sector). The lack of projects in this area is not the general situation in South African cities, however. In Johannesburg, for example, there is ongoing innovation in generating energy from solid waste. Part of the municipal fleet is running on this alternative source of energy.

11. The South African government use the term "second" as a synonym for informal.

12. These regulations faced particular resistance from informal parking attendants, who directed the flow of pedestrians and traffic in the congested downtown area. According to the new scheme, in 2001 these attendants were replaced with a company that employed uniformed "parking wardens". Such a policy was referred to by one critic as "socially sanitising public space" (Miraftab, 2007).

13. Between 1988 and 2003, Bogotá's mayors experimented with nearly every plausible policy for street vendors, including microcredit, worker retraining, rotating street fairs, co-operatives, relocation, pacts with "reformed" vendors and public debates on informal commerce restrictions (Donovan, 2008).

14. The importance of SMEs should not be under-estimated. SMEs may compete successfully in the global economy – "Ten lathes in ten different rooms can be operated as efficiently as ten lathes in one room" (Brusco and Sabel, 1981), provided that *i)* they operate in sectors where the

division of labour is possible, *ii)* machinery is kept up to date, and *iii)* co-ordination costs are kept low thanks to the large availability of social capital. To date, such conditions are not in evidence in the Cape Town city-region.

15 . It could claimed that the proliferation of BPO activities does not further technological progress. However, linking these activities to an explicit spatial and relational perspective intended to establish local backward and forward linkages with clients, suppliers, local governments and universities (*e.g.* developing capacity for programming software for mobile phones, centres of technical assistance and incubators linked to university programs, etc.), could definitely encourage endogenous development.

16 . These include The National Building Regulations and Building Standards Act, No. 103 of 1977 (NBR and BS Act), The National Heritage Resources Act, No. 25 of 1999 (NHR Act), The Environment Conservation Act, No. 73 of 1989 (EC Act) and its Regulations 1182 and 1183 of 1997, amended in 1998 and 2002, The National Environmental Management Act, No. 107 of 1998 (NEMA), Western Cape Planning and Development Act, No. 7 of 1999, The Development Facilitation Act, No. 67 of 1995, Municipal Systems Act, No. 32 of 2000, and The Local Government: Municipal Structures Act, No. 117 of 1998.

17 . For additional material on this draft see *www.capetown.gov.za.*

18 . For a more complete description of variables in the land market assessment along with international studies of their implementation, see Dowall (1991, 1994) and Serra *et al.* (2004).

19 . On April 14, 2002 American Planning Association representatives from all 50 U.S. states agreed to a definition of smart growth that incorporated 13 core principles. "Principle H: Efficient Use of Land and Infrastructure" outlines the importance of infill development to smart growth.

20 . The bills include Cal. Gov't Code §65583(a)(3) (1996), Ore. Rev. Stats. §197.296(3)(a) (1996), and Wash. Rev. Code §36.70A.215(1)(a) (1997) (American Planning Association, 2002).

21 . Few authors have studied the premium that residents pay to regularise their homes; an exception is the detailed work of Levy and Lanjouw (2002) who in Guayaquil, Mexico, calculated that the cost of obtaining a title represented 102% of household annual per capita consumption (cited in Donovan, 2007).

22 . Cape Town contains some of the most innovative informal settlement upgrading programs. One upgrading methodology was built upon a

Geographic Information System-based spatial data management framework and identified physical risk, spatial integration and movement within and out of the informal settlement. See Abbott (2003) for an explanation of this model and its implementation in the New Rest community in Cape Town.

23. The annual target is set at 20 000 by the city. This would cost approximately ZAR 679 million on a yearly basis, while available funding only amounts to ZAR 355 million. The discrepancy between the delivery and the high expectations of low-income communities, coupled with the absence of jobs and broader structural urban reform, have led to continued protests (Goebel, 2007).

24. The source of this estimate is from an unpublished City of Cape Town Housing Directorate study.

25. The Metropolitan Spatial Development Framework argued for a restructuring of the metropole for socio-spatial integration; the primary tools it proposed consisted of corridors, a fixed urban edge, and a metropolitan open space system (MOSS).

26. Pilot projects that attempted to integrate "town-building", such as the Wetton-Landsdowne Corridor initiative, which was inspired by experiences in Curitiba, Brazil, revealed the practical, economic and political limitations of a strong model of urban integration and spatial compaction. Metropolitan frameworks at this time were "far too physically based and design-oriented … [and] did not engage with the economic and social forces shaping the city or with the role of private property interests" (Todes, 2006).

27. The "home equity assurance" program was first implemented in the Chicago suburb of Oak Park, Illinois, to discourage flight following a racial transition. Essentially, this successful program enrolls property owners near high-density developments and agrees to pay the difference between the appraised value and the sale value if the home is sold for less. According to Nelson (2003), Oak Park has yet to compensate any property owner under its innovative program.

28. Within the Provincial Spatial Development Framework of the Western *Cape* (2005), scenarios were developed to illustrate that this densification could be achieved by minimally reducing plot size or using two- or three-storey designs.

29. For housing design information about accessory dwelling units, see *www.mass.gov/envir/smart_growth_toolkit/pages/mod-adu.html.*

30 . For model state and local ordinances for accessory dwelling units, see Cobb and Dvorak (2000).

31 . Information provided by Jaco van der Westhuizen, project manager of the Integrated Zoning Scheme.

32 . This legislation was complemented with the Transport Services for Coloured Persons and Indians Act, enacted in 1972.

33 . The subsidy covers 30% of the economic fare at 10 kilometres from the CBD, 65% at 50 kilometres from the CBD, and 71% at 100 kilometres. Some local governments also decide to supplement this amount with subsidies allocated from their own municipal budgets (Behrens and Wilkinson, 2003).

34 . This contrasts with the Province of the Western Cape, where 45% of traffic fatalities killed pedestrians (Provincial Government of the Western Cape Department of Transport and Public Works, 2004).

35 . This only refers to provincial road infrastructure – roads, bridges, and culverts.

36 . World Bank, 2001, cited in Provincial Government of the Western Cape, 2005.

37 . These 27 Social Transformation Areas include such districts as Mitchell's Plain, Khayelitsha, Manenburg, Hanover Park, Nyanga, Elsies River, Bishop Lavis, Delft, Kleinvlei, Guguletu, Phillipi, Muizenberg, and the rural areas of Vredenberg, Paarl and Oudtshoorn. In the 27 Social Transformation Areas, each area receives funding to assist in processes of community engagements, intermediary structure launches, strategic planning and logistical support. The Departments of Community Safety, Social Development, Education, Sports and the South African Police Service intervene with at-risk youth in 165 schools in the Province of the Western Cape. For more information on these approaches and others,, see Budget Speech by Western Cape MEC for Community Safety, Mr Leonard Ramatlakane, for the 2008/09 financial year (*www.info.gov.za/ speeches/2008/08051914151001.htm*).

38 . Another initiative includes the Violence Prevention through Urban Upgrading program, a project in Khayelitsha funded by the City of Cape Town and the German government.

39 . Gasson, 2002; cited in Swilling, 2006.

40 . Specifically the City of Cape Town's City Council has approved the *Framework for Adaptation to Climate Change in the City of Cape Town* (FACT) and the *City Adaptation Plan of Action* (CAPA). CAPA

initiatives include a wide range of policies, such as the City's Biodiversity and Coastal Management strategy, the proposed Western Cape Climate Change Response Strategy and Action Plan, and the City's Air Quality Management Strategy.

41 . At present, the City supports wind generation and solar water heaters. This is reflected by the purchase of power from the Darling Wind Farm, located 70 kilometres outside Cape Town. The City estimates that by sourcing energy from the wind farm, it will prevent the production of 298 125 tonnes of carbon dioxide and the burning of 100 000 tonnes of coal (South African Cities Network, 2007).

42 . Craig Haskins, City of Cape Town.

43 . The Overstrand visitor economy is premised on a number of world-renowned attractions, including the Kogelberg Biosphere Reserve (one of just two such reserves in South Africa), the award-winning Forest Lodge Grootbos Private Nature Reserve, a premier whale-watching and shark-diving destination, and three tourist beaches, Grotto Beach, Hawston and Kleinmond Beaches, that have attained the much-coveted Blue Flag status (Boulle, 2007*b*).

44 . The Kuyasa Fund was set up by the Development Action Group (DAG), a Cape Town-based community development NGO (and a UN-HABITAT Best Practice in 2004). The fund facilitates access to housing finance as a tool for improving well-being and supporting the development of a financial sector for the poor. Access to finance helps to create sustainable households and communities and alleviates poverty. Kuyasa's mission is to provide credit with the aim of improving housing and building social capital, to enable clients to build adequately sized houses that meet their needs and to provide an example of successful lending to the financially marginalised. Kuyasa Fund works with low-income communities with an average monthly household income of ZAR 1 600 (USD 260), and its clients are drawn from those who qualify for the state housing subsidy and who save in community-based savings groups. Women currently comprise 74% of its clients. To date, Kuyasa has disbursed over 4 000 loans at a value of more than ZAR 20 million (USD 3.3 million). Clients have reported positive results from home ownership that are not limited to physical security, but reflect greater household cohesion, a decline in the stress placed on marital and familial relationships by poor living conditions, increased good health and an increased sense of well-being and dignity, as well as greater engagement with their community.

45 . In the United States, a productive debate has surrounded Michael Porter's work on the relevance of policies of dynamic clustering and networking among firms, for the revitalisation of marginalised inner-city areas in the

United States. See, for example, Schweke (1995); Reichert (1995) and Lowery (1996). Smith (2003) also argues that the North American Metropolis may serve as useful benchmarking material for the South African experience.

46 . Local home rule (the large degree of autonomy of local governments to implement local zoning ordinances) facilitated a generalised practice under which officials in more affluent communities used exclusionary zoning practices to exclude poorer segments from entering and living in the same area. Simultaneously, the formal financial institutions started to redline and discriminate against US inner-city neighbourhoods, while federal urban renewal programs frequently aggravated socio-spatial exclusion.

47 . For example, while Provincial Government actively supports the role of SPVs and similar structures aimed at local economic development (information sharing, strategy elaboration, etc.), the City of Cape Town is actually considering withdrawing financial and human resources from such institutions, and recently withdrew its participation from WESGRO.

48 . The evaluation states that "While private sector financial contributions are lower than would be ideal, business people devote a great deal of time to the work of the SPVs. The existence of the SPVs has a positive effect on communication and information sharing within each sector and between government and business more generally. Private sector involvement is maintained precisely because the SPVs are narrowly focused on particular sectors – and sometimes on particular barriers to the growth of a sector".

49 . As already discussed above, one of the limits of agencies and SPVs is that they are poorly funded. Overall, they receive less than the 1.25% of the combined budget of the Municipality of Cape Town and the Province of the Western Cape.

50 . There are some cases in which the lack of co-ordination among agencies operating in adjacent fields clearly reduces operative capacity and effectiveness. Such is the case, for instance, of the regional branding policy. The Municipality of Cape Town and the Province of the Western Cape unified their marketing agencies in 2004 to create the Cape Town Routes Unlimited (CTRU), a special purpose vehicle whose mandate is to market Cape Town and the Western Cape domestically and internationally. It also aims to distribute the benefits of tourism more widely across the regional population. CTRU focuses on expanding existing markets, growing emerging markets, linking markets to emerging entrepreneurs, and improving the ratio between business and leisure tourism. The tourism market is seasonal because of the wet and stormy winter, and one of its key objectives is a sustained campaign to promote

the city-region as a year-round destination. Although it is currently passing through a difficult period, CTRU has made important gains in its first three years, and has the potential to form the core of a wider marketing drive that promoting the Cape as a destination for for tourism, investment, film-making and academic studies. Although CTRU represents a remarkable effort of co-ordination between the two governments, its brief is narrowly limited to tourism, which reduces its ability to develop broader branding policies. For instance, CTRU cannot target international investors and other sectors not directly related to tourism. After integrating the CTRU with WESGRO, the SPV in charge after four years, the organisation is still struggling with a complex variety of external and internal issues.

Chapter 3

Metropolitan Governance in Cape Town

Since the birth of democratic South Africa in 1994, the nation has witnessed a dramatic institutional transformation. Impressive efforts to reform and strengthen existing institutions of governance accompanied the transition from apartheid to a non-racial liberal democracy. At the same time, completely new social, legal, economic and institutional frameworks were built to address complex imperatives of economic growth, redistribution, social welfare and nation building. This overhaul period was marked by a sweeping reorganisation and demarcation of local authorities in 2000, when the number of local authorities was reduced from over 1 300 to 283 nationwide. The effects of this transformation were legion: over a short time local governments administered larger jurisdictions, collected revenue for the first time, deracialised public service provision, and instituted democratic, non-racial elections at the local and national levels. Few international precedents exist for such rapid institutional change. In Cape Town, the institutional reform gave rise to a large metropolitan municipality that collapsed 61 racially segregated entities into one "unicity" charged with pro-poor service delivery, as well as the standardisation of a range of different land use legislation, computer systems, accounting standards and contracts. The concomitant creation of the Western Cape Province established a vehicle for regional delivery of health services and education and inter-municipal co-ordination. Cumulatively, these reforms prepared regional and local governments to play a more prominent role in economic development.

However, as shown in previous chapters, this dramatic government reform left many serious problems unresolved, including congestion, housing deficits, and a shortage of skilled labour. The Cape Town city-region faces these challenges in a context of high immigration, increased poverty and its obligations to improve global competitiveness and foster more inclusive economic development. The ability of government in the region to resolve these issues is made all the more difficult by South Africa's adoption of strict public-spending restrictions, an entrenched legacy of racial inequality, ecological fragility and a volatile political environment. Given these conditions, new "second generation" governance reforms are needed to consolidate what has been achieved and to respond to emerging obstacles.

These main governance challenges relate to:

- *Stimulating intergovernmental collaboration for improved delivery of public policies.* The post-apartheid package of reform created a sub-national institutional framework, but challenges linked with the alignment of functions across spheres of government remain. This especially afflicts the management of the built environment, which perpetuates a spatial structure that imposes significant social and economic costs. Likewise, the limited co-operation among the provincial and municipal levels of government does not contribute to the effective delivery of public services in the Cape Town city-region. Although intergovernmental co-ordination and metropolitan governance is clearly a pressing problem, relatively few agreements adequately address problems that spill over jurisdictional boundaries, such as traffic, the environment, infrastructure and housing. While Chapter 3 of the Constitution encourages "Co-operative Governance", there are few mechanisms in place to ensure co-operation between such departments as Transport, Mineral and Energy Affairs, and Trade and Industry. This nonalignment results in contradictory public policies that ultimately compromise Cape Town's global competitiveness.

- *Building and retaining capacity in the sub-national civil service.* In many cases, well-developed policies and strategies seem to lack human resources to ensure their effective implementation. The public sector is plagued by a relatively high turnover, staff shortages and dependence on consultancies for work normally performed internally. Political volatility among different levels of government in the region further corrodes governmental capacity and administrative continuity. The volatile political environment has made intergovernmental co-operation between provincial and metropolitan government particularly difficult, while rapid changes in formal political control of provincial and local government have compromised bureaucratic stability. Frequent political shuffles have made governance in the region unpredictable; policy priorities are often changed before programmes can be thoroughly implemented, let alone evaluated. Political stabilisation coupled with improved capacity building would help to build a professional bureaucracy that is sensitive to the inevitable political shifts but to some degree independent of them. In the long run, these efforts would increase institutional memory and enhance the quality of implementation.

- *Consolidating and mainstreaming frameworks for strategic planning at the regional/metropolitan level.* The current sectoral focus of major policy arenas such as public transportation, environment and land use, and economic development has militated strongly against a "territorial" approach where various levels of the state work together to maximise economic competitiveness. Policies and funding regimes impacting spatial planning emanate from several different national ministries with objectives that sometimes conflict. The subsidisation of public transportation by the Department of Transport, for example, is at odds with the Department of Housing's funding systems, whose large-scale housing projects for the disadvantaged on cheap, remote land force more people into long commutes from purlieus outside the public transit grid. Such contradictions, coupled with limited delegation of authority on these functions, limit the extent to which spatial plans can reasonably prescribe settlement patterns. At present, there is no systematic evaluation of the spatial effects of national or provincial economic policies. Strategic decisions need to be made at the regional level, given that the Cape Town city-region now encompasses an area of ecological, social and economic flows that extend well outside the administrative boundaries of the City of Cape Town.

- *Creating an efficient public finance framework.* Sub-national public finance has undergone drastic reform in the last decade. Provinces are largely dependent on grants, but local authorities have relatively large powers to tax and generate additional revenue. Issues of concern in this area include the limited revenue-collection capacity, the need to find new tax revenue sources, fine-tuning the equitable share, and financing economic development.

- *Strengthening civil engagement.* Sub-national governments have often limited the role played by nongovernmental watchdog groups to one of "ceremonial participation". More meaningful participation may reduce the deep legacy of distrust between disadvantaged communities and local government. An inclusive economy clearly requires a language of plural governance, both to improve the efficiency of governance and to reduce the dependency of citizens on the state.

This chapter discusses the capacity of the current governance system to stimulate regional economic development and co-ordinate action across multiple levels and scales of government. After offering a primer on the structure of local governance in South Africa for context, the chapter acknowledges recent improvements within this system, including the creation of metropolitan municipalities and infrastructure for harmonising spatial planning. It also points out the key obstacles to governance that block progress on issues identified in earlier chapters, namely inadequate housing and land management systems, poor co-ordination of public transit, dominance of sectoral programming, and inter-governmental impasses. It highlights the ways in which regional development strategies may be hampered by uncertainty over overlapping responsibilities, weak cross-sectoral co-ordination at the central level, and issues connected to sub-national finance. It explores the imperatives for regional co-ordination in the Western Cape and various opportunities for metropolitan governance and intergovernmental co-operation between public, private and social sector organisations, including parastatal agencies. Finally, it deepens the inquiry of the Review to explore the underlying political capacity – in programmes and personnel – of the metropolitan region, focusing on the participation of citizens and civil society groups in policy making. In light of the crucial importance of governance in sustaining economic development, the chapter concludes with some general recommendations for better co-ordination and co-operation in the Cape Town city-region.

3.1. The Cape Town city-region in the South African governance framework

Decentralisation and the evolution of local governance, 1994-2008

Aside from the collapse of apartheid, the functional expansion of local government authority has arguably been the most significant institutional change in South African society in the past generation. There has been a progressive shift in the scale and scope of local government authority in metropolitan areas. These reforms endowed South Africa a strong central government and a well-articulated structure of interdependent but autonomous "spheres" of sub-national governance. The constitutional principles and political accords of the 1996 Constitution enshrined these principles, creating a unitary, sovereign democratic state elected by proportional representation, with national, provincial and local levels of government.[1] The subsequent Municipal Structures Act (1998) operationalised the Constitutional principles and instituted a one-tier local government structure to allow for integrated local development and a greater degree of redistribution of locally funded resources. The Bantustans, apartheid-era homeland governments, were abolished, along with the four provinces and existing racialised agencies, such as the Black Local Authorities (BLAs).[2] In their place, a Delimitation Commission drew up the boundaries for nine new provinces, using the nine economic regions proposed by the Development Bank of South Africa as a point of departure (Spitz, 2000).

During the post-apartheid transition, South Africa established an ambitious agenda to expand the scope of institutional competencies for local government, despite resistance from entrenched local groups. The details of these new structures were finalised in the White Paper on Local Government in 1998 and legislatively empowered through the Municipal Structures Act. This was accompanied by rapid reform of parastatals, with no less than 500 acts passed between 1994 and 1999. This occasioned an expansion of their jurisdictions, with urban local government structures taking control of housing, water supply, and a large number of weak or poorly functioning council bodies. The restructuring of local government, the last level to undergo reform, encountered frequent opposition and crystallised as the site in which existing privilege was most robustly defended. This opposition favoured metropolitan governance arrangements to enable minority parties to obtain a majority in sub-metropolitan structures (Cameron, 2000). However, the national government pushed back against these proposals.

Gradual decentralisation transformed local governments into autonomous spheres with considerable financial independence. Indeed, the share of sub-national expenditure in South Africa amounts to 49.2%, higher than in most OECD countries (Figure 3.1). The provinces' share of total government expenditure is about a quarter higher than for municipalities: provincial governments account for 27.4% of total government expenditure, whereas municipalities account for 21.8%. Though fiscal policy will be discussed in greater detail later in this chapter, it is clear that intergovernmental co-operation and regional planning are obviously shaped by the financial capacity that municipalities and provinces have at their disposal.

Figure 3.1. **Sub-national expenditure of OECD countries and South Africa**

(as share of total government expenditures in 2006)

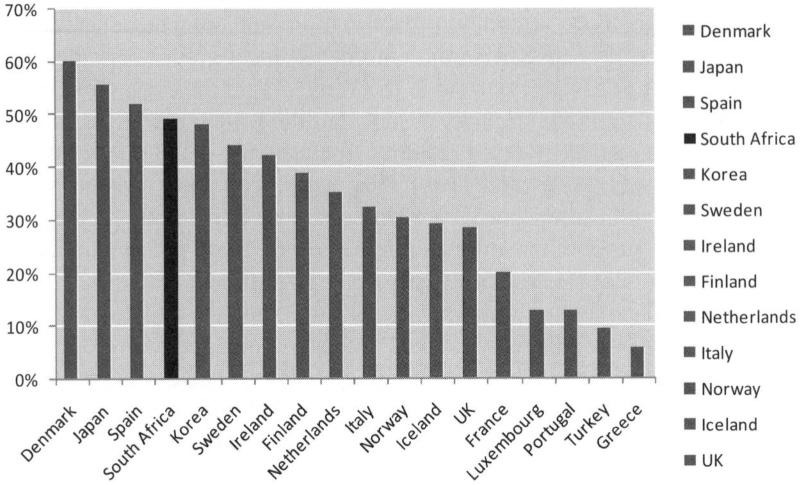

Source: OECD National Accounts Database.

Provinces have relative autonomy in lawmaking and policy development, but a limited capacity for revenue generation. A province's main spending responsibilities include health care (primary and secondary clinics, secondary district hospitals), provincial roads, agriculture and education, which includes primary and secondary schooling, adult education and training colleges. The Constitution [(115 (6)] vests provinces with the tasks of monitoring, support, co-ordination and capacity development of local governments. Essentially, provincial governments are the interlocutor between the macro and micro, translating the national development agenda into contextualised provincial frameworks. Provinces are further empowered to adopt provincial constitutions (as long as these are consistent with the national Constitution) and are represented on the National Council of Provinces. The Western Cape Provincial Government employs around 73 000 people, of whom 90% work in either health care or education (Provincial Government of the Western Cape, 2008*c*). The Western Cape Province is governed by a Premier and a 42-member popularly elected Provincial Parliament, which drafts legislation, approves budgets, and elects the Premier every five years.

Municipalities are charged with providing basic public services – water and electricity distribution, sanitation, municipal road maintenance, refuse removal, and solid waste management – and financing these mainly through user fees and taxation. The *Local Government White Paper* in 1998 outlined this form of local government, placing emphasis on integrated development planning and "developmental local governance".[3] Between 1998 and 2000, the scale and scope of developmental local governance were significantly extended: the Constitution required them to become "*the* primary development champion, the major conduit for poverty alleviation, the guarantor of social and economic rights, the enabler of economic growth, the principal agent of spatial or physical planning and the watchdog of environmental justice" (Parnell and Pieterse, 1998). With this mandate, local governments in the Cape Town city-region employ an estimated 25 500 people on a full-time basis, of which the City of Cape Town accounts for 77.6% (Statistics South Africa, 2007*c*). Cape Town is led by a popularly elected Executive Mayor and a City Council of 210 members, of which 105 are elected as ward councillors and 105 are nominated in terms of proportional representation.

Intergovernmental mandates shared between provinces and municipalities are guided by the constitutional injunction of "co-operative governance" and encompass the concurrent mandates of housing, public transport and land use regulation. The embedded interdependence of spheres of government is reflected both in functional concurrency, a broad set of financial relationships, and the designation of government levels as "spheres" rather than "tiers" (Levy and Tapscott, 2001). A spirit of co-operative intergovernmental relations has not been institutionalised, however, given that the constitutional assignment of functions does not require that the relevant sphere of government be necessarily responsible for direct delivery. By the same token, local governments may perform reimbursable agency functions on behalf of other spheres of government. For example, district municipalities undertake road construction and maintenance work on behalf of the province, and other municipalities may provide library and health services. Other institutional arrangements for service delivery are possible, including the use of the designated public agencies known as special purpose vehicles (SPVs), as well as public-private and community-level partnerships. To put this into effect, the national government has taken a series of legislative measures to stimulate intergovernmental co-operation. At a strategic level, this includes the Intergovernmental Fiscal Relations Act (1997) and the Intergovernmental Relations Framework Act (2005), which provide a framework for consultation and dispute resolution between spheres of government, predominantly through establishing a series of sectoral and budgeting fora for intergovernmental discussion. The responsibilities of different levels of national, provincial, district, and local government present several overlapping responsibilities for which intergovernmental collaboration is essential (Table 3.1).

Table 3.1. **The assignment of government functions in South Africa**

	National	Provincial	Local Government (and Metro)	
			District	Local
Spatial planning	Regulation	Regional planning and development	Regional planning	Local planning and development control
Economic development	Macroeconomic policy	Industrial policy and promotion, regional economic planning	District tourism Promote economic development of community	Local tourism Promote economic development of community
Environment	Regulation	Planning and regulation	Environmental enforcement	
Transport	National roads Rail Major ports	Provincial roads and traffic Public transport	District roads Municipal public transport	Local roads Municipal public transport
Water	Bulk/dams			Bulk and reticulation, limited to potable water supply systems
Waste Management	Regulation			Sanitation, limited to domestic waste-water and sewage disposal systems Stormwater Refuse and solid waste disposal Cleansing
Public Safety	Policing	Policing oversight and traffic management		Metro policing Traffic management
Housing	Regulation	Implementation and policy		Implementation
Education	Tertiary	Primary and secondary		ECD
Health	Regulation	Tertiary, secondary and primary	Municipal health	Municipal health

Source: South African Constitution (Act 108 of 1996).

Debate surrounds the political role of provinces in economic development. To provide as much flexibility for regional variation and differences in potential and capacity, the Constitution loosely defined responsibilities for economic development across all three spheres of government, without giving specific clarification. In South Africa, the current economic agenda is centralised at the national level, and limited amounts of funding are transferred to provinces for provincial roads and minor industrial sector support (agriculture and tourism). In effect, economic development constitutes approximately 12% of total provincial spending, spanning such diverse areas as agriculture, industrial promotion, tourism, trade, regional development and planning, and urban and rural development (National Treasury, 2007c, cited in Robinson, 2007). In this configuration, provinces play a peripheral role in industrial promotion and regional economic development. Though an in-depth legal analysis of South African constitutional law is beyond the scope of this project, another interpretation holds that the expansion of provincial competency in industrial promotion and regional development and planning would be consistent with the Constitution. In other words, regional development is seen as a concurrent national and provincial function. In this configuration, a province would build links upwards to the overarching macroeconomic policy framework at the national level and downwards to the more detailed local economic development plans at the municipal level. Nevertheless, the debate still tends to favour those who believe in a limited provincial developmental role (Robinson, 2007).

The institutional structure of metropolitan planning in Cape Town

Political-administrative reorganisation comprised the central challenge of Cape Town's post-apartheid unification. Before 1994, Cape Town was divided into 61 entities: 19 white local authorities, six local (white semi-rural) councils, 29 Coloured Management Committees and seven Black Local Authorities. In 1994, the Cape Town local government agreed to reduce the number of entities to 39, though the formal political geography of late apartheid was basically untouched.[4] After the first local authority elections took place in 1996, the number of authorities was reduced to six general-purpose local governments under the authority of a single metropolitan-wide authority, the Cape Metropolitan Council. The BLAs of Lingeletu West, which governed Khayelitsha, and Ikapa, which included Guguletu, Langa and Nyanga, were incorporated into historically white and coloured neighbourhoods, *i.e.* Tygerberg and Cape Town, respectively. The Local Government Transition Act, with the Municipal Demarcation Board and its processes, provided local authorities with options of classification. The introduction of A, B, and C category municipalities was determined by factors such as economy, demography, human settlements, transport systems and ecosystems. Thus, all local authorities were compelled to propose their preferred structure, supported by a rigorous analytical justification. In Cape Town, the structure of six local authorities and a metropolitan authority was replaced by a single local authority, the "Unicity" of Cape Town, in 2000

(Jaglin, 2004). The political geography that emerged after 1996 gave rise to 11 elected sub-national public authorities across two spheres of governance in the Cape Town city-region. The Western Cape Province embraces the dominant metropolitan municipality of Cape Town, plus the six ''local'' municipalities immediately adjacent to Cape Town and three ''district'' municipalities located outside the region (Box 3.1).

The creation of a metropolitan municipality exacted the standardisation of services performed by previous local governments and conditioned by national funding allocation. The National Treasury, through such means as conditional grants to local authorities, addresses service delivery failure in poorer areas. This was frequently carried out with a municipal approach that favoured intra-urban equality of service. Consequently, municipal government invested capital in extending water distribution networks, electrification and providing sanitation to disadvantaged areas. This accompanied the so-called Unicity Commission's release of a controversial "rationalisation plan", which created uniform standards of service, contracts and employee benefits across the new metropolitan region. Nevertheless, in some instances, this process is still incomplete, and many different conditions of service (including pension arrangements) continue to exist alongside each other.

The City of Cape Town dominates the new provincial framework, though consensus among varying political groups remains difficult to achieve. While it covers than 2% of the surface area of the province, the City of Cape Town houses 65% of the Province's population and has the largest number of elected councilors (210). Authorities outside Cape Town also represent important constituencies and may voice concerns that reflect the agricultural interests of the 10% of Western Cape's population who live in rural communities (Statistics South Africa, 2006*b*).

Box 3.1. **Structures and functions of government in the Cape Town city-region**

All three spheres of government are represented in the Cape Town city-region. The national government, other than performing exclusive national functions and its regulatory roles regarding sub-national functions, plays an active role in local service delivery, through three key agencies. The Department of Water Affairs and Forestry directly manages the majority of the bulk water supply, including major dams, to the Cape Town city-region and is currently constructing a new dam on the Berg River. Two state-owned enterprises, Eskom and Metro Rail, directly provide electricity distribution and commuter rail services in the Cape Town city-region. National government, particularly through Transnet and the Defence Force, also owns large and strategic land parcels across the metropolitan area.

The Western Cape Province is geographically divided into one single-tier metropolitan (Category A) municipality and five District (Category C) municipalities, each of which is composed of a number of local (Category B) municipalities. While metropolitan municipalities are assigned all the functions of local governments, these must be further divided between district and local municipalities outside metropolitan areas. Because of its enormous size, density and economic complexity, Cape Town is considered a Category A municipality. The city-region's six "local" authorities – Theewaterskloof, Overstrand, Stellenbosch, Drakenstein, Saldanha and Swartland – are designated Category B municipalities. The West Coast consists of the West Coast District Municipality and two of its local municipalities, Swartland Municipality and Saldanha Bay Municipality. The Cape Winelands consists of the Cape Winelands District Municipality and two of its local municipalities, Stellenbosch Municipality and Drakenstein Municipality. Overberg consists of the Overberg District Municipality and two of its local municipalities, Theewaterskloof Municipality and Overstrand Municipality. It should be noted that other local municipalities also fall within the boundaries of each of the district municipalities, but not within the borders of the Cape Town city-region as defined in this Review. This includes the municipalities of Matzikama, Cedarberg and Berg River in the West Coast, Witzenberg, Breede Valley and Breede River/Winelands in the Winelands, and Swellendam and Cape Agulhas in Overstrand.

Source: Province of the Western Cape.

South Africa's provinces and municipalities depend upon different sources of funding and lack hierarchical fiscal relationships. Following the Local Government Transition Act (1993) and the new Constitution, sub-national government reforms modified expenditure assignments, revenue sources and local public management. Reforms also affected revenue generation: a uniform property tax for municipalities was introduced, the business tax was phased out, and the allocation of grants was made more objective. Reforms in public finance management have also had consequences for intergovernmental fiscal relations. The Public Finance Management Act of 1999 introduced regular financial reporting, sound internal expenditure controls, independent audit and supervision of control systems, improved accounting standards and training of financial managers, and greater emphasis on outputs and performance monitoring. In 2003, these budget reforms were extended to local government via the Municipal Finance Management Act.

Planning tools in the Cape Town city-region

Local government currently utilises a wide range of planning tools in the Cape Town city-region. The single most important planning instrument consists of the *Integrated Development Plans* (IDPs), five-year management plans that aim to link the municipal budget to a council's strategic plan and sectoral plans, including spatial frameworks, transport plans, and infrastructure. Although municipalities have no jurisdiction over state-owned enterprises or provincial entities, the IDP should articulate how investments by parastatals, other spheres of government and the private sector will affect local needs, planning frameworks and budgets. Tasked with IDP approval, provincial government is ultimately responsible for approving municipal budgets, as established in the Municipal Financial Management Act (MFMA) (2003). Under this framework, the Province exercises the power to channel its vision and principles to municipalities. Municipalities are required to take national and provincial policies and frameworks into consideration, although in reality, IDPs are frequently not aligned with neighbouring municipal and provincial budgets. For example, "Spatial Development Frameworks" are legally required by the Integrated Development Plans, but municipal capacity, limited vision and vested interests may reduce their quality.

Spatial Development Frameworks (SDFs) offer municipalities a vehicle to reflect long-term (20- to 30-year) vision for the future spatial form and development of the municipality. They also typically contain all relevant supporting built environment sector policy statements. These typically attempt to integrate the forward planning of all sectors that impact spatial development in the city, including Integrated Transport Plans, Environmental Management, Heritage Strategies and Plans, Economic and Social Development Plans, and Infrastructure Investment plans. If approved by the provincial government, SDFs gain legal force and are required to form part of the Integrated Development Plans of local authorities per the Municipal Systems Act. Though SDFs tend to be indicative given the lengthy time horizon these plans address, the level of specificity in the SDFs should be detailed enough to provide direction both to the five-year IDP, but not so specific that unanticipated changes become onerous to achieve. The City of Cape Town has set up the structure of its forward planning through two mechanisms. On the metropolitan level, it is preparing its overall *Spatial Framework* to establish principles to direct the long-term development of the city and specify the type of alignment between various sectors – housing, transport planning, environmental management and infrastructure – necessary to realise this vision. Second, the City supports the elaboration of District *Spatial Development Plans* for each of the eight planning districts within the metropolitan area that plan for a 5 to 10-year time horizon. The SDPs along with any amendments, only have legal force when they have been approved by the Province as Structure Plans under Section 4(6) of the Land Use Planning Ordinance (1985).[5]

The most detailed level of planning guidance occurs with zoning schemes, which are promulgated in terms of Land Use Planning Ordinance. This is where real rights are conferred that significantly influence the value of properties and stipulate which activities are allowed. In many instances, zoning schemes reflect an outdated vision of how settlements should develop, dating to the late 1940s and early 1950s. For example, the current City of Cape Town zoning scheme was first promulgated in 1948. Its vision is now increasingly obsolete, given emerging problems associated with modernist urban form (*e.g.* the isolated pavilion approach one building sited in the middle of a plot), the unconstrained use of the motor car and the sensitivity of environmental and heritage factors. A number of efforts are in process to rationalise zoning schemes (City of Cape Town, Stellenbosch Municipality, Knysna Municipality, and the New Model Scheme Regulations for the Province). These do not generally attempt to rationalise or influence existing rights but rather to standardise different designations for the same use. Where possible, these scheme revisions are also trying to address current issues that have become apparent since the original zoning schemes were promulgated, particularly with respect to environment and heritage (Western Cape Provincial Spatial Development Framework, 2005). Moreover, not all land developed in Cape Town falls under a zoning scheme, as the Less Formal Townships Act (113 of 1991) allowed, in the interests of rapid land release and low-income settlement development, for the fast tracking and neglect of normal regulations contained in the zoning scheme.

Fiscal Framework

Expenditures

Education and health are the largest budget items of the province of Western Cape; together they accounted for more than 70% of the provincial budget in 2006 (Figure 3.2). This percentage increased recently after social security responsibilities were transferred to the national level, reducing the provincial share of the consolidated budget and raising health and education shares as a proportion of provincial expenditure. As health and education services are highly labour-intensive, this means that a large share of provincial budgets is devoted to personnel-related expenditures. The process of allocating national budgets through conditional grants for social services minimises the flexibility of funding to allow provinces to be more pro-active in addressing some of the challenges facing the region. This introduces rigidity into provincial budgets, especially since social security benefits and many policies are set nationally and provinces have very little control over salaries. The provinces are thus often regarded as mere implementation agencies of the national government. In practice, provinces have little discretion over much of their budget, given the labour-intensity and the centrality of bargaining council agreements in these sectors. In this context, innovation and efficiency of public service delivery have taken on importance (Robinson, 2007). Compared to other South African provinces, the province of Western Cape spends less on education and more on health. 9% of its budget is capital expenditure. In the past, a number of provinces have consistently failed to invest funds in crucial programmes such as building and upgrading of schools, clinics and hospitals. Between 2001/02 and 2005/06, provinces, on average, spent only 87% of their capital budget (Amusa and Mathane, 2007). The delivery performance of provinces has, however, improved: in the 2006/2007 financial year, provinces spent 98% of their infrastructure budgets, with Western Cape spending 94% (AsgiSA, 2008).

Figure 3.2. **Main expenditure categories of the province of Western Cape**

(2006)

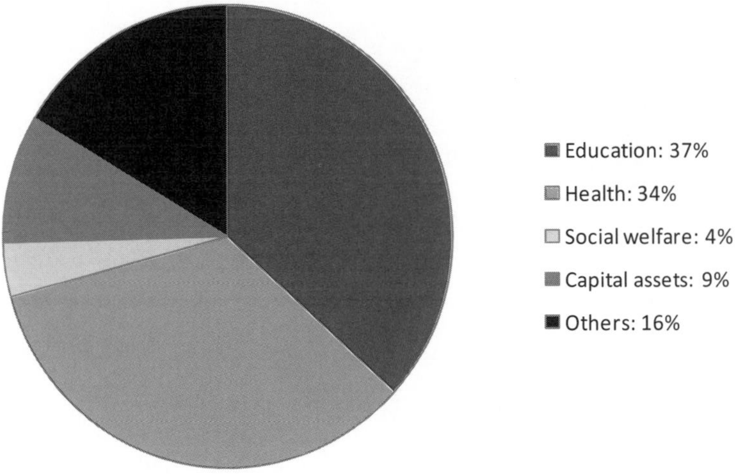

Source: National Treasury database.

The City of Cape Town's greatest expenditures are for basic services and administration, in particular electricity, water, waste and waste-water management. The costs of the administration of Cape Town itself represent a fifth of the budget (Figure 3.3). Expenditures for the built environment (such as housing and roads) are relatively small. As compared with Johannesburg and eThekwini (Durban), its main differences in spending patterns lie in administration and the built environment. Johannesburg spends relatively more on administration and less on the built environment; whereas the proportions in eThekwini (Durban) are reversed. The capital expenditure of Cape Town is above the municipal average for road and bridge construction; and lower on water reservoirs (Table 3.3).[6] There is some variety with regards to expenditure categories of municipalities in the Cape Town city-region (Figure 3.4).

Figure 3.3. **Main expenditures of the metropolitan municipality of Cape Town**

(2006)

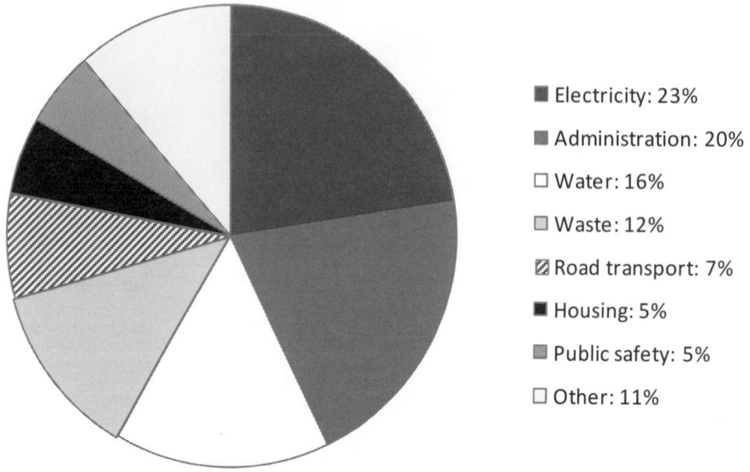

Electricity: 23%
Administration: 20%
Water: 16%
Waste: 12%
Road transport: 7%
Housing: 5%
Public safety: 5%
Other: 11%

Source: National Treasury database.

Figure 3.4. **Expenditure categories in selected municipalities in Cape Town city-region**

(Budgets 2008)

100%
90%
80%
70%
60%
50%
40%
30%
20%
10%
0%
Cape Town
Swartland
Overstrand
Theewaterskloof
Saldanha Bay
Other
Road transport
Waste
Water
Administration
Electricity

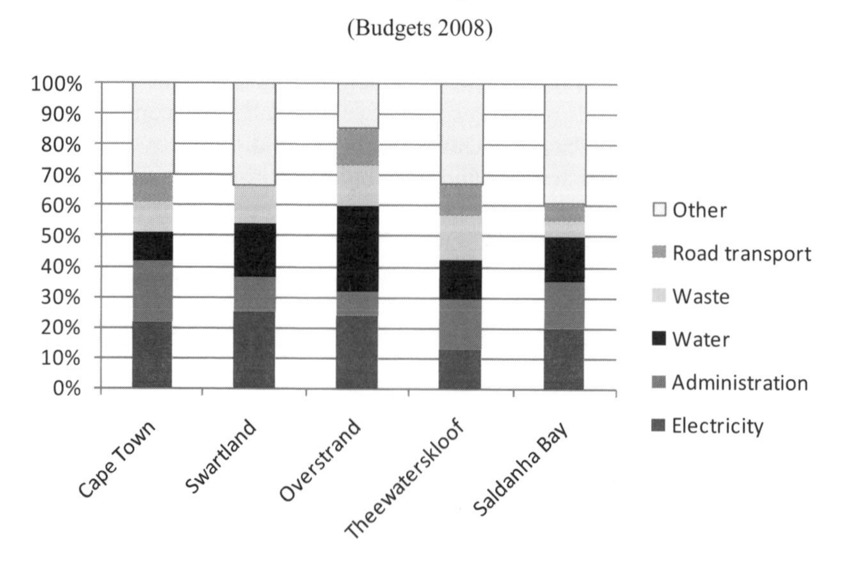

Source: Budgets 2008/2009 of Municipalities of Cape Town, Swartland, Overstrand, Theewaterskloof and Saldana Bay.

Cape Town, as well as Johannesburg and eThekwini (Durban), spend relatively little funds on economic development (Figure 3.5). Some of the municipalities in the Cape Town Functional Region score low on capital expenditure: in a sample of 27 South African Municipalities, both Drakenstein and Saldanha Bay scored below the average. The Minister of Finance is empowered to impose an upper limit on the percentage growth of total municipal expenditure each year, which is achieved through a circular issued by the National Treasury. This budget cap aims at curbing excessive spending, with limited equitable outcomes. Although smaller municipalities might thus be prevented from additional strategic policy interventions, it does not really affect the autonomy of metropolitan municipalities, as they can usually reprioritise expenditures within their budgets.

Figure 3.5. **Expenditure categories in selected South African metropolitan areas**

(Rands per inhabitant, 2005)

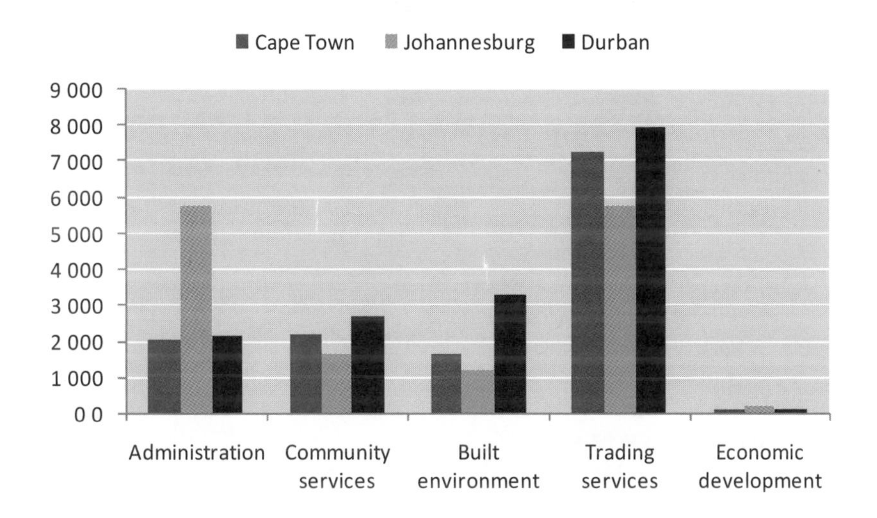

Source: Annual financial statements of the three municipalities, 2005/6 and 2006/7.

Revenue sources

The share of sub-national tax revenues is average from an OECD perspective. Whereas half of government expenditures in South Africa were committed by sub-national governments, only a fifth of total tax revenues are actually generated by sub-national governments. There is thus a vertical funding gap in South Africa, as is the case in all OECD countries. The level of sub-national tax revenues compares to the average in OECD countries (Figure 3.6). A sharp difference between the position of provinces and municipalities, however, distinguishes South Africa.

Figure 3.6. **Sub-national tax revenues of OECD countries and South Africa**

(as share of total government tax revenues in 2006)

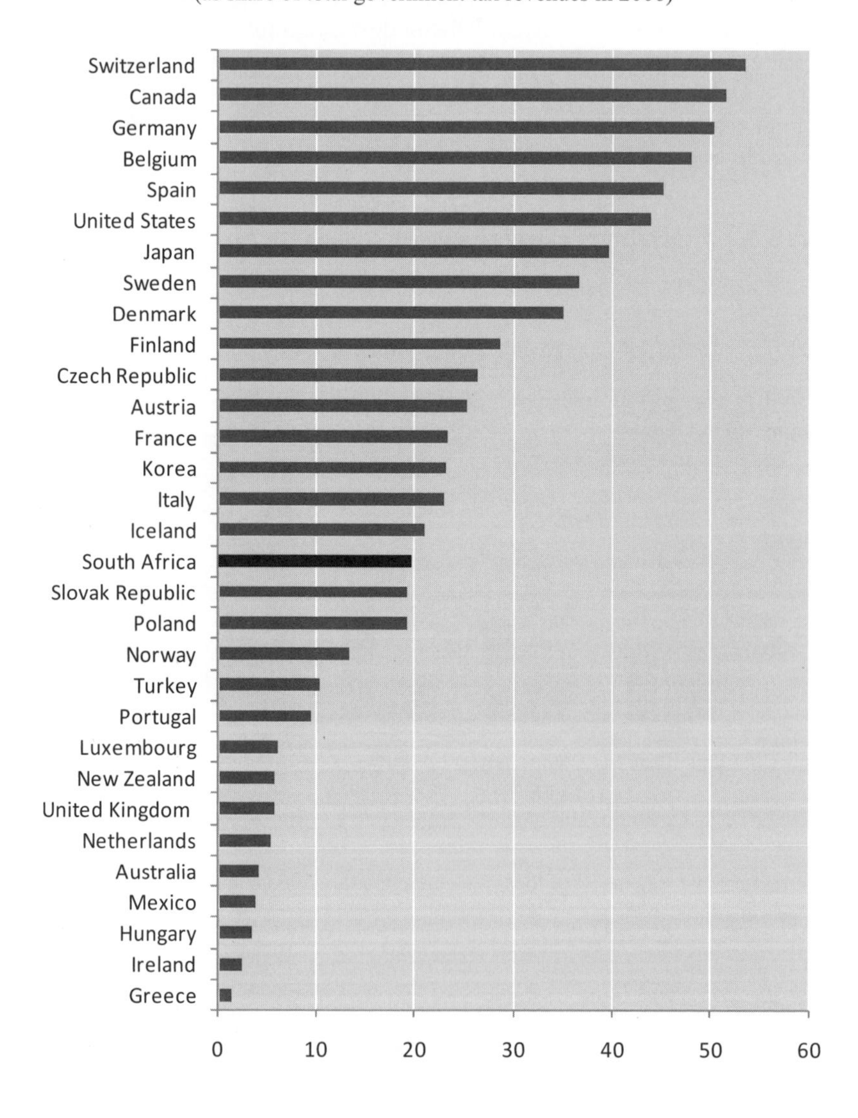

Source: OECD Revenue Statistics Database.

Provinces are mainly financed by grants; their own tax revenues are very small, and they have to deal with a centrally administered fiscal regime. More than 95% of provincial income in South Africa comes from grants (Figure 3.7). By far the most important grant is the general grant, called the "equitable share" in South Africa. Around 15% of provincial revenues come from several conditional grants; there are at least 15 of these conditional grants, in areas such as agriculture, education, health, infrastructure and sports (National Treasury 2007a). The province of Western Cape is less dependent on the equitable share than other provinces in South Africa: it provides 71% of its revenues, against 81% for the average province in South Africa.

Figure 3.7. **Main revenue sources of the province of Western Cape**

(2006)

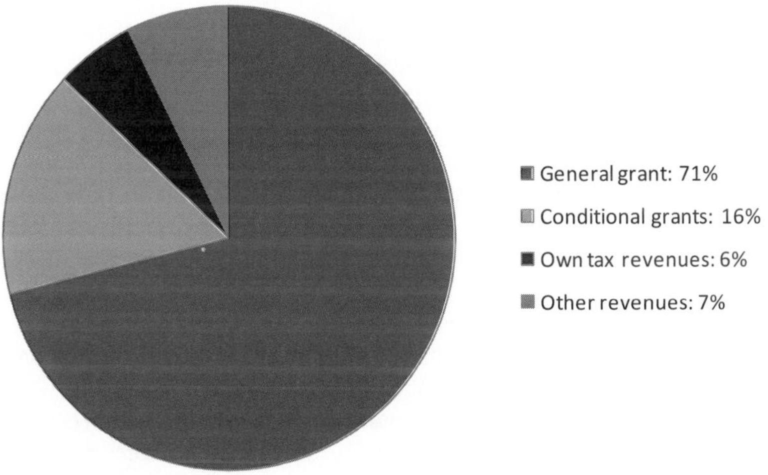

General grant: 71%
Conditional grants: 16%
Own tax revenues: 6%
Other revenues: 7%

Source: National Treasury database.

The allocation of the provincial equitable share is formula-based, taking into account the service for which provinces are responsible. As a result of the negotiated Constitution, national revenue to provinces was allocated according to historical allocations. In an attempt to introduce geographical equity, the Finance and Fiscal Commission designed a formula to redress historical disadvantages. This formula for the equitable share uses criteria such as population, school population, proportion of the population with and without access to medical aid, and components to address backlogs in infrastructure and provision of services. The formula is reviewed and updated every year, taking into account recommendations of the Financial and Fiscal Commission (Robinson, 2007). The introduction of the *Medium Term Budget Policy Statement* (MTBPS) at the national level has improved the predictability of provincial revenue: published annually, the MTBPS states the government's aggregate revenue and expenditure intentions over the next three years, including indicative figures on the division of revenue among provincial governments. Conditional grants are, in contrast with the equitable share, often allocated on an *ad hoc* and discretionary basis. Even if they are phased out, they tend to resurface in another form in later years (FFC 2006). Several provinces do not have the capacity to spend their grants. This was for example the case in 2002/3, when only 76% of the budgeted Housing Subsidy Grants for provinces were spent. Spending capacity of provinces seems to have improved over the last years. The province of Western Cape has usually been able to spend the budgeted grants (as well as the mentioned Housing Subsidy Grant) (Ajam and Aron, 2007).

Provinces are in principle allowed to impose taxes. The Provincial Tax Regulation Process Act of 2001 has added opportunity for increasing provincial revenues. The taxes that provinces can impose are all those other than income tax, VAT, sales tax, rates on property and customs duties. Provinces can, in addition, levy flat-rate surcharges on any tax base, except on those areas mentioned. However, provinces make little use of these possibilities. The four major sources of self-generated provincial revenues are casino licences, motor vehicle licences, sale of non-capital goods and interest income. The province of Western Cape collects a quarter of total provincial tax revenues, being the second-largest collector after the province of Gauteng. In addition, the province of Western Cape scores highest on the provincial average collection of motor vehicle licences. The Western Cape is also known to make use of its freedom to change tax rates and has been the only province to submit a proposal to increase provincial own revenues by introducing a new tax, a fuel levy (Khumalo *et al.,* 2006; Robinson, 2007). The potential revenue generated by this new levy would amount to ZAR 1.6 billion, but part of these revenues might be offset by lower income taxes, due to negative economic effects of the levy (McDonald *et al.,* 2006). This tax, however, has not been introduced: in the 2008 national budget a slice of the national fuel levy was instead allocated to provinces based on their share of economic activity.

The City of Cape Town collects a large share of its revenue through its own taxation and fee collection. Revenue mainly derives from property tax and fees and charges for services such as electricity, water and sanitation (Figure 3.8). Around 20% of the budget of the City of Cape Town is currently financed by grants; due to exceptional circumstances, this share is higher than usually is the case for Cape Town.[7] This is 25% for the average municipality in South Africa, but there is much variation: some rural municipalities depend almost completely on national government grants. The composition of revenues in the metropolitan municipality of Cape Town does not differ much from those of the other municipalities in Western Cape. Cape Town is slightly less dependent on grants and fees and has a little more revenues from the property tax. There is a difference between the average municipality in Western Cape and South Africa: those in Western Cape are considerably less dependent on grants and fees.

Figure 3.8. **Main revenue sources of the metropolitan municipality of Cape Town** (2006)

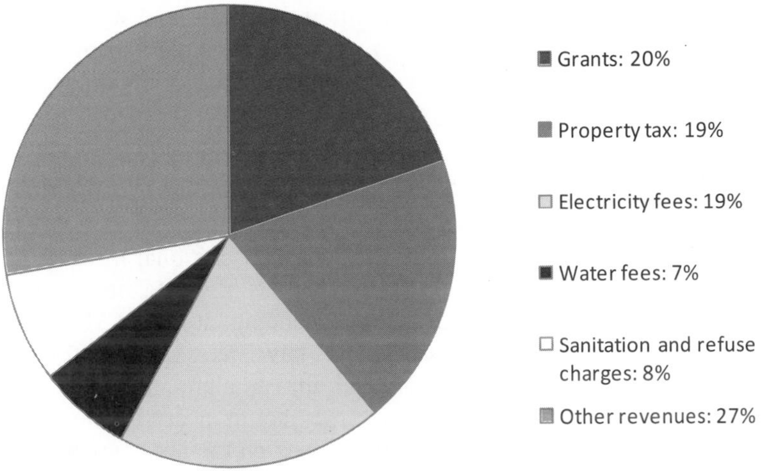

Grants: 20%
Property tax: 19%
Electricity fees: 19%
Water fees: 7%
Sanitation and refuse charges: 8%
Other revenues: 27%

Source: National Treasury database.

The main municipal tax consists of the property tax. This is a tax on the market value of land and the improvements of a property. There is a uniform valuation method and a uniform set of procedures for appeals and rate-setting. Municipalities have the right to set their own rates. The property tax does not apply to the large proportion of property that is illegal or unregistered with municipalities. More uniformity and a broadening of the tax base were achieved by the Municipal Property Rating Act of 2004. Even before this reform, the intensity of the use of the property tax in South Africa was large from an international perspective. The share of property tax revenues as a percentage of GDP in 1995 was comparable to that in industrialised countries and much larger than would have been predicted (Bahl, 2001). Municipalities used to have a local business tax, the Regional Services Council (RSC) levy that was recently abolished.[8]

The general grant (equitable share) for municipalities is guided by design principles similar to the one for provinces: a grant allocated by a predetermined formula. Evidently, the formula for municipalities is different from the one for provinces, as they have different functions and thus different costs to be taken into account. Another difference is that the formula for municipalities takes more account of revenue-raising capacity: as municipalities have more own resources than provinces, there is more need to compensate for these differences. Other important grants are the infrastructure grants, one of which is the 2010 FIFA World Cup Stadiums Development Grant, which provides a vehicle for national funding of stadiums, transport systems, such as airports, railways and stations. As local capacity continues to be a concern, the national government decided to develop municipal capacity by providing capacity-building transfers. ZAR 1.4 billion has been made available to modernise local government budgeting and financial management systems and to improve compliance with national government regulations on financial management (Republic of South Africa, 2007*b*).

The 2010 FIFA World Cup has channelled additional national funding into the City of Cape Town. The World Cup has triggered significant public investment over and above normal grant spending; at least ZAR 5 billion in national funds, which may otherwise not have been spent in the Western Cape, has thus far been invested in local infrastructure and facilities. Mega-events, such as those in Cape Town, may act as a catalyst to secure the public consensus on putting these investments on the fast track by attaching first priority to public expenditure programmes. In addition, mega-events increasingly function as key international governance regimes for the dissemination of current expressions of universal world views, such as human rights, civil equality and environmentalism. However, though the FIFA World Cup represents an opportunity for the development of the Cape Town city-region, it could also turn into a threat. Local and regional authorities need to reduce the environmental impact of the event as much as possible (Matheson, 2006), evenly distribute the economic advantages and pay particular attention to the economic sustainability of the total investment. A primary challenge is in fact that of avoiding a misfit between the structure of the destination and the structure of the event in terms of size, infrastructure and interest or attitude of the local population (Hall and Hodges, 1996).[9] New facilities and infrastructure should be well integrated into the structure of the city-region and constitute a built legacy that citizens may use for the long term once the event is over.

Metropolitan municipalities, including Cape Town, can borrow substantial amounts of money. Municipalities are allowed to borrow for capital expenditure. National guarantees for municipal loans are obliged. The national government does not establish municipal credit limits. Loans to finance current expenditure are allowed on the condition that they are repaid within 12 months. The municipal borrowing market is dominated by two institutions: the Development Bank of Southern Africa (DBSA), a public sector lender, and the Infrastructure Finance Corporation (INCA), a private sector lender. The outstanding debt of the city of Cape Town was ZAR 2.2 billion; this represents 13% of its revenues and ZAR 2 888 per household. The relative debt levels of Johannesburg and eThekwini (Durban) as of June 2007 were twice as high. Provinces do not have the possibility to borrow.

Fiscal equalisation

Fiscal equalisation in South Africa mainly takes place via the equitable share. The allocation criteria aim at providing the possibilities to provincial and local governments to provide comparable levels of public services. In addition, various conditional grants programmes provide additional resources to sub-national governments, each with their respective allocation criteria. The local equitable share is negotiated through the South African Local Government Association (SALGA). The allocation of the provincial equitable share has mixed consequences for Western Cape: although it is the province with the highest public health expenditure per capita, it has one of the lowest expenditures per capita on education. Although regional disparities in funding were reduced, this does not seem to have influenced the variability of educational outcomes across provinces. Additional fiscal resources seem to have made only a limited contribution to improving educational outcomes (Ajam and Aron, 2007). One of the challenges is the lack of regional specificity in their application, which may explain the less regionally differentiated outcomes, given the limited scope for regional intervention.

The local equitable share is understood to incorporate redistribution, because it channels much of the grants to smaller and poorer municipalities, which often happen to be rural municipalities. The average per capita grant for municipalities with less than 10 000 inhabitants is for example ZAR 381, more than twice the amount of the average per capita grant for large municipalities (those with more than 500 000 inhabitants). These large municipalities receive 38.4% of the total local equitable share, while accounting for 41% of the national population. The allocation formula of the equitable share takes account of poverty: it distinguishes between poor households provided with service and those provided with lesser or no services, and recognises water, electricity and sanitation as core services municipalities are mandated to provide. The service costs for poor households in the formula are set at ZAR 130 per month (Amusa *et al.*, 2006).

Financial accountability

The medium-term budget process in provincial and local government has expanded the information available on financial and service delivery performance. Mid-year performance assessment reports are now being generated by municipalities, and it is likely that this will lead to a greater emphasis on performance and financial monitoring in future. The Municipal Financial Management Act (2003) requires municipalities to develop Service Delivery and Budget Improvement Plans that seek to strengthen the alignment between Integrated Development Plans, multi-year budgets and the detailed spending plans of municipalities. As this requirement has only recently been introduced, it is likely to take some time to mature.

The National Treasury plays a key role in the monitoring of financial performance in the Western Cape Province and its large municipalities (Cape Town and Stellenbosch).[10] Budget data, including information on revenues, expenditures and debt, is evaluated annually, and revenue and expenditure performance is collected, analysed and published quarterly[11]. The Provincial Treasury has the delegated authority to monitor the budgets of all other municipalities, with the same periodicity, and this is also consolidated (and now published) on a national basis. The Provincial Treasury has recently expanded its capacity to engage municipalities on fiscal challenges and choices in the course of their budget processes. Annual reports are now constructed by the Provincial Treasury and used as the basis for regular reviews and discussion with municipalities. In addition to this monitoring, the National and Provincial Treasuries also monitor all intergovernmental transfer programmes on a monthly basis. The National Treasury, in conjunction with the South African Reserve Bank, also monitors municipal borrowing, through a quarterly survey of lenders. These monitoring systems generate significant amounts of unaudited financial information that are increasingly becoming publicly available.

The annual audits conducted by the Auditor-General and the electoral process comprise external accountability for provinces and municipalities. Provincial and local governments conduct regular consultation exercises with citizens to determine needs and preferences, and these theoretically translate into strategies and expenditure plans whose progress is monitored through ward committees and performance audit committees. Most municipalities now regularly prepare expanded annual reports, including their financial statements, which has begun to provide an avalanche of (often unstructured) information to the public. Delays in the submission of financial statements and the finalisation of audit reports have been frequent. The Auditor-General is actively addressing these issues, as these delays can undermine public accountability and may prevent a direct translation of findings into mitigating actions. Audits are largely compliance focused, but performance audits in the future have been discussed. Various accountability instruments, such as audits, participatory planning, disclosure requirements and performance improvement programmes, do not seem to be linked up.

3.2. Intergovernmental collaboration and regional planning

Streamlining intergovernmental relationships

Intergovernmental co-ordination is essential for service provision in any metropolitan area. Due to the complex nature of many public services, in almost all OECD countries, several government tiers are involved in the regulation, provision and oversight of public services. This calls for intergovernmental co-ordination, so that duplications or contradictions do not arise. Due to the fact that the functional metropolitan areas usually span different municipalities and that there are inter-jurisdictional spillovers, some form of metropolitan co-ordination is required. This is particularly needed to make sure that sectoral policies within a government tier are linked up, or at least not contradictory. This section looks at the metropolitan governance and intergovernmental relations in the Cape Town city-region, the mechanisms that are in place, their effectiveness and improvements that could be made.

Vertical intergovernmental co-ordination

Legal ambiguity obscures which government tier in South Africa is responsible for government functions. One of the causes of this problem lies in the phrasing of the Municipal Structure Act (1998), which leaves room for interpretation. The Act often delegates responsibility to the municipality unless it has a broader regional effect, in which a higher level of government, such as the district municipal level, is called for.[12] This ambiguity impedes regional economic development, including critical infrastructure investment (national, provincial, local and parastatals), industrial policy and investment promotion. This lack of clarity on concurrency feeds into the budget process, reducing not only effectiveness and impact, but the amount of resources that are allocated and spent across the spheres for interventions intended to enhance regional or spatial economic growth and competitiveness.

The concurrency of responsibility across spheres of government, combined with numerous overlapping functions, create points of confusion that necessitate intergovernmental co-operation, particularly those where a provincial functional area includes or encompasses a local functional area (Table 3.2). The Municipal Systems Act (2000) attempted to clarify the allocation of powers and functions to local government through the assignment of special delegation powers, but did not provide a completely unambiguous allocation of responsibilities over government tiers (van Donk and Pieterse, 2006). This has been exacerbated by other laws where the definition of responsibilities of district municipalities intrudes upon the tasks assigned to local municipalities. The National Health Act of 2003 illustrates such a case. It allocates to the district government a supervisory role over water-quality monitoring, food control, waste management, health surveillance of premises, environmental pollution control and disposal of the dead. In so doing, it produces overlaps with the Municipal Structure Act, which ascribes the following functions to local municipalities: "potable water supply systems", "licensing and control of undertakings that sell food to the public", "solid waste disposal sites", "markets", "air pollution", "noise pollution", "refuse removal", "facilities for the accommodation, care and burial of animals", and "local cemeteries" (Steytler and Fessha, 2005). Given comparable examples throughout government, the Human Sciences Research Council concluded, "[t]here is confusion whether or not municipalities have the authority to perform a function. In some cases municipalities are simply not sure whether they have the authority at all, even when they actually do perform some activities."

Table 3.2. **Overlaps in municipal and provincial policy areas per the Constitution**

Embedded local functional area	Provincial functional area
Air pollution	Pollution control, environment
Beaches and amusement facilities	Environment
Billboards and display of advertisements in public places	Environment
Building regulations	Provincial cultural matters
Child care facilities	Health services
Cemeteries, funeral parlours and crematoria	Health services
Control of undertakings that sell liquor to the public	Liquor licences
Facilities for the accommodation, care and burial of animals	Animal control and diseases
Fencing and fences	Provincial roads, agriculture
Firefighting services	Disaster management
Licensing of dogs	Animal control and diseases
Licensing and control of undertakings that sell food to the public	Consumer protection, health services
Local sport facilities	Provincial sport
Markets	Agriculture
Municipal parks and recreation	Nature conservation
Municipal planning	Regional planning, urban and rural development
Noise pollution	Environment, Pollution control
Pontoons, ferries, jetties, piers, harbours	Environment
Pounds	Animal control and diseases
Refuse removal, refuse dumps and solid waste disposal	Environment, health services
Street trading	Trade
Trading regulations	Trade
Traffic and parking	Road traffic regulation

Source: Steytler and Fessha (2005), based on the Constitution of the Republic of South Africa (1996).

Vaguely defined concurrent mandates can compromise the delivery of key services throughout the Cape Town city-region. First, citizens may receive a poorer level of service if there is confusion over respective mandates and responsibilities; even worse, services may not be delivered if financially stressed governments blame the other level of government for failure to deliver services. A similar scenario occurs with road maintenance, given the uncertainty about responsibility for particular roads. Uncertainty may also generate perceptions of "unfunded services". This question is particularly acute in the Western Cape, where municipalities alleged that they performed 29 functions on behalf of the provincial government (Western Cape Provincial Treasury, 2005). In sum, "[w]hile the extent of the 'unfunded mandates' is contested, it nevertheless indicates that where uncertainty prevails, a municipality may easily find itself in a situation where it provides a much-needed service that, legally speaking, does not fall in its domain. Without sufficient funds [or an unwillingness to use its taxing powers] an inadequate service may be the result" (Steytler and Fessha,

2005). In other instances, political disputes may hamper intergovernmental co-ordination even if a clear mandate and definition are provided.

Future initiatives should be informed by serious evaluation of mechanisms established in previous attempts for co-ordination. A wide range of intergovernmental platforms has been launched in the Cape Town city-region, such as the Premier's Metro Co-ordination Forum (PMCF), Provincial Co-ordination Forums (PCF), District Advisory Forums (DAF), and Integrated Development Planning Committees. Traditionally, these forums, especially the PCF, have facilitated relationships between the two spheres of government and disseminated knowledge from the Provincial Government of the Western Cape to municipalities and vice versa (Smith, 2001). Other initiatives, such as the District Advisory Forum, established provincial monitoring and enhanced capacity of local government to achieve their functions. Meetings networked local government officials: municipal authorities frequently provided detailed information about the current challenges of implementation, while provincial authorities offered their expertise on strategic and aggregate matters. Often the participation in meetings required institutions to create technical bodies that addressed particular areas of concern, *e.g.* the Chief Financial Officers Forum, District Youth Forum, Public Transport Technical and Steering Committee, and the Disaster Management Forum. Nevertheless, monitoring of the effectiveness of these forums is scant. Future evaluations are needed to analyse the level of participation, membership, frequency of meetings, quality of technical support, and the ability to improve service delivery (Steytler *et al.*, 2005). Given that few of these forums contain established dispute resolution mechanisms, additional studies should clarify which conflict management tools could be adopted.

Despite political attention, effective intergovernmental co-operation still suffers from several barriers, particularly with housing delivery and land management. The Constitution foresees "co-operative governance" based on co-operation between the levels of government that are interdependent. President Thabo Mbeki's State of the Union speech in 2006 stressed the need for integration of planning and implementation across government spheres.[13] However, despite this political attention to greater co-ordination, the results have been limited in practice. The paucity of intergovernmental co-operation has produced project delays, especially in land development, where inconsistent regulations and inter-jurisdictional conflicts have increased fees and transaction costs in projects. For example, the N2 Gateway project, which intended to demonstrate an intergovernmental community consultation for rapid, high-density housing delivery, has been bogged down in problems ranging from delays, inadequate community consultation, cost overruns, inadequate construction materials, and contestation between the City of Cape Town and the National Housing Department over defining the beneficiaries of this project. Outside of this project, budgets and responsibilities on housing are often not aligned: various housing delivery functions are provided by local government, while funding flows from the provincial government, which is supposed to maintain an overview of housing delivery, including its location in appropriate and well-located areas. Likewise, land reform budgets rest with the national government, whereas decisions on most land reform programmes have been decentralised to the provincial directors of the Department of Land Affairs (Berrisford *et al.*, 2008). Tensions here relate to the fact that Land Affairs is primarily concerned with historical land claims and restitution, whereas agricultural departments in provincial governments are also concerned with providing water rights, economic opportunities and ensuring access to markets, among other issues.

The use of different budget and planning cycles between municipalities and provinces complicates timing and synergy. As provincial and municipal public officials represent two different public services, they are under no mandate to synchronise their cycles or co-ordinate their budgetary processes. Funds often take time to "flow", and the use of different financial years makes timing between the Province and municipalities all the more difficult. Though the Municipal Finance Management Act (2003) stipulates that South African municipalities begin their financial year on 1 July, it does not provide guidelines for co-ordinating budgets with Provinces.[14] Limited intergovernmental co-ordination reduces the efficacy of IDPs, as underscored by the IDP Hearings in 2005, which encouraged tests for intergovernmental alignment. This incongruence reduces synergy between the provincial and municipal levels of government and produces few moments of confluence. A discussion is ongoing on the future of provincial and local government in South Africa, which will be the subject of a forthcoming White Paper from the national Department of Provincial and Local Government. Intergovernmental co-ordination will play a key role in this debate.

Horizontal intergovernmental co-ordination

In any metropolitan area, there is a need for metropolitan governance. Administrative boundaries of municipalities hardly ever coincide with functional metropolitan areas. This is of particular importance for networks that need interconnection, such as transport networks. In addition, inter-jurisdictional spillovers and externalities make co-ordination necessary to prevent over- or under-provision of certain services. This is also the case in Cape Town: the functional area is larger than the city boundaries, and co-ordination will be needed to provide effective public services.

National legislation in some sectors provides a framework for intergovernmental co-operation, but this is not always successfully invoked and executed, particularly with respect to the management of the built environment in the Cape Town city-region. There are a number of reasons for the disjuncture between local, provincial and national allocation of powers. The Constitution explicitly required spheres of government to tackle the same problems from different angles. The issues of concurrency, unfunded mandates and unclear roles and responsibilities between the three spheres of government call for a review of legislation and the Constitution to clarify the assignation of powers and delegations that have been conferred on as many as three spheres of government. Whereas the design of the system may also have assumed more capacity in all three spheres of government, a review is certainly necessary.

The creation of a new regional planning institution would greatly improve the co-ordination of regional development. Given that different sectors – land use planning, housing, and economic development – are intrinsically connected to the spatial economy, a cross-sectoral body would offer paramount coherence. This would not itself have financial resources, but would allow its delegates the decision-making power to co-ordinate their separate investments in issues that affect the region, such as housing. Representatives from the national, provincial, and municipal government would sit at its table and be given enforcement powers through a formal, legally binding tripartite agreement framed in legislation, complete with a mandate and an accountability framework to measure progress towards the achievement of commonly defined outcomes. Central to this mandate would be the sole responsibility to oversee/monitor implementation of all spatial/transport/development plans currently in existence for the Cape Town city-region and to report these results to legislatures and citizens. This regional authority would also have the capacity to create a regional transportation or regional economic development agency if its members agreed. Through this development, channels of communication between municipalities and the national government could be improved. Municipalities stand to benefit from an institutionalised, ongoing opportunity to influence policy, planning and investment decisions on matters that affect them but over which they do not have jurisdiction. This would not only institutionalise a co-operative approach to addressing the nexus of issues governing housing, transport/transit and land use, but lead to their depoliticisation. The Vancouver Agreement was structured along these lines and may provide useful reference for governance reform in the Cape Town city-region (Box 3.2).

Box 3.2. **The Vancouver Trilateral Agreement**

The Vancouver Agreement (VA) is an urban development initiative that promotes partnerships within and between governments, community organisations and business to make the city a healthy, safe and economically and socially sustainable place in which to live and work for all residents. The agreement was negotiated between the governments of Canada, British Columbia, and the City of Vancouver, signed by the representatives of the three governments in March 2000 for a five-year term and recently renewed to March 2010. The Agreement was a response to a public health emergency in the city's Downtown Eastside, caused by drug-overdose deaths and epidemic rates of HIV infection, throughout the mid-1990s. By 1999, this part of Vancouver had deteriorated to the extent that 61% of Vancouver's drug related arrests and 18% of the city's crimes against persons took place there, even though it comprised only 3% of the city's total population. Before the Agreement was initiated in 2000, each level of government had some jurisdiction over issues central to the creation of the VA: economic development, employment, social housing, HIV/AIDS treatment, drug rehabilitation and policing. While each level of government provided different services directed at the same people, issues were addressed separately with little collaboration.

While collaboration between various levels of government in Canada is not unique, the Vancouver Agreement led to new and innovative partnerships not only between, but within the three levels of government. This therefore involved not only vertical collaboration, but also horizontal co-ordination. In other words, responsibility centres within each level of government co-ordinate their activities. Each tier of government had to harmonise its own programs, planning and service delivery structures to ensure that together, the three partner governments could work toward the achievement of commonly defined policy outcomes. Collaboration between the government partners is facilitated by regular meetings at a number of levels, from elected officials to a working group of mid-public servants. The main governance body of the VA is the Governance Committee and the Management Committee. Supporting these committees is a small secretariat, comprised of an Executive Co-ordinator and staff dedicated to administration, communications, and evaluation, and overseeing of the day-to-day work of the Vancouver Agreement.

As an urban development agreement designed to co-ordinate the work of three governments, the Vancouver Agreement has had many successes. It has succeeded in forging shared objectives and in helping to correlate multiple agencies in a common effort to deal with multi-faceted challenges. Indeed, improving the health and quality of life of Downtown Eastside residents was a significant catalyst for creation of the Vancouver Agreement. Health-related projects and initiatives supported by the Vancouver Agreement have led to reduction of death rates due to alcohol and drug use, alcohol and drug overdoses, HIV/AIDS and suicides. Moreover, addiction-related issues, which also affect other aspects of community life like safety and security and economic revitalisation, are being addressed with a range of services and initiatives.

Since its inception, the Vancouver Agreement has also supported various economic development and employment initiatives, which achieve business and social goals in the Downtown Eastside. Economic revitalisation and employment-related projects and initiatives to date have shown increased development confidence and a changing economic climate in the inner city. Lastly, enforcement-related projects and initiatives have contributed to increased safety and security, but equally important, have improved the physical appearance of the community, making it more attractive and inviting for residents and visitors.

A metropolitan umbrella organisation could have the capacity to provide co-ordination in regional transportation, environmental or economic development bodies, if its members agreed. These agencies, in turn, would receive a seat at the table of the regional co-ordinating body. In terms of transportation, consensus has been reached on the importance of a more efficient system in Cape Town but a regional transportation body has not been established. Significant institutional designs have been crafted in several OECD metropolitan areas, such as in Frankfurt or Chicago that may offer resonance in forging sub-regional consensus on transportation challenges. They could also pursue the creation of regional environmental governance institutions and economic development agencies, such as the models of Helsinki's Metropolitan Area Council and Milan's "Metropoli" agency, discussed in Chapter 2. Another option would include the strengthening of existing structures and the reinforcement of promising experimentation.

Consensus has been reached on the importance of a more efficient transport system in Cape Town, but a regional transportation body has yet to be formed. The *iKapa Growth and Development Strategy* (2008) identified transportation as one of the three most important path-breaking interventions for government. This priority was echoed in City and District IDPs.[15] Early efforts to confront the fragmentation of public transit across the region culminated in the establishment of an Intergovernmental Transport Steering Committee on transportation issues between the Province of the Western Cape, the City of Cape Town, and the National Department of Transport, together with the South African Rail Commuter Corporation. Currently, the Province of the Western Cape is seeking the adoption by the Provincial Cabinet of legislation of a Public Transport Operating Entity. This would include the aforementioned actors plus the district municipalities, to ensure aligned planning between spheres of government (Provincial Government of the Western Cape, 2007*a*). The City of Cape Town contests this design, arguing that the Constitution, the National Land Transport Transition Amendment Bill and the Cabinet's National Public Transport Strategy vest responsibilities for transport in municipalities if it falls within municipal boundaries.[16] The City of Cape Town also bases its interpretation on forthcoming legislation that stipulates that the City would be derelict in fulfilling its mandate if it were to "delegate" its duty to provide municipal transport to the Provincial Government. Consequently, the City seeks to create a transportation authority charged with integrating activities among both public and private transport operators within only the City. Neither of these two options has been adopted so far, and in the meantime, public transport remains highly fragmented, with no co-ordination of the fare systems between each mode. Significant institutional designs have been crafted, such as in Chicago or Frankfurt, that may offer resonance in the Cape Town city-region (Box 3.3).

Box 3.3. **Regional Transportation Authorities in Chicago and Frankfurt**

The Regional Transportation Authority (RTA) operates as the second-largest public transportation system in North America, providing financial oversight and regional planning for the three public transit operators in northeastern Illinois: the Chicago Transit Authority (CTA), Metra commuter rail and Pace suburban bus. Created in 1974 as a special-purpose unit of local government and a municipal corporation of the state of Illinois, it provides more than 2 million rides daily and oversees assets valued at more than USD 27 billion. The origins of RTA can be traced to 1974, when residents of six counties in northeastern Illinois – Cook, DuPage, Kane, Lake, McHenry and Will – approved its creation in a referendum.

In terms of governance, the RTA's Board of Directors provides oversight responsibility and approves an annual budget and two-year financial plan. The 16-member RTA Board consists of 15 directors who are appointed from within the six-county region: five directors by the Mayor of the City of Chicago; four directors by the suburban members of the Cook County Board; one director by the President of the Cook County Board (from Suburban Cook County); and one director each from DuPage, Kane, Lake, McHenry and Will counties, who are appointed by the Chair of their respective county board. The chair, its 16th member, is elected by at least 12 of the 16 appointed members. The RTA Board is required annually to review and approve a five-year capital plan, which is a blueprint of the capital activities to be funded by the RTA and executed by the CTA, Metra, and Pace. The levels of service, fares and operational policies are left to the discretion of the respective boards of the CTA, Metra and Pace. Currently the RTA conducts regional mobility analysis, enforces paratransit guidelines, researches intelligent transportation systems (ITS), and administers a regional discounted fare programme for senior citizens and the disabled.

The Frankfurt Rhein Main transport authority (RMV) organises the public transport in the area of Rhein Main, which comprises two-thirds of the state of Hessen. RMV also co-ordinates the regional public transport system in close co-operation with the local transport organisations. Decisions about transport facilities and tariffs are made at a political level, and the RMV and the local transport organisations implement these decisions. Transport enterprises such as the national railways or bus enterprises are answerable to the RMV through performance contracts. The 130 enterprises within the territory of the RMV are allowed independence in carrying out their contracts and achieving the required performance levels.

Although the RMV does not have its own rail network or materials, it can plan for the construction of new rail networks, stations and material. One of the priorities when the RMV was first created in 1995 was to harmonise about 100 tariff systems that existed in the area that it covered. It created one universal tariff and a single ticket that can be used on all the means of public transport, no matter how many transfers are made. The price is set depending on the number of tariff areas crossed. Every December, the schedules of regional transport in the RMV area are adjusted. The RMV informs the public about any changes in the 14 local transport systems and the one regional transport system.

Source: Regional Transportation Authority (2008).

Enhancing regional planning mechanisms

Regional priorities at both national and local levels reflect a tension between the need to balance dynamic economic growth and to redress extreme social inequality. The unresolved debate within the country as to how spatial inequities should be addressed is illustrated in the limited co-ordination in the field of regional planning. Though the publication of the *National Spatial Development Perspective* (NSDP) in 2003 sparked renewed interest in urban spatial policy, gaps in governance gaps have stalled the development of regional economic development policy. For example, conflicting growth models stymied co-ordination between the National Department of Trade and Industry and the provincial level. The *National Industrial Policy Framework* selects a relatively large number of priority sectors based on criteria concerning the importance of a specific sector within the GDP and its ability to withstand negative external factors (such as the strength of the currency), among others. However, only a minimal level of ''cross-cutting spatial logic" informs sectoral investment decisions around infrastructure, housing, transportation and land use. Through a heightened involvement, provincial government would be able to address patterns of spatially entrenched racism and exclusion by intervening with policy, strategy and implementation. This would require that provincial governments have clearly defined roles and functions and that they are appropriately resourced. For national government to achieve its shared growth and development targets, it needs a strong centre, equally strong provinces and financially robust local governments. The combination of these elements will help to improve, planning, budgeting and implementation and consequently, developmental outcomes.

The *National Spatial Development Perspective*, housed in the Presidency, provides guiding principles for settlement and regional economic development, though on a neighbourhood scale, disagreement over the location of nodes often occurs. Typically the *Spatial Development Frameworks* developed by the Province of the Western Cape and municipalities in the Cape Town city-region concur with the overarching principles outlined in the NSDP. The NSDP tracks history over the last 30 years and works on the assumption that areas with existing and demonstrated economic potential provide greater opportunities for overcoming poverty and providing livelihoods and that poor people continue to relocate to areas where opportunities exist. Recognising these agglomeration effects, the NSDP identified 26 activity corridors and nodes linked to the main growth centres across South Africa (Figure 3.9). Nevertheless, on the micro scale, agreement around the location of nodes, the development of corridors and other specific planning issues are often contested or left unresolved. Given the autonomy of local government and the absence of delegated authority, any attempts to pursue an agreed line of action by one party can be checked by the independence of the spheres of government.

The NSDP calls for government to ensure that policies and investment spending target economically vibrant areas to maximise growth. This view corresponds with that of many OECD countries, which have over the last decade increasingly decided to shift the focus of regional policies, abandoning their former exclusive emphasis on lagging regions in favour of promoting development, particularly in regions with high economic potential. This philosophy recognises the ongoing migration to high-growth areas. For instance, places such as Cape Town, with higher-than-average national growth rates, vigorously attract more people than areas with low growth rates. In brief, the higher the potential for economic growth, the more the location attracts the unemployed from areas with lesser potential.

Figure 3.9. **Priority areas for human resource development and minimum basic services in South Africa**

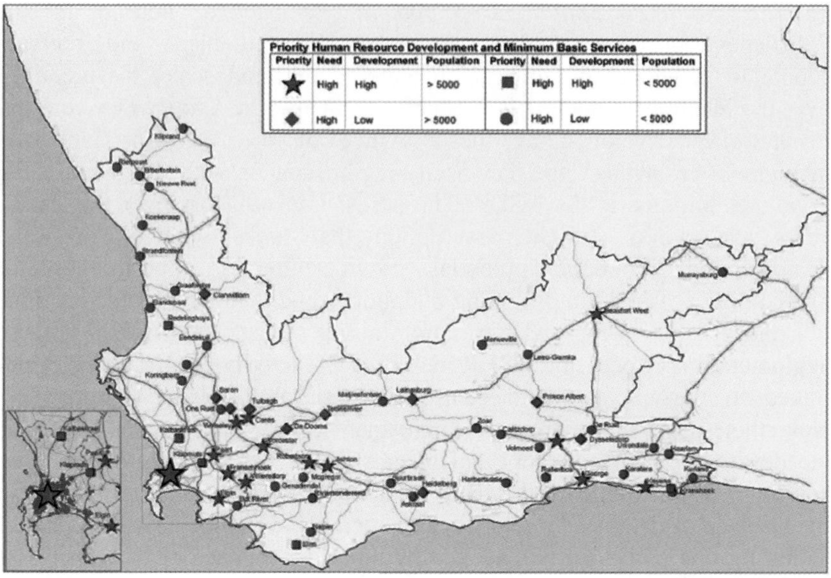

Source: National Spatial Development Perspective (2003).

The *Western Cape Provincial Spatial Development Framework* (PSDF) provides a conceptual framework for regional planning, although the absence of a budget and sanctions vis-à-vis municipalities undermines its implementation capacity. Aligned with the *National Spatial Development Perspective*, the PSDF focuses on reducing inequalities and supporting areas of economic growth or economic potential in terms of government spending on fixed investment. The PSDF favours densification, the use of urban growth boundaries ("urban edges") and mixed land use for socio-economic integration. These principles, though widely accepted by municipalities throughout the Cape Town city-region, often remain rhetorical, given that the Provincial government does not have a significant budget for economic development and is confined to an oversight role. Through various district intergovernmental forums, the Provincial Government attempts to align spatial planning, although municipalities approve their own SDFs and therefore do not legally need to be aligned with provincial policy. The co-ordination embraces the City of Cape Town's Spatial Development Framework and eight district spatial plans (Figure 3.10). Despite political tensions, there has been a high-level of engagement in the PSDF and its complementary technical meetings.

Figure 3.10. **Relationships among Spatial Planning Frameworks (SPFs)**

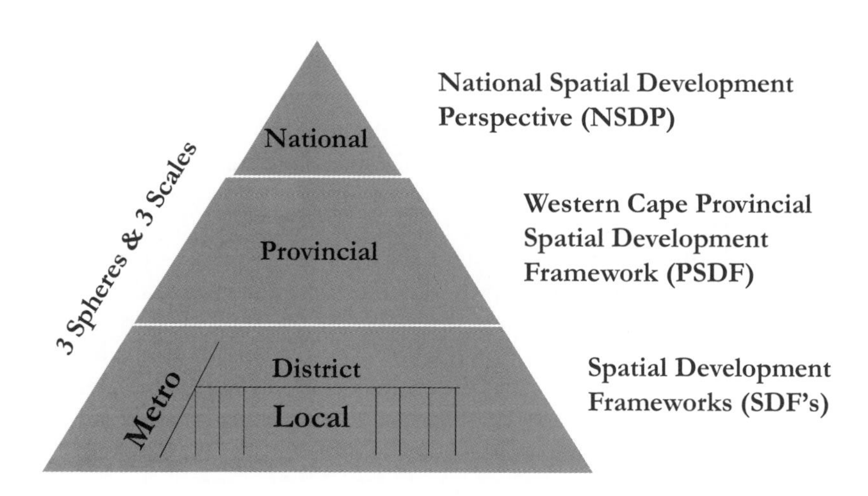

Adherence to and co-ordination among spatial development frameworks could be strengthened by additional reforms. The Western Cape Province, though a co-ordinator in the municipal development of IDPs, has been challenged to harmonise municipal plans with provincial and national thinking. Though on paper there is alignment between spatial planning frameworks at the national, provincial and local levels, at times co-ordination falls apart at the level of implementation. SDFs at the local level often reflect vested local interests, although they are required to take the *Western Cape Provincial Spatial Development Framework* and newer policy documents, such as *Isidima*, into account. Legislation will be introduced by the end of 2008 that has the potential to bolster enhanced co-operation. The Provincial Development Bill, if approved, would require that SDFs be approved as more binding "land use planning acts". This would encourage municipalities to align land use with the thinking of the provincial and national sphere. Future land development may be better guided through legislation such as this, which seeks to provide enforceable norms binding on both municipal and provincial government.

On the municipal level, governments have generally not encouraged development in the private sector to synchronise with regional planning efforts. Preoccupied with internal transformation, local authorities, including the metropolitan government of Cape Town, have not sufficiently contained or directed developer actions, either spatially or in ways that ensure greater economic cohesion, social inclusion and ecological sustainability. Although the *Isidima* policy has been launched, there is no legislated regional spatial plan for human settlements development, and little attention has been paid to the sequencing of public investment or to overall impact assessment. Zoning and other planning regulations have yet to be transformed by local authorities and the means of universal enforcement adequately institutionalised and resourced. By and large, housing in the Cape Town city-region is not embedded within or informed by, broader spatial development visions and policy agendas associated with urban and regional planning. In this sense, the measures outlined in Chapter 2 – densification, inclusionary housing, and improved land management – could empower municipalities to better regulate privately owned land, in pursuit of the collectively determined goal of a *Spatial Development Perspective*. Efforts such as the Integrated Human Settlement Co-ordination Committee show promise in minimising duplication and facilitating co-operation at all stages of planning and implementation of housing projects.[17]

3.3. Sub-national capacity

Despite ambitious recent reforms to improve the quality of staff of sub-national governments, challenges remain. In light of the national and regional trends indicating a diminishing skills pool, government as a whole is often not positioned to deliver services effectively and efficiently in all areas of service delivery. The Portfolio Committee on Provincial and Local Government (2003) noted the challenges in employing skilled officials, especially for smaller municipalities: "To attract highly skilled, efficient managers, municipalities often have to compete with high private sector salaries. Often, the municipalities most in need of highly skilled municipal managers are the smaller and rural municipalities who can least afford them. Yet to draw the requisite skills, these municipalities have to offer high salary packages in competition with the financially better-off municipalities." The transformation into a flexible, participatory and entrepreneurial civil service that the national government wants to achieve, and the increasingly strategic role of spatially oriented regional economic development policies, has undoubtedly increased the demand for new human and institutional capacity (Nel and Bins, 2002). Improved public management has been mandated by several reforms since the advent of South Africa's democracy. This has been driven by the need to reorient public administration as a "developmental" agency for the state in terms of both the objectives and outcomes (equity of access to services) and the process of administration itself (fairness and transparency in decision making). At a national level, these objectives are captured in *Batho Pele*, the national policy framework for public service reforms.

The Province of the Western Cape and the City of Cape Town each employ diverse workforces, both in gender and race, although equity improvements still need to be made at senior management levels. In the Province of the Western Cape, 65% of public servants are women, whereas in the City of Cape Town, 73% of the employees are men. Any comparison, however, should take into account to the quite different services that each level of government provides. In terms of senior management positions, 76% and 80% of senior management positions are occupied by men in the Western Cape and City of Cape Town, respectively. Coloured workers comprise the majority of the public labour force in the Provincial Government of the Western Cape (60%) and in the City of Cape Town (61%). Though African, Asian, and Indian coloured groups comprise large amounts of the provincial public work force, more than 30% of the senior management positions were occupied by white men in 2008. Likewise, in the City of Cape Town, white males occupy 47% of the senior management positions (Tables 3.3 and 3.4). From 2002 to the present, the Province and the City of Cape Town witnessed a steady increase in representation of African people and an overall decrease in the proportion of white public servants (Tables 3.5 and 3.6).

Table 3.3. **Gender and racial representativity per salary band level, Provincial Government of the Western Cape, 2008**

	African		Indian		Coloured		White		Total
Salary Band	Female	Male	Female	Male	Female	Male	Female	Male	
Lower skilled (Levels 1-2)	863	1 060	2	4	2 645	2 220	83	55	6 932
Skilled (Levels 3-5)	2 328	1 340	38	17	7 581	3 741	881	344	16 270
Highly skilled production (Levels 6-8)	5 098	2 039	161	71	14 590	6 934	5 371	1 674	35 938
Highly skilled supervision (Levels 9-12)	1 086	679	171	173	3 875	2 930	2 764	2 645	14 323
Senior management (Levels 13-16)	25	47	5	17	35	92	43	119	383
Total	9 400	5 165	377	282	28 726	15 917	9 142	4 837	73 846

Source: Provincial Government of the Western Cape (2008*c*).

Table 3.4. **Gender and racial representativity per salary band level, City of Cape Town, 2007**

	African		Indian		Coloured		White		Total
Salary Band	Female	Male	Female	Male	Female	Male	Female	Male	
Not assigned	141	284	1	2	296	748	38	62	1 572
Unskilled and defined decision making	204	1 739	1	8	498	3 627	8	36	6 121
Semi-skilled and discretionary decision making	663	1 094	9	11	1 470	4 063	475	322	8 107
Skilled technical and academically qualified workers, junior management, supervisors, foremen and superintendents	472	425	8	23	896	1 808	509	1 087	5 228
Professional qualified and experienced specialists and mid-management	52	95	3	14	133	357	172	667	1 493
Senior management	12	22	1	4	8	28	10	77	162
Top management	1					1			2
Total	1 545	3 659	23	62	3 301	10 632	1 212	2 251	22 685

Source: City of Cape Town (2007*d*).

Table 3.5. **Racial and gender representativity in the Provincial Government of the Western Cape**

(2003 and 2008)

	African		Indian		Coloured		White	
Time period	Female	Male	Female	Male	Female	Male	Female	Male
January 2003	8.77%	5.20%	0.30%	0.30%	40.50%	23.1%	13.30%	8.44%
May 2008	12.81%	7.04%	0.50%	0.36%	39.22%	21.72%	12.27%	6.08%

Source: Provincial Government of the Western Cape (2008*a*).

Table 3.6. **Racial and gender representativity in the City of Cape Town, 2002 2007**

	African		Indian		Coloured		White	
Time Period	Female	Male	Female	Male	Female	Male	Female	Male
2002	4.48%	14.60%	0.08%	0.35%	12.69%	49.42%	6.36%	12.02%
2007	6.81%	16.13%	0.10%	0.27%	14.55%	46.87%	5.34%	9.92%

Source: City of Cape Town (2002, 2007*d*).

Institutional capacity varies within the Cape Town city-region. An indication of this is given by the varying assessments made by the national government of the local capacity to achieve programme objectives. Cape Town is considered to be a high-capacity municipality, whereas other municipalities in the region get lower scores for capacity. Theewaterskloof municipality appears to be the weakest municipality in the Cape Town city-region from the national government's perspective, although Overstrand is the only municipality to have received an adverse audit opinion in 2004. If financial management capacity is measured by accuracy and timely submission of annual financial statements, the picture is hardly satisfactory. Overstrand, Saldanha Bay, Swartland and Theewaterskloof municipalities have all submitted financial statements late to the Auditor-General at least once during the 2004-05 and 2005-06 financial years. Swartland, Drakenstein, Stellenbosch and Theewaterskloof have received qualified audit opinions, and Overberg Local Municipality has received an adverse audit opinion, in the last two years.[18] In at least one instance, the Province of the Western Cape has employed powers under Section 139 of the Constitution to intervene in the affairs of a "failing" municipality.[19]

Political Context

Shifting power bases within and between political parties, as well as rapid changes in formal political control of provincial and local government structures in the Western Cape, have eroded administrative continuity in the Cape Town city-region. Unlike much of the rest of South Africa, provincial and metropolitan governments in the Western Cape are made up of different political parties. The ANC, which leads governments in the country and the Western Cape Province, does not currently hold the majority in Cape Town (Figure 3.11). This reflects in part the demographic make-up of the region. The urban Cape Coloured population, regarded by political parties as the determining vote, has shifted its support from the New National Party to a variety of parties. This has to a large extent given rise to the multi-party arrangements in the City of Cape Town. The shift away from the ANC is to some extent based on the perception that that Africans have received a preferential allocation of resources since 1994, particularly in housing policy (Hendricks, 2005).

The City of Cape Town's government, led by the Executive Mayor, is formed by the party that wins the majority of votes in municipal elections. Over the last few years, the Democratic Alliance (Figure 3.11) has not managed to win an absolute majority and has been obliged to form a coalition with other parties to form the city government. The ANC constitutes the main opposition party in Cape Town and currently commands leadership of the Provincial Government. As was previously mentioned, this configuration differs from other large metropolitan areas in South Africa, where the ANC often leads both the municipal and provincial levels. The political differences between the City of Cape Town and the Provincial Government of the Western Cape may interfere with intergovernmental co-operation and effective public service delivery, where alignment of objectives is essential. Political fluidity is further corroded by "floor-crossing", which currently allows members to change parties every two years in non-election season. This is particularly controversial because South African MPs are elected by proportional representation under the South African electoral system, which mandates that citizens vote for a political party rather than for an individual MP. Thus, "floor-crossing" may create situations where the composition of the elected bodies no longer represents the popular vote count. Given the problems of the current system, legislation to end floor-crossing has been introduced in Parliament and awaits approval.

Figure 3.11. **Political representation in the Western Cape Provincial Parliament and Cape Town City Council, 2008 (share of seats)**

Western Cape Provincial Parliament, 2008

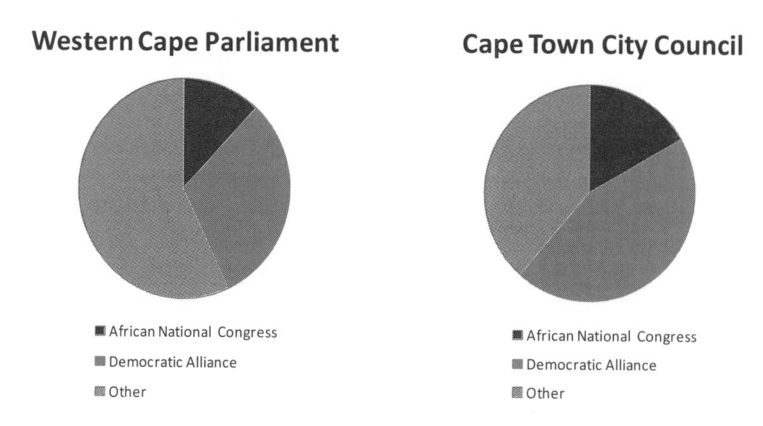

Sources: Western Cape Provincial Parliament (2008) and City of Cape Town (2008).

Staff levels and personnel management

The Cape Town city-region is endowed with a substantial public sector. Local governments in the Cape Town city-region employ around 25 500 people, amounting to 25.6 public servants per 1 000 households, a level 48% above that of the average municipality in South Africa. The size of the public service has expanded as functional responsibilities of the sub-national civil service were increased (Statistics South Africa, 2001).[20] Several new responsibilities and requirements for governance and service delivery have emerged, such as (1) participatory strategic planning at the municipal level, specifically *Integrated Development Plans*; (2) multi-year budgeting at both provincial and municipal levels; and (3) enhanced reporting requirements for local governments.[21] Unfortunately, structural reorganisation has not always been effectively co-ordinated with the introduction of new systems and procedures. This has tended to compound staff uncertainties and negatively impact the morale of personnel, who have become overwhelmed by the pace and scope of changes. However, in several municipalities, the situation seems to show signs of stabilisation. The City of Cape Town has announced that it is now a "time to invest", suggesting it may expand the scope and quality of services, particularly in roads and bulk infrastructure. Drakenstein and Stellenbosch Municipalities appear to share these emerging priorities. In other municipalities in the region, similar forward-looking strategies are emerging.

Cape Town spent less on general administration per household in 2004/5 and 2005/6 than did Johannesburg or eThekwini (Durban). At the same time, it has a larger number of civil servants per capita than those two cities. This situation is difficult to interpret. It might imply comparative state efficiency, in that less "bureaucracy" was needed to deliver key public services and public facilities. Whelan (2002) has argued that one of the main goals of post-apartheid urban policy is to force municipalities "[to] use their resources more efficiently and [to] cut expenditure that is considered unnecessary". It is possible to argue that *relative* to other large urban areas in South Africa, Cape Town is succeeding in this respect, even if its civil service is larger in per capita terms than the average municipality in South Africa. It may, however, also disguise certain capacity issues.

Although public servants enjoy a high degree of lateral mobility, frequent political shuffles have affected the quality of senior-level administrators. Competitive lateral movement between sectors – that is, job seekers applying to work in another department or sphere of government – is more common between the national and provincial government, which share a single public service with the same conditions of service. The municipal level does not have a single public service system, although municipalities voluntarily collaborate on employment benefits (medical and pension plans). Local government officials in bigger municipalities, including Cape Town, are paid more than national or provincial officials. Senior local administrators, however, are disproportionately affected by political transitions. Many of these positions have remained vacant for extended periods as new political leadership introduced new priorities and sought to remove the administrative leadership of their predecessors.[22] This approach has meant considerable executive turnover in many Cape Town city-region municipalities. Nevertheless, municipalities in the Cape Town city-region have fairly low vacancy rates (7.3%) in comparison with the average for metropolitan municipalities in South Africa (25.7%) (Statistics South Africa, 2001). In the Provincial Government of the Western Cape, 21.22% of the posts are vacant (Provincial Government of the Western Cape, 2008*c*).

Capacity building

Various measures have been put in place to encourage skills development for municipal, and to a lesser extent, provincial employees. All local governments are required by law to contribute 1% of their payroll towards skills development, which is channeled through the Local Government Sector Education and Training Authority, supported by SETAs (Sector Education and Training Authorities) operating in other sectors (such as Water and Energy). Municipalities are required to develop *Work Place Skills Plans* and are guaranteed to receive at least 50% of their contributions back for specific skills development programmes in their organisations. Similar legal skills development programmes exist at the provincial level, such as Western Cape's Administrative Academy at Kromme Ree.[23] Universities, exchange programmes, peer networks of city managers and institutions such as the South African Network of Cities, play a role in capacity-building initiatives, though a limited one. To date, however, the extent to which these structural reforms have led to the creation of a more developmentally oriented public administration is difficult to establish.

The National Government plays a key role in providing extensive resources for the upgrading of local institutional capacity. The National Treasury offers performance-based grant funding through the Local Government Restructuring Grant. This programme has, since 2002/03, allocated ZAR 328 million to the City of Cape Town to enable a restructuring of its fiscal and financial management. The grant is disbursed based on performance relative to improvements in pre-determined indicators of revenue, expenditure and debt and has been used to fund "high-return" priority programmes identified by the City itself. These appear to have been fairly small-scale projects that may have struggled to attract private funding, such as a new "auction storage centre", small IT investments and a quality management improvement programme. The Theewaterskloof municipality benefits from a Development Bank of Southern Africa's Siyenza Manje programme, which provides technical assistance and grants to help municipalities overcome capacity constraints in implementing infrastructure improvement programmes. The National Treasury provides advisors to selected large municipalities, and small grants to all municipalities, to assist them to implement prescribed financial management reforms. Advisors are assigned to larger municipalities (including Cape Town and Stellenbosch) for 28 to 24 months, where they work with grant-funded municipal finance personnel. The national government also provides grant funding and technical assistance for performance improvements at the provincial level. The Department of Provincial and Local Government provides support to selected municipalities through Project Consolidate and the Municipal Systems Improvement Grant.[24] No comprehensive evaluation of the skills gaps and explicit policies for staff retention seem to be in place. This is ironic in light of the ambitious hiring programmes, such as the employment equity programme. Emphasis in many of the programmes for upgrading local institutional capacity seems to be on fiscal transparency and fiscal discipline, rather than pro-active development capacity.

Several options need to be considered to improve the civil service. First, given the shortage of qualified government officials, governments need to work better with universities in establishing public service training academies, continuing education courses for project management, and integrating relevant public administration course materials into the classroom. The joint City of Cape Town-Provincial Government of the Western Cape partnership with the five regional universities that form the Cape Higher Education Consortium, to promote and facilitate skills development in the region as well as for government staff exemplifies such an approach. Partnerships with universities could also be further extended to local government, to include more extensive student internship programmes at local government offices, which would offer students experiential learning and facilitate the transfer of knowledge from universities to government. Similarly, local governments may take advantage of the expertise of academics when forming regional plans. Much could be learned, for example, from the partnership between the Municipality of Stellenbosch and the University of Stellenbosch, which have developed a plan to promote the city as a "sustainable university town" and bolster the municipality's capacity, by tapping shared intellectual capital to address the developmental needs of the region. Second, given the frequent migration of civil servants to the private sector and the technical expertise of companies in such fields as finance and technology, local government needs to continue building partnerships with such organisations as the Cape Town Regional Chamber of Commerce and Industry.[25] Third, vertical mobility between provincial levels of government and municipal levels needs to be encouraged, irrespective of whether the proposed national Single Public Service Bill passes. This would promote better collaboration and enable employers who have acquired public administration skills to shift to other spheres if they are attracted by a particular project or do not see opportunity for advancement.

3.4. Sub-national finance issues

The main urban finance issues in Cape Town will be in revenue collection, finding alternative local revenues sources and financing economic developments. These issues are connected with future developments with regards to fiscal decentralisation. The collection of fees, charges and taxes is an issue that will likely intensify; making better use of existing provincial revenue sources will remain a challenge. Alternative local revenue sources will have to be found after the phasing out of the RSC levies and re-structuring of the electricity sector. Finally, more incentives will be needed for financing of economic development, as current framework conditions do not stimulate coherent policies.

Improving revenue collection

Many municipalities, if not the City of Cape Town, have been unable to collect their own revenue sources. In several municipalities, the debtor collection period exceeds 175 days. This does not seem to be a case for the municipalities in the functional area of Cape Town (Schoeman, 2005). There are various explanations for this, from an inability to pay, poor financial management practices, poor customer relationships, poor municipal enforcement capacity and the low level of trust in local government (Fjeldstad, 2004). There are indications that the situation has improved recently: the average debt collection period for all municipalities in South Africa fell from 322 days in 2003/4 to 136 days in 2004/5 (Auditor-General, 2005). It has been suggested that, when taking into account future demographic and macro variables, the debt-ratio of municipalities will grow more than two-fold over the next decade (Schoeman, 2005). A distinction can be made between rate-generating property, largely provided by the private sector, and housing, which is financed by subsidies and for which no rate revenue is collected. This can have an impact on the bankability of municipalities; those in the Cape Town region have a relatively large share of rate-generating property, which makes a well-functioning collection service all the more important.

The implementation of the Property Rates Act of 2004 requires local capacity that many municipalities do not have, to update valuations, conduct land and property assessments and for the valuation of land improvements. The wide variations in the administrative capacity and tax structure of municipalities mean that implementation of a uniform land tax and improvements base has been slow, with urban municipalities able to effect required changes and national requirements more rapidly than other municipalities. Their lack of an encompassing national property valuation roll has wider consequences: it creates difficulties in approximating revenue-raising capacity consistently across municipalities. To overcome this, the National Treasury uses the relationship between demonstrated capacity as provided by reporting municipalities, and information from Statistics South Africa, to proxy revenue-raising capacity for all municipalities. This approach is pragmatic, but clearly second-best. The fiscal equalisation scheme would compensate better for tax capacity if the data on property tax bases were to improve.

Fees and charges for electricity, water, waste and sanitation provide a substantial part of the municipal budget, but non-payment remains a problem. These revenues are supposed to cover the costs of providing the services concerned. In some cases, such as for electricity, municipalities earn surpluses when municipal electricity distributors charge significantly more for their electricity than it costs to deliver it. However, a major financial problem for municipalities in South Africa is poor compliance and inefficient collection of these fees and charges. The accumulated debt of municipalities due to non-payment has been estimated to be ZAR 28 billion in 2005, the majority of which is owed to the six metropolitan councils, including Cape Town (Fjeldstad, 2004; Treasury, 2005).

Improving the narrow scope of provincial revenue collection would limit grant dependence of provinces. The fiscal autonomy of provinces in South Africa is limited. Fiscal federalism literature would suggest that accountability (and efficiency) of provincial expenditure could be increased by increasing the share of its expenditure financed by its own resources. At the same time, it is clear that many provinces do not make good use of current revenue sources: national frameworks leave room for provinces to introduce new taxes or raise tax rates, but only the Western Cape Province has ventured into this field, with its proposal for the fuel levy.

Different options to improve revenue collection could be considered. The national government has acknowledged that capacity at the sub-national level is problematic: it has made some grants available to improve this. As this is a process that will take time, a parallel process might be considered to improve revenue collection in more immediate terms. The national government could take over some tasks regarding property valuation and the administration and collection of certain taxes and fees; local governments would keep their right to set rates, but would not have to be concerned about the collection of these revenues. Differentiation could be made between local government units: some of them, such as the City of Cape Town, certainly seem to be more advanced than several other municipalities. They might be allowed to keep their responsibilities for revenue collection. This would effectively introduce a form of asymmetric devolution of powers. This asymmetry would be justified on ground of capacity, resource availability and performance-based allocation of rights. It might allow for greater regional specificity and better representation of local interests. Another option would be to stimulate outsourcing of the revenue collection by small units to larger urban municipalities.

Finding alternative local revenue sources

At least three developments might provoke a debate on alternative local revenue sources. First, the restructuring of the electricity sector will reduce local income sources. There are currently around 150 municipal electricity providers charging fees that in many cases cover more than the costs for providing electricity services. The government intends to reshape the electricity sector and form six regional electricity distributors. This would remove one of the sources of municipal income and one of the key credit control mechanisms in case of non-payment of municipal fees. It would also take away the current ambiguous situation in which municipalities make appeals to consumers cut energy consumption and reduce the carbon footprint, while themselves benefitting financially from increased energy consumption.

Second, the withdrawal of the RSC levies has led to a debate on alternative financing options. The RSC levies are temporarily replaced by an unconditional grant that takes historical collection of RSC levies into account. Municipalities are thus compensated, but not necessarily at levels that reflect new economic activity. The RSC levy was a more buoyant revenue source: its growth rates were higher than the growth of the current grant. Options for replacing the RSC levies are currently being debated. Options under consideration include a local business tax, or revenue-sharing arrangements on national taxes such as the VAT and the fuel levy.

Third, the equitable grant for municipalities currently takes only basic services into account. Urban municipalities might have problems in funding services for what has been defined as "near-poor" urban population, as the equitable grant does not take these services and population groups into account. Revision of the allocation formula of the equitable grant could be considered, or the issue could be taken into account in the discussion of alternative local revenues.

A wide range of sub-national taxes exist in OECD and non-OECD-countries. The property tax, also available to municipalities in South Africa, is the most common sub-national tax in many OECD-countries. In addition, several other tax bases are used, as the property-tax revenues alone cannot raise enough revenue to fund sub-national governments with a wide range of functions. Income taxes in several Nordic countries are shared by sub-national and national governments. Several continental European countries have sub-national business taxes, whereas several federal countries have a sub-national sales tax or VAT. There are differences between developed and developing countries in this respect. Although local income taxes have occasionally been levied in developing countries, they are far from common. Local income taxes in several transitional countries (such as Russia, Bulgaria and Poland) resemble a tax-sharing arrangement more than a truly local source of revenue. A potentially promising alternative answer for sub-national revenues might be to rely on the VAT. Canada and Brazil use the VAT as a sub-national revenue source. Other sub-national tax resources that are used in several non-OECD countries are taxes on professions (India), taxes on hotels and restaurants (Indonesia) and taxes on vehicles shared with the national government (India, Indonesia and Pakistan).

An important criterion for new sub-national tax sources in South Africa is that it can be collected relatively simply, considering the substantial difficulties in sub-national tax revenue collecting. This could suggest a sub-national tax that piggybacks on an existing national tax base, where collection could be carried out by the central government, but where sub-national governments would be free to set their tax rate. Considering that Cape Town is one of the drivers of national economic growth, it might be considered that a sub-national tax base should be buoyant, so that part of the tax revenues that will be generated in the region and that are connected to economic growth will stay in the region to continue to stimulate national economic growth. Considering the large inequities in South Africa, a sub-national tax revenue that is not regressive might be recommendable. This could in principle be the income tax. There have, however, been concerns as to whether the South African Revenue Service would have the capacity to add a sub-national surcharge on the personal income tax to its current responsibilities (Katz Commission, 2008).

Fine-tuning the equitable share

The design of the local equitable share might work to the disadvantage of large urban areas such as Cape Town. The local equitable share focuses on poor households and a relatively limited set of services.[26] Many urban areas in South Africa, however, contain large populations of what has been defined as "near-poor" households. Their income is just above the poverty threshold and they might be able to afford paying fees, but their income will certainly not be enough to generate revenues that can cover the full costs of services related to water, electricity, sanitation and solid waste removal. These gaps between service costs and the ability to pay citizens may be more substantial in urbanised areas, where the definition of basic municipal services can be much broader and also include street lighting and storm water management. An additional disadvantage in this respect is reported to be the allocation of funds based on residential address rather than work address. Such a criterion does not compensate the Western Cape for the large stream of migrant workers and work seekers from the Eastern Cape, who live and work in the area and use its infrastructure. The Western Cape receives only 9% of the resources transferred to South Africa's nine provinces, and its equitable share diminishes every year. The allocation criteria in the local equitable share scheme could be adjusted, so that the cost structure of large urban areas such as Cape Town is better taken into account.

There are some concerns that the provincial equitable share does not take into account current challenges for the Western Cape. One of the allocation criteria is population, but this is based on the past Census, which does not represent current trends or population projections. As future Censuses are scheduled to be held only once a decade, growing provinces will continue to receive relatively less grants per capita than declining provinces. It is not clear that the provincial equitable share takes into account all current realities of economic growth demands for infrastructure and migration of the population into urban areas.

Inter-provincial inequity results from a variety of factors: apartheid and racially biased inequity; economic equality based on an uneven distribution of natural resources; and spatial inequality. In order to minimise the impact of past inequality, the *National Spatial Development Plan* could be tailored to allocate resources where the economy has the most chance of success. An area's propensity to grow and its capacity for job creation should further allow it to receive funding to achieve this objective. This might result in more investment in certain activities in order to ensure that future outcomes are achieved.

Financing economic development

There are not many incentives in current governance frameworks that stimulate sufficient financing for economic development. Many of the overlapping mandates of municipalities and provinces fall within in this field, leading to co-ordination issues. Many provinces do not utilise their capital grants, and there seem to be backlogs in infrastructure investments. The funding of economic development is not helped by the grants system.

The grant system is characterised by a high number of conditional grants, many of which are distributed on an *ad hoc* and discretionary basis from national line departments. This *ad hoc* and discretionary character implicates duplication of aims and objectives, and unnecessary burdens on implementation. Many different programmes targeting job creation, water, roads, housing, electricity and transport require would require integrated planning, but the disbursement mechanisms are relatively fragmented and there is a lack of co-ordination between policy and budgeting units at national and local level (Amusa and Mathane, 2007).

Effective financing for economic development calls for less fragmented funding. A comprehensive effort should be made to merge conditional grants into a block grant for regional economic development. This would lead to more coherent investment decisions and could increase both metropolitan governance and intergovernmental co-ordination. It would reduce stove-piping at the national level and could stimulate alignment of central and regional goals, depending on the design of the block grant. A model that might be followed is that of the French *contrats d'agglomération* (Box 3.4), so that horizontal co-operation at the metropolitan level is stimulated, considering that many public investments have regional externalities that would have to be taken into account.

Box 3.4. **The French "contrats d'agglomération"**

France has been one of the countries most consistent in pursuing policies aimed at the creation of metropolitan institutional arrangements. This process has been accelerated since 1999, when the central government established metropolitan authorities in the 150 largest urban areas. In addition to creating these new *communautés urbaines* and the *communautés d'agglomération*, central government drafted specific model agreements that urban areas must adopt and projects that urban areas must undertake if they want to receive government grants. These have been specified in two 1999 Acts on National Territorial Planning and Inter-municipal Co-operation.

Following these two acts, councils for *communautés urbaines* and *communautés d'agglomération* must approve a so-called territorial project. This territorial project is a five to 10-year plan which concerns infrastructure, economic development, social housing, culture, environment, etc at the metropolitan level. But it is more than a plan since it specifies the amount of funding and details all the operations to be performed to achieve the plan's objectives. Once approved by the *communauté* council, the project is then discussed with the central government. When it is approved by the central government, there is an agreement signed between it and the *communauté*, called a *contrat d'agglomération.*

This agreement guarantees that the central government will finance some of the actions decided in the territorial project (there are therefore negotiations between the central government and the *communauté* regarding government funding). In addition, the law states that the *contrat d'agglomération* must also be signed by the regional council. This means that the actions envisaged in the *contrat d'agglomération* will also be financed by the region and as such will be part of the *contrat de Plan*, a larger five-year agreement signed by the central government and the region. Moreover, this means that European structural funds will feed the general budget of the territorial project.

For instance, the Bordeaux the *contrat d'agglomération* amounts to €1.2 billion over a seven-year period. It has been signed by the *communauté urbaine* of Bordeaux (CUB), the provincial (*département*) council of Gironde, the City of Bordeaux, the regional council of Aquitaine and the central government's representative (the regional prefect). The central government contributes 17% of the total funding, while the CUB contributes 36% and the regional council 15%. Other contributors are the EU, the Department of Gironde, municipalities and national public agencies such as the National Railways (SNCF) or the National Centre for Aerospace (CNES).

3.5. Participatory governance and civic engagement

In a contested space like Cape Town, characterised by relatively volatile and fragmented alliances and the lack of absolute party political hegemony, the issue of building alliances for a more competitive and inclusive city-region becomes imperative. In this context, providing platforms for civic engagement is useful. Consensual solutions among the various stakeholders – national, provincial and local governments, civil society organisations, labour unions, associations of informal workers, and enterprise associations – will not be easily achieved, but will be essential to create solutions and deliver outcomes that are responsive to local needs. Fortunately, South Africa benefits from an impressive number of laws that require public participation in decision-making.[27]

Provisions for public participation in planning and governance

Signs of emerging participatory governance are visible in South Africa, though initial outcomes have lagged behind expectations. On the positive side, vehicles for direct democracy and citizen engagement have thrived following the end of apartheid. At the national level, the National Economic Development and Labour Council (Nedlac) draws representatives of business, labour and government into stakeholder dialogues. Similar partnerships exist at the provincial level, for example the Provincial Development Council which forms a platform for social dialogue amongst organised business, organised labour, civil society and government.[28] There are legal requirements for local government to engage in consultation and participatory processes across a number of activities, such as environmental impact assessments.[29] A series of community engagements, known as *izimbizo*, are also undertaken across the province at least twice a year, to track questions and trends in community response. Beyond Nedlac and *izimbizo*, the national government does not seem to have a common vision for the role civil society organisations can play after the abolition of apartheid.[30] Public participation in decision-making has not often been integrated, which may be partly explained by the provinces' dependence on grants, which may replace incentives for accountability to citizens with compliance with national priorities and requirements. In this effort, they may consider adopting tools developed in Canada, where the central government conditioned the disbursement of the federal excise tax on gasoline on requirements to develop Integrated Community Sustainability Plans (Box 3.5).

Box 3.5. **Integrated community sustainability planning in Canada**

Over the last years, a key focus of the Canadian government has been to upgrade and improve community infrastructure that is of strategic importance to enhancing the country's prosperity, quality of life and international competitive position. The primary financial vehicle for pursuing this objective was a decision to share with municipalities half of the federal excise tax on gasoline, starting in 2005. The Gas Tax Fund (GTF) is delivered to cities and communities by way of formal agreements between the Government of Canada and other levels of government for environmentally sustainable municipal infrastructure. This initiative was deemed so successful that the Government made the GTF permanent in its 2008 Budget. A key component of Canada's GTF agreements is the requirement for signatory provinces/territories to ensure that their municipalities (or regional authorities or clusters of municipalities) develop *Integrated Community Sustainability Plans* (ICSPs) or equivalent planning documents. An ICSP is a long-term plan, developed in consultation with community members, which articulates an integrated vision of what the community (or cluster of communities) should look like in 20 to 30 years, the suggested end of the planning period. The ICSP articulates a framework in which a community can realise sustainability objectives for the cultural, economic, environmental and social dimensions of its identity in pursuit of this vision.

The purpose of an ICSP is to enhance or build upon existing planning instruments and processes, and in essence, "move the planning bar forward". The ICSP planning process is designed to be collaborative and reflect a co-ordinated approach to enhanced community sustainability, through linkages with different types of plans or planning activities – including those of adjacent regions or municipalities. The ICSP should embed indicators within it to measure progress toward the achievement of whatever sustainability objectives have been identified in individual Plans. Some general principles that tend to be included reflect the importance of moving beyond traditional community planning practices. In particular, the ICSP approach focuses on integrating the four dimensions of sustainability into a plan to achieve the community's 20 to 30-year long-term vision. The ICSP process assists in raising public awareness on this planning approach by involving the community in the development of a plan. The plan is therefore driven from the grass roots, as it solicits input from individuals and groups who may not normally participate in the planning process – *e.g.* youth, low-income residents and recent immigrants.

As of April 2008, seven separate jurisdictions already had frameworks or guidelines for ICSP development in place. Of these jurisdictions, three provinces and one territory had also produced detailed guides, toolkits or templates that communities could use to develop ICSPs. As the GTF Agreements do not anticipate individual ICSPs will be completed for several more years, the success of the ICSP approach in Canada will not be determined until the beginning of the next decade, at the earliest. In the meantime, there have been several examples of governance structures at the municipal and regional level that incorporate the principles associated with ICSPs. For example, the resort community of Whistler, British Columbia (site of the upcoming 2010 Olympic Winter Games), following in-depth consultation with local stakeholders, developed a detailed community plan that sets out the strategies and actions for a 15-year vision of sustainability, with the goal of remaining a successful and sustainable community in 2060. Other examples of sustainable community planning include the ICSPs that have been submitted in smaller communities in Yukon and Alberta, and an effort by rural communities in Nova Scotia's Annapolis Valley to pool their resources to harvest the data that will feed into their own ICSPs. The Niagara 10 Project in Ontario, has sought to assess regional and municipal support for aligning trans-boundary issues and opportunities in a four-pillared (environment, economic, social and cultural) cross-border (Ontario-New York State) sustainability agenda with a clear emphasis on the issues and interests that rest within the jurisdictional responsibility of the local and regional governments in the two countries.

The City of Cape Town, like its abutting municipalities, has experimented with various programmes to facilitate community dialogue, though these efforts have been tempered by the limited capacity of the government to translate input into action. This contradiction is exhibited in the Area Co-ordinating Teams (ACTs), which sought to create dialogue between citizens and their elected representatives in various neglected areas of Cape Town. The issues raised at the ACTs are nonbinding, and the Council is not obliged to follow through on any issue raised during the discussion. One former Cape Town planner and observer of this project urged Councils to "actively support ACTs, both by passing appropriate bye-laws to institutionalise them and to draw up a code of conduct that compel officials and councillors to attend and take seriously scheduled meetings and related development planning initiatives" (Williams, 2006). Likewise, community participation in IDPs and the previous mayoral "Listening Campaigns" seem largely ceremonial, given the local government's absence of structures to evaluate and monitor community participation. Monitoring mechanisms need to be improved and complemented by capacity-building of community workers. In terms of monitoring, participatory systems could be developed to evaluate the effectiveness of public participation in achieving development outputs of IDPs. This infrastructure would also serve as a means for residents to hold local government accountable to the policy choices and targets that emerged from the IDP drafting process (Davids, 2007). Clearly, the government could benefit from inventing new spaces of citizenship that transcend mere consultation with citizens.

The Municipal Structures Act provides local government with various options to encourage and facilitate public participation in the decision-making processes of local government. One option in the Act allows the establishment of ward committees, while a second option allows for the establishment of sub-councils. The City of Cape Town has established 23 sub-councils, while many other local governments have opted to establish ward committees. The sub-council option allowed the city to amalgamate wards into groups of four or five wards. In this system, the requirement to address public participation is addressed by the sub-council presenting its *Integrated Development Plan* and its budget to citizens from the wards. The city therefore demonstrates sufficient and necessary commitment to public participation, while not actively driving public decision-making processes. Given that the agenda setting for the sub-council is driven centrally by the mayoral committee and the full council, there is limited opportunity to address matters of concern emanating from the local community. In this model of decision making and budgeting, civil society is relegated to the position of a passive recipient of pre-determined decisions, limited to offering endorsements rather than public engagement around prioritisation and actual decision-making. As a consequence, civil society has a limited role in influencing decisions at the sub-council level and an inadequate institution for structured engagement.

Outside the City of Cape Town, a number of constraints limit the representation of ward committees. Legislated in the Municipal Structures Act to ensure community input and build partnerships for service delivery, ward committees are chaired by a ward councilor and include ten community representatives. Although a few ward committees have mechanisms in power to democratically elect members (Overstrand, for instance), most ward councilors appoint members who have relatively little power to set agendas. Currently, civil society groups do not have a clear institutional path to voice concerns if they disagree with the decision of a ward committee or believe that it is not representative of public opinion in the area. As one expert on participation argues, "[t]he facilitation of community input often therefore appears partial and sometimes superficial, with many ward committee processes presenting pre-determined positions and programmes for limited feedback" (Oldfield, 2008). Ward councilors, who often sit low in political party hierarchies, may also be vulnerable to patronage and clientelism.

Challenges to participatory governance

Participatory governance has been compromised by low levels of social and associational activity scaled up to the level of the city-region. Social trust is difficult to establish beyond the micro-level in urban areas characterised by a history of racial division and unequal provision of services and amenities. A survey conducted in Cape Town found that a large number of respondents felt that most people cannot be trusted and that an even larger number of respondents felt that people would take advantage of them if they had the opportunity, so that they were more trusting of people in their own neighbourhood (Centre for Social Science Research, 2003). These findings, broadly consistent across age, gender and race, suggest that levels of confidence about engaging across racial and income divides are low and apartheid spatial divisions persist in the city-region. Thus, while there is fairly extensive community level engagement in public activity, largely through neighbourhood level organisations, the vehicles have not yet been found to significantly scale up collective action to the city-regional level.

Given that most citizens in the Cape Town city-region have not heard of Integrated Development Plans, community capacity needs to be greatly strengthened. In 2007, the Provincial Government of the Western Cape completed the most extensive survey on the role of community participation in the IDP design process. A total of 100 000 completed survey forms – 60 [2]000 questionnaires for the City and 40 000 for districts outside the City – were analysed as a representative sample of the population of the Province. Overall, only 21% of the interviewees in the Cape Town region responded that they had heard of the IDPs (Figure 3.12). The lack of awareness surrounding the IDPs greatly constrains the efficacy of this planning tool, arguably the most important vehicle for community input in South Africa's planning process. To strengthen public participation mechanisms, municipalities should draw upon civil society networks and build better competence in local politicians who, in turn, could improve participation in the IDP process. Authorities need to address complaints received, especially concerns that isiXhosa-speaking members were not being fully integrated into debates and that IDP Representative Forum members were not compensated by municipal officials for such items as transport to meetings (Davids, 2007). Additional evaluations are needed to analyse the extent to which women are involved in these discussions, given past experiences of alienation and disempowerment.[31]

Figure 3.12. **Public awareness of Integrated Development Plans (IDPs): Cape Town city-region**

Response to "Do you know what the Integrated Development Plan (IDP) is?" 2007

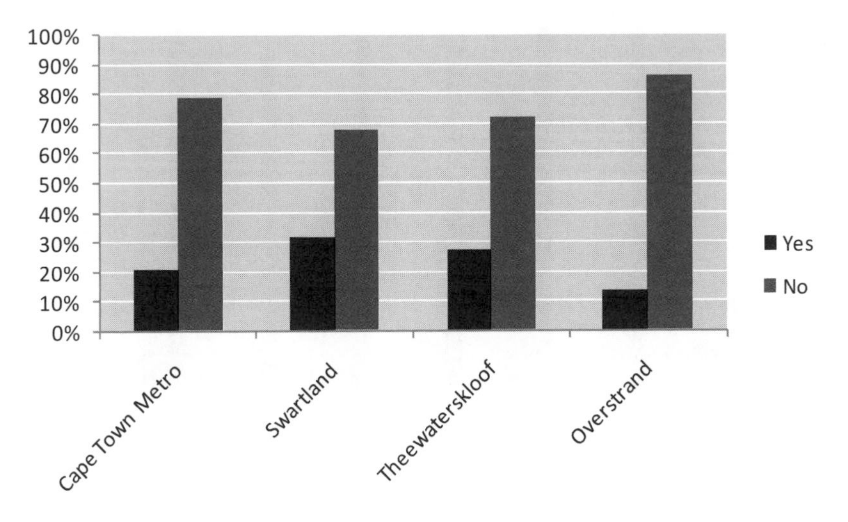

Note: The sample sizes are the following: Cape Town Metro (n=83 305), Swartland (n = 188), Theewaterskloof (n=1 643), and Overstrand (n=2 344). Data were not available for Stellenbosch, Drakenstein or Saldanha.

Source: Provincial Government of the Western Cape. Department of Local Government and Housing (2007), compiled by Foundation for Contemporary Research (2007).

Declining voter participation and increasing political apathy present challenges to engaging the public. Though rates were high after the advent of political democracy in 1994 and in the subsequent 1999 national elections, they have fallen and have been consistently lower for local government elections. In 2004, voter participation fell to 78.2% from 89.6% in the 1999 general election, though this obscures significant neighbourhood differences.[32] For local government elections the national average in both 2000 and 2006 was 48% (Figure 3.13). Decreasing participation in local elections is due to a number of factors, including disillusionment with party politics and service delivery. Nevertheless, participation rates in the Western Cape have been higher than the national average, probably due to the fact that along with KwaZulu-Natal, the Western Cape is the only other province in the country where the ANC has faced serious political opposition at the sub-national level. Overall, declining participation may indicate growing disaffection with formal political processes on the part of significant groups of people, although voter participation remains high compared to the national average.

Figure 3.13. **Voter participation rates in elections in the Cape Town city-region since 1999**

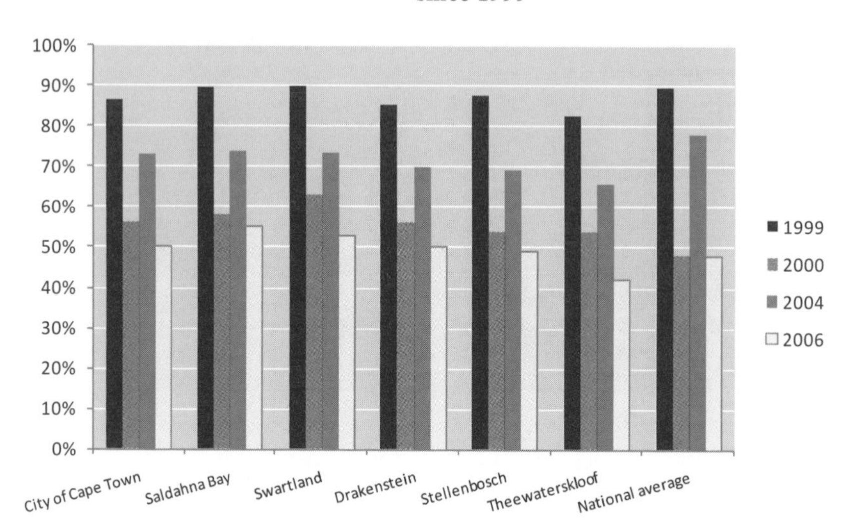

Note: Owing to the new demarcation of municipal boundaries in 2000, the 1999, 2000, 2004 and 2006 election poll results are simply not comparable. This data was constructed utilising the Municipal Demarcation Board's boundary maps to align the results by combining the relevant areas. City of Cape Town: Blaauberg, Central Cape Town, Helderberg, Oostenberg, South Peninsula, Tygerberg. Saldanha: Langebaan, Hopefield Swartland: Yzerfontein, Darling, Malmesbury, Moreesburg and Koringberg. Stellenbosch: Kylemore, Pniel, Franschhoek, Stellenbosch. Drakenstein: Paarl, Wellington, Saron. Theewaterskloof: Riviersonderend, Caledon, Botrivier, Houhoek, Genadendal, Greyton, Grabouw, Villiersdorp.

Civil society

In the post-apartheid era, many civil society organisations have shed their "watchdog" role and become ''extended delivery arms" of the state. The non-governmental sector spans an enormous diversity of housing, religious, and lending organisations, and hundreds of activist organisations were transformed into service providers, undertaking contracts on behalf of local governments.[33] This occurred under a transitional institutional framework, when civil society groups tended to embrace a more collaborationist and co-operative approach. This occurred at the same time as a migration of experienced and high-level staff to government and a shift in donor funds away from nongovernmental organisations to government portfolios. The civic sector has been further atrophied by cases where civic organisations were perceived to be direct competitors of the local branch offices of the ANC (Briggs, 2008). However, emerging civil society groups show a renaissance of the type of critical monitoring exercised by nongovernmental organisations during apartheid. Some groups have mobilised to criticise certain government policies, especially HIV/AIDS and forced evictions.[34]

Popular movements and non-profit organisations in the Western Cape have been unable to develop a cohesive and co-ordinated platform and strategic direction, limiting their influence on politics and policy making. Ongoing strife between the Western Cape Local Government Organisation (WECLOGO) and the South African Local Government Association (SALGA) diffuses the voice of local government officials. Likewise, there is no city-wide umbrella structure to voice common demands and transcend the confrontational encounters that often characterise meetings between government officials and civil society bodies.[35] International experience suggests that movements that are often internally divided and do not have a uniform agenda are limited in their efforts to bring about social change. Brazil offers a positive example of a pro-active and conscious social movement for an urban reform and restructuring. Created in the 1980s, an urban reform movement at the national level supported by housing movements at the city level was instrumental in bringing about a series of land reforms and institutional changes (Box 3.6). Recently, government authorities in Brazil have acknowledged and been responsive to the historic role of social movements in the country, a context that cannot necessarily replicated in South Africa in general and the Cape Town city-region in particular (Heller, 2001). By contrast, it seems that in the Cape Town city-region, associational activity and participation has not always contributed to more accountable and responsive governance. A long-term regional strategy for the Cape Town city-region will have to transcend or bypass party politics and engage organised civil society more creatively in arenas that have resonance for them.

Box 3.6. **The role of the National Forum for Urban Reform in Brazil**

In Brazil during the 1980s, a national movement for urban reform was created comprising a coalition of grass-roots housing movements, NGOs, professionals (*e.g.* the Brazilian Association of Architects and Urban Planners) and intellectuals. The aim was to combat processes of social exclusion through the unfettered workings of urban real estate markets. In Brazil individual property rights are entrenched, making it difficult for the state at any level to increase the size of the market for low-income groups. Consequently, socio-spatial exclusion in Brazilian cities is intense, with around 20% of the population of most metropolitan areas living in slums. At the same time, overall urban development patterns are characterised by gross inefficiencies, including sprawling but densely settled low-income settlements on the periphery, requiring expensive public infrastructure delivery, and declining inner-city areas.

Over the years, the Forum has gained a respectable track record of engagement with the state. Initially, its focus was to enter into the public debate on the new constitution, as a result of which an amendment was introduced on the social function of private property rights, which separated property rights on the one hand from the right to build or use these rights on the other. This introduced into the constitution the possibility of imposing limits on individual property rights when these would infringe on the rights of others, or would have negative city-wide consequences such as socio-spatial exclusion. There were inevitable objections from those with vested interests, but continued pressure by the Forum and its partner organisations pushed through, the Statute of the City (2001), which operationalised specific constitutional clauses for housing rights.

This new national legislation effectively enabled the elaboration of detailed and participatory local master plans and zoning regulations, which provided for negotiated land use changes, fair housing clauses and inclusionary zoning laws. It also increases local government's leverage to act against vacant and speculative land ownership. At the same time, the Statute set specific guidelines for the increased democratisation of urban management through the municipal urban development councils, where the elaboration and implementation of master plans is discussed with social movements, business associations, workers representatives and NGOs, among others.

Source: Souza, 2003.

Despite the region's large housing deficit and large non-profit housing organisations, municipalities have generally not facilitated community-driven housing delivery. The City of Cape Town, for instance, bases its housing delivery scheme on the premise that housing should be driven by the private sector, which, they argue, has the capacity to scale up the delivery of individual housing units. Consequently, Cape Town has not followed the experience of eThekwini (Durban) in experimenting with flexible, community-driven housing delivery; nongovernmental organisations are rarely directly involved in project design. Despite the development of creative housing funds designed to speed up the construction of new housing, *e.g.* the iTshani fund, only 1% of the total flow of funds has gone to traditionally excluded target groups (Briggs, 2008).[36] The City's release of land through leasehold agreements to social housing agencies such as Ilinge Labahlali and the Welcome Zenzile Social Housing Co-ops might be an experience worth replicating and expanding. A greater balance between accelerated delivery and a community-driven approach could be achieved through emulating Cape Town's Masithembane housing project (Box 3.7).

Box 3.7. **The Masithembane People's Housing Association of Cape Town**

The Masithembane housing project involved the provision of 220 houses in Sections U, V and W in Site B, Khayelitsha. The project made use of the consolidation subsidy. A People's Housing Process approach, in which beneficiaries take responsibility for managing the provision of their own housing, was used in the project. In the mid-1990s, people in Site B began to hear about the new housing subsidy scheme and about the People's Housing Process in particular. A group of 20 residents from W Section who lived in shacks on serviced sites formed the Masithembane People's Housing Association in March 1997. The Masithembane People's Housing Association approached the NGO Development Action Group (DAG) for assistance. An application for 220 consolidation subsidies was submitted to the Provincial Housing Development Board in 1998 and approved in 1999.

To empower the community to manage the projects, community members attended DAG's Housing Leadership, Community Housing Development Management and Housing Support Centre Management courses. The Housing Leadership Course is a five-day course that gives some practical leadership skills and an overview of the housing subsidy scheme to committee members. The Community Housing Development Management Course is a five-day course that goes into housing policy in greater detail and gives an overview of the housing project cycle and the roles of different participants in housing projects. The Housing Support Centre Management Course is a 20-day course aimed at the community members who will run the housing support centre, and includes 10 days of theory on project management and building construction, and 10 days of practical construction training. DAG assisted in establishing the housing support centre, which was staffed by community members, setting up the systems and procedures for ordering materials and monitoring construction. Masithembane decided to manage their project themselves, with some assistance from Marnol Projects, a materials supplier. The housing support centre staff (a construction controller and community liaison officer, plus some committee members who worked on a voluntary basis) gave advice to beneficiaries, submitted application forms and managed the implementation of the project.

Beneficiaries in the projects chose their own house designs and builders, and the construction of the houses was monitored by the community construction controller. Most people hired local builders to build for them (28 local builders were involved in the project), and hired helpers to assist the builder. Some people also assisted their builder with such tasks as carrying blocks and mixing cement. The promotion of household savings to supplement the subsidy amount was also an important part of the project. Households were encouraged to save in a variety of forms, which included saving cash, saving on the cost of building materials by reusing materials from their shacks, and saving on labour costs by carrying out some construction tasks themselves. The Kuyasa Fund granted 42 loans, totaling ZAR 132 500, to members of the Masithembane project. Loans were generally in the ZAR 1 000 to ZAR 4 000 range (with an average of ZAR 3 000). Because of the encouragement of individual choice and household savings, and the provision of housing loans by the Kuyasa Fund, these houses meet the specific needs of each household, and are of better quality and larger size (36-66m^2) than houses in most conventional housing projects. Many of the homes incorporate principles of energy efficiency, such as natural ventilation, a ceiling that reduces heating requirements, and the use of non-toxic roof sheeting materials.

The Masithembane project was the first People's Housing Process project to finish building its houses within the allocated time period of 12 months. In 2003, it had over 800 members, many of whom were expanding projects into other development initiatives, including a second phase of the housing project. The Masithembane project has been recognised as a best practice by the National Department of Housing and is a winner of the Impumelelo Innovation Award for its partnerships with the public sector.

Sources: Compiled in Development Action Group (2003); sources include Department of Housing: "The story of people building houses in Khayelitsha", *Sustainable Settlements: Case Studies from South Africa*, Pretoria, 2002; *People's Stories: The People's Housing Process in Khayelitsha*, Cape Town, a video made by the Development Action Group and the Community Video Education Trust for the People's Housing Partnership Trust, 2001.

However, it is important not to over-romanticise community-based organisations. Jenkins and Wilkinson suggest that "local politics is open to manipulation by opportunistic and often corrupt individuals" and that "overtly informal political processes presently limit the reach and effectiveness of formal local government in Cape Town" (2002). Weak formal governance structures in townships and informal settlements leave the way open to gatekeepers "known variously as traditional leaders, headmen, shacklords or warlords" to take charge of allocating sites and other resources in return for financial payments, political loyalty and other favours (Turok, 2001). These gatekeepers also challenge and undermine the authority of democratically elected and legitimate leaders, often in cahoots with criminal elements, leading to frustration and insecurity within such areas. That said, many Community Development Workers (CDWs) and ward councillors who are close to the people play an important and effective role in representing residents of their wards.[37]

Strengthening participatory governance

The streamlining of participation across different departments and levels of government, along with greater public involvement in government decision-making, could enhance participation. Currently, "town hall" meetings resemble silos and occur under the aegis of particular departments and levels of government. Though departmental meetings often offer an appropriate platform, especially if discussions broach technical issues, an excess of meetings may produce "participation fatigue" and impinge upon a broader understanding of complex issues. Local governments in the Cape Town city-region may learn from the case of Rio de Janeiro's Working Group on the Regularisation of Irregular Subdivisions (*Núcleo de Regularização de Loteamentos*), which sponsors bimonthly meetings where residents ask questions about their land claims to a panel of representatives from six different agencies across the state and city government. Through integrating a diverse number of stakeholders, these forums provide useful information to residents on multiple scales – individual, neighbourhood, and departmental – and illuminate the interdependence of institutions. With this rich interaction, planners and residents jointly constructed an understanding of the problems of regularisation, which informed the creation of innovative strategies involving complex issues – urban infrastructure, housing, transportation, and environmental conservation – that are by nature cross-sectoral and multi-jurisdictional (Donovan, 2007).[38] Most important, democratically elected community leaders were given power to help select beneficiaries of government regularisation programmes throughout the year. This empowerment could improve debates in Cape Town and lead to more meaningful and regular participation than the biannual *izimbizos* currently provide.

Clarified functional assignments and a more informed citizenry have the potential to improve community participation. The misalignment of functional assignments between tiers of government leaves many citizens confused as to who is accountable for service delivery. Most people do not distinguish between spheres of government. They expect government to deliver. For example, while the national Department of Housing remains responsible for the budgeting for the provision of houses through their provincial departments, the local municipalities, as implementing agencies, often are called upon to explain the reasons for the lack of housing delivery.

Widespread uncertainty over which sphere of government is responsible for what service means that citizens often do not know who to hold accountable for a service failure (Steytler and Fessha, 2005). Government as a whole must take responsibility, but could also encourage community participation by better informing community members of projects and ensuring that they acquire levels of numeracy and literacy that will facilitate informed participation. Additional efforts could be focused on training community mediators and upgrading civil servants' skills in holding meetings, building consensus and conflict resolution.

3.6. Conclusion

The ambitious institutional transformation of the Cape Town city-region has laid the foundation for more inclusive governance, but created new challenges that confront mature democracies. On one hand, local governments in South Africa have never been as engaged in such issues as pro-poor service delivery, participatory planning, and fiscal responsibility. On the other hand, this reform endowed local government with many new responsibilities over a short period and often failed to clarify responsibilities or offer adequate training for the new work to be done at the municipal level. As previous sections have stressed, the core challenge facing the Cape Town city-region is how to reconcile the huge and growing needs of poor households, ambiguous regional economic performance and a highly inefficient space economy within the relatively tight confines of a threatened natural and fragmented public resource base.

Within this new era, spatial polarisation will continue to haunt an array of governing activities, despite the remarkably effective dénouement of apartheid in the early 1990s by the country's many visionary leaders. Hampered by extraordinary backlogs in appropriate housing, for example, the post-apartheid government at all scales has necessarily emphasised speed rather than space, that is to say, rapid delivery via sectoral channels over regional development. Sectoral initiatives are frequently "siloed" from one another, making effective transportation, infrastructure, housing, and land use policy difficult; this curbs the state's capacity to leverage more completely the economic potential of the region. While integrated development plans promulgated in the late 1990s and early 2000s offer a vibrant policy platform to overcome these problems, plans suffered from insufficient or inappropriate spatial planning and intergovernmental synergy strategies. Consequently, despite progressive intentions, the post-apartheid state has not only been unable to halt problems of social and spatial polarisation, it has sometimes complexified these problems, most notably when intergovernmental and interdepartmental co-operation are required, such as in housing policy. The future is thus being shaping by a present heavily burdened by the past.

A transnational outlook will sharpen policy analysis and implementation in the Cape Town city-region in so far as officials find ways to reshape space, improve inadequate skills, and ensure accountability in ways appropriate to the local history and political fabric of the region. In this sense, the region should not simply look to neighbours within sub-Saharan Africa or colonial ties to the United Kingdom and the Netherlands, but should engage with cities across Europe, Asia, and the Americas that share similar issues of regional planning, intergovernmental co-ordination, revenue collection and local government capacity. The Cape Town city-region could benefit enormously from enhanced engagement in international fora and through city exchanges with "peers" in other coastal regions within middle-income countries and metropolitan regions in the OECD. Such an engagement would build upon South Africa's hosting of the 2010 FIFA World Cup and better position Cape Town on the global stage. In turn, these metropolitan regions would benefit from the multiple lessons Cape Town now has to teach, especially given its experience with one of the world's most remarkable and potentially far-reaching transformations in metropolitan governance.

Notes

1. The primary rationale for decentralisation in South Africa, unlike many other countries, was a negotiated political settlement. Socio-economic considerations were secondary concerns (Momoniat, 1999, cited in Robinson, 2007).

2. In urban areas, the Black Local Authorities (BLAs) were created by the apartheid state in 1982 as part of a political attempt to stabilise and control the urban African population.

3. The *White Paper on Local Government* (1998) defines developmental local government as "local government committed to working with citizens and groups within the community to find sustainable ways to meet their social, economic and material needs and improve the quality of their lives" (quoted in Jensen, 2004).

4. Predominately African areas in Cape Town – communities like Khayelitsha, Guguletu and Nyanga – remained under the local jurisdiction of four BLAs which existed until 1996: Crossroads, Mfuleni, Lingeletu West and Ikapa. Despite often energetic leadership in the 1994-6 stage, BLAs were politically and institutionally paralysed by massive arrears from years of rent boycotts, inadequate cross-subsidies, corruption and, most importantly, insufficient tax bases.

5. Legislation tentatively titled the Provincial Development Act (PDA) or possibly the Land Use Planning Act (LUPA) is planned to replace LUPO and will be submitted to the legislature before the end of 2008.

6. The national government directly builds and operates bulk water facilities in the area of Cape Town and has not introduced an economic pricing regime. Other metropolitan areas in South Africa purchase water from quasi-independent water boards.

7. These circumstances are the replacement of the Regional Services Council levy by a temporary grant and the temporary FIFA 2010 Soccer World Cup grants.

8. Regional Services Council levies were taxes on the turnover and payroll of businesses. They were assigned to district and metropolitan councils,

who administered them directly and had some flexibility to set tax rates (although these were typically kept at very low levels). Revenues were intended to be used for infrastructure development, though this was not enforced. The levies were abolished, as they were regarded as regressive and unconstitutional as a local government tax. In KwaZulu Natal, they were known as Joint Services Board (JSB) levies.

9. For instance, the local government of Montreal built multiple new facilities for the 1976 Summer Olympics, including the grandiose Olympic Stadium, and wound up with a debt totalling some USD 1.2 billion. The debt was not paid off until 30 years after the Games (Matheson, 2006).

10. The National Treasury directly monitors the budgets of large municipalities, defined as the top 30 by budget size. Without this intervention, the Cape Winelands District Municipality has emerged as an acknowledged leader in the monitoring and evaluation of public activities in its jurisdiction. Its initiatives will reportedly be used as a case study and rolled out nationally.

11. Other agencies that monitor sub-national government financial accountability in the Cape Town city-region include Statistics South Africa (Stats SA) which releases annual reports on financial and non-financial aspects of municipal performance (P9114 and P9115 respectively), the South African Reserve Bank, which releases consolidated data on government finances, and the Auditor-General of South Africa, which conducts annual financial audits of municipalities and departments in the Provincial Government.

12. This is illustrated in the case of airports: Schedule 4 Part B of the Municipal Structure Act confers the functions of municipal airports to local government and thus, local municipalities, while Section 84(1) ascribes responsibility to district municipalities over municipal airports that serve the "area of the district as a whole". To this end, a district municipality may only be responsible for municipal airports in so far as that airport services the district as a whole. The problem remains then how to clarify the designation of every airport in the district in terms of this requirement. Other unclear phrases that produce overlap include "for more than one local municipality" (solid waste disposal sites) and "of a major portion of the municipalities in the district" (markets and abattoirs). Given this language and the absence of a standard benchmark, one municipal district could define "a major portion" as three municipalities in a district, while another manager could define the same concept as four of the five municipalities in a district (Jordan, 2006).

13 . In his 2006 State of the Nation Address, President Thabo Mbeki argued, "Integration of planning and implementation across the government spheres is therefore one of the prime areas of focus in our programme for the next term of local government."

14 . Municipalities operate on a financial year running from 1 July to 30 June, while national and provincial government financial years begin on 1 April and end on 31 March.

15 . In the "Moving South Africa Action Agenda," launched by the National Department of Transportation in 1999, the densification of transport corridors was indicated as a key strategy for reducing commuting times and system costs. The document also called on local government to "jointly agree on a common framework to achieve denser, more public transport friendly settlements". Finally, the National Land Transport Transition Act (No. 22 of 2000) established a statutory relationship between transport and land use planning, stating that "all role players must strive to achieve an effective land transportation system through integrated planning, provision and regulation of infrastructure and services". The same Act provides that local governments may agree to set up specific regional transportation agencies for the inter-municipal co-ordination of transport.

16 . The draft National Land Transportation Act provides for the establishment of Metropolitan Transport Authorities that would be jointly controlled by municipalities within a functional metropolitan area and the relevant provincial government.

17 . Agreement has also been reached that spatial planners will assist the long-term planning efforts of the Department of Local Government and Housing by including land identification for housing as a central element of the IDPs.

18 . A qualified opinion means that the Auditor-General highlights significant matters in the report, but that the overall financial statements still present a fair view. An adverse opinion means that significant matters are highlighted, and that the financial statements do not present a fair view.

19 . Formal interventions, however, have typically entailed extensive litigation, and provincial governments have typically avoided them until absolutely necessary.

20 . The City of Cape Town has an even larger number of civil servants per capita, averaging 28.7 per 1 000 households. This figure surpasses that of Johannesburg (25.0) and eThekwini (21.9). However, this number may be elevated, given that the City performs a range of services that

have been privatised by other cities, *e.g.* Johannesburg has outsourced water provision.

21. This is most evident in requirements for annual reports (including annual financial management statements) that are now being issued by all municipalities in the Cape Town Metro Region. The Auditor General has increased efforts to audit municipal financial statements on a timely basis, and is increasingly expanding the scope of auditing to include greater performance auditing.

22. The top levels of senior management in both provincial and local government are subject to political confirmation of their appointment, based on renewable, performance-based contracts that are typically tied to the electoral cycle. Performance agreements and assessments are required of senior management in all spheres of government, municipalities, but may have not penetrated to all levels of municipal administrations on a coherent basis.

23. The Provincial Government of the Western Cape's Skills Development Strategy has embarked on two projects. The first process consists of a co-ordinated bursary and scholarship plan that targets priority skills areas such as engineers, architects, physicians and specialists. The intention is to provide employment contracts on graduation and thus secure future government staff. Currently, more than 1 500 people have participated. The second process program aims to improve the quality of high school graduates to ensure improved university enrolment and graduation.

24. The Systems Improvement Grant provides small grants to all municipalities (approximately ZAR 200 000 per year) to support the introduction of systems required by the Municipal Systems Act.

25. The City of Cape Town's Electricity Department's private partnership with the Society for the Blind offers an innovative approach. The Cape Town Society for the Blind approached the City to develop a "blind friendly" prepayment metreing system in conjunction with the metreing supplier, Conlog. It was agreed that the City make the device compatible with current technology and refrain from using proprietary technology. Currently, the City has just completed the scoping phas,e and Conlog is busy sourcing/manufacturing the various interfaces required to address the brief. The intention is to pilot the project with 10 participants from the Society. Currently, Conlog's participation in this endeavour has no financial implications for the City of Cape Town, as it is counted as part of its social responsibility activities.

26. The provincial equitable share allocation formula consists of six components, which capture the relative demand for services between

provinces and take into account specific provincial circumstances. The components of the formula are neither indicative budgets nor guidelines as to how much should be spent on those functions. Rather, the education and health components are weighted broadly in line with expenditure patterns to provide an indication of relative need. Provinces have discretion regarding the determination of departmental allocations for each function, taking into account the priorities that underpin the division of revenue. The weights of the component are education (51%) based on the size of the school-age population (ages 5-17) and the number of students (Grade R to 12) enrolled in public ordinary schools, health (26%) based on the proportion of the population with and without access to medical aid, a basic share (14%) derived from each province's share of the national population, an institutional component (5%) divided equally between the provinces, an income poverty component (3%) reinforcing the redistributive bias of the formula and an economic output component (1%) based on GDP by region (GDP-R), although the latter is somewhat dated.

27. These include stipulations in the South African Constitution (1996), Municipal Structures Act (1998), Municipal Systems Act (2000), Municipal Finance Management Act (2003), and the Municipal Property Rates Act (2004).

28. Another example is the Provincial Youth Commission, which was established by the Province to promote and advance the interests of youth.

29. Another promising initiative was the Non-Profit Organisations Act 71 of 1997, designed to create an enabling environment for non-profit organisations (NPOs) and to set and regulate standards of governance, accountability and transparency. The Act created a voluntary registration facility for NPOs, *e.g.* Section 21 companies, trusts, voluntary, and non-profit associations.

30. In one view, civic movements would be de-politicised and become temporary single-purpose entities, like social movements in the United States. According to that model, social movements would work with government and other stakeholders to resolve a certain issue and dissolve after the issue was settled. Another view holds that civic organisations would have a permanent role, as in models of participatory governance in such countries as Brazil and India (Mayekiso, 2003). Political alliances with trade unions and civic associations, however, may complicate the inclusion of social movements.

31. Focusing specifically on the experience of African women in low-income communities in Metropolitan Cape Town, McEwan argues that reform of local government offers exceptional opportunities for engagement with

citizens in ways that respond to the gendered concerns of women alongside men. Nevertheless, in practice, African women experience a sense of alienation and disempowerment from structured participatory approaches in which they feel they are being involved but not in a significant fashion (McEwan, 2003).

32 . South Africa's Independent Electoral Commission (IEC) maintains data on the ward level of participation in provincial, district, and national elections. Their data illustrate lower voter turnout in low-income wards.

33 . According to the database of 391 social sector NPOs operating in the Western Cape, which was made available for the OECD Review by the Department of Social Development in the Western Cape, most non-profit organisations were engaged in activities related to development and housing (28.4%), religion (18.9%) and culture and recreation (15.6%). A further 89 NPOs registered with the Department for Social Services fell into an economic support category, undertaking activities such as micro-credit and job creation. While large membership-based organisations appear to be the preserve of the middle classes, low-income and poor people participate in a myriad of small, unregistered local organisations including "friends groups," "stokvels" or savings and credit clubs, as well as burial societies, where people club together to save for and support each other during funerals. A long-standing tradition in South Africa, burial societies have taken on a deeper significance in the time of HIV/AIDS.

34 . For example, the Treatment Action Campaign challenges state policy on HIV/AIDS and demands the universal roll-out of antiretroviral treatment by using horizontal institutions of accountability such as the Constitutional Court and Human Rights Commission, as well as through public demonstration and protest. In the Western Cape, the Homeless People's Federation, together with the People's Dialogue, employs conflict negotiation and constructive involvement in policy making to try and extend housing provision. Finally, the Western Cape Anti-Eviction Campaign (AEC) in Khayelitsha claims to provide multi-dimensional support to communities and aims to open up new spaces of citizenship (Briggs, 2007).

35 . Street traders and vendors, as well as other informal producers and service providers in the city, belong to one of the seven informal trade associations in the city of Cape Town.

36 . The fund was created by an alliance between the Homeless People Federation and the People's Dialogue on Land and Shelter. These organisations had been created in 1994 with support from professionals, and with intensive involvement of hundreds of low-income shack-

dwellers in several South African cities. The model had a remarkable similarity with what had been tried out in the Indian context by well-known organisations such as SPARK. By 2002, this network had grown to about 80 000 members, and 2 000 affiliated savings clubs.

37. In metropolitan and local municipalities, half of the councillors are elected as ward councillors in each ward, while the other half are councillors who come to power on the basis of votes for a specific party, not a specific person or neighbourhood.

38. The Working Group on the Regularisation of Irregular Subdivisions has been lauded for regularising 106 000 individual lots from 1984 to 2004 (Jesus *et al.*, 2005).

Bibliography

Abbott, J (2003), "The Use of GIS in Informal Settlement Upgrading: Its Role and Impact on the Community and on Local Government", *Habitat International*, No. 27, pp. 575-593.

Ajam, T. and Aron, J. (2007), "Fiscal Renaissance in a Democratic South Africa", *Journal of African Economies*, Vol. 16, No. 5, pp. 745-781.

Allerts, S. Kleynhans, T.E., and Vink, N. (1998), "Fynbos Exports from the Western Cape Province: A Problem of Logistics", *Agrekon* 37(4), pp. 588-596.

American Planning Association (2002), "Commentary: Monitoring Land Markets" in American Planning Association, *Growing Smart Legislative Guidebook*, American Planning Association, Chicago, pp. 7-92 & 7-100.

Amusa, H., and P. Mathane (2007), "South Africa's Intergovernmental Fiscal Relations: An Evolving System", *South African Journal of Economics*, Vol. 75, No. 2, pp. 265-292.

Archer, Ray W. (1983), "The Use of the Land Pooling/Readjustment Technique to Improve Land Development in Bangkok", *HSD Working Paper No. 10,* Urban Land Program, Human Settlements Division, Asian Institute of Technology, Bangkok.

Arora, V. and L. Ricci (2006), "Unemployment and the Labour Market", in M. Nowak and L. Ricci (eds.), *Post-Apartheid South Africa: The First Ten Years*, International Monetary Fund, Washington, D.C.

Arvanitis, A. (2006), "Foreign Direct Investment in South Africa: Why Has It Been So Low?", in M. Nowak and L. Ricci (eds.), *Post-Apartheid South Africa. The First Ten Years,* International Monetary Fund, Washington, D.C., pp. 64-75.

Atzema O.A.L.C., J.G; Lambooy, A. van Rietbergen & E. Wever, (2002), *Ruimtelijke Economische Dynamiek*, Coutinho, Bussum, Nederland.

Bahl, R. (2001), "Fiscal Decentralization, Revenue Assignment, and the Case for the Property Tax in South Africa", *International Studies Program Working Paper Series*, at AYSPS, GSU paper 0107, International Studies Program, Andrew Young School of Policy Studies, Georgia State University, Atlanta.

Behrens, R. (2004), "Child and Learner Travel in Cape Town: Problems and Prospects", *Urban Forum*, Vol. 15, No. 3, pp. 254-278.

Behrens, R. and P. Wilkinson (2003), "Housing and Urban Passenger Transport Policy and Planning in South African Cities: A Problematic Relationship?" in Harrison, Huchzermeyer and Mayekiso (eds.), *Confronting Fragmentation: Housing an Urban Development in a Democratising Society*, UCT Press, Cape Town, pp. 154-172.

Bellini, N. (2002), *Cluster and Regional Development Strategy:The Italian Case*, LINK Research Centre, Scuola Superiore Sant'Anna, Pisa.

Berrisford S., D. DeGroot, M. Kihato, N. Marrengane, Z. Mhlanga and R. van den Brink (2008), "In Search of Land and Housing in the New South Africa: The Case of Ethembalethu", *World Bank Working Paper*, No. 130.

Bond, P. (2003), "The Degeneration of Urban Policy After Apartheid", in P. Harrison, M. Huchzermeyer and M. Mayekiso (eds.), *Confronting Fragmentation: Housing and Urban Development in a Democratising Society,* UCT press, Cape Town.

Boulle, J., S. Parnell *et al.* (2007), *Economic and Institutional Inclusion", draft for internal RDS discussion*, unpublished technical report, Cape Town.

Bhorat, H., N. Pranushka and C. van der Westhuizen (2004), *Shifts in Non-Income Welfare in South Africa: 1993-2004*, University of Cape Town, DPRU Working Paper No. 06/108.

Boraine, A., O. Crankshaw, C. Engelbrecht, G. Gotz, S. Mbanga, M. Narsoo and S. Parnell (2006), "The State of South African Cities a Decade after Democracy*"*, *Urban Studies*, Vol. 43, No. 2, pp. 259-284.

Brent, R.S. (1996), "South Africa: Tough Road to Prosperity", *Foreign Affairs*, March/April.

Briggs, X. (2008), *Democracy as Problem Solving: Civic Capacity in Communities Across the Globe*, MIT Press, Cambridge.

Brusco, S. and C.F. Sabel (1981), "Artisan Production and Economic Growth", in F. Wilkinson (ed.), *The Dynamics of Labour Market Segmentation*, Academic Press, London.

Burchell, R.W., G. Lowenstein, W. R. Dolphin, C.C. Galley, A. Downs, S. Seskin, K.G.Still and T. Moore, 2002. TCRP Report 74: *Costs of Sprawl – 2000*, Transportation Research Board, National Research Council, Washington, D.C.

Cameron, R. (1993), "Regional Services Councils in South Africa: past, present and future", *Public Administration,* Vol. 71, No. 3, pp. 417-439.

Cameron, R. (1995), "The History of Devolution of Powers to Local Authorities in South Africa: the Shifting Sands of State Control", *Local Government Studies,* Vol. 21, No. 3, pp. 396-417.

Cameron, R. (1996), "The Democratisation of South African Local Government", *Local Government Studies,* Vol. 22, No. 1, pp. 19-39.

Cameron, R. (2000), "Megacities in South Africa: A Solution for the New Millennium?", *Public Administration and Development,* Vol. 20, No. 2, pp. 155-165.

Cameron, R. (2001), "The Upliftment of South African Local Government?", *Local Government Studies,* Vol. 27, No. 3, pp. 97-118.

Cameron, R. (2002), "Central-Local Financial Relations in South Africa", *Local Government Studies,* Vol. 28, No. 3, pp. 113-134.

Cape Metrorail (2005), *Current Public Transport Record: 2004-5, www.capemetrorail.co.za/Marketing/Marketing_Research/2004-5_current_public _transport_record/extract_from_CPTR.pdf.*

Cape Town Partnership (2007), Creative Cape Town, *www.capetownpartnership.co.za/files/Creative%20Cape%20Town%20Presentation%20Dec%202006.pdf.*

Centre for Social Science Research (2003), *Cape Area Study*, University of Cape Town, Cape Town.

Chamberlain, D. and A. Smith (2006), "Recent Findings on Tax-Related Regulatory Burden on SMMEs in South Africa. Literature Review and Policy Options", *Working Papers 9612*, University of Cape Town, Development Policy Research Unit.

Christianson, D. (2003), "The Investment Climate in South Africa – Regulatory Issues: Some insights from the high-growth, export-oriented SME sector", Small Business Project, Republic of South Africa.

Christopher, A. (2005), "The Slow Pace of Desegregation in South African Cities, 1996-2001", *Urban Studies,* Vol. 42, No. 12, pp. 2, pp. 305-2 320.

City of Cape Town (2002), "Staff2002.xls", Department of Human Resources.

City of Cape Town (2005*a*), Sustainability Report, *www.capetown.gov.za/en /EnvironmentalResourceManagement/publications/Documents/Sustainability_Report_2005.pdf.*

City of Cape Town (2005*b*), *Traffic Accident Report City of Cape Town 2005,* Transport Roads and Stormwater Department, Capetown.

City of Cape Town (2006*a*), *Cape Town 2030: An Argument for the Long-Term Spatial Development of Cape Town*, draft document.

City of Cape Town (2006*b*), *Cape Town Energy and Climate Change Strategy*, Environmental Planning Department.

City of Cape Town (2006*c*), *Current Public Transport Record*, Department of Transport.

City of Cape Town (2006*d*), *Informal Dwelling Count (1993-2005) for Cape Town*, Prepared by Elvira Rodriques, Janet Gie and Craig Haskins of the Information and Knowledge Management Department, City of Cape Town.

City of Cape Town (2006*e*), Integrated Transport Plan for the City of Cape Town 2006-2011, Draft for Public Consultation, Technical Draft, June.

City of Cape Town (2007*a*), *Air Quality Monitoring Laboratory. http://web. capetown.gov.za/wcms/eDocuments/Air_Quality_Monitoring_at_Vissershok__202200811037_267.pdf.*

City of Cape Town (2007*b*), *City Statistics, www.capetown.gov.za/en/stats/ Documents/City%20stats%20summary%20page.htm.*

City of Cape Town (2007*c*), *City of Cape Town Sustainability Report 2006, www.capetown.gov.za/en/EnvironmentalResourceManagement/publications/Documents/Sustainability_Report_2006_2372007132223_ 465.pdf.*

City of Cape Town (2007*d*), *Staff2007.xls*, Department of Human Resources.

City of Cape Town (2008), *Councilors Online, http:web1.capetown.gov.za/ web1/newcitycouncil/councilsearch.asp?choice=1/*, accessed 11 June, 2008.

City of Cape Town (2008*a*), *Five Year Plan for Cape Town: Integrated Development Plan (IDP), 2007/8-2011/12. 2008/09 Review, http://web2.capetown.gov.za/en/IDP/Documents/IDP_review_Jun_08_ web.pdf.*

City of Cape Town (2008*b*), *Service Levels by Ward: 2006, http:web.capetown.gov.za/eDocuments/Ward_2006_Service_Indicators_ 3112006132426_359.pdf.*

City of Cape Town (2008*c*), *Strategic Development Information and GIS, www.capetown.gov.za/en/stats/Pages/default.aspx*

City of Johannesburg (2007), *State of the Air Report*, *www.joburg-archive.co.za/2007/pdfs/air_quality/stateofair2007.pdf.*

Clark G., Dexter, P., Parnell, S. (2007), "Rethinking Regional Development in the Western Cape", discussion paper for the Integrated Development Planning Provincial Conference, Isandla Institute, Cape Town, 7-8 May 2007.

Cobb, R.L., Dvorak, S. (2000), *Accessory Dwelling Units: Model State Act and Local Ordinances*, American Association of Retired Persons Public Policy Institute, *http://assets.aarp.org/rgcenter/consume/d17158_dwell.pdf.*

Cross C., P. Kok, M. Wentzel, K. Tlabela, G. Weir-Smith and J. Mafudze, J. (2005), *Poverty Pockets in Gauteng: How Migration Impacts Poverty*, unpublished report to the Gauteng Intersectoral Development Unit, HSRC, Pretoria.

Davids, I. (2007), *Action, Comrades, Action!: A Review of 10 Years of Public Participation in Democratic Local Government with Recommendations for Future Practice*, Foundation for Contemporary Research, *www.fcr.org.za/work-in-progress/publications-in-progress/ten-year-review.pdf/download*, accessed 28 May, 2008.

Davies, R.J. (1981), "The Spatial Formation of the South African City, GeoJournal", Supplementary Issue No. 2.

Deloitte and Touche, Ltd (2007), "Contact Centre and Business Process Outsourcing in Cape Town; 2006/7 Key Indicators Report", *Cape Town, Calling the Cape Department of Science and Technology (2007)*, Annual report 2006/2007, *www.dst.gov.za/publicatins-policies/annual-reports/Annual%20Report%20200607%20in%20pdf%20format.pdf.*

Department of Science and Technology (2005), *Annual Report 2004/2005*, www.dst.gov.za/publications-policies/annual-reports/annualreport-05.pdf.

Devey, R., Skinner, C., Valodia, I. (2006), "Second Best? Trends and Linkages in the Informal Economy in South Africa", *Development Policy Research Unit Working Paper* 06/102, School of Development Studies, University of KwaZulu-Natal, Durban.

Development Action Group (2003), *Review of International and National Trends and Best Practices in Housing*, draft report prepared by the Development Action Group on behalf of the Western Cape.

Dewar, D. (1995), "The Urban Question in South Africa: the Need for a Planning Paradigm Shift", *Third World Planning Review*, Vol. 17, No. 4, pp. 407-419.

Dewar, D. and F. Todeschini (1999), *Urban Integration and Economic Development in South Africa*, Franklin London.

Dierwechter, Y. (2006), "Geographical Limitations of Neo-liberalism: Urban Planning and the Occluded Territoriality of Informal Survival in African Cape Town", *Space and Polity*, Vol. 10, No. 3, pp. 243-262.

Doebele, W. (1982), *Land Readjustment: A Different Approach to Financing Urbanization,* Health and Company, Lexington Books, Massachusetts, D.C.

Donovan, M.G. (2007), *At the Doors of Legality: Planners,* Favelados*, and the Titling of Urban Brazil*, "Ph.D. dissertation, Department of City and Regional Planning". University of California, Berkeley.

Donovan, M.G. (2008), "Informal Cities and the Contestation of Public Space: The Case of Bogotá's Street Vendors, 1988-2003", *Urban Studies* Vol. 45, No. 1, 29-51.

Dorrington, R. E., Bradshaw, D., Johnson, L. and Daniel, T. (2006), *The Demographic Impact of HIV/AIDS in South Africa. National and Provincial Indicators 2006*, Centre for Actuarial Research, South African Medical Research Council, Actuarial Society of South Africa. Cape Town, *www.mrc.ac.za/bod/DemographicImpactHIVIndicators.pdf.*

Dowall, D. (1991), *The Land Market Assessment: A New Tool for Urban Management*, World Bank Urban Management Program Policy Paper, No. 4.

Dowall, D. (1994), "An Overview of the Land-Market Assessment Technique", in Jones and Ward (eds.), *Methodology for Land and Housing Analysis,* Lincoln Institute of Land Policy, Cambridge, pp. 24-43.

Du Toit, A. and Neves, D. (2007), "In Search of South Africa's Second Economy: Chronic Poverty, Vulnerability and Adverse Incorporation in Mt. Frere and Khayelitsha", *CPRC Working Paper 102,* Chronic Poverty Research Centre, Manchester.

Economist Intelligence Unit (2008), *Country Report*, Monthly Review, January, South Africa.

Farvacque, Catherine and Patrick McAuslan (1992), *Reforming Urban Land Policies and Institutions in Developing Countries*, World Bank Urban Management Program Policy Paper, No. 8.

Financial and Fiscal Commission (FFC) (2006), *Annual Report, 2005-2006*, Midrand.

Fjeldstad, O. H., (2004), "To Pay or not to Pay? Citizens" Views on Taxation in Local Authorities in Tanzania", *CMI Working Papers No. 8*, CMI (Chr. Michelsen Institute), Bergen.

Foster, A. D., Rosenzweig, M. R. (2008), "Economic Development and the Decline of Agricultural Employment", in Shultz T., Strauss, J., *Handbook of Development Economics,* Volume 4, North Holland, Amsterdam.

Foundation for Contemporary Research (1999), *Making Your IDP Work,* Foundation for Contemporary Research, occasional paper, Cape Town.

Foundation for Contemporary Research (2007), *Survey on Public Participation in Integrated Development Plans and Municipal Budgeting Processes*, Foundation for Contemporary Research web site, *www.fcr.org.za/projects/participatory-democracy-projects/microsoft-word-idp-survey-report_website-july-2007.pdf/download, accessed 28 May, 2008.*

Gasson, B. (2006), "The Ecological Footprint of Cape Town: Unsustainable Resource Use and Planning Implications", paper presented at the National Conference of the South African Planning Institution, 18-20 September, Durban.

Goebel, A. (2007), "Sustainable Urban Development? Low-Cost Housing Challenges in South Africa,", *Habitat International,* Vol. 31, pp. 291-302.

Goldin, I. (1987), *Making Race: The Politics and Economics of Coloured Identity in South Africa*, Longman, London.

Hall, C.M., Hodges, J. (1996), "The Party's Great, but What About the Hangover? The Housing and Social Impacts of Mega-Events with Special Reference to the 2000 Sydney Olympics", *Festival Management and Event Tourism: An International Journal*, Vol. 4, pp. 13–20.

Harrison, P., Huchzermeyer, M., Mayekiso, M. (eds.) (2003), *Confronting Fragmentation: Housing and Urban Development in a Democratising Society*, University of Cape Town Press, Cape Town.

Heller, P. (2001), "Moving the State: The Politics of Decentralization in Kerala, South Africa and Porto Alegre", *Politics and Society* Vol. 29, No. 1, pp. 131-163.

Hendricks, C. (2005), "Debating Coloured Identity in the Western Cape", *African Security Review,* Vol. 14, No. 4, pp. 117-119.

Hirschman, A. O. (1973), *Journeys Toward Progress: Studies of Economic Policy-Making in Latin America*, Norton, New York.

Hoover, E. M, (1971), *An Introduction to Regional Economics*, Alfred Knopf, New York.

HSRC (2004), *Fact Sheet: Poverty in South Africa*, Pretoria, Human Science Research Council.

Huchzermeyer, M. (2003), "Addressing Segregation Through Housing Policy and Finance", in Harrison, Huchzermeyer and Mayekiso (eds.), *Confronting Fragmentation: Housing and Urban Development in a Democratising Society*, University of Cape Town Press, Cape Town, pp. 211-227.

Humphrey, J. and H. Schmitz, (2002), "How Does Insertion in Global Value Chains Affect Upgrading in Industrial Clusters?", *Regional Studies* Vol. 36, No. 9, pp. 1 017-1 027.

Humphries, R. (1991), *Whither Regional Service Councils? Apartheid City in Transition*, in M. Swilling, R. Humphries and K. Shubane (eds.), Oxford University Press, Oxford.

Humphries, R. W. James and M. Simons (1992), *Administrative Politics and the Coloured Labour Preference Policy in the 1960s. Class, Caste and Color: A Social and Economic History of the South African Western Cape*, Transactions, New Brunswick, New Jersey.

Independent Electoral Commission (2008) *Election Results*, *www.elections.org.za.*

Industry Canada, Government of Canada (2003), Small Business Policy Brand, *Industry Canada*, Vol. 5, No. 2.

Instituto da Pesquisa Econômica Aplicada (2004), *Segurança*, *www.ipea.gov.br/sites/000/2/livros/radar2006/06_seguranca.pdf*

International Monetary Fund (IMF) (2007), South Africa: 2007 Article IV Consultation – Staff Report; Staff Statement, Public Information Notice on the Executive Board Discussion; and Statement by the Executive Director for South Africa, IMF Country Report No. 07/274.

Isandla Institute (2007), "Culture and the Right to the City. Diversity in the Cultural Ecology of Cape Town", discussion document.

Jackson, S. (2003), "Being and Belonging: Space and Identity in Cape Town", *Anthropology and Humanism*, Vol. 28, No.1, pp. 61-84.

Jacobs, J. (1969), *The Economy of Cities*, Random House, New York.

Jaglin, S. 2004, "Water Delivery and Metropolitan Institution Building in Cape Town: The Problems of Urban Integration", *Urban Forum,* Vol. 15, No. 3, pp. 231-253.

Jenkins, J and Wilkinson, P. (2002), "Assessing the Growing Impact of the Global Economy on Urban Development in Southern African Cities", *Cities*, Vol. 19, No. 1, pp. 33-47.

Jensen, M. (2004), "10 Years of Democracy – Where to with COSATU?", *Alternatives*, Vol. 2, No. 8, pp. 5-6.

Jesus, Ângela Regina Lima de, Antônio Augusto Veríssimo, and Sônia Maria da Silva Pereira (2005), *Núcleo de Regularização de Loteamentos e Programa Morar Legal: um relato da experiência de regularização de loteamentos da Cidade do Rio de Janeiro*, unpublished mimeo.

Jordan, Janis (2006), *Towards Co-operative Relations Between District and Local Municipalities*, LL.M. Thesis, University of Western Cape.

Khumalo, B., H.A. Amusa, N. Madubula (2006), *An Analysis of Provincial Own Revenue Trends*, Technical Report supporting the Financial and Fiscal Commission's Submission on the Division of Revenue 2007/08: Recommendations from the FFC Review of the Transfers in the Intergovernmental Fiscal Relations System in South Africa, Financial and Fiscal Commission, Midrand, South Africa.

Koebel, T., R.C. Lang, and K.A. Danielsen (2004), *Community Acceptance of Affordable Housing*, National Center for Real Estate Research, *www.realtor.org/wps/wcm/connect/53c08d0048be37cab4a1fe0c8bc1f2ed/koebellangfr.pdf?MOD=AJPERES&CACHEID=53c08d0048be37cab4a1fe0c8bc1f2ed.*

Kok, P. and Aliber, M. (2005), *The Causes and Economic Impact of Human Migration: Case Studies of Migration from the Eastern Cape, Northern Cape and Limpopo to the Nine Major Cities in South Africa,* Department of Trade and Industry (DTI).

Krugman, P. (1996), "Urban Concentration: The Role of Increasing Returns and Transport Costs", *International Regional Science Review*, Vol. 19, No. 1-2, pp. 5-30.

Kruss, G. (2005), *Financial or Intellectual Imperatives. Working Partnerships in Higher Education, Industry and Innovation*, HSRC Press, Cape Town.

Lam, D., Leibbrandt, M., Mlatsheni, C. (2007), "Education and Youth Unemployment in South Africa", Prepared for the conference on Labour Markets in Transition and Developing Economies: Emerging Policy and Analytical Issues, An International Conference Organised by Cornell University and the University of Michigan International Policy Center, Ann Arbor, Michigan, 25-27 May.

Lambooy, J. G. (1981), *Ekonomie en Ruimte, Deel 2: Stad en Ekonomie*, Van Gorcum, Assen., Nederlands.

Lemanski, C. (2006), "Desegregation and Integration as Linked or Distinct? Evidence from a Previously 'White' Suburb in Post-apartheid Cape Town", *International Journal of Urban and Regional Research*, Vol. 30 No. 3, pp. 564-86.

Lemanski, C. (2007), "Global Cities in the South: Deepening Social and Spatial Polarization in Cape Town", *Cities*, Vol. 24, No. 6, pp. 448-461.

Levy, N. and Tapscott, C. (2001), *Intergovernmental relations in South Africa: The challenges of Co-operative Government*, IDASA, Cape Town.

Lewis, J. D. (2001), *Policies to Promote Growth and Employment in South Africa*, Discussion Paper 16, World Bank, Washington, D.C.

Limtanakool, N., M. Dijst, and T. Schwanen (2007), "A Theoretical Framework and Methodology for Characterising National Urban Systems on the Basis of Flows of People: Empirical Evidence for France and Germany", *Urban Studies,* Vol. 44, No. 11, pp. 2 123-2 145.

Lorentzen J., G. Robbins and J. Barnes (2007), "The Durban Auto Cluster: Global Competition, Collective Efficiency and Local Development", in B. Oyelaran-Oyeyinka and D. McCormick (eds.), *Industrial Clusters and Innovation Systems in Africa: Institutions, Markets and Policy,* Chapter 9, UNU Press, Tokyo.

Low, I. (2003), "Space and Reconciliation. Cape Town and the South African City Under Transformation", *Urban Design International*, No. 8, pp. 223-46.

Mabin, A. and D. Smit, (1997), "Reconstructing South Africa's Cities? The Making of Urban Planning 1900-2000", *Planning Perspectives*, Vol. 12, No. 2, pp. 193-223.

Macnamara, W. (2008), "What Power to the People? South Africa is Stricken by a Crisis of Electric Capacity", *Financial Times*, 14 February, p. 7.

Marshall, A. (1920), *Principles of Economics*, Macmillan and Co., London.

Matheson, V. A. (2006), "Mega-Events: The Effect of the World's Biggest Sporting Events on Local, Regional, and National Economies", College of the Holy Cross, Department of Economics, Faculty Research Series, Paper No. 06-10.

Mayekiso, M. (2003), "South Africa's Enduring Urban Crisis: The Local State and the Urban Social Movement with Particular Reference to Johannesburg", in Harrison, Huchzermeyer and Mayekiso (eds.), *Confronting Fragmentation: Housing and Urban Development in a*

Democratising Society, University of Cape Town Press, Cape Town, pp. 57-75.

McEwan, C. (2003), "Bringing Government to the People: Women, Local Governance and Community Participation in South Africa", *Geoforum*, No. 34, pp. 469-481.

McKinney, C. (2005), *A Critical Analysis of Learning Materials Used in South African Schools*, HSRC, Pretoria.

Meldolesi L and V. Aniello (1996) (eds.), "Invisible Italy: Flashes on the Missing Italian Mezzogiorno", special issue of *Rivista di Politica Economica,* pp. 10-11.

Merrett, Christopher D. and Norman Waltzer (eds.) (2004), *Cooperatives and Local Development: Theory and Applications for the 21st Century*, M.E. Sharpe, Armonk, New York and London.

Midgley, G.F. *et al.* (2005), *A Status Quo, Vulnerability and Adaptation Assessment of the Physical and Socio-Economic Effects of Climate Change in the Western Cape*, Report to the Western Cape Government, Cape Town, South Africa. CSIR Report No. ENV-S-C 2005-073, Stellenbosch.

Miraftab, F. (2007), "Governing Post Apartheid Spatiality: Implementing City Improvement Districts in Cape Town", *Antipode*, pp. 602-626.

Mohamed, H. (2007), "Spatial Development Patterns: Policy Responses – A South African Case Study", paper presented to the International Policy Workshop on Spatial Disparities and Development Policy in preparation for the World Development Report 2009, 30 September, Berlin.

Momoniat, I. (1999), *Fiscal Decentralisation in South Africa: A Practitioner's Perspective*, World Bank, Washington, D.C.

Mukheibir, P. and G. Zierfogel (2007), "Developing a Municipal Adaptation Plan (MAP) for Climate Change: The City of Cape Town", *Environment and Urbanization*, Vol. 19, No. 1, pp. 143-158.

National Ports Authority (2006), "Summary of Cargo Handled at Ports of South Africa January-December 2006", *www.transnetnationalports authority.net/documents/pdf/portStats/Calender%20Year%202006.pdf*.

Nel, E. and T. Binns (2002), *Evaluating Local Economic Development Initiatives in South Africa: Evidence from the Cities*, unpublished paper presented at the Africa Studies Association Conference, Birmingham, UK. 11 September.

Nelson, A.C. (2003), "Let's Get Efficient About Affordability", *Housing Facts and Findings*, Vol. 5, No. 1, pp. 3-7.

Nicholls, R. J., S. Hanson, C. Herweijer, N. Patmore, S. Hallegatte, J. Corfee-Morlot, J. Château, R. Muir-Wood (2008), "Ranking Port Cities with High Exposure and Vulnerability to Climate Extremes: Exposure Estimates", *OECD Environment Working Papers*, No. 1, OECD publishing, doi:10.1787/011766488208.

Nigrini, M. (2002), "Empowering Poor Rural Villages in South Africa: A Preliminary Investigation into Financial Service Cooperatives", *South African Journal of Economics*, Vol. 70, No. 2, pp. 172-180.

Nowak, M. and L. Ricci (2006), *The First Ten Years after Apartheid: An Overview of the South African Economy. Post-Apartheid South Africa: the First Ten Years*, International Monetary Fund, Washington, D.C.

OECD (1996), *Innovative Policies for Sustainable Urban Development*, OECD, Paris.

OECD (1998), *Integrating Distressed Areas*, OECD, Paris.

OECD (2002), *OECD Guidelines Towards Environmentally Sustainable Transport*, OECD, Paris.

OECD (2003), *Environmentally Sustainable Buildings*, OECD, Paris.

OECD (2004), *Regional Integration, FDI and Competitiveness in South Africa*, OECD, Paris.

OECD (2005), "Table 7: Urban Air Quality. Trends in SO_2 and NO_2 concentrations in selected cities", in *Environment at a Glance: OECD Environmental Indicators*, OECD, Paris.

OECD (2006*a*), *Competitive Cities in the Global Economy*, OECD, Paris.

OECD (2006*b*), *Review of Agricultural Policy, South Africa*, OECD, Paris.

OECD (2007*a*), *OECD African Outlook*, OECD, Paris.

OECD (2007*b*), *OECD Factbook 2007*, OECD, Paris.

OECD (2007*c*), *OECD Reviews of Innovation Policy. South Africa*, OECD, Paris.

OECD (2007*d*), *OECD Reviews of Regional Innovation. Competitive Regional Clusters*, OECD, Paris.

OECD (2007*e*), *OECD Territorial Reviews. Madrid, Spain*, OECD, Paris.

OECD (2008*a*), *OECD Factbook 2008*, OECD, Paris.

OECD (2008*b*), *OECD Economic Assessment of South Africa*, OECD, Paris.

OECD (2008*c*) *Reviews of National Policies for Education: South Africa*, OECD, Paris, forthcoming.

OECD (2008*d), OECD Territorial Reviews. Istanbul, Turkey*, OECD, Paris.

Oldfield, S. (2008), "Participatory Mechanisms and Community Politics: Building Consensus and Conflict", in M. van Donk, M. Swilling, E. Pieterse, S. Parnell (eds.), *Consolidating Developmental Local Government: Lessons from the South African Experience*, University of Cape Town Press, pp. 487-500.

Pandey, K.D., D. Wheeler, B. Ostro, U. Deichman, K. Hamilton and K. Bolt (2006), *Ambient Particulate Matter Concentration in Residential and Pollution Hotspot Areas of World Cities: New Estimates Based on the Global Model of Ambient Particulates (GMAPS),* World Bank, Washington, D.C.

Parnell, S (2004), *Constructing a Developmental Nation the Challenge of Including the Poor in the Post-Apartheid City*, conference Paper Overcoming Underdevelopment in South Africa's Second Economy, jointly hosted by UNDP, HSRC and DBSA 2 and 29 October 2004, Development Bank of Southern Africa, Midrand.

Parnell, S., and Mabin, A. (1995), "Rethinking Urban South Africa", *Journal of Southern African Studies*, Vol. 21, No. 1, pp. 39-61.

Parnell, S. and E. Pieterse (1998), *Developmental Local Governance: The Second Wave of Post-apartheid Urban Reconstruction*, Isandla Institute's Dark Roast, occasional paper no. 1.

Pieterse, E. (2005), "From Divided to Integrated City? Critical Overview of the Emerging Metropolitan Governance System in Cape Town", *Urban Forum*, Vol. 13, No. 1, pp. 3-37.

Pillay, U. (2004), "Are Globally Competitive City-regions Developing in South Africa? Formulaic Aspirations or New Imaginations?" *Urban Forum*, Vol. 15, No. 4, pp. 340-64.

Pillay, U. and R. Tomlinson (eds.) (2006), *Democracy and Delivery: Urban Policy in South Africa*, Cape Town, HSRC Press.

Pirie, G. (2006), "Africanisation of South Africa's international air links, 1994–2003", *Journal of Transport Geography*, Vol. 14, pp. 3-14.

P Platzky, L. and C. Walker (1985), *The Surplus People, Forced Removals in South Africa*, Johannesburg, Ravan Press, Johannesburg.

Portfolio Committee on Provincial and Local Government on the Local Government: Municipal Systems Amendment Bill [B 49 – 2003] (National Assembly – sec 75), dated 3 September 2003, *www.pmg.org.za/docs/2003/comreports/030908pclocalreport.htm.*

Powell, A. (2008), "Cape Town Neglect Blamed for Blackouts", *Cape Times*, 5 February, p. 1.

Provincial Government of the Western Cape (2005), *State of the Environment Report 2005*. Western Cape Department of Environmental Affairs and Planning. Provincial Government of the Western Cape (2006a). *Micro-Economic Development Strategy for the Western Cape (MEDS)* Cape Town. *www.capegateway.gov.za/eng/pubs/reports_research/M/165989.*

Provincial Government of the Western Cape (2006*a*), *WCED Literacy and Numeracy Strategy 2006 – 2016.* Cape Town, *wced.wcape.gov.za/documents/literacy_numeracy_strategy/e-LitNumStrat.pdf.*

Provincical Government of the Western Cape (2006*b*), *Western Cape Integrated Human Settlement Plan.*

Provincial Government of the Western Cape (2007*a*), *Background Report to the OECD Territorial Review Process*, Cape Town.

Provincial Government of the Western Cape (2007*b*), *Department of Transport and Public Works Annual Performance Plan: 2007/08 to 2009/2010*, Department of Transport and Public Works.

Provincial Government of the Western Cape (2007*c*), *Draft Western Cape Integrated Energy Strategy Discussion Document*, Department of Environmental Affairs and Development Planning.

Provincial Government of the Western Cape (2007*d*), *Provincial Growth and Development Strategy, Draft White Paper,* Cape Town.

Provincial Government of the Western Cape (2007*e*), *Road Map to Dignified Communities: Western Cape Sustainable Human Settlement Strategy*, Department of Local Government and Housing.

Provincial Government of the Western Cape (2008*a*), *Employment Equity at a Glance,* Cape Town.

Provincial Government of the Western Cape (2008*b*), *Employment Equity Target Recruitment Model as of 30 April 2008,* Department of the Premier, Institutional Improvement and Development Branch.

Provincial Government of the Western Cape (2008c), *Western Cape Provincial Administration: Race, Gender and Post Distribution on 5 May 2008*, Department of the Premier, Institutional Improvement and Development Branch.

Public Service Commission (2008), *State of the Public Service Report 2008*, Pretoria.

Pycroft, C. (1996), "Local Government in the New South Africa", *Public Administration and Development*, Vol. 16, No. 3, pp. 233-245.

Pycroft, C. (1998), "Integrated Development Planning or Strategic Paralysis? Municipal Development During the Local Government

Transition and Beyond", *Development Southern Africa*, Vol. 15, No. 2, pp. 151-163.

Pycroft, C. (1999), "Restructuring Non-Metropolitan Local Government in South Africa," *Public Administration and Development*, Vol. 19, No.2, pp. 179-192.

Pycroft, C. (2000). "Democracy and Delivery: The Rationalization of Local Government in South Africa", *International Review of Administrative Sciences*, Vol. 66, No. 1, pp. 143-159.

Regional Transportation Authority (2008), "About RTA", *http://rtachicago.com, accessed 5 June, 2008.*

Republic of South Africa, Department of Local Governments (2004), *Khayelitsha Nodal Economic Development Profile,* Pretoria.

Republic of South Africa, National Treasury (2007*a*), *Intergovernmental Fiscal Review*, Pretoria.

Republic of South Africa, National Treasury (2007*b*), *Medium Term Budget Policy Statement 2007*, Pretoria.

Republic of South Africa, National Treasury (2007*c*), Provincial Budgets and Expenditure Review 2003/04 – 2009/10.

Republic of South Africa, the Presidency (2006), *National Spatial Development Perspective*, Pretoria.

Robinson, S. (2007), *South Africa's Intergovernmental Alignment/ Misalignment in Respect of Industrial Policy and Regional Development*, background paper for "Understanding the Relationship between Knowledge and Competitiveness in the Enlarging European Union (U-Know)" project.

Robinson, S., O. Crankshaw, and J. Boulle (2007), "Overview on Cape Town Region Competitiveness and Priority Sectors", overview paper for the Territorial Review Process and Background Report, Cape Town.

Rodrik, D. (2006), *Understanding South Africa's Economic Puzzles*, CID, Harvard University, Working Paper No. 130.

Rogerson, C. M. (2006), "The Market Development Approach to SMME Development: Implications for Local Government in South Africa", *Urban Forum*, Vol. 17, No. 1, pp. 54-78.

Rogerson, C. M. (2006), "Creative Industries and Urban Tourism: South African Perspectives", *Urban Forum*, Vol. 17, No. 2, pp. 149-166.

Serra, V., D. Dowall, D. Motta and M. Donovan (2004), "Urban Land Markets and Urban Land Development: An Examination of Three Brazilian Cities: Brasília, Curitiba and Recife", *Institute of Urban and*

Regional Development Working Paper Series. No. 2004-03, University of California, Berkeley.

Simkins, C. (1999), "The Political Economy of South Africa in the 1970s", *South African Journal of Economic History*, Vol. 14, No. 1, pp. 11-36.

Smetherham, Jo-Anne (2008). "City's Solar Water Heating Byelaw Caught up in Red Tape", *Cape Times*, 13 February, Edition 2.

Smith, D. (2003), "Urban Fragmentation, Inequality and Social Justice: Ethical Perspectives", in Harrison, Huchzermeyer and Mayekiso (eds.), *Confronting Fragmentation: Housing and Urban Development in a Democratising Society*, University of Cape Town Press, Cape Town, pp. 26-39.

South African Cities Network (2006), *State of the Cities Report 2006,* Braamfontein, South African Cities Network.

South African Cities Network (2007), *Cities Warm to Climate Change*, South African Cities Network, Braamfontein.

South African Community Epidemiology Network on Drug Use (2007), "Treatment Centres: Cape Town", in *SACENDU Proceedings (January-June 2007), www.sahealthinfo.org/admodule/report11capetown.pdf.*

Southern African Migration Project (SAMP) (2006), *The Brain Drain of Health Professionals from Sub-Saharan Africa to Canada*, Queen's University, Kingston, Ontario.

Souza, M. Lopes (2003), "Urban Planning and Management in Brazil: Instructive Examples for other Countries in the South?" in Harrison, Huchzermeyer and Mayekiso (eds.), *Confronting Fragmentation: Housing and Urban Development in a Democratising Society. Cape Town*, University of Cape Town Press, pp. 190-208.

Spitz, R. and M. Chaskalson (2000), *The Politics of Transition: A Hidden History of South Africa's Negotiated Settlemen*, Wits University Press, Johannesburg.

Standish, B. (2002), *Cape Town International Convention Centre: The Projected Economic Contribution*, Cape Town, University of Cape Town Development Policy Research Unit.

Statistics South Africa (1996), *Population Census*.

Statistics South Africa (2001), *Population Census*.

Statistics South Africa (2005), *General Household Survey*.

Statistics South Africa (2005), *Labour Force Survey*, Pretoria, Statistics South Africa.

Statistics South Africa (2006*a*), *Labour Force Survey*, Pretoria, Statistics South Africa.

Statistics South Africa (2006*b*), *Migration and Urbanisation in South Africa*, Pretoria, Statistics South Africa.

Statistics South Africa (2006*c*), Non-Financial Census of Municipalities, June.

Statistics South Africa (2007*a*), Community Survey, Pretoria, Statistics South Africa, *www.statssa.gov.za/Publications/Report-03-01-21/Report-03-01-212007.pdf.*

Statistics South Africa (2007*b*), *Gross Domestic Product, Annual Estimates 1993-2006, Annual Estimates per Region 1995-2006, Third quarter: 2007*, Pretoria, Statistics South Africa.

Statistics South Africa (2007*c*), *Labour Force Survey*, Pretoria, Statistics South Africa.

Steytler, N. and Fessha, Y. (2005), *Defining Provincial and Local Government Powers and Functions: The Management of Concurrency*, unpublished, Community Law Centre, University of the Western Cape, Cape Town.

Steytler, N., Y. Fessha, and C. Kirkby (2005), "Status Quo Report on Intergovernmental Relations Regarding Local Government", Community Law Centre, University of the Western Cape.

Swardt, C. De *et al.* (2005), "Urban Poverty in Cape Town." *Environment and Urbanization*, Vol. 17, No. 2, pp. 101-111.

Swilling, M. (2006), "Sustainability and Infrastructure Planning in South Africa a Cape Town Case Study", *Environment and Urbanization*, Vol. 18, No.1, pp. 23-50.

Swilling, M (2008), "Local Governance and the Politics of Sustainability", in M. van Donk, M. Swilling, E. Pieterse, S. Parnell (eds.), *Consolidating Developmental Local Government: Lessons from the South African Experience*, University of Cape Town, Cape Town, pp. 77-108.

Tendler, J. (1988), "What to Think About Cooperatives: A Guide from Bolivia," in S. Annis and P. Hakim (eds.), *Direct to the Poor: Grassroots Development in Latin America*, Lynne Rienner Publishers, Boulder and London.

TIMSS (2003), *International Report on Achievement in the Mathematics Cognitive Domains Findings from a Developmental Project*, International Association for the Evaluation of Educational Achievement (IEA), Amsterdam.

Thomas, L. and J. Leape (2005), *Foreign Direct Investment in South Africa, the Initial Impact of the Trade, Development and Cooperation Agreement between South Africa and the European Union*, CREFSA.

Todes, A. (2006), "Urban Spatial Policy", in U. Pillay, R. Tomlinson and J. du Toit (eds.), *Democracy and Delivery: Urban Policy in South Africa*, HSRC Press, Cape Town.

Toroyan T. and M. Peden (eds.) (2007), *Youth and Road Safety*, World Health Organization, Geneva.

Turok, I and V. Watson (2001), "Divergent Development in South African Cities: Strategic Challenges Facing Cape Town", *Urban Forum*, Vol. 12, No. 2, pp. 119-138.

Turok, I. (2001), "Persistent Polarisation Post-Apartheid? Progress towards Urban Integration in Cape Town", *Urban Studies*, Vol. 38, No. 13, 2 349-2 377.

Tustian, Richard. (2000), "Inclusionary Zoning and Affordable Housing", in *Inclusionary Zoning: A Viable Solution to the Affordable Housing Crisis?* New Century Housing 1(2), The Center for Housing Policy, Washington, D.C.

UNAIDS (2006), "ANNEX 2: HIV and AIDS estimates and data, 2005 and 2003", *2006 Report on the global AIDS epidemic*, United Nations.

UN-HABITAT (2006), *State of the World's Cities 2006/7: The Millennium Development Goals and Urban Sustainability: 30 Years of Shaping the Habitat Agenda*, Earthscan.

Urban Sector Network (2003), "Scoping Study: Urban Land Issues", unpublished document prepared for DFID.

Vanderschuren, M. and Ojungu-Omara, I. (2006), "Ways of Reducing Accidents on South African roads", presentation to the 25th South African Transport Conference, 12 July.

van Donk, M. and E. Pieterse (2006), "Reflections on the Design of a Post-Apartheid System of (Urban) Local Government", in U. Pillay, R. Tomlinson and J. du Toit (eds.), *Democracy and Delivery: Urban Policy in South Africa*. HSRC Press,Cape Town.

van Ryneveld, P. (2006), "The Development of Policy on Financing of Municipalities", in U. Pillay, R. Tomlinson and J. du Toit (eds.), *Democracy and Delivery: Urban Policy in South Africa*, HSRC Press, Cape Town.

Visser, G. (2004), "Second Homes and Local Development: Issues Arising from Cape Town's De Waterkant", *Geojournal*, Vol. 60, No. 3, pp. 259-271.

Watson, V. (1998), "Planning Under Political Transition. Lessons from Cape Town's Metropolitan Planning," *International Planning Studies*, Vol. 3, No. 3, pp. 335-50.

Watson, V., R. Behrens, K. Hennessy, and W. Smit (1994), "Subletting: Towards an Appropriate Policy Response", Urban Problems Research Unit, Cape Town Working Paper No. 52 (Occasional Paper No. 39), Cape Town.

Wells, M. (1981), "Alienation, Work Structure, and the Quality of Life: Can Cooperatives Make a Difference?", *Social Problems*, Vol. 28, No. 5, pp. 548-562.

WESGRO (2005*a*), *Tourism Sector Brief, Cape Town*, WESGRO: The Western Cape Trade and Investment Promotion Agency.

WESGRO (2005*b*), *Exotic Meat and Leather Sector Brief*, Cape Town, WESGRO: The Western Cape Trade and Investment Promotion Agency.

WESGRO (2005*c*), *Oil and Gas Sector Brief, Cape Town*, WESGRO: The Western Cape Trade and Investment Promotion Agency.

WESGRO (2005*d*), *Essential Oils Sector Brief*, Cape Town, WESGRO: The Western Cape Trade and Investment Promotion Agency.

WESGRO (2005*e*), *Automotive Sector Brief*, Cape Town, WESGRO: The Western Cape Trade and Investment Promotion Agency.

WESGRO (2005*f*), *Film and Multi-Media Sector Brief*, Cape Town, WESGRO: The Western Cape Trade and Investment Promotion Agency.

WESGRO (2005*g*), *Demographic Statistics 2005,* WESGRO: The Western Cape Trade and Investment Promotion Agency, *www.wesgro.co.za/asset library/assets/281814428.pdf.*

Western Cape Provincial Parliament (2008), *Political Composition*, www.wcpp.gov.za/Political/politicalComposition.asp, accessed 5 June, 2008.

Western Cape Provincial Treasury (2005), *Provincial/local interface: Functions-Situation Analysis: Functions between the provincial and local spheres of government in the Western Cape*, mimeo.

Western, J. (1996 [1981]), *Outcast Cape Town*, University of California, Los Angeles.

Whelan, P. (2002), "*Local Government Finance Reform.*" in Parnell S., Pieterse, E., Swilling, M., and Wooldridge, D. (eds.), *Democratising Local Government: The South African Experiment*, University of Cape Town Press, Cape Town, pp. 233-250.

Wilkinson, P. (2000), "Cape Town. City Profile", *Cities*, Vol. 17, No. 3, pp. 195-205.

Wilkinson, J., Rocha, R. (2006), *Agri-processing and Developing Countries*, Background paper for the World Development Report 2008.

Williams, J.J. (2006), "Community Participation: Lessons from Post-Apartheid South Africa", *Policy Studies*, Vol. 27, No. 3, pp. 197-217.

World Bank (2001), *PRSP Guideline Reports: Transport, Infrastructure, and Services*, Washington, D.C.

World Bank (2007), "Table 3.13: Air Pollution", in *2007 World Development Indicators*.

YTV (2008), "Helsinki Metropolitan Area Council (YTV)", *www.ytv.fi/eng*, accessed 7 May, 2008.

Also available in the series of Territorial Reviews on Urban and Metropolitan Regions:

Helsinki, Finland (2003)

Öresund Copenhagen/Malmö, Denmark/Sweden (2003)

Vienna/Bratislava, Austria/Czech Republic (2003)

Melbourne, Australia (2003)

Athens, Greece (2004)

Montreal, Canada (2004)

Mexico City, Mexico (2004)

Busan, Korea (2005)

Seoul, Korea (2005)

Milan, Italy (2006)

Stockholm, Sweden (2006)

Newcastle in the North East, United Kingdom (2006)

Randstad Holland, Netherlands (2007)

Madrid, Spain (2007)

Istanbul, Turkey (2008)

Forthcoming:

Copenhagen, Denmark (2009)

Toronto, Canada (2009)

OECD PUBLICATIONS, 2, rue André-Pascal, 75775 PARIS CEDEX 16
PRINTED IN FRANCE
(04 2008 08 1 P) ISBN 978-92-64-04963-5 – No. 56373 2008